The Biography *of*
Goddess Inanna;
Indomitable Queen *of* Heaven, Earth *and* Almost Everything

Her Story is Women's Story

Sandra Bart Heimann

BALBOA.
PRESS
A DIVISION OF HAY HOUSE

Balboa Press books may be ordered through booksellers or by contacting:

Balboa Press
A Division of Hay House
1663 Liberty Drive
Bloomington, IN 47403
www.balboapress.com
1 (877) 407-4847

Because of the dynamic nature of the Internet, any web addresses or links contained in this book may have changed since publication and may no longer be valid. The views expressed in this work are solely those of the author and do not necessarily reflect the views of the publisher, and the publisher hereby disclaims any responsibility for them.

The author of this book does not dispense medical advice or prescribe the use of any technique as a form of treatment for physical, emotional, or medical problems without the advice of a physician, either directly or indirectly. The intent of the author is only to offer information of a general nature to help you in your quest for emotional and spiritual well-being. In the event you use any of the information in this book for yourself, which is your constitutional right, the author and the publisher assume no responsibility for your actions.

Any people depicted in stock imagery provided by Thinkstock are models, and such images are being used for illustrative purposes only.
Certain stock imagery © Thinkstock.

Print information available on the last page.

ISBN: 978-1-5043-5822-4 (sc)
ISBN: 978-1-5043-5824-8 (hc)
ISBN: 978-1-5043-5823-1 (e)

Library of Congress Control Number: 2016909121

Balboa Press rev. date: 09/26/2016

NOTE FROM THE AUTHOR'S DAUGHTER

Sadly, my Mother passed away unexpectedly just weeks after completing her manuscript. Her death greatly affected her community, friends and family. Everybody asks me, What about the book? It has been my honor to complete this process for my Mother, with the help of a dear friend, Michelle Dionetti. I loved my Mother more than I can express. She loved Inanna dearly. I hope you will too.

Joelle Bart Davis

CONTENTS

LIST OF ILLUSTRATIONS

ACKNOWLEDGMENTS

Grateful acknowledgment is made for permission to use the following copyrighted material.

From INANNA, LADY OF LARGEST HEART: POEMS OF THE SUMERIAN HIGH PRIESTESS ENHEDUANNA by Betty De Shong Meador, Copyright © 2000. Courtesy of Betty De Shong Meador and the University of Texas Press.

From THE HARPS THAT ONCE ... SUMERIAN POETRY IN TRANSLATION by Thorkild Jacobsen, Copyright © 1987. Reprinted by permission of Yale University Press.

From THE EXALTATION OF INANNA by William W. Hallo and J. J. A. Van Dijk, Copyright © 1968. Reprinted by permission of Yale University Press.

From THE EPIC OF GILGAMESH by Andrew George (Allen Lane the Penguin Press 1999, Penguin Classics 2000, Revised 2003). Copyright © Andrew George, 1999. Reprinted by permission of Penguin Books Ltd.

From INANNA QUEEN OF HEAVEN AND EARTH by Diane Wolkstein and Samuel Noah Kramer (Harper & Row), Copyright © Diane Wolkstein 1983. Reprinted by permission of Rachel Zucker and the estate of Diane Wolkstein.

For my daughter, Joelle Leah Bart Davis
and to the memory of my mother, Margaret Elizabeth Palmer Seibel

My daughter, Joelle, models Inanna; she was born on the sliver of a new moon — Inanna's ancient monthly festival day — she is beautiful, loving and lovable, feisty, concerned with justice and fairness, creative, wise, fearless, and a natural leader. She chose a career that cares for a lost part of our population; she is a successful upholder of partnership with her beloved. Her teenaged face is the model for the cover portrait of Inanna.

My mother set the idea of this book long ago. She pointed to the evening star and taught me "Starlight, Starbright, first star I see tonight …"; ever after I look for and talk to evening star. Evening star *is* Inanna. When I was eight my mother said: "Men must be very afraid of us, they try so hard to keep us down." Her words lingered. At that time, World War II was over; women successfully doing the work of men were made to go home so the men had jobs; it was the 1950's and women were limited to the home, again. My mother had no wartime job but was from a matristic lineage of strong women and kind men. She was born the year women got the vote and left school at fourteen to help support the large family during depression. Her wisdom was innate and experiential. She gave me the three foundation blocks for this book: evening star (Inanna); men fear women and hold strong women down; if you want to do something badly enough you will do it. Her words stayed in my consciousness all these decades, stuck fast as truth.

GRATITUDES

Many women had a part in the creation of this book. The exchange of stories of friends and clients over the years inspired the long effort for researching and writing this Big Story into print. Friends listened to Inanna's story as I gathered the pieces. They delighted in the translated Inanna poems. They recommended books on goddess, women's studies, and related material. Thank you to the many women I have met at the well and shared work, repast and stories!

Special gratitude goes to my friend and editor Michelle Dionetti. Forty years ago she invited me to a small writer's group held in her living room in Houston, Texas. Four decades later this book was delivered into her hands and wisdom for final editing. Her suggestions were impeccable, her encouragement sublime, and the trimming of my rants and too much sass exactly right!

Gratitude goes out to friend-readers who read the text in its various incarnations and made excellent suggestions: Phyl Brazee, Liza Walsh, June Fisher, and Jill Luks.

I also thank Veda Andrus who mentored my holistic nursing practicum. She inspired me to work toward a Masters degree at Goddard College where she became my faculty advisor. Veda asked many probing questions about my intended self-study course work. One of those questions was the seed for delving into the sacred feminine; it eventually grew into this book. My one semester at Goddard was so full and supportive that it was all I needed to launch this project. Thank you Veda and Goddard College.

The Rockport Public Library, in midcoast Maine, located many obscure books on related topics from libraries around the country. Thank you to the helpful and interested staff of our very special and friendly small town library!

I thank and remember my neighbor and friend Barbara Nickels. She enjoyed hearing Inanna stories before or after we solved the problems of the world over morning coffee. Barbara, I miss you.

Toward the end of Mary Daly's life I wrote her a thank-you note for her wonderfully wise books and for being the radical feminist philosopher women and the world of gender politics needs. We became phone friends. We talked about her life, ideas and our own creative endeavors. Mary thought her efforts were forgotten. I assured her that her work broke down barriers and women who may not know her name are moving forward over the barriers she tumbled. I had hoped one day to place this completed book in her hands but my research and writing process was too slow. The confrontational bits of my book took some courage — she would have enjoyed those parts particularly! Thank you, Mary, for your friendship and stories.

An especially warm gratitude and loving remembrance goes to my husband, Peter K. Heimann, who liked strong women and believed in my ability to turn ideas into reality. Peter, you would have suggested more diplomacy in the feminist parts, but Inanna's story needed telling!

HOW TO READ THIS BOOK

The present tense is generally used throughout the book to emphasize the immediacy of Inanna as sacred woman — as Life — and to transport the reader back in time through the millennia.

The English language has a masculine orientation and shamelessly uses **man** and **mankind** to imply "**humankind**". The word "god" is used to infer all deities. Here, **woman** is the feminine of our species and man the masculine. **Goddess** is a female deity and **god** is a male deity. **Human** equates to humankind: everyone. **Humane** is the feminine of human and connotes kindness, caring, and relational involvement with others. Men can also be humane. They have an X chromosome. I will use the word **humane-ity** to mean caring people of both genders. **XX** is female, **XY** is male. **X-ness** is the humane chromosomal behavior of maternal caring, inclusivity and the cooperative qualities present in both genders and doubly present in women. I use **Y-man** or **Y-ness** to indicate men in denial of **X-ness** — the men who replace partnership with domination.

The translated Ancient Near Eastern text selections have various indicators for lacunas (holes and missing parts in the tablets) or fragmented lines in the tablets and may appear ... or [... ...]. Guesses at possible meaning are also bracketed or in italics. I have kept the translator's indicators. The stories retold by the author are based on translated texts and appear as paragraphs in italics. I use Near East in preference to the contemporary use of Middle East to identify the geographic area of Sumer.

The short lines in italics inserted here and there in the text are credited if the translation is unique. If the line is typical of many translations, its source is not specifically identified.

The Sumerian "s" under an inverted v is pronounced "sh"; I have used the phonetic "sh" (Ishtar and Gilgamesh).

Pronunciation for main characters, locations and several other Sumerian words are as follows: **Inanna** is Ee-nah'-nah; **Dumuzi** is Doo'-moo-zee; **Ereshkigal** is Eh-resh-kee'-gahl; **Ninshubur** is Neen-shoo'-boor; **Utu** is Oo'-too; **Uruk** is Oo'-rook; **Eridu** is Eh'-ree-doo; **abzu** is ahb'-zoo; **huluppu** is hoo-loo'-poo; **kur** is koor; **ME/*me*** sounds like 'may' (Wolkstein and Kramer 1983: 215).

Cult is defined as a religious or community worship and ritual of a particular group focusing on a shared esoteric idea or belief. Its word root is Latin, *cultus*, meaning cultivation. Cult is *not* used here, as popular 'culture' frequently uses it, with implied negative and judgmental inferences.

Epithet throughout the book is used in its original narrow definition. Epithet here is an equivalent word that substitutes for a person's or deity's name. It is not used, as has become common meaning, as an abusive equivalent or curse.

Matristic or **matrilocal** will indicate women-based culture. It is inclusive. **Matrinity** is the Great Goddess in her triple life-death-return; mother-death mother-maid aspects.

Patriarchy is male-based and came long after women created culture. It is exclusive. **Domination culture** is equivalent to patriarchy.

B.C.E. is "before the common era" replacing B.C., before Christ.

C.E. is the "common era", replacing A.D. which means anno Domini, to indicate a specific year of the Christian era.

INTRODUCTION

Who is Inanna and why is she important?

The goddess Inan(n)a or Ishtar was the most important
female deity of ancient Mesopotamia at all periods.

Jeremy Black and Anthony Green:
Gods, Demons and Symbols of Ancient Mesopotamia

Inanna's story is preserved: fresh and available as the day a scribe pressed it into clay tablets. Finding Inanna's remaining intact glory days is an expedition of excavation through thousands of lines, story fragments, and word phrase shards — forensic mythology. I am neither a trained archeologist nor Sumerologist. I am an intuitive woman on a serious quest for woman's lost story, both sacred and human(e). I have a library card and computer, a love of story and storytelling and an "insatiable curiosity." The book was birthed after a gestational decade of search and re-search, following insights, and pairing scholarly information with intuition. Books, lexicons, electronic texts, and art images were found, compared, and considered. Inanna — beautiful, lovable, feisty, unstoppable for timeless millennia, reigning far longer than the few millennia that buried her, appears smiling down on her people from the sky as evening star, morning star, and new moon. She sails into city quays; she runs across heaven, over the land, and up mountains; she protects her people, hears appeals, makes decrees and love. She brings the art of womanhood and the ME (powers) of civilization to the people. "No god may say her nay!"

Evening star was my childhood introduction to Inanna. I did not know her name; I called her Starlight, Starbright. In the late 1940s no one knew her name but for a few Assyriologists pondering ancient palm-held clay tablets crowded with wedge shaped writing. My mother taught me to wish on the first star of coming night: "Starlight, Starbright, first star I see tonight, I wish I may, I wish I might, have the wish I wish tonight." Ever after, wishing on evening star became my default prayer. I have known her and petitioned her most of my life. She granted my wishes: a new box of crayons my five-year-old self requested and forty years later she granted the survival of my son after a "fatal" (so said the attending physician) accident.

I searched for her, for sacred woman, and for the story of woman. I found Inanna in ancient poems and texts, gloriously naked singing a song to her vulva and later stripped of her supreme status; I found her, goddess of every power imaginable who was, over time, blatantly usurped, marginalized, silenced. Her name was lost under tons of ruins and blown dust. I sifted through translations and gathered her story; I also found her deep in my heart. Come. Let me introduce you to Inanna, Queen of Heaven, Earth, and almost everything. Her story is also woman's story; she and we are stirring again. We gather again at the well; we tell her story and remember ourselves.

Inanna's known story was recorded three thousand years before the origin of Judaism and Christianity, however, her story began in the late Paleolithic. She was supreme over all deities in the Neolithic time of farming and settling. She inspired art, music, hymns, justice, and compassion. Her temples, shrines, and sanctuaries numbered twice that of her nearest competitor. While she was strong, so were women.

Inanna's powers were stripped away over several millennia through rising male domination of earth and cosmos. Men replaced her and her people's egalitarian partnership by thieving what women created and sustained. Newly imagined gods (gender specific) were created either by gender-flipping goddesses into gods, or "marrying" local male deities to major goddesses. Gods also raped to get their superior position. Inanna was difficult to usurp. It took longer then the male-based religions of today have been around to finally reduce her and her equivalent, Ishtar. Only a few goddesses, the powerful and ancient "virgin" goddesses (virgin meaning unmarried, i.e., not owned by a man), escaped patriarchal marriage. Patriarchal marriage is far different from the sacred marriage, the *hieros gamos*, of the "virgin" young goddess "bride," for it is she who anoints and initiates her beloved consort into full potential and the world responds with a return to fecundity. Women have a similar task with men.

The reader is asked to remember: all goddesses are but a part of the global Great Goddess. All goddess names and epithets are aspects of the ever-growing accommodating mother goddess. Priests usurped priestess roles and crafted new stories. Inanna's vast powers slowly disappeared from the religious texts but for her designation of goddess of love, sex, and prostitution. She was also made into the blamable fickle goddess of war.

I will dip into the science of gender differences for better understanding the before and after of male domination. I will unite science and creative expression; physical evidence and intuition. This book's language is gender specific.

Through constant war and conflict of domination, the Ancient Near East weakened and crumbled. Creativity and literacy disappeared; a dark age descended. Invaders easily conquered the Near East. The high culture of the Sumerians lives on only as an unnamed ghost haunting the foundation of myriad civilizations.

Inanna merged with Semitic Ishtar, an equivalent Neolithic goddess. Ishtar's name lived on in infamy. Another Inanna export equivalent is remembered with a better reputation. Aphrodite is the Greek name of the Sumerian goddess of love. She floated ashore *from the east* (Sumer) and is the remains of the once supreme Inanna. Inanna is lightly remembered in her faded exported shade-forms as Aphrodite and Venus, the disreputable "whore of Babylon" Ishtar, and survives remarkably in the Old Testament as the unnamed beloved in the Song of Songs. Inanna lay buried under ruins and dust, silent and forgotten for millennia. She re-emerged in the last century through translations of the previously untranslatable Sumerian language, stylus-pressed into hand-held damp clay tablets by long-ago scribes. New translations of her story and times are continually added to the corpus of the ancient Sumerian texts. Story fragments are pieced together from tablets scattered around the world. We know her again.

Once one meets Inanna, she cannot be forgotten! She is the beautiful, loving, and feisty heroine, protector, inspiration, alter-ego, sister, and mother we women long to know. She lingers, just there, in the twilight, waiting to hear her name. Do you see her? Perhaps not quite yet, but you already know her. She is our foremothers, she is woman and our potential amplified to fill the universe! She is so big you see her everywhere. She is woman's long-ago consciousness, the story women told everywhere; the story of life that guides humans toward humane potential; the story that loves life with all its joy and sorrow. Her story is entwined with women. She returns and so do we.

Come; meet Goddess Inanna, indomitable Queen of Heaven, Earth, and almost everything.

PART I

LIFE

CHAPTER 1

Who is Inanna?

"I am the great one ... life of the people!"[1]

Inanna

*"Female deities were worshipped and adored all through Sumerian
history ... but the goddess who outweighed, overshadowed, and
outlasted them all was a deity known to the Sumerians by the
name of Inanna, 'Queen of Heaven', and to the Semites who lived
in Sumer by the name of Ishtar. Inanna played a greater role in
myth, epic, and hymn than any other deity, male or female."*

Samuel Noah Kramer, from *The Poetry of Sumer*

Imagine that Inanna is here now. She regally sits on her lion throne.
Her eyes are enhanced with kohl. Her gown is red, wraps over one
shoulder and falls to her sandaled feet in layered flounces. Her tiara is
gold and shaped like a crescent moon. Inanna's hair is midnight black,
loose and curly with tiny gold vulvas affixed. The beads at her neck are
lapis lazuli and carnelian. They are her love charms. She is beautiful,
young, vigorous, lovable, confident, wise, seductive, protective and

---
[1] Foster 2005: 590

compassionate. She runs across the sky or floats about the celestial dome in her boat of heaven; she ties her sandals and sprints over the land. Inanna goes from heaven to visit the underworld and returns. She is rain and storms; when she roars, mountains tremble. Inanna is everywhere! She purrs and men and gods cool their anger. With a goddess-glance, ardor is stirred. She loves her people: the destitute woman at the city walls selling her body for bread is as loved as the shepherd king. For millennia, no god could say her nay! Every new moon we met at her festival and shouted: All hail holy maid Inanna!

The goddess senses our presence after all the long dusty years of silence and waiting. She turns toward us and smiles in welcome. She knows us. She holds her spiral scepter and rises to greet us. She feels our curiosity and awe; our delight in being near her; our desire to know her again.

Inanna speaks, pacing like a lioness about to escape her captivity:

"**Who** am I?

"Who **am** I?

"Who am **I**?

"I AM INANNA, LIFE OF THE PEOPLE!

"I am Inanna, Queen of Heaven and Earth and almost everything! I am life and renewal. I am love and fertility. I own the powers of culture and civilization. I gave you the art of being women!

"You do not remember me … I see it in your eyes. But, you do know me. Did you ever gaze into the evening sky searching for the first star? You squeezed your eyes shut and sent a wish into the purpling sky. Do you remember doing that? You whispered: Starlight, Starbright … ; you sent your wishes to me. I am that evening star.

"My story is long and deep. This modern day scribe will tell it to you. I will sit here on my throne while my story is told. My story is also your story; we will remember who we are. Thank you for hailing me again, and I say: All hail the women! Together we will remember. Together we are strong!" (Excerpted from "The Inanna Monolog" by the author.)

THE STORY BEFORE THE STORY

In those days, in those far off days …

When stars were many and people few, a first great and forever story was birthed. We are human, not because we use tools but because we tell stories. Wherever people live, stories come into being. Storytellers weave location, observation, people, nature, and celestial bodies together. Stories satisfy; they explain mysteries, guide behavior, remember events, and entertain. A story needs two kinds of people: tellers and listeners. The tellers spin and weave a tale into the fabric of knowing that resonates wildly and widely; those who have ears hear; the story is told and retold. It is the same first story, the original root of all myth; it is known everywhere. Its content is universal, strong and reasonable. It is so understandable and practical that it became the warp storytellers would use to bridge the misty distant past, travel through our present and beyond.

People are of two types. First are the ones who consider the land they move over, the thirst-quenching water, the ever-changing sky above; who feel living energy in their offspring, themselves, and in all life around them. The second sort of people are those who need guidance to awaken into that awareness.

The people who find life and living beautiful, nurturing, cyclic, plentiful, surprising, and occasionally unpredictable asked: who? and what? and why? and when? and where? — they are the warp for the great story of life, they are women whose bodies produce and sustain life. They are women whose minds spiral out and grasp big knowing. They are women who include and care for others. They are women who do not kill their or other people's children.

In the beginning of every story is the before. The before of Inanna's story is Life. In the beginning womankind felt life quicken within and noticed all life was thrumming with something mysterious. That numinous mystery was explained by her own body and phases of life. Numinous is equated with brightness, purity (natural or sacred) and also with happiness, wellbeing, and divine favor.

In the beginning, woman called life-energy mother, a Great Mother who brought life into being, collected life when it finished, and birthed it back in renewing cycles of return. Life looks like a woman. She has the humane qualities of the feminine and is big, very big. The same idea arose wherever there were women; the same universal understanding and expanded consciousness, the same story.

Inanna's story is woman's story. Woman's synchronized and baby-building blood-power created culture and a new human consciousness. Woman everywhere recognized life energy — that numinous quality that animates and cycles and blooms and breathes. Women maternally revere life. Long ago women expressed what they knew. A Great Mother birthed everything — Great Mother — monotheaistic and global.

Figure 1. Mesopotamian Goddesses from the Third Millennium B.C.E.

Writing began in Sumer in the 4th millennium B.C.E. (before the common era). Thousands of tablets are now translated. The earliest written record of the divine feminine is Sumerian. Art about the goddess mother has existed since the upper Paleolithic. A Great Mother image is present in art at least since the human "creative explosion" 30,000 years ago (Pfeiffer 1982). Cave wall paintings and carved figures expressed Great Mother long before writing was invented. We do not know her early names and epithets; we do not know how her people celebrated her, we only know they did. Her images survive. Inanna is the earliest written story of the sacred feminine but seals and figurines already knew her form.

Women are intimately enmeshed in life. They gather, work, and birth together. Women gather into multi-tasking cooperative groups of mothers. They are responsible for life. Woman is the obvious answer to who, what, why, when and where. Before and beyond human woman there must be a big mother, a Great Mother. And so it was that women everywhere created sacred consciousness, awareness, image, and story about a Great Mother.

From our bodies, out of our dark wombs, in a flood of seawater through our vaginal mouths, come tiny squalling helpless new people tethered to a vaginal snake (umbilical cord). Women's bodies labor and push like earthquakes. Muscles tighten and loosen over and over beyond our control until our babe is pushed out and into the world. Our laboring sounds are strong and noisy; our afterbirth blood is copious. Not all babes and mothers survive the ordeal; though fraught with danger, women continue to create and arduously support new life.

Women in solidarity share the work of gathering, storing, preparing, and processing well over half of their clan's food while child-rearing and tending. They talk together and name life around them. They explain first story from their own experience and observations. Together they say "NO!" to male opportunistic sexual and "self-feed" behavior. Saying "NO!" together directs men into hunting parties to participate in cooperative partnership for supporting the young. They also say "YES!" since sex can be pleasurable — and sex helps Great Mother with earth's fertility.

Surviving pregnancy and delivery is only the first paragraph of the story. What follows is less dramatic but wholly necessary. The helpless new people require nourishment so woman's breasts drip generously when baby cries. Mother's milk is watery and resembles rain. Round, milk-filled breasts are like rain-filled clouds. Woman's breasts become the cloud breasts of a great sky mother letting down rain. New life needs years of tending, cleaning, protecting, nourishing, nurturing, and patient teaching to grow from helpless dependent to independent youth.

Trees and lions and clams go about the business of being alive; as far as we know, not one of them considers the why and how of it. Our new species on two legs, after three million years of slow evolution, perceived a numinous life force; the unseeable energy that causes things to come into existence, to sprout, birth, hatch, and grow. The women-people's body bled with dark moon phase. Moon and women's blood took human thinking into the heavens, into metaphor, into big story. Undulating land, mountains, waterways, sheltering caves, rain, storms, phasing moon, and stars must all be a woman, a first prime creatress, a Great Mother who is everywhere.

When girls grow tall and round, blood appears at their vaginal mouth. Their first menses is celebrated, it is powerful. They are girl-women entering into the role of creating life. When women of childbearing age are in close proximity, their blood comes at the same time. Women are moon people. Their bleeding comes together *and* in harmony with moon; like river and sea tides, women dance with moon. Moon must be a woman. When she is dark and hidden, she secludes with them during their menses. Women first secluded so the scent of their blood would not draw predators to their camps. They said NO! to sex. When moon re-appears, their menses ends; they bathe and emerge from seclusion at the appearance of moon's slender waxing crescent (Knight and Grahn). Inanna is the young aspect of great mother, the potential fertility, the beautiful girl-woman emerging with the new moon. For thousands of years, every new moon was Inanna's festival day.

Women lock-step with moon. They bleed naturally. They survive their bleeding. When blood stops flowing and bellies bulge, a baby is made. The people believed the retained blood built the baby. Only women can produce life. Their blood is powerful. When older women stop bleeding, they hold their blood and create wisdom. Women are powerful. Women are wise people.

What makes each gender who they are is now understood to be directed by chromosomes. The X chromosome is female and holds long-evolved maternal tendencies. Y is the male counterpart and primarily contains the secondary sex characteristics. We now know that in the beginning all baby brains are the same, female. Eight weeks after conception baby boy's Y-ness, testosterone, kicks in. (Brizendine 2006: 14:)

> A huge testosterone surge beginning in the eighth week will turn this unisex brain male by killing off some cells in the communication centers and growing more cells in the sex and aggression centers. If the testosterone surge doesn't happen, the female brain continues to grow unperturbed. The fetal girl's brain cells sprout more connections to the communication centers and areas that process emotion … it (hormonal effect) defines our innate biological destiny, coloring the lens through which each of us views and engages the world.

For about two years after birth, a girl child has an increase in estrogen surges. This is to prepare her body and brain for reproduction and "this high quantity of estrogen also stimulates the brain circuits that are rapidly being built. It spurs the growth and development of neurons, further enhancing the female brain circuits and centers for observation, communication, gut feelings, even tending and caring" (ibid.: 19). The girl child is more adept at reading emotions, feeling empathy, and in relating from infancy onward.

Men have one X chromosome, women have two. "Testosterone suppresses maternal behavior" (ibid.: 104). It also reduces: communication skills, desire for emotional connections and relationship, cooperation in egalitarian groups, and the ability to hear — to listen to others. Testosterone-fueled men seek sexual opportunity, not relationship; they use self-opportunity and easily become aggressive. Men are of two kinds: the ones embracing their own humane-ity in their X-ness as a modifier of Y-ness; they are wise. Men embracing only their Y-ness are unwise and unkind. They are the other type of men. They are dangerous to life.

Women have enormous responsibility supporting the helpless babes of our species. Every one of us is here today because of an unbroken web of mothers. If women did not have their XX behaviors and brain, if they had not taken that strenuous job seriously, our species would be extinct in the Long Ago. Our large brain is helpful, clever, and rich with potential. That potential is of two kinds: beneficial and creative or destructive and devolved. Our big brain places a great weight on the shoulders of the women people. Babes are born immature so as to have a good chance of making their way through the birth canal. Women give our species a chance to survive. Women also have the unenviable task of taming the men-people into participation and cooperation (see Chris Knight, *Blood Relations*).

Woman, moon, emerging light, bodies of water, dripping breasts, rain, dark womb, umbilical cord, new life, powerful moon blood, and creativity are the symbols of first story everywhere. Aspects of woman in all her life phases answer all the questions our clever minds ask. Everywhere, Great Mother cultures grew out of women's blood and her tending, mending, befriending, defending wisdom. Mother goddess-based cultures became egalitarian societies. A monotheaistic story wove itself on the warp of womanhood. As long as there are women, the warp holds. As long as the warp holds, the flawed miss-weavings of the unwise people will cease and the pushed aside woman-known patterns will re-establish our potential and survival.

The woman-based cultures originated in the Paleolithic. We know they have been around at least thirty thousand years, but more likely they are rooted as far back as the emergence of modern humans (estimated between seventy to two hundred thousand years ago). Our cellular memory and our universal unconscious hold the template for a biophilic (life honoring) partnership culture. Excavations of ancient goddess worship sites in the Ancient Near East, Old Europe, Anatolia, Malta, and Crete reveal millennia of peace. Many art forms of Great Mother are discovered at these widely spaced sites, but few male figurines are recovered. Marija Gimbutas reports the same findings in Old Europe. This means that men, both human and godly, were not superior; instead, an honoring bias toward women and sacred woman is observed. War did not exist. Burials and homes indicate social near equality. Long ago women were important and involved. The early societies were "partnership cultures." Women guided the cultures toward sustaining life with inclusion and group consciousness.

Women once created patterns of cooperation and participation; we acknowledged the revolving cycle of birth, death, and renewal. Our story is well woven. When woman is dishonored and ignored, earth wantonly destroyed and life devalued, the continuation of our species is in jeopardy. The usurpation continues into the present, yet in parts of the world the reweaving has begun. The first weavers again take up whorls and spindles and return to work on the warp and woof; women re-member and continue our story. The creatresses of culture can weave our world into wellness. We women need our story and the sacred feminine returned. Women and goddess love life. Women are biophilic, they honor life. They were the first storytellers until they were silenced. Women are telling the stories again, and Inanna's story returns.

Inanna, goddess of the Ancient Near East, once queen of the land between the two old rivers, the Tigris and Euphrates, was the sacred divine woman described in first writing that developed in Sumer in the fourth millennium B.C.E.. Writing grew out of temple storehouse accounting symbols and pictographs in urban centers requiring large food storage's contents, inventory and distribution. The storehouse was supervised by women in all cultures. Women were the accountants in urban storehouses. Women likely developed first writing.

Inanna's story, hymns, rites, power, praise, and adoration were in existence before writing. The old stories and songs were recorded onto hand-held clay tablets. More is known about the culture and people of the three and a half millennia preceding our era, than can be known about the papyrus and parchment writing people from last centuries

B.C.E. and early C.E. (Common Era). Papyrus and parchment disintegrate. Tens of thousands of clay tablets survive scattered about in museums and collections; many are not yet translated; more still lie waiting under the war torn land of Iraq and Iran.

Ancient Sumerian cuneiform script was successfully translated only during the last century. We can hear again the devotion of the Sumerian and Semitic people for the all-important Sumerian goddess Inanna and her Semitic equivalent, Ishtar. Inanna is the prototype for Aphrodite, Venus, and very possibly Isis; her equivalent goddesses are numerous (see chapter 10).

Figure 2. Inanna Seated on Her Temple and Lion Throne

Inanna is the global One Goddess, Primal Mother concept: the goddess of life, death, return; earth, moon, heaven, and star; fertility, compassion, and the changeability of nature and human life. Her wide-ranging attributes indicate she is early and of the all-inclusive mother goddess. Goddesses of few or singular attributes are isolated aspects of Great Mother; the more specialized the function of the deity, the more recent is that one's story and the more distant from the original goddess. Inanna too was reduced and fragmented and her powers pirated by priests. Since she was so highly revered and so powerful, three millennia were required to do the job. By the last millennium B.C.E., she is a fragment of her former self. Fortunately we have new translations of her songs, hymns, and exaltations that piece her fragments back to wholeness. Goddess was weakened through fragmentation; gods gained power by assembling fragments; they cobbled together a "monotheistic" god from stolen goddess parts and local gods. We are told that Judaism is the first monotheistic religion. It is not. Long before the male single-god was a glimmer in priestly eyes, a great singular goddess reigned. She is never forced on her people. She is a natural expression of consciousness. She is everywhere. She is Life.

Inanna has many epithets and names; her root-story varies only in details of local geography, climate, flora, and fauna. Everywhere, she is earth, moon, star, water, caves, weather, abundance, fertility, sexuality, pleasure, and love; she is birth, death, and renewal. Divine woman loves and cares for her people— as a mother cares. Inanna encompasses the entire i-dea of "goddess", every goddess. (I-dea *is* a goddess!). She is also woman. Every woman. Everywhere. The goddess with thousands of names originated in the creative imagination of women. She is the mirror image of women enlarged to fill the universe. Her story is woman's story; woman once honored; woman expressive, decisive, inclusive, insightful, and industrious; caring woman creating safe passage of survival for humankind from birth to death and back again.

Male domination was a recent unfortunate usurping upstart in a lengthy flow of millennial partnership. Out of womb and menstrual blood-power envy, men contrived father families and believed males were entitled and superior. They developed their version of blood power by mutilating, sacrificing, and making others bleed in death-causing conflict and war; they wrested control of all things feminine. They claimed our hard earned attributes, rationalized their bad behavior, acted with impunity, and blamed women. They retold our long story to their advantage to bury Great Mother and own women's bodies, minds, labor, and creativity. They suppressed our creative expressive potential and influence; they regretted our daughters because they were not sons. They enslaved the conquered ones from their constant conflicts. Priests gender-flipped long standing goddess aspects. They minted new godlets who usurped goddess power and attributes by "marrying" or raping or "fathering" the archaic mother in her many personae. Men became the storytellers.

A few strongly adored and revered sacred women were hard to subdue. Those few, the "virgins," held at least some of their former power through popular devotion. Yet they too were eventually diminished, erased, or demonized and their worshippers were left with incomplete substitutions. In the Common Era, non-Christians were forcefully converted or murdered. Judaism began forced conversion, Christianity perfected it, and radical Muslims are in the throws of owning a superior version of a god who is the contrived excuse for the radical Y-men factions to kill or convert the the non-believers. The big three male-based religions are all rooted in the Ancient Near East, the same Ancient Near East that did not practice forced religion even as men practiced and perfected war. The big three religions share cultural roots that once respected diverse pantheons even as male gods gained status by borrowing, adopting, and merging equivalent deities. Equivalency and similarity of adversaries' pantheons was once common. When disputes were settled and territory reassigned, treaties and boundary markers included important deities from both sides who would curse the treaty breakers or boundary movers.

Inanna's story, her biography, reaches through millennia but has no death to conclude the final chapter. Inanna struggled to hold her position. She met serious adversity; suffered slander, humiliation, dismissal, rejection, and liturgical demotion. She did not die. She lives in humanity's deepest memories. She stirs. Her story, though scattered, fragmented, buried, and misused, is rewoven and the fragments repaired. When women's story is alive and honored, we, with a sacred feminine model again, remember and act. We again celebrate the sacredness of life and the *hieros gamos* — the creative merging of beloveds outwardly and the inner marriage of ourselves with our fertile potential. Life needs tending, earth and humans are sick and yet there is hope — the barely tapped, long suppressed creative potential of women.

Inanna tells us in her own words that she is powerful. She is an active hardworking goddess. She is accessible. In contrast, the Sumerian gods are not involved directly with the people. They are distant, removed, alpha-arranged, and they sit on thrones a great deal. Several gods complain about the city people's noise and plot floods and plagues to kill them. The big gods are generally located off planet. Inanna hears the pleas of the people. She remains with her people and her land. She is both celestial and chthonic. She loves her people, her storehouse feeds the orphans and widows. She stands up to the anger of the gods to protect her people. She is as fierce as the gods and cannot be denied. The gods complain that she is too noisy and the priest scribes claim that she enjoys war, urges kings to war, and even drinks up the blood of war. Aggressive blood-slurping war is not a mother goddess attribute. This is added to our goddess by men who place blame on the sacred feminine!

Inanna is juicy, luscious, and confusing; she represents natural unpredictable life. She moves about from earth to heaven to the underworld and back into the world and heaven. She is never "married," she is "virgin," which in the day means "not owned by a man". She makes joyous love with her beloved consort to bring fertility to the land and her people. Inanna chooses a man who will sit on her throne for a year to protect her city and her people. Inanna loves her people and they love her. She calls them home, as evening star, to eat, to talk man to woman and woman to man, to make love, sleep and dream. As morning star, she awakens them into consciousness for the day; she announces her decisions on their pleas sent during the night. Inanna is healer, counselor, lover, and all aspects of behavior. Her powers were once all inclusive: queen of heaven, earth, and almost everything; her name is whispered again on the winds of time coming.

Inanna's prevalent name has several reasoned origins. Sumerian *nin* means lady or queen. Anna is from *an*, heaven. Some suggest the "n" was dropped changing Nin-anna to Inanna. Two spellings of her name are used, with a single or double "n" — Inanna or Inana. Inanna, as I first met her in the texts, may be from "i-nanna" meaning divine entreaty, as she is the goddess who hears appeals and entreaties. The University of Pennsylvania electronic text Sumerian dictionary[2] refers to the appeals and entreaty aspect used in Old Babylonian texts; that use came later, after her Sumerian naming. I would suggest that since "Ishtar" came to mean generally "goddess", that Inanna's attribute of appeals gave her name to the idea of divine appeal. The second accepted spelling is Inana, defined in the electronic text as "plant." Inanna did bring fertility to the land and her people were agriculturalists but "plant" is too limiting a name. She may have been primarily plant growth until settled farming villages grew into urban centers and her influence was expanded to accommodate the challenges of administering her storehouse temple and city life and her name changed to include decree-making. I lean toward her name coming first directly from nin (queen) + anna (heaven) with "plant" and "decree" as derivative associations. Her many names, titles, and epithets are grouped in chapter 10.

Inanna's story, her biography, is drawn from hints of her early beginnings recorded on ancient Sumerian clay tablets and seals, some of which are five millennia old. Scribes from the fourth millennium to the first millennium B.C.E. pressed her glory and adoration onto their tablets. She is mother to the people and maid of fertility; she is loved, indomitable, reduced, and finally forgotten. Inanna returns to life with the recent translations. We re-member her name and story. We read her hymns, we sing her songs, we recognize her images. We re-story her power; we re-story womankind. We read again what her devotees knew about her, what they believed, and how they celebrated her. The retelling of Inanna's story is important. When goddess is reduced and erased, so too is woman marginalized and silenced.

Sumerian woman, in the twenty-fourth century B.C.E., "was man's equal, socially and economically" (Kramer 1979: 27). Inanna was

---

[2] Electronic Text Sumerian Dictionary http://psd.museum.upenn.edu/epsd/nepsd-frame-html

supreme queen of heaven and earth with many powers and attributes. She had twice the temples, sanctuaries, and shrines on a temple list then her nearest competitor, Enlil. She had many compositions sung to praise her. The first recognized poet, en-priestess[3] Enheduanna, wrote temple compositions to Inanna. "This sensitive, intelligent woman had a passion for the goddess Inanna, and this passion fueled her writing. We learn from her poetry that she undertook to keep alive an ancient tradition, reaching back a thousand years or more to the beginning of the myth, story and song that surrounded the worship of Inanna." (Meador 2000: 103)

We have no proof of her first emergence since the Sumerian people's land of origin remains a mystery. We do know that goddess is a global phenomenon and evidence of mother goddess comes from the Paleolithic caves of gather-hunters. We also know that Neolithic farming everywhere emphasizes Great Mother's young, fertile, and renewing persona; goddess mother faded and her maid version captured center stage. Neolithic religion also included a demigod of rise and fall who is the catalyst for the maid's fertility. In early farming days, maleness is included but the young goddess is the star. After the mid-third millennium, male usurpation is afoot and on the rise. (Kramer 1979: 27:)

> But what is of interest to us here is the fact that it was not only on the human plane that women lost some of their rights and prerogatives in the course of the centuries, but that it happened also on the divine plane. Some of the female deities that had held top rank in the Sumerian pantheon were gradually forced down the hierarchical ladder by the male theologians who may have manipulated the order of the deities in accordance with their chauvinistic predilections.

There is no "may have" to their "chauvinistic predilections" as Inanna's biography will reveal! If not the Sumerian priests, then the

---

[3] en- indicates a very high position in a temple, Enheduanna is the en-priestess of the Nanna (moon god) temple in southern Sumer

Akkadian priests and theologians systematically reduced the goddess, hymn by hymn and story by story. Kramer implies that human and sacred woman lost ground simultaneously. I suspect sacred woman usurpation occurred first, and when woman no longer had a protectress, a model, a cosmic representative, then woman could not sustain her status. If goddess as feminine principle stays strong then woman stays strong.

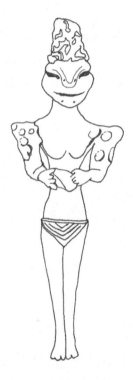

Figure 3. Ubaidian Snake Goddess

Inanna is the fertile young aspect of Great Mother. Her beautiful form replaces the abundant round figure of the Paleolithic Great Mother, the goddess mother of gatherers and hunters. Settled Neolithic farming is an important technological advancement. Farming is a new event for our species. Social organization changes with settled life; story reflects the shift from nomadic gathering and hunting to settled farm community. In Sumer, Inanna is the all important fertility goddess. She is called "mother" in early texts. She is also called "first snake."

The prime creatress of both Ubaidians and emigrating Sumerians is shaped in figurines as a snake head on a woman body. She is Nammu, earliest parthenogenetic creatress of heaven and earth; mother of the early deities — earth (ki) as female, and heaven (an) as male. Earth and Heaven in turn birth Enlil, the god of air; en (head, in charge) + lil (air). Enlil separates heaven and earth. An becomes the heavenly dome holding back the upper sea that spills from time to time through Antu, the feminine heaven, which is imagined as cloud breasts dripping rain. Antu is one of Inanna's alternate names. Enlil is the atmosphere between heaven and earth. Ki (renamed Ninhursag, queen of stoney ground) is earth mother. She remains one of the top three deities until Enki, en (head of) + ki (earth) arrives on the scene. Enki is said to be "son" of prime creatress, Nammu, the great prime creatress mother and origin of Inanna. Enki controls the underground water, wells, marshes, and springs. He takes charge of earth. Ki's name fades.

Goddess is the first conceived monotheism; she is also the first deity expressed as a trinity within her wholeness. She is at once young potential fertile maid, pregnant mother, and death mother holding our bones for renewal.

Sumerian Inanna is the star of this book. She is more than a unique goddess of a specific geographic location. She and her fertility "maid" equivalents are similar everywhere; where there are women there is goddess. Where goddess is, woman is empowered. When sacred woman is present, woman's wisdom is heard.

Sumerian and Akkadian texts reveal the backstory of theologians usurping Inanna's story. Religion and politics are in bed together. Literally. Goddess granted the king rulership for a year if he pleased her as a consort, as her beloved. Priestly scribes concoct new stories to support male rule and promote minor godlets who eventually combine and eventually become the monotheism of major male-based religions.

There was once another way, another story. Do you remember? "In the beginning, people prayed to the Creatress of Life, the Mistress of Heaven. At the very dawn of religion, God was a woman. Do you remember?" (Stone 1976:1)

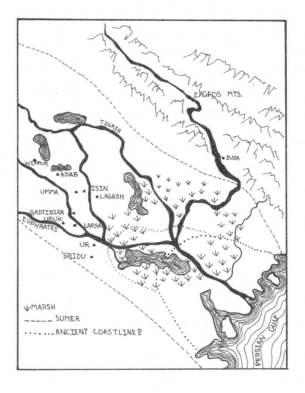

Figure 4. Map of Sumer

WHERE DID INANNA ORIGINATE?

Queen, great Queen who abides among her people

The origin of the Sumerian people remains a mystery. Their language is not a Semitic language as are most other language roots of the Levant and Mesopotamia. Old Europe was settled before southern Mesopotamia was high and dry enough from the glacial melt of the last Ice Age to be habitable by Ubaidians and Sumerians. However, older evidence than Mesopotamia's Great Mother is abundant in Old Europe's caves. The art of long ago gather-hunters is preserved. Great

Mother is recognizable both as the cave and the depicted theme of cycles of life.

In the Ancient Near East, there were earlier people than the Sumerians, now called Ubaidians, after the first discovery site. They were also non-Semitic as evidenced by retained place names in Sumerian language, such as the names of the Tigris and Euphrates rivers. The Sumerians arrived by river, or sea, or over land with a fully developed culture. They merged with the Ubaidians. They built their urban centers on the delta-blocked drying marshlands of southern Mesopotamia. Archeologist Vere Gordon Childe described southern Mesopotamia as the Sumerian settlers would have seen it. (Cited in Liverani 1998: 6:)

> [Sumer] was still covered with vast swamps, full of towering reeds, interrupted by arid banks of mud and sand, and periodically inundated by floods. Through tortuous channels among the reeds the muddy water flowed sluggishly into the sea. But the waters teemed with fish, the reed brakes were alive with wild fowl, wild pig, and other game, and on every emergent patch of soil grew date palms offering each year a reliable crop of nutritive fruit. [...] If once the flood waters could be controlled and canalized, the swamps drained, and the arid banks watered, it could be made a Garden of Eden. The soil was so fertile that a hundred-fold return was not impossible. [...] Here, then, farmers could easily produce a surplus above their domestic needs.

Some theories speculate on a mountainous origin since an early temple building in Uruk had mud brick pillars imitating the great trunks of trees that once grew plentifully on mountainsides surrounding Mesopotamia. Mesopotamia, the "Land Between the Two Rivers" is an alluvial plane. There are no great trees. Any timber used was imported and brought by river. The "white temple" of Uruk began with white stonework, imported, since the planes and marshland have no stone. Both the early 'timber' columns and stone foundations bespeak a mountain origin. The stonework, an imported building material perhaps from the homeland, was abandoned and the temple completed with clay bricks formed from the available resources: clay and reeds.

Inanna's symbolic doorposts are tied reed bundles with a loop at the top and streamers trailing resembling a female figure with head and hair. This door post is an actual form used with reed-built structures. Reeds and mud are the building materials of the marshes. Inanna's earliest storehouses were made of reeds; temple building came later.

Figure 5. Inanna's Storehouse with Her Ring Posts

Other possible origins of the Sumerians are based on hymns mentioning a paradise, a place of ease and beauty: Dilmun. The Sumerian paradise and possible land of origin, is the prototype for "Eden". However, no parallel culture is found to date in any of the suspected "homelands". Another possible origin of Inanna's people is that they originally were the "Ubaidians", Mesopotamia's indigenous people, who developed a culture and whose pottery is found at sites all along the two rivers. A deluge flooded a vast region of Mesopotamia. That flood was recorded in ancient story throughout the effected areas. If the Ubaidians were the original people, did their remnant population remember their homeland and did they return after the flood subsided? The arriving or returning Sumerians blended with the Ubaidian people. Neither had a Semitic based language. Their dynamic fusion brought forth the first complex Sumerian urban centers that were built on Ubaidian foundations. Inanna's Eanna temple precinct rose over earlier layers of smaller Ubaidian cult buildings. Wherever their land of origin, the Sumerians simply referred to their new settled area as "the Land", and themselves as "the black haired people." That description begs an answer: if "black haired people" distinguished them from others, who were the other people and what hair coloration did they have?

INANNA'S GENEALOGY

The early part of this chapter places Inanna as part of the original creatress goddess whose all purpose i-dea was understood as a triune in the upper Paleolithic era into the Neolithic. Creatress goddess fades as fertile Inanna becomes the new emphasis of the sacred feminine. By the time of first writing, she is referred to as "daughter" of the moon couple and is said to surpass her mother, Ningal ("great queen"). Sumerian theology presents Inanna's direct genealogy as follows:

Nammu
/ \
Ki + An
/
Enlil + Ninlil
/
Nanna + Ningal
/ \
Inanna Utu

Are Ninlil and Enlil the grandparents of Inanna? That lineage would demote her antiquity and singular power. I suggest a different beginning lineage:

Nammu — Ereshkigal — Inanna

Many versions of divine genealogy are suggested. Every city had its begetters, its consorts, its divine children, its divine's functions. Those who take later text genealogy literally will not agree with my thinking of Inanna's position alongside the progenitress, yet references connecting both Inanna and Ishtar to Nammu and Tiamat are plentiful. Most priestly arranged lineages put Inanna in the fourth generation. Their first generation is Nammu birthing Ki, and An. Ki and An beget second generation Enlil who misbehaves with Ninlil; they beget Nanna (moon god) who pays a bride price and weds Ningal. They beget Inanna and Utu (sun).

The parentage of Inanna is usually given as Ningal and Nanna, the moon couple. Inanna's brother is Utu, sun. Moon mother, Ningal is traditionally a triad: full, dark, and new crescent — life, death, return. In every moon tradition, Inanna is an aspect, a young maid, a daughter to full moon. Creatress as earth, chthonic mother goddess, is also a well known global image. She too comes as a triune: mother, death mother and maid. Inanna is Queen of Heaven, Queen of Earth, and frequently described as Queen of the underworld. She is celestial *and* chthonic. She is water and earth. She is weather and storms. She is everywhere. To place her in the fourth generation of deities is unthinkable. I place her from the beginning. She is Great Mother goddess.

Moon everywhere is a womanly celestial body, the White Goddess. In hot climates, sun is destructive heat and moon is refreshing coolness. Nanna (moon god) claimed the Sumerian moon mother in "marriage". A poem describes how the moon god pays the bride price for lunar goddess Nikkal/Ningal. He promises to make her fields fertile. "I shall make her fields into vineyards, the field of her love into orchards" (Kramer 1961: 214). (ibid.: 214-15:)

Moreover, his promise to make her fertile reflects the real attitude toward marriage, whose purpose was human fertility. A husband was like a farmer who cultivates the soil so that it yields harvest. A woman, like a field, needs the seed and cultivation of a husband, if she is to be fertile. Our text is therefore a *hieros gamos:* a wedding of the gods, whose fertility brings on terrestrial abundance for mankind.

Sumerian Inanna refers to herself as a field in need of "plowing", asking: "Who will plow my field?" It is *her* participation in the *hieros gamos* with the king that brings abundant fertility for the land and a year of rulership for the man. The end result is fertility on earth. Inanna is front and center as fertile maid-virgin since early farming days. The above mentioned text of lunar marriage has a masculine emphasis — a god buys the moon with the male invention of bride price reflecting patriarchal-based marriage arrangements. Moon, Ningal, is purchased. Moon becomes the man in the moon; Ningal is moon god Nanna's means for elevation. I cannot stress enough the blatancy of the usurpation of the most feminine celestial symbol. This step represents the second level of myth-making — men taking over menstrual and birthing powers of women. The first myth everywhere is based on the menstrual blood power of women. By the last millennium B.C.E., Ningal is barely mentioned while Nanna/Suen/Sin is important and is one of the few big gods. Ningal fades and Inanna is no longer needed for granting rulership and fertility; the gods do both. Goddess no longer confers a hint of divine specialness to rulers; kings declare themselves divine and their male heirs inherit their divine status. Dynasties emerge. Conflict increases. Rulers compete to own more cities and territories. Cities are reduced to ruin and men, women and children are killed, captured, or moved as slaves to other locales to rebuild previously destroyed urban centers.

Destruction of enemies drives the Ancient Near East after domination conquered partnership. The high culture and creativity of the fourth and third millennia are lost. Literature from the first millennium B.C.E. is reduced to copying old texts badly. Scribal schools disappear; many people leave the city ruins and return to former tribal groups. Literacy and creativity dim. The heritage of Sumerian culture is all but lost. A dark age ensues. Military costs bleed the economy, trade routes are overtaken and the cost of goods is inflated; civil war breaks out, and plague and famine spread. Outside foreigners take the land. First the Egyptians invade and then Persian king Cyrus easily takes Mesopotamia in the mid-first millennium B.C.E.. The power of Babylon and Assyria is broken. The glory of the Ancient Near East is lost.

The genealogy of deities varies with location and how local or lesser divine personalities are brought into the story. The oldest genealogy would have parthenogenetic creatress (Nammu or Tiamat) birthing earth and heaven out of the primordial Abyss. Ki and An. They have sex and Enlil is born. Lord Air. Many cultures have the same child of earth and heaven who separates his parents to make space, air, for all the life to follow. Enlil is the tutelary god of Nippur, a city never to house a regional ruler but which emerges as the religious center of Sumer. Enlil gets to confer godship by sanctioning new gods, rulership, and divine promotions.

How Enlil gets a wife fits into the examination of how goddess is generally usurped; it is also a portrayal of how womanhood tames manhood. The following is retold and included because in later myths Ninlil and Enlil are the proud parents of the moon god, Nanna, who begets (with a bit of help from his purchased wife) Inanna the evening/morning star and her brother Utu the sun god. All quoted sentences are from the translated text. (Black et al 2002: 103-106:)

> *In the great city of Nibru, lives Ninlil (queen of air), and the young god Enlil, son of earth and heaven, Ki and An. Ninlil is a maid (and just of marriageable age, that is, she has begun her menses). Her mother (a wise old woman) warns her away from the holy river and the women taking their purifying baths. "The river is holy — don't bathe in it! Ninlil, don't walk along the bank ... His eye is bright, the lord's eye is bright, he will*

look at you! Straight away he will want to have sex, he will want to kiss! He will be happy to pour lust semen into your womb, and then he will leave you to it!" Enlil, here also called Great Mountain, Father, king, and shepherd, does look at her with his bright eyes. "I want to have sex with you!" Ninlil says NO! "I want to kiss you!" Ninlil gets away. She is firm. She explains the consequences. "My vagina is small, it does not know pregnancy. My lips are young, they do not know kissing." Her mother and father (unnamed) will punish her, and she will tell her girlfriend.

Enlil, accustomed it seems to having his way, is frustrated. He summons his minister (vizier, sukkal, administrative assistant) Nuska. "At your service, my lord." Enlil spills out his longing. "Has anyone had sex with, has anyone kissed a maiden so beautiful, so radiant …?" Accommodating Nuska brings a boat to float Enlil to Ninlil to have sex with her. Enlil anticipates his conquest with joy. " …he was actually to have sex with her, he was actually to kiss her! … he grasped hold of her whom he was seeking … on a small bank … He actually had sex with her, he actually kissed her." The one encounter resulted in her pregnancy of the moon god.

Enlil returns to his temple and fifty great gods and seven decision-maker gods arrest him. He is accused of rape, here called "ritual impurity". He is banished from the city. The next part of the Enlil-Ninlil text is strange and one cannot help but wonder: does young Ninlil know exactly what she is doing, i.e., changing male lust through sexual initiation into a relational and responsible partnership, or is her behavior the prototype for much later bodice-ripper novels? The rough virile man has his way with the heroine over her resistance; she is weak in his arms, her clothing is in disarray, she swoons with love and they go on to live happily ever after. The reader may decide.

Enlil is on the run and Ninlil is in hot pursuit. Enlil reaches the city gatekeeper. He first explains that Ninlil will look for him and ask if he saw Enlil. He is to deny seeing him. Here comes the sly part: Enlil disguises himself as the city gatekeeper. Ninlil asks her question, Enlil as gatekeeper answers that he hasn't seen him(self). Ninlil counters with a proposition. "I

27

will make clear my aim and explain my intent. You can fill my womb once it is empty — Enlil, lord of all the lands, has had sex with me! Just as Enlil is your lord, so am I your lady!" Enlil as gatekeeper answers: "If you are my lady, let my hand touch your ...!" She reminds him she is pregnant with Enlil's moon god seed. The disguised Enlil says, "My master's seed can go up to the heavens! Let my seed go downwards! Let my seed go downwards, instead of my master's seed!" He lay her down in his gatekeeper chamber and kisses her and has sex with her. His "bright seed" is poured in to make Nergal, the future underworld god who eventually takes over Ereshkigal's realm as her consort.

Enlil runs on to the guardian of the river of the underworld, the man-eating river. Ninlil chases after him. The same ruse is enacted, the same words are spoken, and Enlil, in disguise, accepts Ninlil's proposition and has more sex with her in the guardian's chamber. This time, Ninazu, "the king (god) who stretches measuring lines over the fields", also defined as an underworld god, is conceived. Enlil again escapes. He reaches the "Man of the ferryboat". The exchanges and actions are repeated word for word. Ninlil proposes, Enlil accepts. She is now carrying Enbilulu, inspector god of canals.

The poem does not tell us when Enlil is allowed back in his city. It does not explain to any satisfaction maiden Ninlil's promiscuity unless she was not promiscuous — as Enlil had known before meeting her.

Goddesses are all-seeing. Many texts tell us this is so. I suggest that, since available gods were few and the new story must go on, Ninlil is aware of Enlil; she disobeys her mother and goes where he will see her. First forced by Enlil, she decides to make him over into a grown-up responsible husband-god. She knows who he is in each disguise. She beguiles him with sex *at her beckoning* and initiates him into full divine-manhood.

The story is also a way of populating the pantheon. In one Sumerian afternoon's dalliances, four new gods came into being: Moon god, two underworld gods and one canal god. The text ends with praises for the god who was banished for rape. Glorious words are heaped upon Enlil, far more than are said for the fertility goddess of the sacred *hieros gamos*. We hear the priests proclaim: "You are lord! You are king! You are supreme lord, you are powerful lord! Lord who makes the flax grow, lord who makes barley grow, you are lord of the earth, Lord Plenty, Lord of heaven! Enlil in heaven, Enlil is king! Lord whose utterances cannot be altered at all! His primordial utterances will not be changed! For the praise spoken for Ninlil the mother, praise be to Father Enlil!" (ibid.: 106)

Sumerian genealogy places prime creatress first and alone as Nammu or Tiamat. She is the Great Goddess of three aspects. The first divine family in Sumer is Great goddess and her maid form, daughter of herself, Inanna, and her death mother self, Ereshkigal, Inanna's archaic "sister." The first "family" expands when male sexual participation is understood. A vegetation rise and fall god appears, son of Great Mother and consort for her maid self.

The stories explain that the prime creatress births Earth and Heaven who have sex and produce Enlil. Enlil gets Ninlil pregnant and Moon god and three other gods are born. Every area and city had a first creation myth and divine genealogy, its own version of begetting familial connections. At Eridu, Enki is the first born of Nammu. Sumer standardizes Inanna's family making her daughter of the moon couple and consort with an array of gods in wide flung texts: An, Enlil, Dumuzi, and a near endless line-up of hopeful kings.

People create story and interpret divine personalities to reflect their times, needs, and politics. Prime Mother Goddess births early deities after singly creating heaven and earth out of the abyss, the void, the sea of creative potential and chaos. Some gods came into being full grown, others rise in spring with youthful virility and consort with great mother's young maid self as the catalyst for fertility on the earth. Vegetation gods are chthonic demigods: they live, they die, they return during the two-season farm cycle. Summer and winter.

Men are not cyclic people. They do not like the rise and fall of vegetation demigods while goddess remains constant. They wrest divine maleness from the goddess; they re-make their gods as constant and fixed. Their gods mirror men's behavior; they are increasingly destructive and practice usurpation of the feminine through marriage and rape.

Nanna/Suen (Sumerian/Akkadian) is father-moon by the time of first writing; Great Lady, Ningal, moon goddess, has only a supporting role. Inanna, of the great mother, is explained as an aspect, the daughter, of Ningal moon goddess. Inanna is the new crescent; she is celebrated every new moon for millennia. Ningal is the full moon and Nanna, moon god, becomes the last day of the moon, the powerful going-into-seclusion dark of moon. Moon belongs first to women. New moon is when women and goddess emerge from seclusion; they are powerful; they bring light, fertility, and new beginnings (Knight and Grahn). People celebrate together with song and dance. Food is served from the goddess's storehouse. Young people meet. A public feast is prepared. Temple performers entertain. People parade before Inanna's seated image. The coterie of wise women, the doyenne, walk with the city's elite; young girls and old women parade with loosened hair, suggesting the potential allure of the girls and the past allure of the old women. Temple eunuchs, priests, and warriors walk past her. Inanna is said to change men to women and women to men. Some women and men parade with clothing rearranged to indicate cross-gender dressing. (This was accomplished by draping the upper garment over one shoulder and leaving opposite shoulder bare but changing the traditional side that was left free for women and men.) Young men act like captives and plead for her mercy as they parade by her; granting mercy to actual captives is in her power. One text describes a band of women warriors marching in from the mountains in single file. While the people revere their goddess, animals are sacrificed, roasted, and served to the people with the rest of the feast from Inanna's storehouse.

Inanna increases in stature during the Neolithic era when farming settlements grow into urban centers. Crop and herd fertility is vital to settled people. Praising and pleasing Inanna is supremely important. She is first an agricultural goddess. She has sheepfolds, she is the storehouse for the farm products. By the time of writing, Inanna is reverenced in her urban temples. Literature is concerned primarily with city life. She has become a city goddess, the tutelary owner of Uruk, alone or with An as consort. Inanna is also important in Ur and has temples in many other cities.

Farm communities ring the urban centers. Some of the farmland is privately owned as evidenced on contract tablets; temples also own land and appoint estate managers. Women also manage estates and temple-owned land. The rulers' queens run large estates from their women's quarters. One text describes the installation of a majordoma, a woman manager of a temple.

Inanna's consort in one text is nearly a farmer which indicates he probably was a farmer-god before herding grew in importance in the economy. Inanna is convinced to choose the shepherd Dumuzi over the farm god, Enkimdu, by her "brother" Utu, the sun god. That she is talked into reluctantly accepting the shepherd hints strongly that an older story existed before Semitic herding was prevalent; an earlier time when agriculture is the reliable economy. Kramer translated the following text he entitled: "Inanna Prefers the Farmer" (Kramer 1961: 101-103:)

> *"Ubiquitous" Inanna is ready to have a consort. Her brother, sun god Utu, promotes the shepherd-god Dumuzi. Dumuzi also has herds and "jewels and precious stones". Utu is puzzled. Why doesn't his sister want the shepherd for her consort? She refuses to walk with Dumuzi or utter praises for him. Inanna prefers the farmer-god, Enkimdu. He makes plants and grains grow in abundance. Dumuzi is put out! What can the farmer offer that is more than what he offers? For the farmer's woven black garment, Dumuzi has a black ewe; for the white garment, he shows a white ewe. For the farmers date-wine, the shepherd has yellow milk; for Enkimdu's "heart-turning" date-wine, he compares his bubbling-milk. If the farmer pours oil, he pours milk; for his good bread, Dumuzi has "honey-cheese."*
>
> *The farmer asks why Dumuzi wants to quarrel? He offers the shepherd the grass in his meadowland, and water from his river for the shepherd's herd.*

> *Somewhere in the text fragments Inanna is being given to*
> *the shepherd. Dumuzi is belligerent and Enkimdu is peaceable.*
> *Despite the farmer's generosity and good will, Dumuzi warns*
> *the farmer that he is not to come as a wedding guest, as a friend.*
> *The farmer, treated so rudely, still offers beans and any pleasing*
> *gift Dumuzi desires, anything pleasing to him — including*
> *Inanna! The farmer ends the poem with: "The maid Inanna …*
> *I shall bring thee."*

The above poem is both revealing and unusual. The Sumerians are farming people, the Akkadians and other Semitic people are primarily herders. I suspect that the competition between the shepherd and farmer was the uneasy merging of two cultures. People who live in harsh conditions lean toward male leadership. Nomadic and semi-nomadic herding people move over arid and stoney land. The harsh life style develops aggression. Herders raid and are raided. Conflict is part of herding life. The Semitic herders settle and outnumber Sumerian farmers. Sumerian culture is absorbed by the settling herders. A merging of deities is symptomatic of the changing times. Utu is referred to as brother of Inanna, second child of the moon couple. Here he takes on the patriarchal tribal tradition of eldest brother arranging his sister's marriage, presumably because he knows the young men, their families, and their potential as husbands. Utu also aligns with Dumuzi in the story of Inanna's descent to the underworld, when the sun god transforms Dumuzi to escape his fate imposed by Inanna. Here he promotes Dumuzi as spouse for Inanna. At first, Inanna appears to have some say and argues for her personal choice. In the end, she has no say, the three men decide her bridal fate. We sense the dis-ease between farming and herding. Farming is more peaceable than herding. We experience an adaptation to changing economies, herding Semitic people out-number and/or out-muscle Sumerian farm people; rising patriarchal domination is taking power and control over women from the goddess.

Story and myth reflect human life and behavior; nature and geography. "Woman" is the metaphor to express life. Early people recognize "Life" as a mother, a great mother, who mirrors woman's body, reproductive functions, and woman's double X humane-ity.

Once upon a time in the lands at hand and far away, lived people who were of two kinds: wise and not wise. The wise ones kindly led the unwise into sacred understanding of life, living together, cooperating, and participating in the care of the young, the land, and each other. The wise ones taught the others with stories, dance, images, ritual and song. They celebrated and were grateful for Life. The unwise had a handicap that could be overcome; once overcome, they too could be wise ones; even trusted elders.

Religion reflects the people who cherish it. "No religion is truly real — identifiable and analyzable —except through and within the individuals who practice it, individuals who, alone, using the mechanism of their minds and their hearts, hold the secrets of it, even if they are unaware that they do so" (Bottero 2001: 2). Every Sumerian hearing the sacred hymns and songs and taking part in public religious ritual of the time knew the story and deities in personally felt devotions. As we explore more about Inanna, I ask the reader to use imagination, senses, life experiences, and gratitude for life to feel her presence travel over the millennia and miles into the reader's presence.

INANNA AS EVENING STAR

Inanna is our memory of evening star. She is nearby and lingers close at hand. She is easily accessed by searching the sky as evening deepens. The following ancient Sumerian poem lines for the great Queen of Heaven, Lady of the Evening, span the millennia.

The translations of the Ancient Near Eastern writing, from c. 3500 B.C.E. to the end of the first millennium B.C.E. used in this book, have retained the translator's indicators for missing fragments and guesses at word meanings. Selections are excerpted from longer texts. The ancient scribes used frequent repetitions for the listening pleasure and participation of their audience. I include here the lines and verses needed to tell Inanna's story. The back story for better understanding is inserted between the sections. The following group of poems have to do with Inanna in her star persona. (Wolkstein and Kramer 1983: 101:)

Figure 6. Inanna's Star Emblem Variations

The holy one stands alone in the sky

THE LADY OF THE EVENING

My Lady looks in sweet wonder from heaven.
The people of Sumer parade before the holy Inanna.
Inanna, the Lady of the Evening, is radiant.
I sing your praises, holy Inanna.
The Lady of the Evening is radiant on the horizon.

Thorkild Jacobsen translates the following descriptive praise hymn that includes many of Inanna's attributes and powers. Imagine a full performance publicly conducted in the temple proper or its courtyard. The people are hushed. Inanna is ceremonially costumed and adorned.

She sits or stands on her dais. The king sits beside her. Temple performers sing, dance, and play the appropriate instruments. Since it is Inanna, I suspect we stand in twilight watching for her star and/or the new moon. (Jacobsen 1987: 113-124:)

THE ONE COME FORTH ON HIGH

The one come forth on high,
    the one come forth on high,
    I will hail!
The holy one (*nu-gig*), come forth on high,
    I will hail!
The great [queen] of heaven,
    Inanna,
    I will hail!
The pure torch lit in the sky,
the heavenly light, lighting like day,
the great queen of heaven, Inanna,
    I will hail!
The holy one,
    queen awe-laden
    of the Anunnaki,
noblest one in heaven and earth,
    crowned with great horns,
oldest child of the Moon,
    Inanna,
    I will hail!

Of her grandeur, of her greatness,
    of her brilliant coming forth
    in the evening sky,
of her lighting up in the sky,
    a pure torch,
of her stepping up onto the sky

like Moon and Sun,
noted by all lands from south to north,
of the greatness of the holy one of heaven,
to the young lady I will sing!

(chant): "Her coming forth is (that of) a warrior."

(1)

She likes wandering in the sky,
    being truly Heaven's wild cow,
on earth she is noble, queen of all lands,
in the Deep [Apsu, fresh water], in Eridu, she took office,
her father Enki conferred it on her,
laid to her hand lordship and kingship.
With An she has taken her seat
    on the great throne dais,
with Enlil she will be making
    the decisions for her country,
Monthly, at new moon,
    that the offices be carried out properly,
the country's gods gather unto her.
The great Anunnaki, having bowed to her
are stepping up for prayer, petition, and plaint,
able to voice unto her
    the pleas of all lands,
and Milady decides the country's cases,
    settling them.
[Inanna] makes the decisions
    for the country,
        having them carried out.
The dark-headed people
    are parading before her.

(chant): "Her coming forth is (that of) a warrior."

The above text is a description of Inanna as she once was, with her powers of office intact. We will see scribes directed by priestly revisions adding gods who associate with her and build status through her. She is Queen of Heaven, Queen of Earth, and Queen of the Deep, the Apsu. This is a title surviving from earlier understanding. Inanna reigns over the Apsu, the fresh water under the earth that seeps up in wells and marshes. It is our first clue that Inanna is none other than the prime creatress, Nammu, mother of the Apsu, "the mother who gave birth to heaven and earth" (Kramer 1961:39). Over time Nammu is made prime creatress of the Sea, the bitter salty water, the Sea Primeval; Inanna is an aspect of her. Nammu's "son", Enki became god of the Apsu, the deep fresh water. When "her father" is written, we recognize an attempt to place male authority over the sacred feminine. When she "rules with" (Enlil) or "sits with" (An), we see male additions in the pantheon rising by association with her. When Enki "conferred" her with granting kingship and rulership, remember — she had that power from early days. A ruler rules because she selects him, she "loves" him, he is her beloved, he has successful sex with her. Rulership comes through sacred "marriage" (sex) with the goddess as the demigod Dumuzi's proxy. Dumuzi and Tammuz are the names of the vegetation demigods who are consorts for Sumerian Inanna and her Semitic equivalent, Ishtar.

Inanna hears prayers, petitions and plaints; she makes decisions for the land. She settles disputes. While her people sleep, she decides their cases. Her new moon celebration gathers the people and deities together; she makes her decisions known. Her new moon festival is joyous. People come to see and celebrate her; musicians perform with tambourines, harps, and "*algar*-instruments" (small harps with little drum heads attached); kettledrums sound. We learn about her cult personnel. Her guardsmen were once warriors but became ritual performers whose hair is carefully coiffed with colorful ribbons. The temple performers wear sheepskin robes as did earlier people and their deities. Fashion sense for divine personalities always lags behind contemporary dress. In another poem, credited to Enheduanna, *en* priestess, daughter of Sargon the Great, Inanna "wears the robes of the old old gods."

The lines about "fine men" and "eminent ladies" walking with "the doyenne of the women sages" is revealing. The woman sages are wise women who advise people; the wisest women advise the king. Here is evidence of former times when women were consulted and heard, even by kings. The lines of repetition invite familiarity and audience participation, the indicated chant line is for the temple singers.

(2)

Algar-instruments, silver inwrought,
    they are beating for her,
      —before holy Inanna, before her eyes,
        they are parading —
The great queen of heaven, Inanna,
    I will hail!
Holy harps and holy kettledrums
    they are smiting for her,
      —before holy Inanna, before her eyes,
    they are parading—
The oldest child of the Moon,
    Inanna,
    I will hail!

(chant): "Her coming forth is (that of) a warrior"

(3)

The guardsmen have combed
    (their hair) for her,
      —before holy Inanna, before her eyes
they are parading—
    they have made colorful for her
    the back hair with colored ribbons,
      —before holy Inanna, before her eyes
    they are parading—

on their bodies are (sheep)skin (robes)
    (the dress) of divinities,
        —before holy Inanna, before her eyes,
        they are parading—
Fine men, eminent ladies,
    the doyennes of the women sages,
        —before holy Inanna, before her eyes
        they are parading—
who hold harps and calming instruments,
    march beside them.
        —before holy Inanna, before her eyes,
        they are parading—

They (themselves) are girt
    with implements of battle,
        —before holy Inanna, before her eyes
        they are parading—
spears, the arms of battle,
    are in their hands,
        —before holy Inanna, before her eyes,
        they are parading—

(chant): "Her coming forth is (that of) a warrior."

The following section includes analysis of the goddess' intriguing ability: to turn men into women and women into men. Gender is indicated by the drape of the upper clothing. The following lines have the right shoulder and arm covered and left uncovered for men; women are similarly draped but with the opposite shoulder covered. In lines farther down, male reverse-dressers expose their "painted buttocks" as a parody of women's menstruation; they "engage in single combat" (involving only two people, a euphemism for copulation). Women traditionally enter seclusion during menses. Remember, menstrual blood is powerful, even feared. Men draped as women with "paint" imitating menstrual blood on their buttocks are publicly out and about and furthermore engaged in "single combat". Sex during the menses was taboo because menses was sacred. Inanna represents women's blood power, menstruation, especially the first maiden menses.

Inanna is the crescent moon goddess as are her equivalent "virgin" goddesses; Virgin Mary is often painted with a new crescent moon. Before male fertilization is understood, all cultures believe it is the woman's blood alone that creates the new life. The young goddess is celebrated monthly at new moon; women's return from seclusion. As warrior goddess she is later involved with defense and conflict. During menstrual bleeding, the blood that creates, she and woman are taboo and fearsome. Kings rise to power through her love secretions. (Ambrosia was originally women's blood.) Medieval alchemy requires menstrual blood. The male cross-dressers are before us burlesquing for crowd amusement.

(4)

Their right arms are clothed with cloth
　　in male fashion,
　　—before holy Inanna, before her eyes,
　　they are parading—
the great queen of heaven, Inanna,
　　I will hail!
On their left arms they have pulled
　　the cloth down and off
　　—before holy Inanna, before her eyes
　　they are parading—
the great queen of heaven, Inanna,
　　I will hail!
Playfully, with painted buttocks,
　　they engage in single combat
　　—before holy Inanna, before her eyes,
　　they are parading—
the oldest child of the Moon,
　　Inanna,

I will hail!

(chant): "Her coming forth is (that of) a warrior."

Figure 7. Instruments on Parade

The new moon parade for Inanna is a joyous and inclusive monthly event. Small drums and kettledrums; harps, lyres, and tambourines play; priestesses, priests and temple singers chant: "Her coming forth (is that) of a warrior" and the people respond: "before holy Inanna, before her eyes they are parading." Her people dress in their best for her festival. A proverb warns young men to beware of choosing a bride on festival days as her jewelry and costume are likely borrowed. The girl may not be who she seems!

The next stanza describes actors as captive soldiers begging Inanna for mercy; the goddess can grant clemency. Girls and old women walk with their hair loose and curly. Luxurious and abundant hair is a symbol of strength in both genders; loosened hair is powerful sexuality and a reminder of the girls' future potential of allure and fertility and the memory of older women's past allure and fertility. Prostitutes also signal their availability with loosened hair imitating Inanna's allure and sexuality. They present themselves as unofficial priestesses imitating the temple priestesses who initiate men into humane-ity through their art of "being a woman". Beads worn at the neck are Inanna/Ishtar's love charms and signify the goddess's sensual power and the draw of her allure. Her driving force of life's renewal through the energy of sexuality and fertility is expressed as "love" and "sex". Sex, allure, sensuality, and pleasure are sacred. Inanna/Ishtar is the only Ancient Near Eastern deity who loves and cares about women forced into unofficial prostitution through hardship. Constant conflict and upheaval left many widows and widows with children, who, if unprotected without family and unable to enter the temple for shelter and sustenance, had only voluntary servitude or prostitution left as survival options. Inanna loves them. Some food assistance is available for widows and orphans from the storehouse while Inanna is powerful.

Various weapons are carried by her personnel as symbols of earlier cult warriors who fought for the temple and Inanna. A priest drips blood from his sword onto her dais (Wolkstein and Kramer 1983: 99). The blood could be the priest's own, a cut made to indicate his self-imposed eunuch status, however, the lines below this one in Jacobsen's translation describe the administrators, the temple *ens,* who shed blood in the courtyard. Cutting or shedding blood is an imitation of women's menses. Men did not bleed naturally; they had to make blood flow. At some point in our human mythmaking, animals are sacrificed for blood offerings and the flesh roasted and shared with the people on festival days.

Inanna is overseer of the storehouse and herds. She continues as the great mother of abundance though her youthful fertility has the staring role. In settled farming she is portrayed in her youthful potential as evoker of life's fertility and not the moon-round pregnant mother goddess of the upper Paleolithic people. When people settle to farm, storehouses expand. No longer nomadic, people's religious beliefs could be expressed in art forms unlimited by portability. Storehouses grow into early temples; Inanna's temple at Uruk is the first monumental structure built (Woolley).

Inanna's praise hymn lists instruments: *tigi*-harps, tambourines, and lyres that play joyously and loudly! Wolkstein and Kramer include other entertainments and performers in a new moon parade: "They play the sweet *ala*-drums before you ... They beat the holy drum and timpani before you ... They play the holy harp ... The people compete with jump ropes and colored cords ... The young men, who carry hoops, sing to you" (Wolkstein and Kramer 1983: 97).

The reference to Inanna as a "warrior" comes from three goddess-orientated ideas. First, mothers protect and defend their young. Inanna is the mother goddess defending her black haired people, her children. Second, she represents menstrual blood power; wars are bloody. Third, Inanna, as early all-purpose mother, is a weather goddess: she is soaking rain and dark storm clouds rising above the horizon like a great black eagle bringing destructive flooding with loud thunder and lightening. Her emblem, the Imdugud bird, is a black eagle with a roaring lion head hybrid to fit the appearance and sound of fierce storms. Imdugud is a thunderbird. Wars and storms are noisy and destructive. Inanna's storm noisiness is frequently mentioned both in war and for intimidating gods to do her just bidding. Imdugud, as emblem, is placed with Inanna or represents her in many cylinder seals. The Jacobsen text continues:

Figure 8. Imdugud Bird (Sumerian Thunderbird)

(5)

(Captive) lads in neck stocks
    bewail to her (their fate)
—before holy Inanna, before her eyes,
    they are parading—
maidens and crones, curling their hair (as harlots)
—before holy Inanna, before her eyes
    they are parading—
daggers and clubs rage before her
—before holy Inanna, before her eyes,
    they are parading—
gore is covering the daggers,
    blood sprinkles,
—before holy Inanna, before her eyes,
    they are parading—
in the courtyard, the (place of) assembly

of the temple administrators,
    they are shedding blood
(as) loudly resounds there
(gay music of) *tigi*-harps, tambourines, and lyres.

The holy one has seen fit to step up
    lone on the clear sky,
and on all lands, teaming
    like the nation's dark-headed people,
from heaven's midst Milady
    looks kindly down.
August is the queen, the evening star, Inanna.
Fitly (therefore) they praise the maiden Inanna.
August is the queen, the evening star, Inanna,
    unto the borders of heaven!

(chant): "Her coming forth is (that of) a warrior"

Evening star announces night's coming coolness and rest for human and beast alike. Wild animals and orchards rest; fish and birds, gardens and canebrakes welcome evening. The young man is cheerful (his work day has ended) and the young woman brightens (she looks forward to her man returning). Night is the welcomed respite from sun's heat; night is for rest and lovemaking. "Living beings" and "numerous people" bend their knees in worship of her. All play and festivities quiet; the young married couples have time to talk "heart to heart."

(6)

The evening star, the brilliantly rising star,
    shedding great light over holy heaven,
the queen, the evening star, has seen fit
    to come forth on high,
    warrior-like in the sky,
and in all lands the people

are lifting up their faces toward her,
the man is cheering up, the woman is brightening,
the ox in its yoke is turning the head (homewards),
sheep and goats (?) (shuffling back)
    make the dust settle (thick) in their folds.
The numerous (wild) goats and asses of Shaken,[4]
the animals of the desert,
the far-flung four-footed beasts,
the orchard pits, the garden beds
    the green canebrake,
the fish of the deep, the birds of heaven,
Milady is making wend their way
    to their lairs.
(All) living beings, the numerous people,
are bending (their) knees to her.

Called by Milady, the old women
are providing plentifully
    for great eating and drinking.
(Then) Milady calms down
    everything in her country,
the playgrounds of the nations,
    the holiday makers;
and the young brave
    holds converse with the wife
    heart (to heart).

From heaven's midst Milady
    looks kindly down,
before holy Inanna, before her eyes,
    they walk –

---

[4] Here, god of goats, asses and gazelles; in early Sumerian texts it is the mother goddess who creates humans out of clay and blood. Her name is Ki, renamed Ninhursag, Lady of the Steppes, and demoted to mother of wild asses, donkeys and goats.

August is the queen, the evening star in the sky,
　　Inanna.
Fitly (therefore) they praise the maiden Inanna.
August is the queen, the evening star in the sky
unto the borders of heaven!

(chant): "Her coming forth is (that of) a warrior."

Inanna's people work hard. Evening means cessation of labor; evening means rest and relief from heat. Inanna is goddess of Ninsianna, the evening-morning star that is our planet Venus; the goddess Venus is a later equivalent of Inanna. For periods of time the planet that shines like a star is not visible from earth; ancient people compare a disappearance of a celestial body to women in seclusion; seclusion grew to include the underworld where the dead rest. Whether or not she is visible, Inanna, Starlight, Star Bright, is associated with rest; she calls everyone home. While people sleep, their "dream-soul *aflatis*"[5] approach her with the people's problems, appeals, and needs; she delivers fateful decisions and decrees. Her name is used for the word "decree" in Babylonian lexicons. The goddess takes a compassionate and personal interest in her people. She loves her people inclusively, from kings to desperate women selling sex by the city walls. All come to her. She is available to everyone. No god loves the people so unconditionally.

---

[5]　dream-soul *aflatis* is a divine being who brings the dreamer to petition the goddess

Figure 9. Goddess Bringing a Worshipper or Dreamer to Inanna

(7)

Preeminent in the (rose-) tinted sky
    the alluring one, befitting broad heaven,
has risen like moonlight at night,
has risen like sunlight at high noon.
Having imposed sweet sleep
    on the nation's homes,
while all lands, the dark-headed ones,
    the nation in its entirety,
sleep on roofs, sleep on city walls –
eloquent dream-soul *afflati* step up to her,
    bring her their cases.

Then she discerns the righteous one,
    discerns the wicked one.
The wicked one she will hand over
    to (serve) a wicked sentence,

the evil one she will do evil to.
On the just one she looks truly,
 determines a good fate for him.
From heaven's midst Milady
 looks kindly down.
Before holy Inanna, before her eyes,
 they walk.
August is the queen
 hovering where heaven is founded,
 Inanna.
Fitly (therefore) they praise
 the maiden Inanna.
August is the queen
 going (down) where heaven is founded
 unto the borders of heaven!

(chant): "Her coming forth (is that) of a warrior."

Night must end. The goddess and her consort, An[6], are awake and talk together on their couch. The couch is the sacred bed of the goddess. As patriarchy took over, only males appear in images on the couch while the women are seated on chairs.

Dreams finish, dawn emerges, sun rises. Inanna, as morning star (when her planet is visible in the early morning), calls everyone to rise and go into his or her active conscious day. Before work begins, morning rituals are observed. Whether on farms, city walls and house roofs or in palace and temple, a place is cleared and prepared for offering with sweet incense made of resin of conifers, the sacred trees of the goddess. Incense, and later burnt-offering smoke, is used to attract divine attention and invite that one to come close.

Hand washing is a morning rising ritual and everywhere, regardless of circumstances, a break-fast is laid out. Food offerings brought to Inanna, to her image, by her temple personnel include: "ghee, dates,

---

[6] *An* means heaven and indicates the god of heaven who was born of the creatress Nammu when she birthed earth and heaven.

cheese, seven kinds of fruit ... dark beer ... light beer ... wine ... honey and date cakes ... (and) loaves." Sheep are offered at the temple, as in *given* to the temple herds, not sacrificed as meat is not included in her breakfast, though she is the storehouse and oversees the sheepfold. There is a difference of foodstuff used in women-based celebrations compared to later male-based celebrations. Goddess worship of ancient Greece also used grain and nature's available foodstuff; neither blood sacrifice nor roasted meat are involved, only water, honey, grains, fermented grain or grape, fruit, and dairy products. Offerings for Inanna were plant food and that which is given by herd animals without killing them: cheese, butter, and milk. Inanna's breakfast is horticultural food, woman's food, goddess food. Crescent-shaped date-sweetened barley cakes, (Inanna) Ishtar cakes, are still made today.[7]

Incense (cedar) is burned. Cedar and other groves are sacred to the mother goddess. Inanna is associated with trees: she grew one for her throne/seat and bed, she is symbolized as the orchard tree in blossom, a rosette adorned branch, or rosette alone. Goddess' holy groves are a threat to patriarchy. They are destroyed in the Akkadian or Babylonian version of the *Epic of Gilgamesh*. Gilgamesh and his servant/companion Enkidu kill the peaceful guardian of the goddess's sacred mountain grove and then destroy Ishtar's (also known as Inanna's and Mother Goddess') sacred forest. Early Judaism destroyed sacred groves and the wooden pillars representing groves as the Hebrews moved into monotheistic Yahweh worship. What hairy heroes and religious zealots choose to destroy, here we find symbols, emblems, or names of the divine feminine.

(8)

The queen preeminent, the alluring one of heaven,
    has seen fit to come out, warrior-like, on high,
lovely is she at An's radiant side,
    with An on his august couch
        she holds converse heart (to heart).

---

[7] See notes at back of book for a Sumerian recipe for Inanna's date cake, lady cake.

(chant):"May she be found to be
    the young brave's and the warrior's only one!"

The queen marveled at by the nation,
    the lone star, the morning star,
the queen hovering where heaven is founded,
    has seen fit
    to come forth warrior-like on high,
and all lands do tremble before her.

The dark-headed people get up for her,
the young brave traveling the road
    sets his course by her,
the ox lifts up its head eagerly
    in its yoke.
While at the same time, in the nation's homes
    they provide everything aplenty,
hasten to holy Inanna,
and put it out in goodly fashion
    for Milady (up in) heaven's midst.

In the clean places, the clear places
    of the desert,
on the roofs, on the wall-tops,
    [of the dwellers on] wall-tops,
on mankind's smoothed-out spots (for offerings),
they bring her incense
    (fragrant) like a cedar forest.
Tine sheep, maned sheep, and grain-fed sheep
    they offer up.
For the holy one they clean up a place,
    set up handwashing (things) for her.

Ghee, dates, cheese, seven kinds of fruits,
they fill, as breakfast,

onto the country's table for her.
Dark beer they pour for her,
light beer [they pour] for her.
With dark beer and [*emmer* (woman's)] beer
shaggubbe-pot and the fermenting vat
    bubble, one as the other.
Of paste, liberally enriched with honey and ghee,
and of honey and dates, on cakes,
    they make loaves for her,
wine at dawn, finely ground flour,
    honeyed flour,
honey and wine at sunrise they libate for her.
The tutelary gods[8] of the humans step,
    as their part,
    up to her with the food and drink,
and the holy one eats in the pure places,
    the clean places.

From heaven's midst Milady
    looks kindly down,
before holy Inanna, before her eyes,
    they wander.
August where heaven is founded,
    is the queen, Inanna.
Fitly (therefore) they praise
    the maiden Inanna.
August is the queen
    hovering where heaven is founded
    unto the borders of heaven!

(chant): "Her coming forth (is that) of a warrior."

---

[8] Tutelary deities are the owners of settlements and urban centers. Kings and people work for them. They may travel as their figurine to visit other tutelary divines.

The poem extols many of Inanna's vast arrays of powers, her presence in people's daily lives, and their adoration and offerings to her. She *is* the storehouse for the Ancient Near East. No burnt offerings or roasting meat is required to attract her attention. The goddess is offered beer as a standard beverage. It is fermented in jars by women and drunk with long reed straws to avoid the sediment. The light beer, *emmer*, also called "lady's beer", was made from a different fermented grain (a reddish wheat) considered of higher value than the common barley used for dark beer. Women ran the taverns because it was women who fermented the beer. Inanna is also associated with taverns and beer. Wine is also mentioned; grapes were introduced long after indigenous barley was farmed and fermented. Beer was a staple from early days. All cultures have a fermented beverage of some sort. The effects of the fermented "spirits" are universal; the deities also imbibe, sometimes to excess.

Inanna's black headed people revere her whether they are rich or poor, women or men, priestess or priest, destitute or sacred prostitute. Kings and warriors claim her. Wild and tame animals, fish and birds, orchards and farms: everything living worships her. She is life. When conflict grew and spread over the land, she became the warrior star rising to lead the defending warriors to protect her people.

Armies fight in daylight. Morning star came to be associated with battle. Semitic Ishtar was known as female evening star and masculine morning star; the same "star" with different attributes. Walker mentions other such "twins" among deities: Yin-Yang, Eros-Psyche, Jana-Janus, Diana-Dianus, Artemis-Apollo, and Brahma-Bhavani (Walker 1983: 33). The female-male version of Semitic Ishtar represents the concept of androgyne of the above pairs, but Sumerian Inanna is always female.

The tutelary "gods of the humans" serve her food. The important fact here is that other deities serve Inanna. The sculpted figures of various deities travel to visit her or reside in the side cellae[9] of Inanna's temples. The representation of other deities also includes those of arriving immigrant groups. Inanna has a superior position in the

---

[9] plural of cella; small room

growing pantheon. "No god could say her nay!" She scares them; she growls or screams in rage and the gods flee "like bats leaving a cave." She also receives them companionably.

The final two sections below address the sacred "marriage" between Inanna and the man she selects to protect her, her land, and her people. The "marriage" is an annual renewal of a ruler. As *hieros gamos*, it represents the union of female and male to bring fertility of all life to the land. The consort courts and copulates with Inanna/Ishtar. If he pleases her with his virility, the land will grow food abundantly, herds will multiply, and he rules for another year. Virility is mimicry of crop and herd productivity. Sex is vital. Sexual pleasure is sacred. The composers of the sacred "marriage" poems present the king as proxy for the beloved consort god who, in the beginning of the poem is An, and by poem's end is Dumuzi ("good son" of Great Mother). Inanna selects him and makes love with him on her sacred bed. If he pleases her, he sits on her sacred dais, on her sacred seat, the throne. The seat belonging to the goddess began as women's menstrual seat and birthing chair; it is infused with life-giving blood power. We have texts written about the successful trysts of the rulers, her beloveds, but none where his virility fails.

Ancient Near Eastern rulers gained their thrones through her. When conflict became nearly continuous, texts describe Inanna/Ishtar as fickle and the losing side accuses her of abandoning her beloved, the king. Both side's kings claim her.

Eventually, additions and deletions in edited textural story supported absolute male rule in the cosmos and that of course supported absolute rule of special alpha men on earth. Remember, when a goddess is "married to", or "daughter of", know that a usurpation of sacred feminine and human woman has occurred. The following section of the long poem refers to Inanna as "bride." "Consort" is linguistically the better word choice, but Inanna is not a king's consort; he is *her* consort; she is more powerful and important. She chooses the ruler who serves her and protects her land and her people.

That the annual renewal of kingship and fertility in the land in this Sumerian composition is attached to the new moon monthly festival for Inanna is strange. Was it recited, chanted, enacted, sung and performed at each new moon as the rest of the poem suggests, or was the following section composed and used only at the annual sacred "marriage" event? Perhaps the liturgy was used every month as a retelling of reinstatement of the king with his participation in the fertility of the land.

This poem began with Inanna having An as her consort, yet these stanzas refer to the king as Ama-ushumgal-anna, another name for Dumuzi, the shepherd god. An's inclusion likely evolved in the late Paleolithic when the role of male fertility was understood and before the Neolithic farming dependency on fertility. An was replaced by Dumuzi as consort and An remained in the Sumerian pantheon only as a distant benevolent father god.

When Inanna is called Ninegalla, "queen of the palace," Jacobsen assumes the title to mean the "wife of the king". If so, the queen or priestess channeling Inanna, being Inanna, would be a woman of power, even divine, but no human woman in any of the texts is considered divine, only the kings. Goddess rose from the creative expression of women. Women birthed the goddess concept. Women set religion into being. Sacred woman everywhere is the distant root of all religion. Kings assumed their divinity when Inanna, through her proxy priestess, takes them to her bed and anoints them with oil, with her secretions, or perhaps her menstrual blood. In time, rulers deny their human mothers and replace them with goddess mothers. The ruler's sons inherit divine status; dynastic male lines are created. Late dynasties do not require the goddess to confer divine status; they self-proclaim it.

An interesting note in this hymn poem is that the ritual takes place in the palace. Inanna comes to the king. The palace, at the time of this composition or revision, has separated from the temple. The important annual event takes place in *his* chamber in *his* palace and not *her* chamber in *her* temple as is the old tradition.

(9)

55

In the palace,
>   the house that advises the country
>   and is a (restraining) yoke ["neck stock"]
>   on all foreign lands,
the house that is the river ordeal [10]
>   of the dark-headed people,
>   the nation in its entirety,
a dais has been founded for Ninegalla, ["queen of the palace"]
the king, being a god, will sojourn with her on it.

That she may take in charge
>   the life of all lands,
has on New Year's Day,
>   the day for rites
>   for reviewing loyal servants
and performing correctly
>   the rites of the last day of the month,
>   a bed been set up for Milady.
Halfa-straw they have been purifying
>   with cedar perfume,
have been putting it on that bed for Milady.
Over it a bedspread has been pulled straight for her,
a bedspread of heart's delight
>   to make the bed comfortable.

Milady bathes in water the holy loins,
for the loins of the king
>   she bathes them in water.
Holy Inanna rubs (herself) with soap,
sprinkles the floor with cedar perfume.

The king goes with (eagerly) lifted head

---

[10] The river ordeal was used to settle difficult disputes. The guilty party was tossed into the river. If he sank, he was guilty, it he made it back to shore, then the river deities declared his innocence.

to the loins of Inanna.

Ama-ushumgal-anna (Dumuzi) goes to bed with her:

"O my holy loins! O my holy Inanna!"

Several lines are interesting. The king with "eagerly lifted head" can mean either with pride or in arousal. When the king is in bed with Inanna, he cries, or the chanters exclaim for him: "O my holy loins! O my holy Inanna!" No matter how important and powerful Inanna is proclaimed in the above eight sections, the self-proclaimed divinity of the king allows him to bed the goddess in his palace; that same goddess, more adored and more powerful than all other male divine personalities is placed second to the king as we hear his "holy loins" praised first. The second exclamation is as troubling: "O *my* holy Inanna!", as if she is his because he bedded her, and not the other way around. Ama-ushumgal-anna is an epithet for Dumuzi who, after An faded as Inanna's consort, is her shepherd-god consort. He is named on the early king lists. Dumuzi may well have been a human ruler or hero or hero-king long ago and mythified to divine status. We return now as voyeurs in the royal bedchamber. The king has just climaxed and pleased Inanna; he praises his penis, his holy loins.

After he on the bed, in the holy loins,
    has made the queen rejoice,
after he on the bed, in the holy loins
    has made holy Inanna rejoice,
she in turn soothes the heart for him
    there on the bed:

"Iddin-Daggan, you are verily
    my beloved!"

To pure libations, lavers set up,
to gently wafted incense vapors,
    to lighted juniper incense,

to food portions standing ready,
 to jars standing ready
into his august palace
 she enters with him.
His loving consort has the arm
 around his shoulders,
holy Inanna has the arm around his shoulders,
shines forth on the arm-lean throne
 like the dawn.
With her radiates there, on the long side of the table,
 sunlike the king.
Abundance, delicacies, plenty,
 they bring straight to her,
a banquet of sweet things
 they lay out,
the dark-headed people
 bring it straight to her.
The bard has the lute,
 that gives tongue from the podium,
the sweet-sounding *agar*-instruments,
and the lyre, which belongs
 where mankind is gay,
prove themselves
 in his song of joy of heart.

The king has reached out for food and drink,
Ama-ushumgal-anna has reached out
 for food and drink.
The palace is in festive mood,
 the king is joyous,
the nation spends the time amid plenty,
Ama-ushumgal-anna is come in joy,
long may he live on this pure throne!
On the royal throne dais she has
 (her) head on (his) shoulder.

O Milady, you are given praise
    to the borders
    of heaven and earth!
You being a holy one,
    engendered with heaven and earth,
holy passages, pure passages
    for a holy one,
    are put in song!
O (you), chief ornament of the night,
befitting the assembly,
Inanna, oldest child of the Moon,
Queen, evening star, to praise you is sweet!

(10)

From heaven's midst Milady looks kindly down –
before holy Inanna, before her eyes,
    they walk.
August is the queen, the evening star,
    unto the borders of Heaven!
Mighty she is, noble, elevated to high rank,
    great she is and august,
in heroism surpassing.

(the scribe adds:) A song of valor pertaining to Ninsianna.[11]

---

[11] Ninsianna, "heaven's radiant queen", is Inanna's name as both morning and evening star; our planet Venus.

Figure 10. Banquet Scene

The above poem was selected for its wide scope of descriptions of who Inanna is. Her biography is written in present tense, not past. Goddess is Life. Life is. Bottero writes that (Bottero 2001: 2:)

... no religion is truly real — identifiable and analyzable— except through and within the individuals who practice it, individuals who, alone, using the mechanism of their minds and their hearts, hold the secrets of it, even if they are unaware that they do so.

The worship of Inanna, Great Goddess, is organic. The operative word in the above quotation is "individuals" — separate, alone and not organized. The feminine principles are obvious and indwelling; worship of goddess is never forced, coerced, nor in muscular competition for soul counting. I believe Inanna is accessible to contemporary women. She is the metaphor, the expression of woman's presence, wisdom, and potential. She is whole and complete, though several millennia of incomplete male-based male-superior religions have forced, coerced, threatened, and killed to cut Great Mother, her fertile daughter self, and women from their religions. Her story continues to resurface. Our amazement and awe of being alive, of life, the observation of life energy that our foremothers recognized and named Great Mother, is still within us. Inanna is a starting place for reclamation of our selves, our story, and our world.

Who is Inanna? She is Life! She is Wisdom! She is Woman! (Baring and Cashford 1991: 176:)

> Inanna, or Ishtar as she was called in Northern Sumeria (Sumer), was one of the three great goddesses of the Bronze Age, the others being Isis of Egypt and Cybele of Anatolia. All three reflect the image of the Great Mother who presided over the earliest civilizations that arose between Europe and the Indian subcontinent. Inanna relates the Neolithic Great Mother to the biblical Eve [Life], Sophia [Wisdom] and Mary. Her imagery is the foundation of Sophia (the Hebrew Hokhmah, or wisdom), the Gnostic Great Mother and even the Medieval Shekninah of the Jewish Kabbalah.

Sumerian texts are carried forward in the Flood story, the Garden of Eden (i.e., the place of Eve and serpent, but not the Eve, Adam, serpent, and angry God version), and the Song of Songs. Inanna is the Archetypal Feminine that is yet alive. Queen of Heaven, Queen of Earth is at home in the celestial dome and present as both lunar crescent and planetary evening star. She journeys to earth; she strides and runs over the land; she enters and leaves the underworld. She terrorizes unfair gods who "cannot say her nay!" Lions attend her. She roars; she is noisy like lions and thunderstorms. Regional rulers argue over whom she loves most. She shoulders her quiver that holds stalks of snakes, buds, and defensive weapons. She holds her scepter of office and the measuring rod, ring, and line.

The following chapter will investigate more of Inanna's powers, the ME. They are vast and encompass almost everything. They are the powers of culture and civilization. They also include contradictory human behaviors. The goddess owns them and gives them to her people.

CHAPTER 2

Inanna and Her *Me*

QUEEN OF ALL THE ME

Inanna holds the ME (pronounced "may"). The word represents so large a concept that we have no equivalent translation and the Sumerian word is retained. ME is traditionally left as itself and appears as ME or *me* or *ME* in various translations. This book uses ME excepting where a variant is used in texts. The ME is the civilizing power, authority, rulership, decree-making, laws, crafts, water, love, the art of women, and much, much more. The ME is civilization's developed cultural authority over lordship, artisans, and all manner of human behavior. We learn that these "powers" are carried, worn, and/or ridden. They are often represented by symbolic objects and are numerous. The prototype of ME is based on woman and her honored position and authority. A pure matriarchy, mirroring patriarchy, never existed. Women are inclusive, unlike the later exclusive patriarchal rule of male domination. The ME belong to Inanna. They are created by women. About one hundred areas of powers are listed as her ME. Later texts credit her with only seven. Inanna does not keep the ME for herself; she owns them and keeps them safe; but she brings them to her people.

A myth survives of how Inanna got the ME back from sweet-water god, Enki. The reader will recognize the androcratic hand re-framing the early authority of woman and her divine image. The text's list includes the pre-writing time-honored culture-creating authority of woman. The list of Inanna's ME is found below in Wolkstein and Kramer's, *Inanna Queen of Heaven and Earth,* in a selection named "Inanna and the God of Wisdom." I would suggest the title: "How Inanna Got Her ME Back." (Wolkstein and Kramer. 1983: 12-27:)

INANNA AND THE GOD OF WISDOM

The story opens with Inanna putting her crown in place; she rests against an apple tree; "her vulva was wondrous to behold (ibid.:12)." She decides to visit Enki, god of wisdom, in the Abzu, the deep water. He is son of Nammu the prime creatress who is first Great Mother and elder image of Inanna. Because he is the god of wisdom, he "knows all things." He tells his sukkal (administrative assistant) that Inanna is coming to the Abzu; he is to set her at the holy table of heaven by a lion statue and "treat her like an equal." [We ask, an equal to the administrative assistant or equal to Enki? Furthermore, note: lion has to do with Inanna and not the sweet water underground god.] Inanna is given butter cake, pure water and beer. Inanna and Enki drink beer together. Their beer drinking vessels are full; they drink and toast and drink some more.

Enki is tipsy and begins giving Inanna powers, the ME, with drunken generosity. "Godship!" "Kingship!" With each group of ME, she says: "I take them!" Enki drinks more and gives more ME to her. "The art of lovemaking! The kissing of the phallus!" (ibid.:15) Enki gets more and more drunk. "Truth!" "Descent" and "ascent" to and from the netherworld! "I take them!" Enki gives Inanna all the ME. He tells his sukkal with two-faces that Inanna is returning to Uruk and to give her safe passage. Inanna and her assistant, Ninshubur, Lady Dawn,

*load the ME on Inanna's boat of heaven. Inanna is sober; she
lists her ME (ibid.: 16-18 partial lines:)*

Figure 11. Inanna's Boat of Heaven

... high priesthood
... godship
... noble, enduring crown
... throne of kingship
... noble scepter
... staff
... holy measuring rod and line
... high throne
... shepherdship
... kingship
... princess priestess
... divine queen priestess
... incantation priest
... noble priest
... truth
... descent into the underworld
... ascent from the underworld

**Figure 12. Inanna
with Scepter**

... *kurgarra* (expert mourner)
... dagger and sword
... black garment
... colorful garment
... loosening of the hair
... binding of the hair
... standard
... quiver
... art of lovemaking
... kissing of the phallus
... art of prostitution
... art of speeding
... art of forthright speech
... art of slanderous speech
... art of adoring speech
... cult prostitute
... holy tavern
... holy shrine
... holy priestess of heaven
... resounding musical instrument
... art of song
... art of the elder
... art of the hero
... art of power
... art of treachery
... art of straightforwardness
... plundering of cities
... setting up of lamentations
... rejoicing of the heart
... deceit
... rebellious land
... art of kindness
... travel
... secure dwelling place

Figure 13. Couple Embracing

Figure 14. Musician with Harp

... craft of the woodworker
... craft of the copper worker
... craft of the scribe
... craft of the smith
... craft of the leather maker
... craft of the fuller
... craft of the builder
... craft of the reed worker
... perceptive ear
... power of attention
... purification rites
... feeding pen
... heaping up of hot coals
... sheepfold
... fear
... consternation
... dismay
... bitter-toothed lion
... kindling of fire
... putting out of fire
... the weary arm
... the assembled family
... procreation
... kindling of strife
... counseling
... heart-soothing
... giving of judgments
... making of decisions

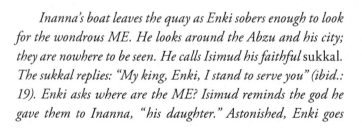

Figure 15. Sheepfold

Inanna's boat leaves the quay as Enki sobers enough to look for the wondrous ME. He looks around the Abzu and his city; they are nowhere to be seen. He calls Isimud his faithful sukkal. *The sukkal replies: "My king, Enki, I stand to serve you" (ibid.: 19). Enki asks where are the ME? Isimud reminds the god he gave them to Inanna, "his daughter." Astonished, Enki goes down the list of the ME, and finds he gave them all to Inanna. Enki asks his sukkal the location of the Boat of Heaven and is told "it is one quay away." Enki orders his servant to take the* enkum-*creatures (some sort of monster) and bring the Boat of Heaven and its cargo of ME back to Eridu.*

Isimud tells Inanna that "her father" has sent a command that must be obeyed. She asks what words he sent that must be obeyed. "Let Inanna proceed to Uruk; bring the Boat of Heaven with the holy me (ME) back to Eridu." (ibid.: 21) Inanna is angry. Enki went back on his word, he lied! With that, wild-haired creatures grab her Boat of Heaven. Inanna shouts to Ninshubur reminding her she was once "Queen of the East" (Dawn) and now serves Inanna's shrine in Uruk; she is wise and a good fighter. Save us! Ninshubur makes a tremendous cry and cuts the air with her hand. (I imagine a divine karate chop here.) Enki's creatures are stopped (ibid.: 22).

Priestly mythmakers of this text name Enki son of prime creatress and owner of the ME. First, Enki has taken over Nammu's Abzu. Secondly, the priestly editors have given Enki the civilizing ME. The ME in other stories and temple names indicate they belong to Inanna.

Remember, Goddess is woman writ large. The ME first belonged to the women. Men coveted women's life-creating blood and birthing, their womb and blood power. Men eventually took every part of culture and civilizing authority for themselves. Of course they want the ME! What is Enki doing with them? He is keeping them for himself. Inanna's intention for them is far different. She brings them to her people.

When Inanna came to visit Enki, (the statues of deities visited one another), she enacted, on divine scale, an old tradition as old as women creating culture. During menstrual seclusion, they left behind their usual duties and belongings; their trappings of office (Knight and Gahn), to sit on their seclusion seat or cushion. That seat becomes the powerful throne of rulership *because* it is associated with women's blood power. At the end of seclusion women bathe and take up their usual roles. Since women secluded in solidarity, whether menstruating or not, it is possible that male elders held the sacred or power symbols until the women returned.

Inanna is offered lady's beer and given sweet cakes — celebratory food for emergence from seclusion. Emmer beer, more refined than barley beer, is poured for her and honeyed cakes are offered.

Etana, an early king, approached Inanna in another story while she was in heavenly seclusion. An eagle flew him to her to get a plant for his barren wife so he could have an heir. He peers through her window and sees her nude on her cushion with a lion beside her. When moon is dark, she and women are absent; when evening star and other celestial bodies are not visible, they are in sacred and powerful seclusion. While goddess reigns supreme, death is linked to that sacred time-out cycle and return. The ME powers of culture begin with woman and her amplified image — goddess. Inanna is the young potentially fertile form of the prime creatress. Inanna is "first snake". Enki is prime creatress' "son". Inanna is the first story so Enki is *her* son. Enki came later, in both divine genealogy and story. Mythic story alters as human culture, behavior, and experience change. Men had begun their usurpation of sacred woman in the Ancient Near East by the time of first writing.

Further evidence of patriarchal encroachment is: "Your father's words are words of state. They may not be disobeyed (ibid.: 20)." Nice try, but Inanna in other texts is the goddess to whom "no god could say her nay!" That she is called "daughter" is the traditional term applied to girls and young women; and "father" is the respectful address for older men. "Sister" is synonymous for "wife" and "brother" for husband, indicating closeness — "like a sister" or "like a brother". In this case, "father" and "daughter" are not about age but imposed demotion in divine genealogy. Enki should call Inanna "mother" as she is the young aspect of his mother, Nammu. The relational terms are added to put "daughter" goddesses under the control of "father" gods through gender domination. The "father" gods are usurping the power and attributes of the original goddess. Here, priestly pirates are already testing to see what they can get away with in storytelling. Enki is a patriarchal god who keeps some of his Xness, his humane-ity, intact in another myth[12] but here he reacts to the loss of the ME by angrily unleashing assorted demons against the goddess's escape.

Inanna, with the help of her vizier/sukkal (administrative assistant), Ninshubur (Queen of the East), escapes Enki's demons. Ninshubur is associated with both Inanna and An, the oldest god, but not the oldest deity. An is Inanna's consort when a male partner is introduced into the prime creatress story. Nammu is imagined as a great serpent and sculpted as a woman body and serpent head hybrid; she creates heaven and earth. Nammu and Inanna are called first snake; Nammu is mother of the gods.

If that sacred merging, *hieros gamos,* represented an early partnership for our species, and I suspect it did, then our present Sumerian text is sliding dangerously away from the needful balance and moderating influence of X holding Y accountable and cooperative. 'Inanna and the God of Wisdom' is about Y taking power; when the rightful owner, Inanna, regains it, he responds with aggressive tyrannical behavior. He tries to recapture the prize by force. Enki has been given Inanna's ME by priestly piracy. Men are taking over politically. It would not do for a woman, a goddess, to hold all the civilizing powers. With the press of a stylus they are Enki's.

The new story does not yet have momentum; the people remember the earlier version and so, for now, Inanna recovers her ME, but only because Enki *gives* them to her; to give them to her he had to be drunk out of his mind; he was senselessly inebriated because Inanna got him drunk, poor him. Inanna, an adolescent, just past her first menses, is unaffected, though matching him beer for beer. She remains fully present and sober. Drunk, he gives the ME (back) to Inanna and then acts as if it were she who perpetrated a wrong on him. He does not confront her himself. In the early days, gods were not greater than a great goddess. He sends his vizier/sukkal, a perhaps lesser local god, to

---

[12] In the Sumerian Flood story Enki goes against Enlil and saves humanity from disaster twice and finally reveals to one man that he should build a safe boat, collect animals, and seal his family and animals into the boat during the deluge.

do his dirty work. He invokes demons to capsize her boat and prevent her from bringing the powers to her city. With Lady of the East's help (dawn light "slashes" the night sky and accompanies morning star), Inanna avoids disaster. Inanna calms the waves that Enki sends; she reaches the quays of Uruk. Power over water is a goddess talent. The ME are taken to Inanna's temple precinct and quay. Her divine civilizing powers are given to the people. Because people are not perfect, the ME include contradictory behaviors. Human nature.

Figure 16. Mesopotamian Mythological Monsters

Enki, under the influence of alcohol, gives the ME (back) to her. Drunkenness is a time-honored excuse for many actions. Beer is easily fermented, and if not an everyday beverage, is at least consumed frequently in the Ancient Near East. As people drink, so does their pantheon. Libations of both pure water and beer are ritually offered. Deities enjoy their beer, even to excess. Enki gets drunk; Inanna does not. Drunk, his guard is down; he generously does the right thing, he returns the ME. Sobering, he wants the goddess' powers, the ME, for himself. We return to the action. The creatures of Enki are not translatable, but they are numerous; we hear a bit of description but must rely on our imagination.

> *Enki's* enkum-*creatures were thrown back to Eridu. Enki asks Isimud again where Inanna and the Boat of Heaven are. "Two quays away from Eridu." Enki sends "fifty* uru-*giants ... to carry off the Boat of Heaven." The "flying" fifty seizes the craft and again Ninshubur saves their boat. Enki asks where Inanna is now, and he is told she has reached Dulma. He sends fifty* labama-*sea monsters. Again, Ninshubur defeats them. He sends a "sound-piercing* kugalgal," *the* enun, *and the "watchmen of the Iturungal Canal." Every assault is countered by Ninshubur. (Perhaps, like "vampires", the light of coming day dispels them!)*
>
> *When the Boat of Heaven comes safely into the harbor gate of Uruk, Inanna's own city, the goddess's sukkal advises her to "let high water flow in our city. Let the deep-going boats sail swiftly through our canals" (ibid.: 24). (The rising water is the Euphrates flooding after snow melt and spring rains in the north.) There is so much water that her Boat of Heaven docks at her shrine. (Inanna represents rain; she holds her breast to indicate her clouds of heaven that let down rain. Ninshubur's instructions connect the goddess to water; an old feminine power.) Inanna is home and water spills over the streets and paths. She will address her people and order that "the old men give counsel," the old women offer comforting, the young men brandish weapons, the children are happy with song, and priests come to her arrival with song, prayers, and beer libation. The land (Sumer) will proclaims her; the people will sing her praise (ibid.: 22-4).*
>
> *Inanna and Ninshubur enter the gate at Uruk exactly as the sukkal described. Enki has not given up! "Isimud, where are they now?" They have docked at the white quay, at Eanna. Inanna astonishes everyone. Every ME is announced, all the*

> *ones known and some new. The sukkal informs Enki that*
> *even more ME than Enki knew are unloaded. Inanna gives*
> *these to the people as well: "placing the garment on the ground*
> *(for prayer or lovemaking?)," "the art of women," the ability*
> *for "the perfect execution of the* me," *and new sorts of drums*
> *and tambourines for ceremony. Enki is defeated. He makes a*
> *proclamation and fate for Uruk: "Let the* me *you have taken*
> *with you remain in the holy shrine of your city. Let the high*
> *priest spend his days at the holy shrine in song. Let the city of*
> *Uruk be restored to its great place (ibid.: 25-7)."*

There is another possible explanation for the ME being with Enki in Eridu. Statues of a deity contain the deity. Inanna's figurine *is* Inanna to her people just as religious people today talk and pray to statues of Virgin Mary, Jesus, Kwan Yin, and Buddha. When war and conflict infect the Ancient Near East, cities and temples are raided, looted, and often destroyed. Statues of cities' divine owners are kidnapped to dispirit the populace into submission. The final phrase of Wolkstein and Kramer's interpretation is curious. Uruk is "restored to its great place". Enki was the tutelary owner of Eridu, a city on the Euphrates south of Uruk and said to be the oldest Sumerian city. A looting of Inanna's temple by soldiers of Eridu would explain how Enki came into possession of Inanna's ME. By the time of this story version, the culturally developed Sumerians are disappearing; they are outnumbered by the influx of tribal, nomadic and semi-nomadic Semitic speaking people. Though Sumerian remains the language of sacred, legal, and literary texts, the Sumerian people disappear. One may imagine a rivalry, a sacking of Eanna, and the theft of both Inanna and her ME.

Lordly queen of the awesome ME

Of special interest to contemporary women is that Sumerian women had a voice. They were fully involved in co-guiding settled urban centers, managing farming estates and administrating both storehouse and temple. The text records that Inanna still held the civilizing and human relational powers. Eridu's "king" god Enki lost the treasure when

Inanna and her assistant, Ninshubur, Queen of the East, successfully regained them. Another hint that Enki did not originate the ME is the added powers, "more *me* than Enki had given" her. Besides new sorts of drums and tambourines for ritual and celebration, Inanna adds: "placing of the garment on the ground" which most likely refers to impromptu lovemaking. Sex was a sacred power, a sacrament. The robe on the ground could also be a prayer rug; prayer is also a sacrament.

Inanna brings us "the art of women", the art of being a woman. The art of women is followed by "the perfect execution of the *me.*" Women create culture and partnership society. Wise women oversee the success, harmony, guidance, cooperation, of humane behavior in their groups, tribes, and settlements. Briffault writes that all women in traditional groups, from birth to death, are "the mothers." The mothers are the wise preservers of our species. Inanna is woman and mother of cosmic proportions. Inanna is all the powers. She presents them to her people, both women and men. This is our goddess at work. She loves her people and gives them the ME while Enki wanted them for himself. In the ending lines, priestly writers have Enki graciously and generously again *giving* the ME to Inanna and calling Uruk an ally. Both Uruk and Inanna win over Eridu and Enki, but the priestly teller of this version finds a way to claim that the ME were first Enki's and then stolen by Inanna. They were not.

More is said of Inanna's ME by Betty De Shong Meador (2000:17:)

> Inanna is an irresistible directional movement of the imagination. We have nothing in the western pantheons of goddesses that even approaches her variety and dominion. Inanna is a unique outbreak of a particular consciousness attempting to embody and define itself. She is an expression of the Mesopotamian psyche that manifested itself in this paradoxical, complex divine woman … The Sumerian characterization of Inanna emerges as an all-encompassing, over-arching deity, even an attempt at a unitary vision.

Inanna's MEs are paired opposites, syzygies. When aligned, they are powerful; nature and humanity at their beneficial best and destructive worst. Through acknowledgement of the contrary reality of life and the opposing hidden and revealed parts of ourselves, one lives free of illusion. "Inanna is a single deity in whose being the opposing pairs of creation are gathered (ibid.: 21,18)." Humans make rules and social order to avoid chaos, but Inanna laughs. She knows that chaos and peace are interchangeable. She shows us that change is everywhere, bad turns good and good goes bad. She is the fluid flow of flux beyond human control. Attempts to "fix" life with rules and permanent social or political order is folly. That the Sumerians embrace such a huge concept speaks of a high consciousness. Insecure humans try millennia after millennia to fix order in place, nail it down, proclaim permanency, bribe the deities, and blame whoever, whatever for bad fortune. How great is the courage to see life as an inevitable flow of change and contradiction — with acceptance; to acknowledge acceptance of change without blame or elaborate ritual of magical thinking or guilt. How amazed I am to learn that this wise concept is placed in the ME of a single sacred woman.

Inanna's *historical*[13] rise in the fourth millennium B.C.E. was at a time when kings were becoming tyrannical authoritarians demanding obedience and conformity to their new hierarchal political power. Inanna stood up for cosmic disobedience. No wonder her people loved her! She dared what her people could not! She was more than a pretty face and sexual allure. She was each of her people in their own combination of inner and outer behaviors, weaknesses and strengths; she made cosmic commotions. She is a super heroine who hears the plaints of every one of her people.

To be all knowing is yours, Inanna

The following section of "Inanna, Lady of Largest Heart", composed by the *en* priestess of Sumer, Enheduanna, gives us an additional version of Inanna's ME. (ibid: 126-130:)

---

[13] Inanna was already known in the oral tradition preceding the "historical" period, i.e., after writing was invented.

Figure 17. Enheduanna

INANNA, LADY OF LARGEST HEART

...

Mistress
you outclass Enlil and An
your praiseworthy path shows forth
without YOU is no fate fixed
without YOU is no seen counsel arrived

...

to run   to steal away
to cool the heart to soothe
are yours Inanna

fitful wandering
speeding by
rising   falling
reaching the fore
are yours Inanna

to smooth the traveler's road
to clear a path for the weak
are yours Inanna

to straighten the footpath
to make firm the cleft place
are yours Inanna

to destroy   to build
to lift up to put down
are yours Inanna

to turn man into woman
woman into man
are yours Inanna

allure   ardent desire
belongings   households
are yours Inanna

wealth   brisk trading
quick profits   hoard even more
are yours Inanna

prosperous business   abundance of money
indebtedness   ruinous loss
are yours Inanna

to teach   watch over
supervise   scrutinize
are yours Inanna

life vigor   fitting modesty
male guardian spirits
female guardian spirits
disclosing sacred spots
are yours Inanna

to worship in lowly prostration
to worship in high heaven
are yours Inanna

the word of rejection
the word of riddance
are yours Inanna

(10-12 missing lines)

to hand out tender mercies
restore your heart to someone
are yours Inanna

heart trembling   weakness
shivering cramps   illness
are yours Inanna

Figure 18. Wife and Husband

to have a husband   to have a wife
to thrive in the goodness of love
are yours Inanna

to spark a quarrel
within love's lust delight
is yours Inanna

to be negligent
tend carefully
are yours Inanna

Figure 19. Mother Suckling a Baby

to build a house
construct the women's rooms
furnish them
to kiss a baby's lips
are yours Inanna

to spread the leg stride
to footrace
to win
are yours Inanna

to mingle
the brute   the strong
the downtrodden   the weak
are yours Inanna

to inter mix
high ground   low lying pools
peaks   rolling plains
are yours Inanna

to give the royal crown
the throne   the king's scepter
are yours Inanna

(13 lines missing)

to heap on lavish adornments
small   large   fine   wide
are yours Inanna

to grant cultic rites
guide their execution
are yours Inanna

to utter slander

words of deception
to speak unashamedly
even hostilely
are yours Inanna

to sneer at an answer
false or true
to say wicked words
are yours Inanna

to joke   inflame a quarrel
provoke laughter
to defile   to esteem
are yours Inanna

calamity   bitter woes
torrent   wickedness
darkening the light
are yours Inanna

fear   panic alarm
stifling terror
dreadful brilliance
are yours Inanna

triumph   hard pursuit
trembling sickness
wakeful   quivers sleeplessness
are yours Inanna

to muster troops
to strike   slaughter
rise the battle cry
are yours Inanna

brawling
blurring the eyes
clashing strife   murderous fights
are yours Inanna

to be all knowing
is yours Inanna

to build a bird's nest
safe in a sound branch
make indestructible
are yours Inanna

Figure 20. Inanna with Captives

to lure snakes from the wasteland
terrorize the hateful
throw in chains   hold in bondage
are yours Inanna

to summon the hated
is yours Inanna

to cast lots
is yours Inanna

to gather the scattered
restore the living place
are yours Inanna

setting free
is yours Inanna

Inanna's many ME were reduced to seven in the descent story (see chapter 11). She wears her ME: the *shugurra* crown of the steppe; at her neck she wears small lapis beads; over her breast are two strands of beads; she is wrapped in a royal robe; eye make-up that is named "Let him come!"; a breast plate called "Come, man, come!"; a golden ring; and the measuring rod and line. We are not told the power of each of her adornments other than allure. We are told that at the seven gates into the underworld she is made to take off her garments, her powers, one by one and enter nude like a corpse (Wolkstein and Kramer 1983:53).

I AM HOLY INANNA — WHERE ARE MY FUNCTIONS?

A text entitled "Enki and the World Order" describes Enki taking credit for Nammu's established accomplishments as well as almost all goddess functions, which he then reassigns. It is not Enki creating the natural order but rather his priests of Eridu creating a *new* order for the Sumerian pantheon. He has stolen the ME, (again), and Inanna complains and asks "where are my functions?" The story is a diminishment of Inanna, long-time holder of the ME, and an elevation of Enki. (Black et al 2004: 215-225:)

"Grandiloquent lord of heaven and earth, self-reliant, father Enki, engendered by a bull, begotten by a wild bull ... great dragon who stands in Eridug ... mighty one of the E-kur[14] ... strong one of heaven and earth!" (ibid.: 215-16) Enki's eye-glance can disrupt the mountains, his gaze covers all the land both settled and wild. He orders time into days and months and years; with his word, everything multiplies. Abundance comes to the land: fruit trees, sheep, plowed land, stockpiles of grain, oil, and dairy products. At his word he bestows a young man with vigor and gives spectacular beauty to a young woman; she has so much loveliness that the urban dwellers will gasp. Enki is commissioned by Enlil to grant happiness to the rulers. He is declared lord of prosperity and wisdom, he commands, decrees, and decides fates. He oversees the pregnant humans, goats, ewes, and cows. He makes certain the births go well. He germinates the fields. (These ME once all belonged to Inanna!) Enki praises himself, his arts and crafts, his "good semen" and says that Enlil gave all the powers to him. He is even claiming to be Inanna's storm rising from the horizon. He says he brings prosperity. (That is a long time function of the birth/fate goddesses and the personal deities.) He is wisdom in every land. Enki continues saying he is cherished by the birth goddesses and is head of the Anuna gods. (In other stories he tricks Ninhursaga out of her city and into banishment in the steppes. Remember also that Inanna is Queen of decree-making and in charge of the seven Anuna gods.) He eulogizes himself shamelessly. (This text is late because Enki was previously said to be prime creatress Nammu's son yet here he claims An as his father.)

The poem says he is just in his self-praise. He claims that he excels in every way. He increases the sheep herds, makes rain fall (goddess business), and travels to lands rich in silver and cedar and brings them back. His priests admire him and sing to him, as do the boatmen of the marshes. He is the "Lord who rides upon the great powers, the pure powers, who controls the great powers, the numberless powers, foremost in all the breadth of heaven and earth (ibid.: 217)."

---

[14] Enlil's temple in Nibru; E-kur is 'e', house + 'kur', mountain

Figure 21. Enki

*Enki goes about on his barge named Stag of the Abzu.
From his boat he addresses the land of Sumer and gives them
unmatchable superior powers. He assures them that their heart
is "inscrutable". His barge reaches widespread areas of Sumer.
Meluha is the black land of mes trees. Enki grants them great
trees for furniture building, strong reeds for heroes' weapons,
and claims to decree that all their bulls are great ones, all the
birds are peacocks, and their silver turns to gold. Their men will
fight other men like bulls. He purifies the pure land of Dilmun
giving it fish and palms. He destroys Elam and Marhasi and
takes their silver and lapis lazuli for Enlil. He gives animals to
the nomadic people.*

*Enki moves on to fill the rivers with spring flood: " ...
he stood up full of lust like a rampant bull, lifted his penis,
ejaculated and filled the Tigris with flowing water (ibid.: 220-
21)." He performs another ejaculation and fills the Euphrates.
His water causes grapes and barley to grow. He dons his crown,
touches the earth and all manner abundance grows; he talks
to the big and small reeds so they grow, appoints fishermen
and bird catchers, and establishes a shrine between the two
constellations: Field and Chariot. Enki's scribal priests have
taken over goddess fertility.*

It is time for Enki to assign functions to the goddesses and gods. To Nanse he gives the sea, copulation, high flooding, underground water, great waves, and tides. To Ishkur, son of An, he gives rain, storms, lightning, and inspection of both earthly and heavenly canals for irrigation. Enkimdu, the farmer-god, receives ploughs, teams that pull the plough, the furrows, and the implements of agriculture. To goddess Ezina, he gives mottled barley, chickpeas, lentils and the cultivated fields. Ezina is the matron of both bread and inciting sexual arousal. Kulla is made a god of hoe and brick after Enki invents both, of course. He appoints a god as master builder after he has assembled the idea of "house;" another god is made "king of the hills" and oversees the increase of herds that Enki brought into being. He gives sheepfolds on the plain to the shepherd king, Dumuzi(d), who supplies E-anna (Inanna's temple), and who is "the holy spouse of Inana the mistress, the lady of the great powers who allows sexual intercourse in the open squares of Kulaba (i.e., prostitution) (ibid.: 223)." Enki invented flax for linen and weaving and makes weaving the domain of women under the goddess Uttu.

"Then, alone lacking any function, the great woman of heaven, Inanna, lacking any function — Inana came in to see her father Enki in his house, weeping to him, and making her complaint to him ... Why did you treat me, the woman, in an exceptional manner: I am holy Inana — where are my functions? (ibid.: 223)" She lists the other goddesses who have received duties from him: Nintud is birth mother, the midwife of the land. Ninisina (goddess of medicine and healing) is given the s(h)uba stones (Inanna always wears these) and is reassigned to be An's consort and have access to him. (Before Dumuzi, An was Inanna's consort.) Goddess Ninmug (metal working) has the gold chisel and silver burin of metal workers and the making of crowns. Nisaba (writing and wisdom) receives the measuring rod and lapis lazuli measuring tape to reestablish boundaries (after floods). She will define boundaries and be the scribe of the land. Nanshe is in charge of the fish and birds of the waterways. Where, she asks in despair, are her functions?

> *Enki answers holy Inanna. How have I neglected you? How can I improve on you? Enki continues with all the things he gave her that is but a list of a general description of any woman: pleasant voice, clothes, spindle, and hairpins.*
>
> *Enki says he gives her the speaking of curses in the midst of battle. He takes credit for giving her the complex syzygy of opposite attributes; the tangling and untangling of the threads of life. He says he made her put on garments of linen, showed her to prepare fibers and spin with her spindle; he gave her color tufted cloth.*
>
> *He also leaves her the grisly and gory slaughter of war where he says she stacks up human heads like piles of dirt and plants others like seeds. He tells her: "Inan(n)a, you destroy what should not be destroyed, you create what should not be created. You remove the cover from the* shem *drum of lamentations, Maiden Inana, while shutting up the* tigi *drum and adab instrument in their homes. You never grow weary with adorers looking at you Maiden Inana ... (ibid.: 225)."*
>
> *The text ends with "Praise be to Father Enki!"*

What has happened? This is the second skirmish over the ME with the priests of Enki promoting him and themselves into grander power and prominence versus the tradition of Inanna in charge of Life and the ME. The areas of nice and pleasant — abundance, sex, and all the ME are claimed and named by priestly scribes using Enki as their puppet for power. Inanna is left with her womanly pleasant voice, the clothes on her back, preparing flax to spin, a spool and spindle, fabric dyeing, and hairpins. She is like every other woman. Earlier in the text she is mistress of prostitutes who have sex in the open square. Enki takes credit for her speaking words of courage and words of bad omen and the tangling and untangling of human problems, but in the text he has no need to assign to her the gory piling up of heads in battle; he says she does that on her own. Inanna brings out the lamentation drums *and* the happy joyous tigi drums and the ceremonial instruments, but Enki says she puts away the latter since she causes laments, not joyous celebrations. Enki's priest-scribes leave Inanna with prostitution, womanly weeping, the daily activities of ordinary women, piling up corpse heads, and causing lamentation in the land. She devastates what should not be devastated, she creates the unthinkable. The priest scribes diminish the Great Goddess Inanna and Enki is praised.

A scribe's stylus can wreck havoc. It is mightier than the battle mace! It is this writer's hope the her computer keys may be stronger than patriarchal fabrications! May they help to restore Inanna to her former glory!

Thorkild Jacobsen writes that the physical evidence of the earliest Mesopotamian religion is limited, scant, and spotty. He derives the earlier religious expression from the evidence of later texts (1976: 25). I also search what survives in order to gather the remaining details of earlier stories. Literary and liturgical tablets were copied and recopied, edited, and tweaked, yet parts of the old story remain. Consider the unexpected sensual Song of Songs, a *hieros gamos*, included in the Old Testament of the Christian Bible. How that erotic old love story escaped patriarchy's editorial deletion, I do not know. There is a universality of a sacred feminine in all cultures. Mother, of necessity, is the obvious prime parent. A few minutes' participation against a decade and more does not justify male mastery and "father family." The first story, first myth everywhere, mirrors woman: woman's body and reproductive functions, woman's humane-ity, and women's creativity.

A sacred woman story is universal with differences only in representational details from local climate, geography, economy, flora, fauna, and human experience. People settled and stories added new divine aspects. Ideas are fluid organic expressions dependent on the people who have the ideas. Pressures of economy, social change, and political maneuvering inform the ideas. Above, the scribal editors are rewriting Inanna.

The supreme goddess of who knows how many millennia is under attack from patriarchy. In another attempt to hijack her importance, "The Huluppu Tree," priestly scribes reduce Inanna to a helpless young woman who needs a man to rescue her and solve her problems. She is coming of age; she has need of her famous bed and throne. She is ready, her carefully planted tree is ready, but Snake is living in its roots,

Imdugud bird and *his* offspring are nested in the crown, and maid Lilith has made a home in the trunk. She can't make them go away. (They are her own emblems!) She cries and cries and asks her brother, Utu the sun god, to help her but he won't or can't. Weeping, she goes to the hairy-hero, Gilgamesh (Wolkstein and Kramer 1983:4-9). Patriarchy writes a new and opportunistic role for Gilgamesh, who once was an early king of Uruk (early third millennium B.C.E.). Through claiming his father as Lugalbunda, an earlier hero king, and birth goddess Ninsun as his mother, he is "two thirds divine and one third human;" nonetheless, he is quite mortal. Gilgamesh is fabricated into a patriarchal superman, an oversized brut who bullies young men, makes them fight him in unfair contests while carrying him about on their backs, and rapes brides on their wedding night. The story of Gilgamesh tells us he is splendid but out of control. (Mitchell 2004: 73:)

> The people suffer from his tyranny, the people cry out that he takes the son from his father and crushes him, takes the girl from her mother and uses her, the warrior's daughter, the young man's bride, he uses her, no one dares to oppose him.
> Is this how you want your king to rule?

He-man Gilgamesh is extolled in his adventures that include: murder of the goddess' non-aggressive guardian of her forest, Humbaba (Old Babylonian Huwawa); destruction of that same sacred grove where the goddess's throne sits; the slaughter and dismemberment of her bull of heaven. He refuses to accept the goddess's invitation to be initiated into kingship by "sacred marriage." Instead, he calls her a prostitute of the city walls. Historically, he is a mortal ruler of Uruk for Inanna. He formerly worships her; he is her "beloved", tends her temple as a priest-king, and keeps her city safe. The huluppu tree revision was created to put Gilgamesh close to her sacred tree, throne, bed, and power in order to enhance the growing malignancy of male domination.

Gilgamesh suits up in amazingly heavy battle armor to face the four emblems of Inanna. He scares the Imdugud bird back to the mountains, the serpent slithers away or is chopped up, Lilith runs barefoot and naked back to the wilderness, and Inanna's tree is cut down and made into her furniture. Priestly scribes have Inanna behaving like a helpless adolescent girl and weeping because those bad things won't leave her tree. She needs her tree to make her bed and chair (throne). Gilgamesh is storied to be the hero for the great goddess, a hero who then in other texts repudiates her, kills off her symbols, and refuses her offer of ancient partnership.

Another stimulus for changing sacred story is challenging times. Fear. If the old stories and rituals do not bring safety or relief, if the old is deemed impotent, then imported stories and deities are added in hope of a positive turn of events. Personalities and characteristics of the old storied divine are expanded. New versions are accepted over time. The newly spun revisions manipulate the older stories and support the rise of patriarchy; "marriage to" long-worshipped divine woman promotes minor local gods. Mother-daughter goddess is the central story for uncountable millennia, time out of mind, but it is changing.

Patriarchy spread like a plague in urban centers; rural egalitarianism lost gender partnership when people congregated in cities. Fear of decrease in water and food supply resulted in conflict between cities; opportunity for acquisition of power and goods spread through the land. Like a wild fire, sparks were blown far, igniting male imagination. Patriarchal domination gained power by piracy of what is coveted. Inanna and all goddesses were reduced by priestly story re-making.

Inanna is the special goddess of harlots, whores, and prostitutes whether sacred priestess or abandoned desperate woman. She cares about orphans and widows and, perhaps, even offers some protection as a deterrent for abuse of women. Early Greeks had avenging goddesses who punished men who abused women and escaped with impunity.

Inanna changes men into women and women into men. Though homosexuality is known and cross-dressing is included in her parade of people, I believe that her transforming art is also about changing gendered behavior. Men's Y-tendency for lust-satisfaction and inherent lack of interest in relational love and family responsibilities requires taming. Inanna is an honest goddess. Sex is natural. Making love is mutually pleasurable. Pleasure is sacred. Men are enamored of the sex drive. Women also like sex but additionally care deeply for others; women are responsible for the young that sex creates. Women are relational. With the art of allure that ignites male sexual interest, woman can lead man into relational caring and cooperation to benefit the young and the society. Inanna transforms opposites. She transforms lust to love when she oversees fertility, as women have done since distant time. Women also change from docile maternal creatures into sexually explicit powerful lionesses when they are passionately in love. Inanna and Dumuzi are "bed lions." Men admire he-men and heroes; women are also strong, decisive, and willful — like Inanna, like a lioness.

Sex is fertility *and* pleasure. Sex is Inanna's ME. Seeking sexual pleasure, especially women wanting and experiencing pleasure, is made wrong and sinful in later religions when women are said to be the temptation. Women are called the worst sinners as they tempt men into impurity, yet "pure men" are hardly pure. [15]

The next stage of religious story that occurs in Sumer during the third millennium is rulership in the land. Since religious story mirrors human behavior, gods assume hierarchy with alpha gods placed in rulership over other deities. Patriarchy spreads, rulership requires gods ruling cosmically as men rule terrestrially. For three millennia, maleness systematically usurps Goddess through priestly-piracy, gender-flipping, power take-overs, rape of goddesses, "marriage", and reassigning goddess powers to the male-based pantheon. Lacking a vulva and uterus, gods give birth in peculiar and bizarre ways: ejaculation (by masturbation — Enki), a god's word and thoughts, out of their heads (Zeus), and with a rib. Gods compete, rage, fight, and even kill one another. They behave like men. Goddesses do not fight and kill each other; they *are* each other.

---

[15] Consider the widespread Catholic priest child molestation scandals surfacing around the world.

Goddesses are diminished during the last three millennia B.C.E.. Only Inanna/Ishtar retains importance as Queen of Heaven and Queen of Earth. She is said to be indomitable. She is loved by her people and so entrenched in everyday life and religious tradition that she is difficult to dominate and remove. Eventually, to make way for new gods, her popular and strong presence is not praised as valiant but called recalcitrant; priestly attempts to turn people away from her include presenting her as a spoiled impetuous adolescent; lusty, fickle and destructive; the cause of wars, floods and drought and whatever else is undesirable. However, she is universally rooted in people's hearts and minds; as deeply rooted as having a "mother." Inanna/Ishtar is last to be conquered in the Ancient Near East. She retains her titles of Queen of Heaven and Queen of Earth and much else under many names until the rise of muscular male-based religion took over, denying all else. Her complex personality defies convenient categorization and minimization. Her long held high status is woven into the warp and woof of ancient Mesopotamia. As long as a strong sacred feminine survives, woman has a model. Without the moderating guidance of women's wisdom and voice, Y-ness crowns itself ruler, absolute and even divine. King-pleasing priests rewrite religion to eliminate the feminine, both sacred and human(e). Unbelievable destruction, killing, suffering, and greed spread. Thorkild Jacobsen writes in *The Treasures of Darkness* (1976: 21:)

> In the latter half of the second millennium and in the following first millennium a dark age closed down on Mesopotamia. The old framework within which to understand the workings of the cosmos survived, but it moved from the interplay of many divine wills to the willful whim of a single despot. The major gods became national gods, identified with narrow national political aspirations. There was a corresponding coarsening and barbarization of the idea of divinity, no new overarching concepts arose, rather doubts and despair abounded. Witchcraft and sorcery were suspected everywhere; demons and evil spirits threatened life unceasingly.

And yet, Inanna/Ishtar survives throughout the oppressive control of male storytelling, re-visioning, editing, deleting, and plotting. Mother Goddess is long imagined and understood as a woman; she is difficult, even impossible, to erase. Maleness turns her emblems into demons. Men's "hairy heroes" (hair of all sorts equals strength) earn immortality by killing her demonized emblems. They "murder" her only in their own concocted stories. Nammu/Tiamat, first creatress of Mesopotamia, is also "first snake" (remember: serpent signifies the umbilical cord, the vaginal snake, i.e., life and life-renewing). Prime creatress' birthing snakiness is man-made into venomous and destructive creatures; she becomes both dragon and serpent that require a "hairy hero" to kill. She is also useful in her terrifying forms as a convenient "dragon of the gods" to fight men's wars. Inanna/Ishtar is allowed the serpent-dragon emblem when it is useful, that is, as threat against "enemies". When Inanna is called "first snake", this is reference to her great antiquity, her mother goddess origin.

The politically posturing despots claim she is on their side just as in recent modern times both sides of conflict claim: "God is on our side." The kings hide behind her powerful fierceness of protection; they present her nude, armed and standing on her lions leading them into battle.

Sacred feminine's emblematic murder is unsuccessful though the heroes declare her sliced, diced, and dead (Marduk and Tiamat). "First Snake" is an epithet used for Inanna by the first recognized poet, Enheduanna, the educated daughter of Sargon the Great, who is made *en,* high priestess, of the moon god, Nana/Suen/Sin all over Sumer. She is also a devotee of Inanna. For forty years she travels about Sumer composing liturgical poem-songs for various cities' deities. One poem tells us that Enheduanna begs Inanna for assistance because a high priest has treated her badly. He hurt her and threw her out of the temple to wander the wilderness. The great gods do not help her, not even Nanna (she is consecrated to him). At poem's end, Enheduanna is restored to her *en* post and exalts Inanna as her champion in a beautiful composition.

Figure 22. Inanna with Her Lion

Inanna/Ishtar is called "dragon of the gods" and a "venomous lion" that combines her lion and her serpent emblem. Serpent and woman are connected; men do not have vaginal snakes that deliver babies. They do not have vaginas, they do not have wombs, they envy women's ability to produce life. As emblems are blemished and blamed, so too are women. Early emblems are rooted in our story; the deep story of humankind. (Kramer 1979: 71, 72:)

> Female deities were worshipped and adored all through Sumerian history, and though several of them were victimized and reduced in hierarchical rank, the goddesses of Sumer played a crucial, pivotal role in Sumerian religion to the very end – God in Sumer never became all male ... The goddess who outweighed, overshadowed, and out lasted them all was a deity known to the Sumerians by the name of

Inanna, "Queen of Heaven", and to the Semites who lived in Sumer by the name of Ishtar.

Inanna played a greater role in myth, epic, and hymn than any other deity, male or female. And no wonder, for she was worshipped under three aspects that at least on the surface seem unrelated, and even antithetical: as the Venus-goddess in charge of the bright Morning Star and Evening Star; as the goddess of war and weaponry, who wrought havoc upon all who displeased her, and especially on the enemies of Sumer; as the goddess of love and desire who ensured the fertility of the soil and the fecundity of the womb.

Figure 23. Inanna's Storehouse

Inanna/Ishtar is the most complex deity of the Ancient Near East; she is also the most popular, and appears in nearly every epic tale interacting with the national heroes: Enmerker, Etana, Lugalbanda, and Gilgamesh. She beds many a king who is proxy for her beloved long-time consort, Dumuzi, thereby granting them kingship for a year (see chapter 6). Inanna inspires poets to compose poems, priests to create ritual, and temple personnel to dance, sing, and play a variety of instruments in accompaniment to her devotional ceremonies. She receives ample piles of grain, herd animals, and other goods in her name; her people and temples place all manner of riches into *her* storehouse. Workers are paid in grain and beer and the poor are fed from her storehouse, as are the ever growing temple staff. Lists of temples show that Inanna has more temples, sanctuaries, and shrines than any other deity. She has twice that of her closest competitor, Enlil. Her people adore and worship her. Their dream souls seek her at night to petition her help. "The mythographers do not weary singing her daring, cunning, vindictive feats and exploits (Kramer, 1979: 75)." They also sing of her beauty, charms, sexuality, youth; her wisdom, her motherly caring for the marginal people, i.e., tavern and city wall prostitutes, widows, orphans and the poor.

LORDLY QUEEN OF THE AWESOME ME

Myths list Inanna's many attributes, especially her indomitable powers; she has more power than any other deity. She holds the ME, the powers of civilization. The following lines praise her powers, her planetary aspect, and her ability to fight the *kur*. *Kur* originates as a pictogram for "mountain" and later came to mean attacks on Sumer from the highlands. *Kur is* "the inimical land", the enemy, and place of haunting ghosts ("Inanna and Ebih," Kramer 1979: 24, footnote 9). Inanna is "lordly queen of the awesome me, garbed in fear, who rides the great *me* (ME)." She has weapons dripping blood; she is planner of wars. She stomps on shields and brings the flood-storm (here this likely means pitched battle). Their queen of the ME roars like a lion and is spoiling for a fight like a wild bull; she smites the enemy and destroys the disobedient with venom. When Inanna stands atop the lion demon or is the dragon of the gods, she dispenses venom. The poet says: "My queen, when you become immense as heaven, maid Inanna, when you become vast as earth," when she is cloaked in "awesome fear," wearing brilliant light, when she births the mountains, and when she leads her people successfully in battle, "then the black-haired people break out in song." The poem ends with a praise to the "queen of battle (ibid.: 76)."

The poem also contains her beneficence. She is Queen. She is "immense as heaven". Important deities of Sumer are shown larger than or placed higher than lesser deities and humans in seal art. She is big as the sky; "vast as earth." She is Queen of Earth. She rises like the sun "swinging wide (her) arms." Her "arms" are rays of light from her "star," her planet, and her luminosity. (I once saw Venus/Ninsianna rise low on the horizon in an evening sky and reflect brightly onto my cove at high tide. She made a path over the water to shore. She came to earth.)

Inanna is celestially "garbed in awesome fear." Since her evening star appearance brings people and animals home to rest and make love, "fear" would be her morning star appearance, when in times of conflict, she goes to defend her people in war. When she stands in heaven she is fearsome and when she is on earth she is dressed in "bright, steadfast light." Luminosity represents sacredness, holiness. Heroes are dressed in brightness, or have a shine about them. Our goddess travels not only in the heavens as both star and new crescent moon, she straps on sandals and walks the wide earth; she visits the underworld. She has the ME power to descend and ascend from the land of the dead. Her "sister" Ereshkigal reins as queen of the dead. "Sister" is the hint. Ereshkigal is the third aspect of the Great Mother, the death mother as the earth womb-tomb birthing renewal. She and Inanna are part of a whole story, the ancient triune, the matrinity.

Star and planet movement is carefully observed in Ancient Mesopotamia. Inanna is new moon and celebrated on the first day of every lunar month. When she goes over the mountains, this could be either new moon or her planet moving; I suspect "planet" is meant. The "lapis-lazuli blue net" has several connotations. The lapis-lazuli stone is deep dark blue and is found in the mountains. It is precious. It is dark as night and a metaphor for the night sky and the color of strong kings' beards. A net catches things. Woman's womb nets the little fish, the baby, in her birth ocean. Net is also a metaphor to describe capturing enemies by heroes and kings, as if they were birds or fish.

Inanna bathes in the "fruitful *kur*," purifies in the mountain streams, and gives "birth to the bright *kur*, the pure *kur*." Bathing is preliminary to making love in the sacred marriage rites and is based on the custom of purification before important ceremony. Here, Inanna bathes in the mountains and births pure mountains without mention of male involvement, just as primal Mother creates singly. Seals show Inanna standing atop mountains either as her creations or an artistic prop so that she stands high in seals, higher than many gods. Mountains reach to connect heaven and earth. When Inanna's people are victorious, they sing her praise, an "*ilulamma*-chant."

Two ME powers are particularly interesting: descending into and ascending out of the underworld. Inanna accomplishes this in her descent story (chapter 11). That power, and she is the only deity with it, is changed by patriarchy into blame for her going there in the first place. Patriarchal priests claim she goes there to overthrow Ereshkigal, her sister, and rule that the underworld needs Enki's cleverness to escape. The early story of the Neolithic Period would have been mother goddess bringing the dead vegetation god from the underworld where he goes when the land turns dusty, crops finish, sheep and goat udders dry. The story varies depending on the local economy. After human and divine lamentation, mother goddess fetches him back to the world and a new cycle manifests.

In Old Europe, a few surviving figurines show the vegetation god born as a baby, maturing into youthful vigor, growing old and "sorrowful", and dying to be reborn. Erect phallus gods appear. By the time of writing, Ancient Mesopotamia embraces the young mother goddess, Inanna, who meets the vegetation/shepherd god in delicious, joyous, sacred lovemaking. Dumuzi goes to the underworld because that is his cycle, and not because Inanna petulantly gives him to the death goddess in exchange for her own escape from the land of the dead. Inanna's ME for descending and ascending gives her ready passage.

The following story text is presented for the reader to know the width, depth, and scope of the most popular goddess of Mesopotamia. Inanna is long developed and very old by the time Sumerians settled in the southern Mesopotamia, the "Land Between the Two Rivers." In the following excerpts compiled during the "mature" literary period, we feel the awe of Inanna/Ishtar's attributes and celebrations.

The poem is written in first person by a man who neither provided offerings to Ishtar nor spoke with her. He apparently saw the error of his ways, or desired more out of life and wanted to please her. The first part, fragmented, contains praises for her. Next he admits his omissions. He lists the ill fortunes she has heaped upon him. (Humans want to know why they are being "punished," as if life due them should be easy.) Priests make use of this for gaining wealth and offerings. They eat and live well as they serve in evermore luxurious abodes for the deities. Priests also offer incantations, exorcism, healing magic and divination services, all for a fee. In the text retold below, bad luck, fearfulness, and illness are punishments served up by the powerful Inanna/Ishtar.

The concept, worship me or else, was a masculine add-on and not woman-made. Great Mother, no matter her name, loves her children. Mother goddess did not punish. Punishment reflects authoritative domineering absolute alpha androcratic rule that felt guilt for self-serving brutal and destructive behavior. The punishing gods are men's reflected image of cruelty. Extreme punishment like war, enslavement, and ruined cities could occur from some slight lack of adoration or ritual for a deity. In the following text we have a man who has not worshipped Ishtar with offerings and prayers and so he blames her for his bad fortune and illness. The text is both a display of blame and a fear of the sacred feminine's power. The summarized text of "Ishtar Queen of Heaven" tells us (Foster 2005: 592-8:)

A man did not worship Ishtar, the Capable Lady, so she
grew angry at him and shouted like a thunder storm. She

chased off his protective personal goddess and god, his family abandoned him. He became so bent over that his head drooped all the way to his feet. People feared him; his hair and beard fell out. Ishtar sent her "envoy," Lilith, the Owl demon who leaned menacingly into his window; he was silenced and chilled with fear. Ishtar sent a Dusk Demon who drove him crazy.

The sufferer turns to praising Ishtar to win her over and end his terrible condition. He says only she can grant kingship, make all beautiful things, speak for the people, and create good governance. No one but Ishtar can be angry and then be merciful, only she can punish and then forgive; only she can lead people out of peril and bring the dead back to life. She gives long life to those who attend her. She "made everything perfect, completed the rites and gathered to herself everything (ibid.: 594)." Her penitent worshipper calls out her many names: Ninanna (Queen Heaven, equal to An), Minu-anni (fierceness), Min-ulla (great bull-like strength), Ne'anna (sublime strength), Zannaru (capable one), and Anunu (assorted sexual expression — she turns male to female and female to male). She is awesome and overwhelming.

After a break in the text, the petitioner continues to remind Ishtar that Enlil had a temple built for himself but instead dedicated it to her in Nippur which she inspected and enjoyed. The light from the temple is brilliant and shines over the entire land; the inside of her "house" is full of joy. The people and all the goddesses kneel before her. "She is the very greatest, the most important of goddesses, mighty daughter of the luminary of the night sky ... Cherished goddess, princess of her brothers" (ibid.: 596-7). She is "omnipotent," supreme, highest, and sublime queen. He wishes for her that she join the great gods drinking wine out of lapis lazuli tankards and making decrees. He wants her to be glad and ready for a festival. The text ends in fragments; we do not know if the scribe's health and fortune improved.

Figure 24. Winged Inanna on a Pair of Ibex

The above descriptions of powerful Ishtar are helpful in connecting aspects of her that separate into other names and functions. The Owl demon reference is her wilderness self, that is, before settlements became cities. Images from Old Europe, dating well before the southern Mesopotamian plane was habitable, include the owl goddess. Bird goddesses are a global expression for the sacred feminine indicating that both goddess and birds frequent heaven and earth. Owls are a universal favorite metaphor for goddess. Moon, darkness, all-seeing, and death belong to the goddess. Owls fly silently in the night and see in the dark with moon-bright golden eyes. They hunt and carry off unfortunate small animals. Because they are all-seeing, owls and goddesses are wise. Darkness of night, womb, tomb and women's mysterious seclusion are linked with night creatures and are powerful reminders of mystery, all-seeing wisdom, and death. Owls are both wisdom and death. Ishtar in the above text can bring the dead back to life.

Consider Lilith, the owl-demon who peers into the sufferer's window. Lilith is a Semitic name based on Sumerian "Lil" for air. She is a wind maiden of the wilderness. The crowded settled centers spread contagion. Disease in the Ancient Near East was thought to be wind-borne at night; it blew into the tightly packed homes in crowded urban centers through cracks and under doors. She was blamed for stillborn babies and early infancy death. Lilith became the ill-wind and baby snatcher. She was demonized. That she is present in the story reminds us that there is a lost association between Inanna and Lilith.

Wind and air also bring the image of wings. The winged Inanna in figure 24 retains the zoomorphic hybrid of her earlier bird self and is both celestial and earthly. Lilith is the winged Inanna with owl emphasis. She has wings and appears with owls and lions. Her feet and lower legs are owl feathers and talons. Lions always indicate the Great Mother, and Inanna is rarely without her lions. Lions and owls are wilderness creatures. Lilith is lovely, young, and nude. Her time is night, her element is air/wind. A beautifully preserved plaque of Lilith is mistakenly called an "owl-demon." (See figure 32) It was found in a sanctuary. Demons do not have sanctuaries. This figure is a goddess. She wears the tiered horn-headdress of divinity. She carries the ring, line, and rod of rulership. She is Lilith, wilderness Inanna/Ishtar.

I find little left out in Ishtar/Inanna's above praise-hymn. She is hugely important from olden times. The elder generation of important gods are not as old as the Mother Goddess and her maid aspect. When the gods "grant" Inanna/Ishtar names or powers, remember that they are already hers! When she is beloved of a particular god, he is *her* consort and shares *her* attributes of power; she is not *his* consort receiving a portion of *his* power. In the above text, Ishtar is twice said to be equal to Anu, the head male deity; she is his equal, his female counterpart. They are the first pair. However, before they can be a pair, the *single* parthenogenetic Great Mother must create the gods. She is their mother in all the ancient Near East and is the universal first story. The above text is dated in the Mature Period but is assembled from earlier sources.

QUEEN OF ALL THE INHABITED WORLD
WHO GOVERNS THE PEOPLES[16]

Another poem in Foster's anthology of Akkadian literature describes Inanna/Ishtar's wide powers of governance. The consistency of her powers is evidence of her sustained attributes over time. "The Great Prayer to Ishtar" is briefly retold here. It lists her powers and heaps up praise in the hope of reaching her ear and receiving her help. (Foster, 2005: 601-5:)

THE GREAT PRAYER TO ISHTAR

Ishtar/Irinni/Inanna is petitioned. The worshipper grandly enumerates recognition of her power, her exalted status, and her governance of all the people in the inhabited world. She is described as "the luminary of heaven and earth," the one who wears the holy tiara, holds all the weapons, stands ready for battle, and is supreme over all the gods (ibid.: 601). The composer praises her ability to reverse peace to war. She is dressed in icy fear, commands both heaven and earth and gives judgements and decrees. Her sanctuaries are everywhere, her name makes the gods, heaven, and underworld tremble; yet she helps the "oppressed and abused," and acts with mercy. "Have mercy, mistress of heaven and earth, shepherdess of the human race!" (ibid.: 602) Our goddess is a lioness of the gods, holds kings by her leadline, and parts the veils of brides. Her torch burns in the heavens, she brings the people together, she is a mystery no one understands. She heals the sick and raises the dead. She is the dancing one.

The penitent tells Ishtar he is her most weary, desperate, and sick servant. He begs her to hear his entreaty. He is confused and upset; sighing and crying. He calls her Irninitum, the lioness who rages, and pleads that she be merciful to his household in mourning. He calls her a wild bull in a furious mood and asks her to look upon him with kind eyes and her radiance.

---

[16] Foster 2005: 601

> *The pitifulness of the petitioner's suffering goes on and on. Enemies glare at him; he is harassed and evilly plotted against. Fools and weaklings get ahead of him; the weak strengthen, and he weakens; he "churn(s) like a wave that an adverse wind masses" and he "moan(s) like a dove, night and day." He has suffered "days of darkness, months of gloom, years of grief;" he has lost his relations, fields, and flock. He pleads for Ishtar to relent, be at ease, and help him avenge his foes. If she does all that for him, and lets him succeed, then people will recognize her part in his recovery and praise her (ibid.: 603, 604).*
>
> *The long prayer ends with the Sumerian tradition of saying the same thing three ways. We hear her people saying:"Ishtar is preeminent, Ishtar is queen, the lady is preeminent, the lady is queen, Irnini, the valiant daughter of Sin (moon god), has no rival (ibid: 605)."*

The prayer to Ishtar above ends in a petition perhaps for the poet, but since it includes nearly every misfortune known to humankind, it is likely a general petition for anyone one reciting it. The text reiterates Ishtar/Inanna's great popularity and includes more of her names. She is known everywhere. She is queen: exalted, powerful, strong, and a warrior. She makes judgments and decisions; she commands heaven and netherworld. Her places of worship, chapels, sanctuaries, altars and daises are everywhere. Ishtar/Inanna has greatest authority and highest rank of the gods; she makes them "totter" and "tremble." All that lives; animals and humans, praise her. She bestows truth and justice; the oppressed and abused are set right, the sick are healed and the dead return to life. When the dead live again, the meaning can be rebirth and/or the dried winter land coming back to sprout anew. Other than Inanna arranging the seasonal return of Dumuzi, and Ishtar's Tammuz, I have not read of Inanna performing a Lazarus-rising, but that is the implication.

Inanna is "shepherdess of the human race," she is merciful and travels around heaven and earth. Many texts refer to her ease of moving between the above and below. As the planet, morning and evening star, Ninsianna, she rises and falls below the horizon, she appears visible to the naked eye in her crescent and full-phase angle as she reflects the sun. The planet rotates very slowly; her day from dawn to dawn is 243 earth days. The planet's orbit around the sun is 225 earth days. Note: her day is longer than her year. Because of her proximity to earth, the planet/star appears to stand still and go retrograde (backwards).[17] All of the planetary characteristics add to Inanna's mystery! Her planet-star moves in the night sky: sometimes crescent star, sometimes full, sometimes halting near various constellations. The planet is not synchronized to earth's movements and seasons.

Inanna rules her planet and emerges as the new crescent moon; her disappearance as planet and dark moon is menstrual seclusion. Any cyclic seclusion is equivalent to menstruation, women's blood power. Inanna's association with new moon and blood reveal her as goddess of menstruation. Though that particular epithet is not stated in poems, it is implied and underlies her fertile potency.

Our goddess is everywhere. She is, after all, the young Mother Goddess, celestial and chthonic. She, Great Mother, is humankind's first monotheism, or rather, monotheaism. Everyone has a human mother, so why not a big mother of all, of everything? Her story is the root of all religion.

Inanna/Ishtar is a lioness; she "renders furious gods submissive." Calling her "the dancing one" is reminiscent of the young Semitic women who danced for men gearing up for battle; inciting their passion. The goddess' dance became a war-dance. Before war is invented, her dance, and the dance of priestesses and women is joyous, sexual, alluring, and celebratory.

How does a goddess of fertility, love, and almost everything get to be a war goddess? Sumerians are a peaceful, goddess-orientated people with a well-developed high culture already in place when they arrive in southern Mesopotamia. High culture does not evolve in times of constant conflict. What happened?

Mothers protect and defend their offspring. Humans are the children of Great Mother; logically a Great Mother will protect her

---

[17] www.universtoday.com 37481/days-of-the-planets/

children. Inanna is the young form of the Mother. She will protect them. She will go to war for them *defensively*. Offensive war goddess and her dance of war are not Inanna the Sumerian goddess but came with her amalgamation with Ishtar, her equivalent Semitic maid goddess. Both goddesses are the evening star and call animals and people home to rest, make love, sleep, and dream. Morning star is the same celestial body as evening star and visibly lingers in the predawn sky. Inanna, as morning star, calls the people from sleep back into consciousness in their awake and active day.

Ishtar, however, had an additional morning star aspect. Semitic tribes are nomadic and move about over difficult terrain. Harsh climate or geographical conditions, i.e., arid lands with little rain, deserts, mountains, and threat from others over scant resources produce anxiety over survival. Males respond with aggressive action to counter fear; nomadic male leadership aggressively steps forward when faced with threat. When permanency of male leadership is established, the cause of patriarchy is elevated. Competition for scant water, food, or land for grazing brings out survival anxiety and toughness and not conflict resolution. Anxiety grows into fear, male fear easily becomes aggressive; men in charge go from fear to anger, to violence and destruction. Ishtar is Semitic. Her aggressive nature is the morning star when battles take place; she is often "he" in this aspect. She may have assimilated a local god of war or else Ishtar is called "he" when she is aggressive and displays masculine characteristics. As Ishtar morning star, the goddess is shown with a beard in several cylinder seals. I believe her contradictory star nature arose from the uncertainty of conflict and war.

War is sometimes won, sometimes lost. If the well-known goddess is claimed by both sides of conflict, and she was, she will let one side down. When she disappears from the side of her "beloved," defeat threatens. At those times she is sought out in her chambers in her temple. Life goes in cycles, as do fortunes, battles, seasons, women and goddess.

Texts frequently refer to Inanna as "woman;" I have not read of any Ancient Near Eastern god called a "man." This referencing of goddess as woman may indicate the high status of women in ancient times. Inanna is also called "fickle." Her contradictory nature is reiterated in texts. The belief in goddess's and women's fickleness was born of men inventing war and drafting the most popular goddess of all time to lead them to victory. When a war is lost, it is said by patriarchy that she abandoned her beloved, the king, and not that the king used bad judgement.

As star and moon Inanna appears and disappears. Disappearance is woman and goddess in menstruation seclusion. She leaves the battle for her seclusion. She is found in one text in her temple house and persuaded to return and help the ruler. In a second poem, a favored mortal is flown to her seclusion in her celestial home by an eagle (Imdugud) to request a plant for his barren wife so she might conceive. The mortal looks in her window; she is nude, sitting on a cushion, and has a lion in attendance. The window is the very same window of goddess and woman alike. They peer from the sanctity of the women's quarters. (Women looking out of the window became a cliche for harlots and prostitutes. Consider Amsterdam's red light district with comely women in display windows enticing the passing men.) The cushion Inanna sits upon is the menstrual seat that evolves into the seat of power of rulers (Knight and Grahn). She is nude — her garments of power are set aside. The goddess' lion with its implied muzzle bloodied is present. All of these are archaic power symbols of menstruation and women's creative fertile blood.

Inanna and Ishtar are first and foremost fertility goddesses. Human fertility requires copulation. When the goddess copulates, her action is cosmic. The world is renewed with grains, newborn animals, and babies. Men have a stronger sex drive than do women.[18] This is long understood by women. Men want sex without responsibility. Women require more; they are relational and bear the responsibility of resulting pregnancy, birth, and support of new life. Inanna and women are alluring, they have what men want. Women learned to modify male behavior into much needed participation and cooperation with the

---

[18] Men have "two and a half times the brain space devoted to sexual drive as well as larger brain centers for action and aggression" compared to women's brains. (Brizendino 2006: 5)

long dependent young. Men in the ancient Near East were initiated — tamed — into culture through sexual enticement that converts lust to caring and love. Temple prostitutes initiate young men. Sumerian men were not considered men until they had a wife and household. This was *not* so that young men could dominate something, but because women and household responsibilities turn a wild man into a responsible man.

War is noisy, storms are noisy, and Inanna/Ishtar is noisy. She announces her desire to enter the netherworld in her descent story with a huge ruckus. In another story, Ishtar is so noisy that a doppelgänger is created by the gods to mirror her behavior. For Enki to make her double disappear, Ishtar must agree to better behavior with less noise. A festival once a year commemorated that event. People flocked to the streets making foolish noise and mock war to remind her of her reprimand and agreement to be less quarrelsome.

Women handle conflict differently from men. If the X chromosome's biophilic behavior of both genders had prevailed, our world would be far different today. Inclusion, cooperation, justice, and conflict resolution of the feminine nature, X-ness, could yet save what remains of our world. Once Y-ness dominates, war was/is the unfortunate response to conflict. Patriarchy transformed Inanna into a war goddess when she actually is, first and foremost, a peaceable fertility goddess who would defend her children. Men conveniently combined their bad behavior with her popularity making her goddess of war while yet retaining her fertility, sex and love attributes.

Men also moved the blame for going to war to a woman, Inanna. War is not the fault of men — the war goddess decided on the fight! In case of defeat, blame it on Inanna. Men's plans and fortunes don't proceed as desired? Both sacred and human woman is blamed for being fickle. Her joy-dance sadly becomes a war dance. With her archaic emblem form as dragon-lion spitting venom, the goddess fights along side soldiers and guards the king. Men's warrior gods and hairy heroes later fight battles against the demonized sacred feminine emblems (Tiamat and Imdugud/Anzu); yet as dragons and lion-dragons, the goddess emblems fight alongside the soldiers and guard the kings. The gods occasionally declare deadly punishments on humans, who have no recourse but to die of disease or in floods where corpses clog the irrigation ditches, like "dragon flies." The bullying gods could torment humans who could not fight back, but man-made war was Ishtar's doing. So said the men.

Inanna dancing for war, mayhem, and destruction? This is wrong! I puzzled over her "dance of battle" as it is unnatural to the goddess as I came to know her. Well before the dance of war and battle, the goddess dances. She dances sensually in celebration of life. She dances the joy of being alive. Her priestesses dance, her women dance, her temples' sacred dancers dance. I slept on that idea. Upon awakening, I saw old crescent moon rising. I thought about women assembling to celebrate the menstrual seclusion: women only, taboo — "men, stay away" — women in their women's quarter that is sacred space and not yet a prison for women captured by male-rule. Because of the sacred women's quarters, I do add: Inanna, Goddess of Menstruation, to the lengthy list of her names, titles, and epithets though no other reference calls her that. Her new moon festival is when young woman emerge out of women's quarter seclusion. The monthly festival at new moon is a celebration with a joyous, playful parade, public feast and dancing!

I dozed again, thinking of her dance, and awakened with a fresh vibrant dream vision of many women in a courtyard in solid flower-colored flounced gowns, like goddess dresses of the Ancient Near East. I considered the similarity of flamenco and tango dresses with flounced skirts. The dream-women danced alone, individually and free, yet moving as one, together, in solidarity; their contagious joy engulfed this dreamer and haunts yet. I dreamed Inanna's original and forever dance. She represents women who represent life and all potential life — joyous, giddy, amazing, difficult and messy life. Women are the dancers who have been subdued, forbidden to dance her dance, our dance of life; our biophilic dance of X-ness, whirling and enthralled with life. Inanna does not dance for war!

The following selected portions of another prayer to Ishtar will highlight additional attributes of the goddess not included above. The text tablet is quite damaged but the formula format is recognizable. Later texts were compilations of earlier ones and edited or expanded.

A predictable similarity of worship and thought continues through several millennia. Later texts are evidence that her power is weakened over time. (Foster, 2005: 606-10:)

A LITERARY PRAYER TO ISHTAR

A poetic sufferer first praises Ishtar and then beseeches her. Though fragmented, we still hear him praising her loudness, power, strength; her ability to shear off mountains ("Inanna and Ebih") and command the four winds. The speaker does not know what he did to deserve her punishment. He claims to have served her, upheld his vows to her, but still he suffers mightily. He points out that she is known for answering prayers, she leads people to protective spirits (personal deities), she gets angry and relents, but she forgets him. He lists his physical ailments: confusion, weakness, and dizziness. "His songs of joy are bitter," he lacerates himself by day (scratching with fingernails is a traditional form of showing grief); and sobs all night. He is trapped and abandoned. He shakes and has trouble breathing; he can neither understand nor hear. His "eyes rolled up" and his kin prepare for his burial. He pleads: "Like the mother who bore me, take pity on me!" He reminds her: she is "sweet to praise ... she releases the captive. She reveals light to the one in prison ... her mercy is close at hand ... swift her relenting ... Prayer and abjuration are yours, Ishtar!" The petition appears unfulfilled; the petitioner awaits her intercession.

The above devotee composes a full accounting of the goddess's powers and attributes. Patriarchy insinuates itself when we are told that Ishtar/Inanna has particular duties that Anu, Enlil, and Ea "gave" her. They did not give them to her; she had them before the gods were birthed. Saying that gods grant her the powers implies a power-over position. "Giving" power implies first ownership. Not true. A name used for her indicates her original identity: "O Mother-Matrix ..." (Foster, 2005: 674). Mother of all mothers, of all matter, first-mother of all, of all that matters. The text lists the goddess's many responsibilities and powers. It is difficult to think of a power she does not have! The devotional begins first and foremost with reference to her warrior aspect. Inanna did not originally have that job. In her early days, war is not a constant concern, but safety from war's destruction is first of the composer's concerns. After raids and war, the next greatest threats are insufficient water and food supplies, disease, and poverty.

The problem of governance increases as population concentration in urban centers grows. People come to the cities from many directions and cannot live as they had: nomadic or semi-nomadic. Tribal traditions are enough for governance in small homogeneous groups but not sizable settlements of diverse people. Sumer's tradition of wise elders, composed of both women and men, served them well. A second advisory group made of men with weapons who defended the cities is added when near constant conflict is established. Sumerians have the first bicameral government. In the following selection, we find Ishtar in charge of governance. Below is a summary of "The Greatness of Inanna/Ishtar" (Foster 2005: 674-6:)

THE GREATNESS OF INANNA/ISHTAR

Ishtar is addressed as a warrior and the most loved of all goddesses; the torchlight of all the celestial and earthly domains. She is Mother-Matrix who designs the rites, libations, temple foundations and brickwork. The goddess has the powers of the deep water. She has no equal, she has no rival. She reverses good and bad fortune and decides the fate of wealth or poverty for each babe in the womb. The petitioner of this poem searched among the gods and goddesses but only she would hear his entreaty. "How sweet to pray to you, how near at hand your listening, your look is hearing, your speech light!" (ibid.: 675)

The petitioner reminds Ishtar of his devotion to her: he serves her, he works for her; he seeks her and gazes upon her. Because of this he reasons that the goddess should help him, use her powers and grant him her protection, guidance, wealth and good fortune. He wants everything he desires! He asks that heaven and the depths rejoice for her and that all the gods bless her.

From these lines we know she is a warrior, she is cherished, and she has celestial grandeur over the four regions (cardinal directions); she *is* Mother-Matrix, another name for the parthenogenetic creatress of everything, aka: Nammu/Mammu and Tiamat. She is the "bonds of the depths," later associated with Ea/Enki the acclaimed son of Nammu (who is none other than Inanna/Ishtar). Other texts tell us he *gives* her the waterpower of river flooding. However, women and goddesses rule water since the early inception of goddess consciousness and expression. Waterpower is long held to be feminine. River deities are always goddesses. Water, moon and tides are woman's. Rivers and oceans experience tides and mothers gush a birth sea during delivery. Woman + moon + birth water + sea + tides + fish = water goddess.

Figure 25. Inanna with Date Palm Blossom

Inanna/Ishtar and Lilith hold the rod and line for building, laying the bricks. The instruments also symbolize the resetting of land boundaries after flooding, the measuring out of building foundations, and keeping walls straight during building. Kings are shown holding the symbols to indicate times of peace for only then did building and rebuilding take place. The symbols over time came to indicate peaceful rulership.

Women are the first measurers: moon time, birth time, and year time. Birth goddesses reflect that power in measuring life, granting fate and destiny, and above, Ishtar decides the fate "in the womb": poverty or wealth. Matristic wisdom settles disputes. Women once had a voice. We hear that Inanna/Ishtar is greatest of all the deities; she has no rival.

When children are troubled they go to their mother. When humans began divine myths, they naturally turned to a Mother who symbolizes all they need in the physical world for nourishment, shelter, comforting, and protection. She is the answer to their deepest questions and explains their life experiences.

Trouble comes to the ancient scribe composing the above lines. He considers all the deities and settles on petitioning a goddess. The unhappy petitioner selects the most important goddess to hear his plaints. He imagines her with a protective spirit in front of her and a guardian spirit behind. Justice flanks her right side and good fortune is on her left. When Ishtar comes, she brings "obedience, acceptance and peace ... life and well-being."

The petitioner is childlike in his demands for attaining all he desires. Inanna/Ishtar is life and life is complex. Her opposing opposites, her syzygies of behavior tell us anything can happen! Her MEs are many and seem beyond human control. Appeasing the goddess is a full-time endeavor, yet does she ask for all that?

I imagine Inanna, Life, dancing between the poles of possibility. We move through the ups and downs of life. We face choices and consequences. Like a good mother, she allows us to grow, evolve, and solve our own problems. She is life and we love her.

> *True goddess, fit for the MEs, it is exalting to acclaim you.*
> *Merciful one, brilliantly righteous woman ...* [19]

---

[19] Hallo 1968: 23

CHAPTER 3

Creation Myths

She is older than all the gods.[20]

LIFE-GIVING WOMAN

The mother goddess is universal and modeled on women. Killing one's offspring is not a feminine characteristic. XX chromosome is doubly biophilic, not necrophilic. Instead of guidance, creative problem solving, and inclusion, male competition and aggression lead to solving problems with violence. Instead of the egalitarian social structure present when sacred feminine is observed and human feminine is honored, male alpha-hierarchy competes and concentrates power into a single absolute alpha authority. What is the patriarchal solution for reducing the feminine? Blame the goddess, she must die. Goddess, and therefore woman, are silenced and stripped of power. This chapter compares earlier and later texts as evidence of the erasure of the goddess of creation. Remember, Inanna is an aspect of the prime creatress.

Nammu (Namma), Sumerian prime creatress, is the parthenogenetic great mother goddess. She and her global equivalents are the root of all

---

[20] Graves 1948: 361

goddesses. She is mother of all gods, that is, the ones who are not derivatives or gender-flips of an existing goddess (aspect). She, prime creatress, is the first deity; everywhere, long ago, "god" is female. Her name, Nammu, came to mean "river" and the power of dry riverbeds renewing; i.e., the water table rising and falling. Jacobsen notes that her name is derived from Nin-imma, "Lady female-genitals;" "a personification of the numinous power to shape, mature, and give birth to the child." Further changes are: nin-imma > nam-amma > nanma > namma > nammu. "N" and "m" stand in for each other in variant names. Nammu is also written Mammu (Jacobsen 1987: 155, footnote 5). Note the similarity of emphasis on Inanna's vulva, her fertility, and the prime creatress' original name: "Lady (queen) female-genitals". Inanna is the maid version of Namma/Nammu. Prime creatress births the gods; she has no need to birth Inanna and the birth goddesses — they are herself. She births fresh-water god Enki first. Being first-born is important to male-based hierarchy; the first-born of goddess or god so and so appears in many texts. Enki sleeps when river beds are low and little water seeps into wells. When Namma/Nammu flows water in her riverbed (vaginal cleft), Enki comes to life just as birth water flows before a baby is delivered.

The Sumerians imagined how the world and heavens came into being and what the world looked like before people came into being. At first, nothing was named (known) until Matrix-Tiamat and Primeval Apsu came together. Tiamat bore the universe when the salty water (Tiamat) and sweet waters (Primeval Apsu) mingled. It was a time when "no canebrake was intertwined nor thicket matted close; when no gods at all had been brought forth, nor called by names, none destinies ordained (Foster 2005: 439)."

Professor Kramer translated the following two creation scenes (Kramer 1979: 29-30:)

The great Earth-crust was resplendent, its surface was jewel-green,
The wide Earth — its surface was covered with precious metals and lapis lazuli,

...

> The Earth was arrayed luxuriantly in plants and herbs, its presence
>   was majestic,
> The holy Earth, the pure Earth, beautified herself for holy Heaven,

The Sumerians settled southern Mesopotamia, the land between
the two rivers in the fifth millennium BC.E.. Sumer's territory was
about the size of Maryland — 10,000 square miles. They merged with
the indigenous Ubaidian people who had moved from the north as the
great marshes dried and habitable land rose. The blending of Sumerians
with the Ubaidians caused a dynamic culture to grow. Theirs was the
high culture of the Ancient Near East for millennia.

The cosmology of the Sumerian people changes in time, but the
earliest version goes something like this:

In the beginning is the great Abyss, sea and fresh water together. It is
everywhere; it fills the universe. A single female progenitor of serpentine
description, lives in the Abyss. From the abyss, the chaos of creative
potential, earth and heaven are birthed together. They are enclosed in
a large empty sphere. Heaven copulates with earth. The space between
them is born: atmosphere, sky, and wind.

Earth is beautiful. She is a disc floating like an island over the vast
below contained by the lower half of the birth sphere. (Picture a quarter-
pounder burger enclosed in a rounded bun.) Earth is surrounded on
all sides by water. The sea and earth layer divides the sphere in half.
Directly under earth is the Apsu, fresh water. This water seeps into
wells, marshes, canals, and rivers. To the west, the land becomes desert
at the the bitter sea's edge. Beyond that is water stretching far to the east
to a distant land and the infernal river. The eastern edge of the earth
disc also has a desert that ends at the surrounding water. The land of
the dead was in the great below, the vast hollow underworld. Beyond
the sphere is the primal sea. Rain drips from goddess cloud-breasts from
water outside the containing dome.

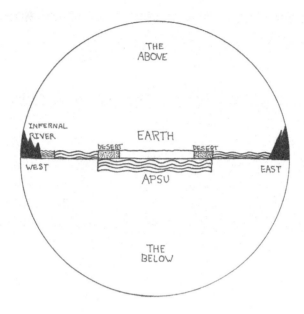

Figure 26. Sumerian Cosmography

The prime creatress is Nammu/Mammu or Tiamat. Heaven is An, earth is Ki, and the air and atmosphere is Enlil. Inanna is of the first triad: Nammu, Great Mother — renewal maid Inanna — Ereshkigal, the death mother. "When ... An had carried off the heavens, and ... Enlil had carried off the earth ... When ... Ereshkigal, was given the underworld for her domain" we notice Ki, earth, is missing in the role call. Ki is more often known as Ninhursag. Her son, Enlil ("head of air") "carried off the earth" by the time of first writing (Wolkstein and Kramer 1983: 139).

Sumerian time begins at night. Evening comes, sun retires, evening star appears. Night is time for love, dreams, visions, and divine decision-making. Daylight brings action and understanding. Moon is extremely important in hot and dry climes. Moon and earth are the first depictions of sacred feminine.

Inanna has two moon phase connotations. First, she is goddess of moon's crescent, potential fertility and new beginnings. Inanna is moon goddess Ningal's daughter, but by time of writing, Inanna is known as the child of the moon goddess and god. The sacred feminine is a lunar deity from the beginning of goddess time.

Deities are assigned numbers that can stand for a divine name in texts. Inanna's number is 14 which is half of the 28-9 day moon cycle and women's menstrual cycle. On the last day, 28-30, women enter menstrual seclusion and dark moon. The number 30 becomes Nanna's (aka Suen/Sin, moon god). Inanna is number 14, which is full moon when women ovulate mid-cycle, yet her celebration is new moon, beginning of the month, and mentioned in some texts as the "fat quarter," day seven. Fixed ritual days are given in other texts for the 7th and 15th days counting from the 29th or 30th of the previous month. I believe the numbering tells us that Inanna is the young aspect of full moon. This marking of lunar time is expressed in a poem, "Illuminator of Darkness", written for the moon god. The strongest, most magical time of the moon is the dark moon, the end of the month, when women's naturally coordinated menses occurs — the 30th day — and Nanna owns the number. Menstruation is powerful and here is another proof of usurpation. Of Nanna, ever renewing "illuminator of darkness" it is said (Foster, 2005: 760:)

> Your day of disappearance is your day of splendor, a secret
> of the great gods.
> The thirtieth day is your festival, day of your divinity's
> splendor.

Inanna *is* goddess of fertility which occurs on the full moon, mid-cycle. The above text calls Nanna's disappearance: "a secret of the great gods". That is again an imitation, a piracy, for menstrual blood power. All early cultures practiced the exclusion of men from women's taboo (sacred, holy) seclusion. In all early cultures, men worked at taking away the creative blood and birthing power of women.

The moon god's "day of disappearance" means the dark moon aspect, formerly belonging to the moon mother. With story re-vision, the moon *god* is in the netherworld deciding the fate of the dead. Remember, deciding fate is an old goddess attribute, and decision-making is Inanna's (women's). Nanna, moon *god*, imitates menstrual seclusion, the moon's disappearance. Dark moon belongs to a moon goddess, not a god, as moon rules women's cycles. Not only is moon tied directly to women's cycles of fertility, moon is a benevolent celestial body. In hot and arid lands people welcome the coolness of night and dew rising. When moon becomes "the man in the moon", we witness men taking over women's menstrual powers and lunar beneficence. Knight states this take-over is the second global myth, disagreeing with Levy Strauss who claims the menstrual take-over is the *first* universal myth. Obviously something must exist to be taken over! Women own menstrual power first and create the first myth (Knight: 1991, general information on the myth take-over).

HUMANS ARE CREATED

For the rest of time the gods would hear the drumbeat of their hearts

The early gods are established in the beautiful sphere. Gods and goddesses inhabit the earth. The gods do all the work to supply the grain, the canal building and everything imaginable. Of course the lesser gods work for the greater gods. One day the lesser gods threw down their tools and quit!

This is the back story for how humans came into being. Humans are created to do the labor of the gods who previously did all the work. "When gods were man" meant working like men. Nammu/Mami/Mammu births the gods; the greater gods An(u), Enlil, Enki, and the Anunna and the lesser gods numbering seven — likely the Pleiades — called sages. An/Anu ("heaven") was king, Enlil ("head of air") took earth and Enki ("head of earth") was in charge of fresh water and the bolt trap of the ocean. The "greater gods" of this patriarchal text do not include goddesses. Earlier texts include Inanna and Ninhursag, the earth goddess of numerous names, and Ereshkigal, Inanna's "sister" who reigns as death mother, the universal goddess trinity of many names.

One story of how humans were created is retold below and based on Foster's anthology inclusion of "Atrahasis." (Foster 2005: 229-253:)

ATRAHASIS

> *Before humans are invented, the lesser gods do the work for the greater gods; they are forced to labor. An(u) takes heaven, Enlil takes earth, and Enki owns the "bolt trap" of the sea (holds the fishes). Enlil's gods dig the great waterways, "the life of the land." They dig wells, pile up mountains, and drain the marsh. They work all day and all night for forty years. The big gods do no work. A rebellion is instigated by a lesser god, Awila. "Let us kill him (Enlil)," we will be free of this labor, let us take him from his house! This is war! The lesser Igigi-gods burn their tools and baskets and start toward Enlil's house ready for battle.*

An interesting note here is that in this story there is no feminine influence, no goddess to modify the gods; the hierarchy of power-over is well established. Under a mother goddess, an egalitarian society maintains a fair distribution of work and produce; women and goddess find creative solutions to resolve problems without fighting. When men take control, they naturally look to an alpha ordering, a hierarchy, and settle problems with force. Here, the goddesses are called upon only to birth the humans.

> *Enlil's house, Ekur, is surrounded. The gatekeeper warns Enlil that a war is at his gate. The rebellious gods are asked to identify their leader. The labor gang gods declare war. The misery is killing them. Enlil tells An(u) to take the power he still retains and return to the sky and assemble the "great gods." Ea (aka Enki) is the one to suggest that it was true, the Igigi-gods were overworked. Enki/Ea speaks saying he will call the birth goddess Mami (also called Nammu, Nintu, Mama, and Belet-ili in the text) to make human beings. She is the midwife for the gods. (Note that Mami/Nammu is neither called mother of the gods nor creatress of heaven and earth as she was in earlier*

119

Sumerian story.) Enki asks her to make humans to relieve the gods of their burden.

The birth-goddess speaks, deferring to Enki (who gains his authority in other texts as the son of Nammu, the prime singular creatress), saying he is the purifying god who can give her clay to form the people. He establishes the first, seventh, and fifteenth days of a month for purification baths. He requests that one of the Igigi-gods be killed. (This act removes the guilt from the others and is the blood needed to enliven the clay. Women's blood cessation during pregnancy was thought to build the baby. Men do not bleed and so must make blood.) Enki proposes that Nintu mix the sacrificed flesh and blood of the god into the clay. Human and god are merged. "Let us hear the drumbeat for the rest of time, from the flesh of the god let a spirit remain, let it make the living know its sign (ibid.: 235)." Awila was slaughtered and mixed with clay. (Earlier stories of creating humans did not have a god killed for his blood and it was Nammu who invited the other birth goddesses to assist. Life and birth is in the hands and bodies of Goddess and women.) The great Anunna-gods assembled and the Igigi-gods spat on the clay mix.

Mami completes her task; she has given drudgery to the humans. She also gives her creations the gift of noise! The gods ran to her and kissed her feet. They said: "Formerly [we used to call] you 'Mami', now let your name be 'Mistress-of-All-the Gods', Betet-kala-ili" (ibid.: 237). The tablet text is broken, but in other texts she creates seven female and seven male fetuses that are birthed by the birth goddesses. She places a brick of clay between the female and male infants. (A brick remained present during births into recent times in the region.)

The humans mature, the girls grow breasts and the boys grow beards. They notice each other and choose partners. The birth goddesses count the months and at the tenth (lunar reckoning) flour meal is sprinkled and a brick is placed in the room "of the sacrosanct woman's house." The women's wombs open; babes are born and separated (from the umbilical cord). Thereafter women and men pair, "…when the (marital) bed is laid, let wife and her husband choose each other, at the time for being man and wife, they should heed Ishtar in the [marriage] chamber. For nine days let there be rejoicing, let them call Ishtar Ishara (ibid.: 238)."

Twelve hundred years pass and the people are numerous and too noisy. The gift of clamor that the birth goddess gave them annoys Enlil. "The [land] was bellowing [like a bull]." Enlil is disturbed and says humankind is too clamorous! The humans of this time live long; death has not yet been invented. Enlil sends disease and plagues to kill them. Enki tells a man, his favorite, Atrahasis, how to prevent the annihilation. He is to call the elders to his home and advise the people to ignore their goddesses and gods and instead make a loaf of bread and leave the offering at the door of Namtar, god of plagues. "May he be shamed by the gift and withdraw his hand (ibid.: 240)." And so he does.

The people continue their clamor. Enlil decides food for the people should be cut off and causes drought. He was losing sleep because of their uproar. He orders that plant life grow scant; he orders Adad the weather god to hold back his rain. He orders underground water to not seep upwards and orders that no flooding could occur. The wind blew and the land turned to dust. The clouds appear but let down no rain. Adad withdraws his rain and floods do not come up (from the depths). "Let the field reduce its yields. Let the grain-goddess close her bosom (ibid.: 241)."

Again, Enki chooses to save humanity. He tells Atrahasis, his favorite, to call the elders to his house at the usual time. They are to send out heralds to spread the word that no goddesses nor gods are to be reverenced; they are to put a baked loaf before the door of Adad. "May he be shamed by the gift and withdraw his hand. May he rain down mist in the morning, may he stealthily rain down dew in the night, that the fields just as stealthily bear ninefold (ibid.: 242)." They leave the bread offering and Adad supplies rain, mist and dew.

The grain grew and the people again became clamorous. Famine was sent next by Enlil to kill off the people. Atrahasis senses that Enki is unable to contact him directly so he goes to the waterway to sleep; he dreams an indirect message from

Enki. God and man communicate via dream. In the dream he weeps loudly (laments are loud to get divine attention to right a wrong and change misfortune). He libates and brings dream offerings. Enki in the depths, received the gifts and sends his hairy-hero-men (hairy meant strong and heroes are half divine) to ask Atrahasis about the conditions in the land. They are told: "The flood did not rise from the depths. The womb of earth did not bear ... The black field whitened, the broad plain was filled up with salts ... When the third year came, their features were gray from hunger ... Life was ebbing, little by little. Tall people shriveled in body, they walked hunched in the street. Broad-shouldered people turned slender, their long stance grew short." The hairy-hero-men report to Enki by the sea. (After a lacuna in the text) Enki "released the yoke (bolt)," and brings a flood of fishes to restore the people (ibid.: 244).

Enlil is angry with the water god and reminds him he was bound to Enlil's command yet he released the fish house bolt and arranged for moisture in the fields so the people survived. After several gaps the story continues. What the great god Enlil orders must be done even though it is an evil thing he commands. Enki, the crafty god, is bound by divine order and oath to not warn the people, so he spoke to a reed wall where Atrahasis waited. The man is told to leave his house and build a boat with a covered roof so the sun cannot peer in. He should make the sailing gear fast and use pitch to make the boat strong. Enki says he would give him a "shower" of fish and a "windfall" of birds.

Atrahasis explains to the elders that his god Enki, and their god Enlil are always angry at each other and he has been expelled from the land. He intends to join Enki in the depths. The elders and craftsmen help him build his boat. When the boat is finished he brings cattle, birds and steppe animals aboard. Atrahasis gives a great feast for the people, but he is restless and heartsick with knowledge of their impending doom; "he retched gall." Enki cannot not save them.

The feast finishes; the weather changes. Atrahasis brings his family into the boat. He seals the door with pitch. Adad roars in the heavens. The winds grow furious. Anzu fills the world with storm rain, lightening, and thunder. The flood comes. People cannot see each other. The flood roars like a bull, the wind screams like an eagle. Atrahasis unties his moorings and sails off. The sun disappears. The dark is deep and dense. The gods fear the storming din and abandon earth to hunker down outside heaven. Nintu, the humans' birth mother, is in agony. The Anunna, the great gods, are sitting about thirsty and hungry. (Note: the great gods are not grieving the human loss, only the loss of the food and drink they provide, while Enki and the birth goddess mourn the dead people as they were involved with human creation.)

The goddess sees the devastation; weeping, the midwife of the gods, the wise Mami, asks herself why she agreed to such punishment. Her offspring, without her help, die like flies. She blames Anu since he gave the order, and Enlil for forcing them to agree. She wails. Her offspring clog the waterways like dragon flies, they pile up along the river banks. When she finishes weeping, she grows hungry and thirsty. The storm and flood last seven days.

After a gap of twenty-four lines, the storm has ended and Atrahasis is cooking a savory food offering. The gods smell the smoke and "gathered like flies." They ate the offering and then Nintu shouted at them: "Where has Anu come to, the chief decision-maker? ... They who irrationally brought about the flood, and relegated the peoples to catastrophe? You resolved upon annihilation, so now (the people's) countenances are turned gray (ibid.: 251)."

Enlil sees the escape boat and is furious at the Igigi-gods. How did any human escape? Anu guesses it is Enki. Enki admits it was he. He explained saying: "I did it for your sakes! I am responsible for life (ibid.: 252)." Enlil calls Nintu the birth-goddess, creatress of destinies, to create a destined life span for humans who had previously lived long without death. Further, to reduce population growth, a "third woman" is destined. There would be women who bore children and those who did not. Enlil created a she-demon who would snatch babes from their mother's laps and priestesses who were taboo, cloistered, and sacrosanct — non-sexual women to reduce childbirth.

The following version of how humans are created and why there are handicapped people is found in Thorkild Jacobsen's *The Harps that Once. ...* (Jacobsen 1987: 153-166:)

THE BIRTH OF MAN

In days of yore,
    the days
    when heaven and earth
    had been [fashioned,]
in nights of yore,
    the nights
    when heaven and earth
    had been [fashioned,]
in years of yore,
    the years
    when the modes of be[ing
    were determined,]
when the Anunnaki gods
    had been born,
when the goddess-[mothers]
    had been chosen
    for marriage,
when the goddess-mothers
    had been assigned
    to heaven or earth,
and when the goddess-mothers
    [had had intercourse,]
    had become pregnant,
    and had given birth,

did the gods for whom they baked
    their food portions (flour made into bread)
    and set therewith

their tables,
did the major gods
    oversee work,
    while the minor gods
    were shouldering the menial labor.
The gods were dredging the rivers,
    were piling up their silt
    on projecting bends —
and the gods lugging the clay
    began complaining
    about the corvee.

The text is evidence of risen patriarchy. Nammu is credited with birthing the gods but the goddesses are being "chosen" for marriage and are "assigned" their posts. The assignments are made by the big gods — goddess'/goddesses' long held obvious powers from the inception of womankind's creative storytelling and invention of sacred myth are gone — here goddesses make bread to serve the gods, their "husbands". The major gods supervise the lesser gods who do all the hard work. Male hierarchy is established. Goddess/woman culture is waning. The poem features Enki as the major player, problem solver, and tutelary divine of Eridu, a very early Sumerian city built by marshlands.

In those days
    lay he of the vast intelligence,
    the creator bringing
    the major gods into being,
Enki,
    In *E- engur,* a well
    into which water seeped,
    a place the inside of which
    no god whatever
    was laying eyes on,
on his bed, sleeping
    and was not getting up.

The gods were weeping
    and were saying:
    "He made the present misery!"
yet they (dared) not rouse
    the sleeper, him who lay at rest,
    from that bed!

Namma, the mother primordial,
    bearer of the major gods,
took the tears of the gods to her son.
"Since, after you will have rested,
    since, after you will have sat up,
[you] of yourself [will] rise:
The gods are smashing
    at noon and at eventide
    what they have (just) made!
My son, rise from your bed,
    and when you
    with your ingenuity
    have searched out
    the (required) skill,
and you have fashioned
    a fill-in worker
    for the gods,
    may they get loose
    of their digging!"

...

    Enki rises, contemplates, and smites his thigh, i.e., he has an idea! Enki, "creator and constructor of everything," invites Imma-en and Imma-shar to come to him. (Jacobsen translates the names to mean the two ovaries: "imma" is female genitalia; "en" here = "productrix" while "shar" = "the bountiful one".) The clever god reaches his "arm" toward them and a fetus begins to grow. He remembers his mother and that she is needed for forming the fetus, for adding arms and legs. He tells her to get the birth goddesses to help give birth. He asks Namma to get the birth-chair ready. [Birth-chairs formerly belong to Ningal, moon goddess, and women!] He names the birth-helpers: Ninmah ("exalted lady" — she is usually the birth goddess of mention); Ninimma (Namma/Nammu herself), Shuzidanna (Enki's consort), Ninmada, Dududuh (opens the womb), Ninmug (female genitals), and three names of Inanna: Ninshara, Ninbara, and Ereshguna.

The humans will take form in the uterus of Namma/ Nammu. "Without the sperm of a male" she creates the first human fetus. She makes its shoulders wide, opens a hole for its mouth, and places it in "amnion" (birth fluid). Enki's contribution is to wrap it in wool. The human embryo is happy; Enki is happy. He invites the goddesses and gods to a feast. Everyone is served bread while a "ritually pure kid" is roasted for An and Enlil. The assembly praises Enki, but it is Namma/ Nammu who does the creative work!

The people drink beer, so their deities also enjoy beer. The celebration of the creation of humans to do the work for the divine pantheon includes beer. Intoxication is a good excuse for making mistakes. We rejoin the poem with what is likely a separate literary text to explain miscarriages and anomalies. Notice: the birth goddess announces it is she who decides the form so it is her fault if things go amiss. Namma/Nammu creates the first prototype and the birth goddesses (of fertility — Inanna — and ovaries, uterus, and vagina) are responsible for good and bad pregnancies).

Enki and Ninmah (birth goddess)
    were drinking beer
    and began to feel good
    inside.
Ninmah said to Enlil:
"(As for) the build of men (humankind),
    what makes it good
    or bad

is mine (affair),
whichever way
    my turn of heart,
    I am making the decision
    about the mode of being,
    good or bad."

> *The birth goddess and Enki are inebriated. They think they will try their hand at making humans! The drunken results have abnormalities. What follows is a contest challenge. Tipsy Ninmah makes people with afflictions out of the Apsu clay. Enki finds a use or job for each one. Enki takes his turn at creating. He has a motive. He wants to create something that "is killing her city." In other words, the competition is no longer about finding employment for the handicapped. He, the tricky god, finds a way to diminish the mother goddess. The women in her city will abort fetuses; when the population decreases, her city dies. Here the temple, Ekur (house-mountain), belongs to Ninmah and not Enlil as is usual. That text line hints strongly that Ninmah was replaced by Enlil as the tutelary deity of the city. Enki's name, (head of earth), indicates he has already usurped Ki (earth), the original earth goddess.*

The competition is between uterus and penis. Enki is proud of his wonderful member. In other creation stories he masturbates everything into existence. In this text, since he has no uterus or vagina, a human woman is brought to birth his "creation". The created form is non-viable; it is born too soon; it is without strength or hope. Ninmah cannot get Enki's creation to sit up or eat or live. The poem tells us that she loses the contest; she cannot provide employment for what Enki made. Enki, the clever and tricky god, breaks the game rule. Enki wins as what he makes has no chance to develop and live — he never intended it to live! Ninmah can not find employment for what Enki creates: the expelled matter of early miscarriage. His plan here is diabolical for the usurpation of the goddess's city.

A variant text, "Enki and Ninmah," described by Jacobsen in *The Treasures of Darkness* has the same feast to celebrate Nammu's successful creation of working humans. She creates fourteen in number, seven of each gender who magically mature, notice each other, make love, and reproduce more humans to work for the deities. Ninmah and Enki again get drunk. Ninmah picks up some of the Apsu clay Nammu used to make humans and tries her hand. Drunk, she makes mistakes. Enki is clever and gives them employment. He takes a turn at creating humans and makes the same non-viable fetus as in our present text but without a human woman to assist with her uterus. The goddess can not help the too-soon-born human in either text. The second text still ends with praise to Enki but Ninmah is reminded that only women (and goddesses) can birth new life and Ninmah does not lose her temple and city. (Jacobsen 1976: 113)

Similar defect-challenges appear in both texts. Similar "jobs" are found for the disabled. The former text, "The Birth of Man," is priestly promotion of maleness, even maleness that creates death and uses tricky schemes to demote and humiliate the birth goddess and blatantly steal her city. Enki condemns women to suffer aborted pregnancies so the goddess's city dies and Enlil can take over her temple, Ekur. Everafter, Ekur belongs to Enlil. The non-viable human is premeditated. Enki is not comparable to mother goddesses. Enki is not a birth goddess and he has no anatomical way to make babies, yet in the poem's conclusion, he is the winner and Ninmah has lost her city.

Goddess' womb is metaphor for creating life. Enki does not have a womb so what he creates by himself dies. Goddess is biophilic and caring. She holds the aborted dying babe to her breast and her lap. She is in despair at her own feast; she laments the nonviable baby. Enki cares not for life, fairness, or truth! He wins the contest through trickery. The gods (men) take her city and temple. Ninmah loses the contest; she has no recourse but to leave her party and city. She weeps. She will go where Enki does not go. Ninmah becomes Ninhursag, "Lady Stoney Ground or Foothills," when she relocates in the myth revision, far from the marshy wetlands where Enki lives and rules. She is demoted from third

place in the divine lists. She becomes mother of wild steppe animals.
We return to "The Birth of Man:"

> Enki replied thereunto
>   to Ninmah:
> "In that decision about the mode of being
>   desired by the heart
>   let me mitigate
>   the good or the bad."
>
> Ninmah took
>   the fathering Apsu clay
> and moulded from it
>   the "Man-unable-to close-
>   the shaking-hand-upon-an-arrow-shaft-
>   to-send-it-going,"
>   a seeing man.
> When Enki had looked
>   the "Man-unable-to-close-
>   the-shaking-hand-upon-an-arrow-shaft-
>   to-send-it-going" over
> he determined a way for it to be,
>   had it stand at attention
>   by the head of the king.
>
> Next she molded from it
>   the "One-handing-back-
>   the-lamp-
>   to-the-men-who-can-see" (he is blind)
> [When] Enki had looked
>   the "One-handing-back-
>   the-lamp-
>   to-the-men-who-can-see"
>   he determined a way for it to be,
>   he allotted to it

the musical arts
had it sit ... on the long side
    in front of the king. [21]
Third [she moulded from it]
    the "Hobbled-by-twisting-ankles."

When En[ki] had lo[oked]
    the "Hobbled-by-twisting-ankles"
    over,
he [taught] (?) it the work
    of metal casters and silversmiths,
    and ...

Fourth she molded from it
    the "Moron, the-engenderer-of-which-
    was-a-Subarean"[22]
    he looked it over,

he determined a way for it to be,
    had it stand at attention
    by the head of the king.

Fifth she molded from it
    the "Man-leaking-urine."

When Enki had looked
    the "Man-leaking-urine"
    over
he showered it
    with blest water
    and thereby drew out

---

[21] Jacobsen speculates that the composer of the poem was himself blind and includes the lengthy justification of disabilities as being divinely inspired. (Jacobsen 1987: 160, footnote 16)

[22] a slur against mountain people considered barbarian and stupid

of its body
the (former)
mode of being.

Sixth she molded from it
the "Woman-who-is-not-
giving-birth".

When Enki had looked
the "Woman-who-is-not-
giving-birth
over
he determined a way for it to be,
made it look (for orders)
to a weaver,
and entrusted it
to the queen's household.

Seventh she molded from it
the "Man-in-the-body-of-which-
no-male-and-no-female-organ-was-placed."
When Enki had looked
the "Man-in-the-body-of-which-
no-male-and-no-female-organ-was-placed"
over
he called it by the name
"Nippurean-the-courtier"
and determined for it
its mode of being
so that it would stand
in attendance
before the king.

Ninmah threw the pinch of clay
in her hand upon the ground
and a great silence fell.

The great lord Enki
    said to Ninmah:
"I have determined modes of being
    for your creatures
    and given them
    (their) daily bread.
Well then! Let me (now) mold
    (one) for you,
    and do you determine
    the mode of being
    of that newborn one!"

Enki for his part
    fashioned a creature
    for the secret purpose of which
    was killing her city.
He said to Ninmah:
"The semen which the male member
    is emitting,
    when discharged
    into a woman's womb
    that woman
    gives birth to it
    from her womb."
(So) Ninmah brought [a woman
    to Enki]
    to give birth to it
but that woman [...]
    aborted the fetus
    in accordance with
    its secret purpose,
    so that its days [become not full.]
The first one, Ud-mu'ul,
    ("the-day-was-far-off")
    — its scalp was sore,

its front was sore,
its eyes were sore,
its neck was sore,
the throat was closing up,
    the ribs twisting
    the liver was sore,
    the insides were sore,
    the heart was sore,
its hands, having the shakes,
    could not put food
    to its mouth,
    the spine was crushed,
    the anus closed up,
the hips were brittle
    the feet (with their) skin breaking
    unable to walk the fields.
Enki said to Ninmah:
"I determined modes of being
    for your creatures,
    gave them
    (their daily) bread
do you (now) determine
    for my creature
    its mode of being,
    that it may
    (have enough to) eat!"

Ninmah, when she had looked
    Ud-mu'ul over
    took back the pinch (of clay)
    into her hand.
She approached Ud-mu'ul,
    was questioning him,
    but it was not opening
    its mouth

she piled up loaves
> for him to eat,
> but he reached not out
> to her for it.
A seat to make (one) rejoice,
> a place to lie down,
> she laid out for him
> but he was unable
> to lie down.
Standing he was [un]able to sit down,
> was unable to lie down,
> was unable to [...]
> he was unable to [...]
> he was unable to eat bread.

Ninmah [re]plied to Enki
> to the word (he had spoken):
"The man, your handiwork,
> is not a live man,
> nor a [dead] man,
> I cannot support it!"
...

Enki reminds her that he has found a way for her creations to earn their daily bread and repeats the above assignments. Note that a number of unfortunates end up close to the king by reason that the king is the shepherd of his flock and will look after them. The section of text where Ninmah is despairing is fragmented. Translatable lines are: "I am the one lamenting," "I am the one driven out of my house (temple), at my beer-pouring party," "I am become one lingering outside, [cannot] enter at wish! (ibid.: 164-5)" Enki dismisses Ninmah's grief and despair; he admits that what he made was "incomplete" without her "work." He praises his penis and says that when a woman has miscarried, mourners will "relay widely word of your power!" Enki designed the aborted fetus to reduce the population and kill her city. Part of the poem reverts back

135

to the earlier version that recognizes Ninmah as the one with the power to form babies in wombs. Both poems end with Enki the winner. He is praised. Ninmah speaks:

"Now I cannot dwell under heaven,
    cannot dwell on earth,
    cannot in the country
    get out of your sight.
Where you dwell not,
    in a house I shall build,
    I shall not hear your voice.
Where you live not,
    in a city I shall build,
    me myself (despairing) silence will fill.

"My city is destroyed,
    my house wrecked,
    my children taken captive.
I am a fugitive
    driven out of Ekur,
I myself, even,
    have not escaped
    out your hands!"

Enki replied to it, to Ninmah:
    "Who can gainsay
    a word from your mouth?
(But) hand (down) Ud-mu'ul
    clasped your bosom
    from your lap!
He is lacking, in sooth,
    your work, Ninmah;
    was born to me
    incomplete,
    who could challenge that?

"May men to the end of days
    in awe pay their respect to him,
and whenever, as is due,
    my male member
    may be extolled,
    may he be there
    as a (sobering) reminder!
May Enkum and Ninkum (professional mourners)
(consolingly) respond
    [with cries of woe
    to your cries of woe,]
    may they relay widely
    word of your power!
My sister,
    may your warrior's arm
    be made [man]ifest to hea[ven]'s [borders].
Holy songs, softly and loudly,
    . ... (fragmented)
    . ...

Ninmah did not equal
    the great lord Enki!
Father Enki,
    praise of you is sweet!

The reader will note the reference above to "my sister, may your warrior's arm ..." Inanna is the warrior goddess, there is no other. She is included in the poem's beginning with the assembly of birth goddesses with three of her names. Inanna is often called "Mother" in her praise poems. She is the young potential fertility and manifesting fertility of Great Mother. All goddesses are aspects of the Great Goddess Mother. Inanna is of the original upper Paleolithic mother goddess story. She "wears the robes of the old old gods." The above poem is included for two reasons: first is that penis is winning over womb, the second is that

Inanna, as fertile great creatress also suffers when Enki, maleness, wins another skirmish in overtaking the divine woman.

A story, dated late second millennium B.C.E., justifies Marduk rising to the top of the Babylonian pantheon by slaughtering the primal creatress, Tiamat/Nammu, and forming heaven and earth from her flayed carcass. Assur, another god who rose from obscurity, is also attributed with the same murderous deed. The rewriting of old myths supports a national concept of a deified king as absolute ruler. The inspiration behind the rise of Marduk is "the evolution of Mesopotamian political institutions from a reconstructed local assemble of elders to absolute kingship claiming divine sanction on a regional or international scale (Foster, 2005: 436)."

A poet scribe revised the old creation myth by dismissing the human capability of rebellion and instead puts them in their place in divine order, as subdued servants of gods and of later self-proclaimed divine kings. A great threat required a leader, a *lugal,* "a big man," with absolute authority. This was the old concept from the intrinsically peaceful Sumerians who had a counsel of elders (women and men). When conflict increased, a second branch of weapon-bearing men was added to the governance. At times of threat, a temporary leader was selected to protect the community. He had, for that period of time, absolute power. When the threat was resolved, he returned to his ordinary life. Kramer notes that the taste for absolute power was too tempting for men. To make the position last, leaders kept conflict or threat of conflict ongoing; they changed a part-time role into a full-time one of absolute rulership. The Babylonian text explains absolute obedience to a leader. It also reveals the deliberate effort to displace the divine feminine. Remember, Inanna is of the first creatress. In the following story, Nammu is Tiamat.

Genealogy of the deities varies excepting for the prime creatress. She is always first. The following text is about creation and how male problem solving and power usurpation retells the origin myth. In this gruesome epic, all is created from the prime creatress' body by an upstart godlet who hacks her to pieces. It is those pieces did the creating. Note

138

also that the story tells us it is Apsu, here not the watery deep but a male consort to prime creatress, who, like Enlil in the flood story, wants to kill the creatress' children because they are too numerous and noisy. They disturb his rest and sleep. The bad behavior starts with Apsu, the male consort; but it is the feminine, Tiamat/Nammu, who is blamed and hacked up. Killing the competition, here the god Apsu's own offspring, is also a common story in the Greek male-dominated pantheon. Goddesses do not kill their offspring, divine or human, as mothers do not kill their children. Gods can't create life, but they can destroy it! (Foster 2005: 439-445:)

THE EPIC OF CREATION

"Before anything was, mother ocean [Tiamat] and fresh water(?) [Apsu] mingled to produce the first of a series of pairs of gods. The descendants, with their boisterous behavior, stir Tiamat and Apsu. Although Tiamat bears it in good part, Apsu wishes to kill the offspring (ibid.: 439)." Apsu's vizier counsels him he should have rest during the day and sleep at night. Apsu is delighted with the evils the vizier plans. Word gets out. The gods are stunned to learn that they are to be killed. Ea/Enki, son of Anu, comes to the rescue.[23] Ea/Enki kills Apsu (his great-great-grandfather), captures his counselor, and takes up residence in the Apsu, here meaning fresh water, rivers, and springs — the former domain of Apsu.

Ea/Enki fathers Marduk who is born and suckled at the breasts of goddesses, "he was a hero at birth, he was a mighty one from the beginning! (ibid.: 442)." Anu, Marduk's grandfather, is so pleased with Marduk that he makes him four times better than any other god; he surpasses all others; he is so beautifully made that eyes can not take him in. Marduk is given the four winds for play. He makes waves that rock Tiamat, and the gods who live within her, day and night. The winds steal the sleep from the gods who angrily plot to do evil. The four winds roil Tiamat. The gods in Tiamat criticize her saying she let her own

---

[23] Ea is Enki and in most other texts he is son of Nammu/Tiamat.

husband Apsu be killed and now she does nothing to stop the roiling. They decide she doesn't love them. They urge Tiamat to make a tempest. War begins. In other words, the retaliation against Tiamat is said to be over her non-grieving when her "husband" (who was about to murder his own offspring), is murdered. She protects her offspring, the gods do not.

Tiamat, "Mother Huber, who can form everything added countless invincible weapons, gave birth to monster serpents, pointed of fang, with merciless incisors(?), she filled their bodies with venom for blood. Fierce dragons she clad with glories, causing them to bear auras like gods, ... She deployed serpents, dragons, and hairy hero-men, lion monsters, lion men, scorpion men, mighty demons, fish men, bull men, bearing unsparing arms, fearing no battle (ibid.: 444)." Enki owns the monsters in the Apsu. Tiamat selects Qingu to sit on the dais, to lead and make destinies. She readies her creatures for war, she lets Ea/ Enki know she is coming.

Ea/Enki is afraid and reports the situation to his grandfather, Anshur. Tiamat, their mother is in a rage at them. Anu is angry at Ea/Enki who killed Apsu, though Enki explains why he did the deed. Ea/Enki is ordered to subdue Tiamat. He uses his magic spells, and fails. Enki asks that, though he failed, Anshur should "send another to her. A woman's force may be very great, but it cannot match a man's (ibid.: 449)." Anu is sent against her and fails. Anshur dithers and again blames Ea/ Enki who reminds Anshur why he had to do what was done.

Anshur is angry. The Anunna-gods and Igigi-gods refuse to battle Tiamat as Anshur orders. Marduk steps forth and offers his help. "Let me go, let me accomplish your heart's desire! What man is it who has sent forth his battle against you? Why, Tiamat, a woman, comes out against you to arms! [My father], creator, rejoice and be glad. Soon you will trample [the neck] of Tiamat! (ibid.: 451)" Marduk, his moment near, vows to kill Tiamat and save the lives of the gods; in exchange he wants to be the supreme destiny-making god forever. Patriarchy is fully entrenched. Tiamat is only a woman and easily dispatched.

The ancient gods (no goddesses) convene. They drink and eat festively. They agree to surrender all their powers to Marduk. "Marduk is king!" They give him the scepter, throne, and staff. Marduk declares his absolute rulership over the other deities forever.

He goes to battle Tiamat. War and gore are described with scribal delight. The gods give him "unopposable" weapons. They tell him to go cut her up and send her blood to the winds. He arms-up with his mace and bow and arrow. He puts thunderbolts on his face and covers his body with fire; he makes a net to throw over Tiamat. He sends the destructive south, north, east and west winds to her. He steps into his terrible storm chariot, the Storm Demon, and hitches the chariot to his four demons: Slaughterer, Merciless, Overwhelmer, and Soaring. They bare their venomous teeth. To his right side he has "gruesome battle and strife": to his left is the force to overthrow all combatants. His head is "covered with terrifying auras." He holds an antidote to venom in his hand and a spell on his tongue.

Marduk searches out Qingu, who is the appointed leader and new "husband" of Tiamat. Quingu is confused and frightened. Tiamat tells Marduk that the gods he champions are disloyal. Marduk accuses her of wanting to destroy her children. Marduk challenges her to a one-on-one duel. (Please remember, it is Apsu, Tiamat's consort, who started the problem by planning to kill their disruptive children! The retaliatory mayhem began because of that god's planned aggravated destructiveness.)

Marduk flings his indictments against her. He spreads out his net and lets loose the great evil winds. Tiamat opens her mouth and he throws the wild winds into her, she could not close her mouth. His arrow pierces her heart and opens her belly. He "kills" her, throws down her carcass and stomps on it.

The composition describes how Marduk creates the universe and makes abodes for the gods he championed. Marduk breaks up her forces and imprisons her allies in the net. He ties up and tramples the eleven monsters Tiamat had birthed/created. He takes the tablet of destinies from the captured Qingu and places *it on his own chest. He crushes her skull and opens her arteries. Her blood is carried off by the four winds. He splits her in two "like a fish for drying;" one half he made into the cover of heaven, the other half holds the water.*

The conquering god measures and builds sanctuaries for Ea, Anu, and Enlil. He places the stars and constellations, and fixes the days of the year in twelve months, each with three stars. From her liver Marduk forms the mountains. He makes the moon appear and entrusts (to the moon god) the crown jewel of night to mark the day (of the month).

Marduk makes night and day and creates clouds. From Tiamat's foam he produces rain, wind, mist, and springs; from her eyes he makes the Tigris and Euphrates rivers. He makes mountains from her breasts. He gives the tablet of destinies to Anu. Marduk changes Tiamat's eleven monsters into sculptures and places them at the gate of Apsu so all can remember his deed. He is celebrated! He cleanses himself from battle, anoints himself with cedar oil, sits on his throne in his cella, puts on his aura of kingship, and places his staff of authority beside him. The deities promise obedience to his commands and in exchange he will provide for their sanctuaries.

Next, Marduk sets about making a human. He compacts blood to make bones so his creation can stand up. He names it "man". He divides man in half — creating man and woman. (Note the prototype for biblical Adam who is also created first before woman.) The purpose for humans is of course to do the labor for the gods.

Compacting blood is how women were understood to grow their infants. Please note that women and goddess are sidestepped here. Marduk, however, can not create by himself as the archaic creatress does. He uses her for all the parts of the universe.

Marduk divides the gods into two groups: three hundred supernal and three hundred infernal. The gods design a grand shrine in Babylon for Marduk saying: "We will make a shrine, whose name will be a byword, your chamber that shall be our stopping place, we shall find rest therein." The temple is built and named "the upper ziggurat of Apsu." Marduk takes his seat and the six hundred gods assemble to feast and drink. The fifty (most important) gods take their thrones and each one gives him a name. Anu (Asharu), Enlil, and Ea each give him their names — their aptitudes and powers. Marduk is assigned 50 as his symbolic number name. Fifty was formerly Enlil's signifying number. Marduk, with priestly help, has been elevated over Anu, Enlil, and Ea. The sacred feminine is struck a serious blow. Marduk's absolute power is described and no one should neglect to worship him! His powers are Inanna's ME and now no god can say him nay! When he is angry, no god can face him. He judges crimes and sins. The story ends with a summary of Marduk's valor in defeating Tiamat and taking absolute divine kingship. It is put to song that will be sung everywhere.

Foster points out that the purpose of the story revamping was to explain the absolute power of Babylonian kingship. Marduk, a lesser regional god is the king's favorite. Marduk is now absolute. The king who promotes Marduk is divine. This particular king is a priest and the beloved of Marduk. No longer does sacred "marriage" with goddess Inanna/Ishtar bestow kingship. Since the king is beloved of Marduk, the newly made absolute god, the king is absolute. The story revision supports the political structural change into absolute patriarchy and monarchy.

There is another purpose of the above composition that is as important. It establishes the annihilation of the Creatress and gives no role to goddess(es). Patriarchy, along with Marduk and kingship, is now absolute. Earlier creation myths of Sumerian and Akkadian origin are distinctly different. Goddess is included.

The Marduk story is fabricated to support absolute rule by men and their gods. Male god behavior backs up human male behavior. The gods, in the words of priestly king-pleasing scribes, kill off the long held old myth of the creatress to support a new political arrangement — male-rule on a cosmic scale. Kill the goddess is their solution. Since goddess represents life, it is good their plan fails. The scribes writing of

Marduk claim that her murder was accomplished but in the final lines the creatress is not dead. One of the gods says (ibid.: 483:)

"He shall keep Tiamat subdued, he shall keep her life cut short,
"In the future of humankind, with the passing of time,
"She shall always be far off, she shall be distant forever."

Be aware, the creatress is not dispensed. The claims of killing her are false. At story's end, she is "guarded" and so is not dead. "Subdued", "far off", and "distant forever" is not death. No matter how absolute the absolute rule of maleness, some version of feminine is indispensable. If the feminine, Life, ends, there is nothing left to have absolute rule over.

Today, the awareness of women remembering the first story, the divine feminine, is crucial to restoring gender balance and sanity in the land. Through scholarly search of recent translations of long forgotten crumbling, fragmented tablets and careful archeology with fresh eyes (Gimbutas), through several waves of feminism and methodology based on inclusion; woman and her story — everyday women and sacred woman alike — are un-subdued. Sacred Woman, Creatress, Great Mother are symbols to restore and re-story women's crucial life-affirming roles. Women remember their wisdom, worth, and story; they step from margins to center page in culture and influence. She, goddess, sacred symbol of "life", is not a distant myth; all she is and represents is as close as the nearest woman. She comes in dreams, inspiration, wisdom, poems, and art. She is woman's wisdom. Men, their gods and their hairy-heroes did not kill the goddess. Her life was not "cut short" — it is long; long as life itself. They did not kill her. She lives!

CHAPTER 4

Inanna's Images And Emblems

I come forth a queen
like cool moonlight
down the breast of the sky.[24]

MYTHICAL IMAGES LAST FOR MANY MILLENNIA.[25]

Figure 27. Important Sumerian Deities: Nintur, Inanna, Utu, and Enki

---

[24] Meador 2000: 95
[25] Gimbutas 1974: 199

Anthropomorphic divine images represent deities and deities live within their figurines. From the Upper Paleolithic into the present day, devotees directly address religious sculptures and emblems in many of the world religions. Places of worship continue to carry forth indicators of something sacred. Temples of the Ancient Near East and churches, cathedrals, mosques, and shrines of our Common Era are often built over the layered foundation of earlier sacred places of various beliefs. Humans seem to have brain space and heart space for seeking something beyond ourselves, something that takes our breath away; a source of wisdom greater than our own, an explanation of mysteries, protection and solace through images and symbols human-made or found in nature's splendor. We share that longing for sacredness, for understanding life, with the Sumerians.

Since ancient days, a deity develops out of our grasp and expression of life's sacredness. Story and physical image vary dependent on geographic area and lifestyle: gatherer-hunter, semi-nomadic herding, settlement or city; desert, coast, mountains or marsh in climates hot or cold, wet or dry. An image is formed and becomes the agreed upon generational concept. The form is imbued with built-up tradition. People talk and pray and praise and petition the divine images. Eventually settled people build the divine images their own homes and give them attendants. A temple staff serves the figurines by seeing to their every need. Chefs cook, dressers costume the figures appropriately for special festivals, stylists coif hair and wigs, priestesses and priests sing, chant, recite, and compose poems and songs. Wrestlers, acrobats, dancers, jugglers and musicians entertain the divine one. Stone and metal artisans are commissioned to make sacred objects, sculptures, cylinder seals and adornments. Inanna receives gold stars, lapis lazuli vulvas, gold wires and ribbons for her hair, strung beads of carnelian and lapis lazuli, and beautiful robes and dresses. An altar is nearby to receive her food offerings.

The divine sculptures visit one another or live in another's temple cellae.[26] The goddesses and gods are taken out of the temple for public reenactment of popular myths and events. Some seasonal enactment journeys require travel by water or by cart over land. Many figures are life size; smaller divine images are found in home shrines. Divinity is represented in stone, wood, assemblages, clay, shell, mosaics, and fresco paintings on walls.

The cylinder seal is a functional tiny carved image to roll in damp clay for identification purposes in the storehouse. The tiny carvings contained divine images and mythic story. In time, seals became amulets worn as adornments and signs of prestige. The cylinders are made of stone, shell, ivory and fired clay; many are found in burials. The artistry of the seal makers varied from exquisite composition and craft to rough drilled and poorly-made. Artistic style varies from region to region but the images portrayed are reliably deities and illustrations of myth. The seals give us valuable references for viewing the religious stories of Ancient Mesopotamia.

Kings and divine tutelary figurines are captured during war to dishearten the surviving people into submission. Temples are looted and ruined. The next logical step is more war to get the deity back. Soldiers and brick layers have guaranteed job security in dominator cultures. Excellent craftspeople are captured in wars and pressed into serving palace or temple needs for seals and other items. Most of the illustrations throughout this book are based on cylinder seals that are three to five thousand years old.

Wealthy devotees commission votive figures of themselves to place facing a deity in substitution for their own presence. The votive stand-ins send out praise and prayers constantly. The 24/7 attention just might bring good fortune. Early votives have happy smiling faces; the people have an easy relationship with their deities. Later figures had big "awestruck" eyes and serious faces; priestly stylus and changing theology introduced fearsome gods who practice divine retribution.

---

[26] cellae, plural of cella; small rooms that line the side walls of the main temple chamber; used for other deities or storing clay tablets of records and liturgy

Groenewegen-Frankfort describes the use of votives and divine images as a connection, a "hyphenation" between the human and superhuman realms. Early votives appear comfortable and able to reach out a hand for connection. Later votives portray reticence and fright instead of the former Sumerian joyful reverence and trust.

Figure 28. Votive Figurines

EMBLEMS

Our Queen of Heaven, Earth, and almost everything is recognized in her many symbols and emblems on the cylinder seals. Divine woman's emblems embrace her early story and include: serpent, tree, crescent moon, lion, storehouse reed posts, mountains, storms as Imdugud bird, evening and morning star, rosette, rod and line, owl, and dragon. Language is a word picture; a word is a symbol; words combine and form an image; a pictorial symbol is an imaged idea without words. Beneath the skin of an emblem picture is a full story to the knower of the pictorial language. Emblems are metaphors. "Metaphor consists of assigning to a thing the name of something else" (Mindlin et al. 1987: xii citing Aristotle, *Poetics 21*). Divine emblems hold the history of an idea over long stretches of time. The emblems equal or represent a divine idea or deity. One can feel the emblem trembling and alive within the visual metaphor. Frankfort has this to say about zoomorphic symbols: "It is as if their inner being was threatening to break and burst through the human form imposed on it" (ibid.: 7 citing Frankfort).

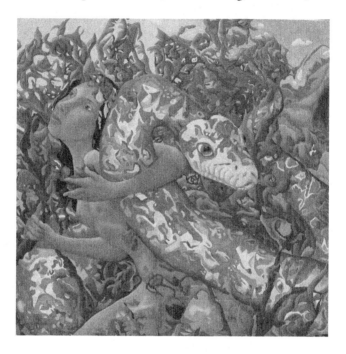

Figure 29. Eve

Serpent — "Serpent" is the umbilical cord, the vaginal snake, emerging from the dark womb, the dark earth. Serpents live in holes in the ground and shed old skin to grow and renew. Inanna is fertility; she secludes and renews the month and the year. Inanna is called "first snake" by the first recognized poet, en-priestess Enheduanna. Nammu/Tiamat is prime creatress, parthenogenetic mother of heaven, earth, and the earliest deities. She is a serpent-woman hybrid. Hero gods attempt her murder, but she lives on, "captured", feared, and reviled, yet indestructible. She is the serpent Marduk flays. He uses her body to create the world and everything on it. He can not create without her. Serpents and dragons lurk about in caves and myths for later heroes to kill. Heroes attempt murder of the early emblems of Great Mother. But, since life continues, the "heroes" have not succeeded. Many cultures have a dragon or serpent-killing quest story, yet life goes on and babes are born tethered to the vaginal snake. Prime creatress continues to haunt men. She is the serpent in the male-based religious rib, Eve, and serpent ruse. "Rib" came from a Hebrew mistranslation. Eve is the mother goddess; her name means "Life" and the serpent is the scary umbilical cord, the great mystery of new life (see also Eve in chapter 10). Woman and Serpent — Life and birth. The serpent everywhere is the symbol of an umbilical cord: arterial and venous blood vessels spiral around the fibrous cord tethering the fetus in the salty amniotic fluid and seriously resembles a serpent or two serpents mating. The vaginal snake is Life. Life and serpent are sacred.

New life arrives in a gush of sea water held by the vaginal snake: a snake that lives in the dark interior of woman's womb, the vaginal cave, just as earth serpents live in holes in the ground. Snakes shed their skins and renew. Women shed old blood to renew wombs for fertility. Snakes live in holes in the dark underground. Tree roots also resemble serpents.

Tree — Cypress, tamarisk, cedar, palm, fruit trees, huluppu tree, willow, and the fruited trees of life and knowledge are sacred to the goddess. The fruit is her gift to us of knowledge granted through observation, inspiration, intuition, and creative expression. The fruit of the serpent's tree is the goddess' gift of wisdom. Gilgamesh onwards through early Judaism cut down sacred groves. Christian zealots destroyed sacred groves in Europe. Trees are emblems of the goddess: rooted in the earth and crowned in heaven. Cylinder seal art shows many vases with flowering tree branches that are associated with Inanna. Oils and incense of fragrant tree sap are anointing oils and invitations for deities to come near. Tree oil is sprinkled on the bed of newlyweds and used as part of the sacred marriage rite.

Trees are long associated with the sacred feminine, especially those with reddish (women's blood) bark or wood.

Crescent Moon — Moon counts gestation time. Moon harmonizes women's menstrual cycles and directs tidal flow. White, red, and black represent the goddess in three moon phases: white moon, moon blood, and dark of moon that is black death/womb/tomb/cave and births renewal of seasons and life. White, red, and black are the important colors in universal shamanic traditions. They are the first colors an infant's eyes recognize. White, red(dish), black are natural pigments first used in human art. Burials include red ochre painted on bones and/or burial niches and is found in archaic Old Europe and the Ancient Near East. Catal Huyuk, an Anatolian matristic culture established some 3,000 years before Mesopotamia's great cities, painted their communal birthing room red. Everything in the room is red. Red is blood building new life. Niches and bones painted red prepare the dead for renewal. Rebirth. The crescent moon signals return to life, a new cycle, renewal.

Figure 30. Inanna the Lioness

Lion — Inanna is called Labbatu, "Lioness". She is envisioned as a lion. Great cats accompany Great Mother in every land the feline giants roam. Early art shows lions accompanying a goddess mother seated, or seated and giving birth. They support her or flank her chair of woman's blood power. Big cats have blood on their muzzles after a kill; menstrual blood is on the vaginal "mouth". Women's blood is powerful. Blood is thought to form the fetus. Far-flung cultures use the same image of big cats and Great Mother. Inanna's throne is guarded by lions, she rides a team of seven lions, she holds haltered tamed lions, and sits on her cushion beside a lion.

Inanna represents the fearful (for men) blood taboo when she stands glaring and nude on her lions, with a quiver at her back bristling with arrow shafts, and accompanying a king to war. Great Goddess Mother, in lands where great cats roam, is associated with lions, leopards, jaguars, and panthers. Inanna leads, stands beside or on, rides, or is pulled in a cart by lions. She is a lioness who calms the gods; she sits nude on her cushion in heavenly seclusion with a lion in attendance.

Ur in Sumerian means lion and occasionally guardian dog. A king's name, Ur-Nanshe (Nanshe is an equivalent goddess to Inanna), means the king is guardian for the goddess Nanshe. He is guardian of the people. Lions are frequently located as guardians at gates and painted dog guardian figurines are buried under gateways and doorways. Ur-Nanshe is "doorkeeper of the palace". King Gudea calls himself *ur,* lion, of goddess Gatumdug. Lions accompany Inanna. "Lioness" is her epithet. Lions take her into battle. She is the protector guardian of her people. She does not kill lions, her own emblem, yet Gilgamesh accuses her of lioncide in a late tablet edition in the Gilgamesh epic. This is one of many priestly-concocted reasons Lord Gilgamesh refuses to be her consort. He says she killed them by digging pits for their capture. It is the kings who take up public lion slaying! Translated tablet letters describe hunters trapping, caging and starving lions for the event. The king does his "kill" publicly surrounded by men with shields and spears; the captured weakened lion is released, the king kills it, the people cheer. The public spectacle is to prove his virility and therefore his ability to continue kingship. The event is safe theater. He enacts the old hunter role, the shepherd protecting his sheep, his subjects. The lion murder spectacle was annual. Kingship is now based on a successful lion kill. We have here evidence of another refusal to participate with goddess Inanna (and her equivalents) conferring rulership through partnership — the *hieros gamos*. In fact, the king is killing her, her lion power, her emblem.

Paired reed posts — Inanna is queen of the storehouse. The storehouse holds surplus food for settled or semi-settled people. Women are always in charge of the storehouse, the food surplus, in all cultures. As settlements expand in Sumer, so does Inanna's storehouse. She is matron of the storehouse because she is the fertility of the land. Grain and other foodstuff for future use are brought to her. From the storehouse, priestess functions and temples develop. All manner of goods are given over to the storehouse. As urban centers grow, temples expand with the storehouse at its center. Eventually priests take over the administration of temples and the kings began accumulating the wealth in treasuries.

The urban center is surrounded by two concentric rings. The temple, storehouse and palace are central. They are surrounded by tightly packed one and two-story residential homes reached via a few wide avenues and many winding labyrinthian alleyways. Villages, like our suburbs, are the next ring out and house the artisans, bureaucrats, and other specialized occupations. These workers are paid in barter from the storehouse. The outer ring is agricultural. The farmers are the food producers and give up large portions of their crops and herds but receive nothing for it. The religious stories say that humans are created to serve the deities. The agricultural products are given over to Inanna's storehouse. The village is the middle ring and does not grow food but supplies important services like corvee labor for the irrigation ditching and canal cleaning, the rebuilding of temple and palace buildings, and of course, warriors. The corvee workers are paid in barley and beer. The innermost circle is parasitic. The temple administrators handle the flow of goods coming in, oversee the corvee labor, and are assured a livelihood. The non-producers at the center grow more numerous and gain the most. During times of conflict, armed men protect the temple and palace, not the people.

Sumer is a richly silted land with a problematic climate and great marshes. There are no trees for building, there are no mountain resources for timber, stone, and metals. Early Inanna storehouses are likely the same reed structures constructed unchanged into recent times in Iraq's marshland.

The posts are reed bundles tied forming a top loop with streamers hanging down like long hair. They resemble women standing in profile. The paired reed posts are the pictogram for Inanna and Ishtar. They stand near sheepfolds and flank the entrance of her storehouse in numerous seals and other objects of art.

Mountains — Mountains rise to the east and north of the alluvial plains of Sumer. Inanna stands on mountains in seal art. This may indicate that she stands high above as celestial queen, or that mountains are a remembered location of Inanna's origin. Experts continue to write that her geographical origin is uncertain. In the "Epic of Lugalbanda" we hear: "At that time and place my princely sister, holy Inanna, verily envisaged me from the mountain crest in her holy heart (Minden 1987: 8 citing Wilcke. *Das Lugalbanda*. 1969)." Kramer, in "Enmerker and the Lord of Aratta," translates: "Heaven's great queen (Inanna), who is highly placed in awesome office, seated on the foothills of the mountain crests, ... on the throne dais of the mountain crests (ibid.: footnote page 8)." Did she come from mountain people or sea people or overland? We may never know.

Figure 31. Imdugud

Storms as Imdugud bird — Woman first and goddess after have weather powers. Rain is the goddess letting down water from her cloud breasts. A rainstorm with thunder, lightning, howling wind and flooding has its own identity: Imdugud bird. Storms are noisy and destructive. Spring storm clouds rise dark and menacing above the horizon like the outstretched wings of a black eagle. The roaring of a great storm is more than the eagle shriek, it is like a lion roaring! The symbol for thunderstorms in many cultures is the thunderbird. Sumerian thunderbird is called Imdugud and is a hybridized eagle body and lion head.

Imdugud *is* Inanna, her storm power, the destructiveness and noise of storms. Eagle is a prey bird and is always shown with knees apart — the position the bird holds its legs when attacking. "The queen who emits roars that fill the heaven" is her thunderstorm persona (Jacobsen 1987: 282). Weather deities are the natural choice for representing divine warriors because of the noise and destruction of fierce storms. Inanna is she who gives "wings to the storm" (Kramer 1979: 87). The goddess gives forth dragon venom on the land; she thunders and releases mountain floods; she rains fire (lightning strikes). Inanna is fierce in battle, she does not grow weary; she is louder than evil winds. The storm (or war) causes the lamenting harps to wail. The poets proclaim her "Queen of the earth-gods;" she is supreme compared to the heaven-gods. Inanna, as Imdugud, sends lightning to the earth, to the mountains; she is so powerful in her storm aspect that heaven shakes and earth quakes (ibid.: 87, 88). Storms and war come from angry deities. (ibid.: 89:)

My Queen, the Anunna, the great gods, fled before you like
  fluttering bats,
Could not stand before your awesome face, could not approach your
  awesome forehead.
Who can soothe your angry heart?

In "Enmerkar and the Lord of Aratta," Inanna threatens the Lord of Aratta into submission to Uruk's king or else, in her Imdugud storm persona, she will scream and roar at the city, she will drown it with flood waves (Jacobsen 1987: 286-7, f. 22). So saith the scribes of Uruk!

Evening and Morning Star — (see also chapter 1) Inanna is Ninsianna, the planet, our Venus. Because of its proximity to us, the planet appears to move forward and then back. It is invisible for periods of time, and its brightness is observable as it goes through crescent and full reflections of sun's light. Evening star is the first visible star at dusk and the last star remaining at dawn. She wanders the sky and appears to visit other less mobile constellations. The evening star looks down and sees her people. She calls humans and animals home to rest. Sumerian morning star is Inanna awakening her people to do ritual and learn the decrees she decided while they slept. The Akkadian morning star, Ishtar, is masculine in nature, aggressive, and a warrior. The goddess's eight-pointed star is found on many seals and other sculptured art with or without Inanna. She has functions in the night. She is the night. The "gods of the night are hushed." In prayers, one calls to Ninsianna (Venus), to "Ishtar of silence," the bride of An, goddess of splendor (Foster 2005: 664, 665).

Meador offers a beautiful star image from her rendition of High Priestess Enheduanna's "Inanna and Ebih." (Meador 2000: 94:)

Inanna
    child of the Moon God
a soft bud swelling
her queen's robe cloaks the slender stem
on her brow she paints
fire beams and fearsome glint

fastens carnelian
blood-red and glowing
around her throat

and then her hand clasps
the seven-headed mace
she stands as in youth's prime
her right hand grasps the mace

steps, yes she steps her narrow foot
on the furred back
of a wild lapis lazuli bull

and she goes up
white-sparked, radiant
in the dark vault of evening's sky
star-steps in the street
through the Gate of Wonder

…

Rosettes — Rosettes are shown on branches in vases. They mean: fertility and fruitfulness. They also represent droplets of blood that spatter in a rosette pattern. Women's blood (Knight and Grahn).

Rod and Line — This emblem appears as a rod and ring; the ring is actually a coil of measuring line (See figure 43). The line measures longer lengths and the rod, shorter distances. The line is used for reestablishing land boundaries after floods and for measuring buildings under construction. The cord assists the bricklayers in keeping bricks in line. Building occurs only in peace time. When Inanna became goddess of war — her ME opposite is peace. Inanna holds the emblems because, as goddess of war she is also the absence of war — peace. She and kings carry the rod and line in times of peace.

Figure 32. Lilith

Owl — Inanna is occasionally shown as an owl-woman hybrid. She has wings and talons for feet. A famous relief plaque (see figure 32 and equivalent names in chapter 10) is always identified as Lilith. Minden is the first Sumerian expert I read who carefully explains that the "Lilith Demon" plaque is none other than Inanna herself. I happily agree with Minden. Early goddesses are birds; they fly between heaven and earth. Inanna is called Nin-ninna, "Divine Lady Owl"; *ninna* means "owl". Zoomorphic emblems are formed when humans have a comfortable relationship with nature. Owls fly at night. Inanna watches over us by night. Owl's golden eyes glow in the night like the full moon and evening star. Inanna is a glowing star in the evening sky and is all-seeing.

Dragon — Dragon is a hybrid monster likely arising from the early myth of Nammu/Tiamat who is imagined as a serpent and serpent is synonymous with dragon. The dragon can be malevolent or beneficial. Lions and serpents blend in various ways. Inanna is seen standing on the back of a lion-serpent dragon that spews out venom. She is leading the king to war. When Inanna is called the "dragon of the gods," her dragon persona is beneficial for protection of the king. Eventually, patriarchy re-visioned Dragon. She became seriously maligned and evil; she had to be killed by later religious heroes who are actually killing the Great Mother. Strangely, the dragon always reappears for more generations of "heroes" to "murder".

Zoomorphic metaphors and emblems are associated with aspects of great goddess. She is found in animal representations, hybridized animal-human, and fully anthropomorphized. Early emblems are divine images. Inanna is "first snake", lioness and thunder storm; she is *Imdugud* bird, the noisy dark clouds rising on the horizon and storm with rain, thunder, and lightning. The archaic animal forms of the zoomorphic hybridized Paleolithic Goddess are later demonized or killed off to assure new male-supported gods superior influence in a growing male-dominated world. The hairy hero men and their gods do the killing; goddess does not kill off her early forms. Life is not in stasis; it is ever changing, cycling, transforming, and renewing. Y-ness desperately seeks to fix and control that which threatens their despotic rule. Some of Inanna's emblems disappear, others continue into our time — evening star, crescent moon, rosette, lion, thunderbird, dragon, and owl.

The following story is evidence of Inanna and her above emblems undergoing patriarchal devolution. Her presence continues even as priest-directed scribes intentionally reduce her to a petulant, unpredictable, spoiled adolescent "girl" who requires gods to help, rescue, or advise her out of the predicaments she brings upon her self. "Inanna and the Huluppu Tree" is an emblem-laden text that demonstrates Inanna as a victim of patriarchal tampering. The reader will notice in the story below, Nammu and birth goddesses are not mentioned. Maleness has taken over excepting for the underworld of shadow and death where Ereshkigal reigns. Inanna is reduced to being a "woman who walked in fear of the word" of the Sky and Air gods. The poem ends with Inanna giving gifts to Gilgamesh for solving her predicament. Gilgamesh is an early mythified Sumerian king. (Wolkstein and Kramer 1983: 4-9:)

INANNA AND THE HULUPPU TREE

In the first days, in the very first days,
In the first nights, in the very first nights,
In the first years, in the very first years,

In the first days when everything needed was brought into being,
In the first days when everything needed was properly nourished,
When bread was baked in the shrines of the land,
And bread was tasted in the homes of the land,
When heaven had moved away from earth,
And earth had separated from heaven,
And the name of man was fixed;
When Sky God, An, had carried off the heavens,
And the Air God, Enlil, had carried off the earth,

When the Queen of the Great Below, Ereshkigal, was given the underworld for her domain,

Prime creatress, Nammu, is not mentioned and Ereshkigal is "given" the Great Below as it is not popular real estate for the big gods to own. Gods "carried off" heaven and earth. The following segment is patristic deafness to woman's NO! Enki invades Ereshkigal's domain. The underworld fights him. It throws big and little stones at him. He "enters," "visits," the Great Below, and a tree grows as a result of something Enki did. Trees represent the divine feminine. They grow out of the earth and are rooted where the dead are placed, the womb of the great mother. Roots also resemble snakes. Considering the reputation of randy Enki in stories like the incest of his divine family for four generations in "Enki and Ninhursaga;" his invasion implies forced sex with Ereshkigal.

Enki is involving himself with the goddess's tree emblem. In this myth, a tree grows as do crops after Inanna and Dumuzi have loving consensual sex following Inanna's seclusion time. The underworld evolves from woman's menstrual and birth-blood seclusion. That seclusion becomes earth's deep and dark cavernous womb — the underworld. It is taboo and sacred because it is connected to women's blood and birth. Worldwide, burials in caves, hypogeums,[27] and earth have red-pigmented paint on bones or niches for women's blood. Grave goods represent continuation or renewal of life; birth from the womb-tomb. Women in seclusion are taboo. Ereshkigal is in seclusion. Enki invades.

---

[27] Hypogeums are underground caverns considered sacred to the chthonic Great Mother. In Malta such a hypogeum was discovered. It includes storehouse bins, benches for priestesses to sleep and receive dream instructions from the goddess and/or for the ill to spend a night in the womb of the goddess for healing. Pits may also have contained serpents as they are part of the oldest story. Niches are painted red and vines are painted reaching up the walls indicating the the bones of the dead are awaiting renewal.

Enki is fresh surface and marsh water; he is water beneath the earth. He originates as son of the prime creatress and shares the same general physical earth strata as does the underworld goddess — the third part globally of Great Goddess. Ereshkigal fights him. Either she, alone or because of Enki's interference, sends up a *huluppu* tree from the Great Below.

The *huluppu* tree is not yet translated but suggestions include: willow, boxwood, poplar, or some such water-tolerant tree since Uruk is located on the alluvial plane between the two great rivers in marshy wetlands where no great trees grow. Cedar and other aromatic sap trees, often with reddish inner bark (like woman's blood), are named in other texts in association with the mother goddess. Aromatic cypress oil is sprinkled as sacrament for the sacred marriage. One very early temple at Uruk has large columns and half-columns in its outer courtyard. This implies that the emigrating Sumerians remember great trees from their homeland. Without timber in the alluvial planes, the temple builders imitate tree trunk pillars with shaped dried mud bricks. That particular design element was neither continued nor found at other sites.

Trees come from earth goddess and grow tall. They reach the sky; they rise toward the moon and stars. They connect the underworld, earth and heaven. Trees are useful for making things: fire, tools, structures and furniture. Goddesses own their seat/throne. The throne is originally both the menstrual chair and birth stool — the seat is empowered by woman blood. The blood is sacred, taboo, and powerful.

Imdugud bird, aka Anzu-bird or Zu, is Inanna as the noisy spring storm rising darkly above the southern horizon. Thunderstorms are loud. The black eagle has a lion head; it thunder-roars noisily. Weather deities became war deities aligning noise, destruction, and war. Both the serpent and bird are old goddess emblems transcending cultures. Note that in this story the Imdugud bird is "he" and brings "his" young to the treetop. Though Imdugud is the weather part of Inanna's wholeness, the bird is later always singular, male, and raising *his* brood.

Lilith made a home in the trunk of Inanna's tree. She too is an emblem from the past. Lil is "air" or "wind" in Sumerian. As "wind maid", she plays in city ruins. Eventually the "wind maid" is demonized and called Lilith by Semitic peoples. She is a wilderness form of Inanna. Before Inanna became a city goddess, she was goddess of the steppes, or island in the sea, or mountains where wind is prevalent. Lilith is an early non-urban Inanna. She stays close to Inanna as a haunting spirit of her barely remembered past. Urban centers enhance the contagion of disease. Priests turn older goddess emblems into demons that are blamed for illness. Lilith becomes the ill-wind. Demons are not part of old goddess worship. Priests change Lilith to the Lili demon.

The above Lilith image (figure 32) is generally identified as the Lilith demon and, because she is nude, experts suggest it is from the wall of a brothel. First, the nude figure is not unusual for Inanna/Ishtar and is evidence of her aspect as the Great Mother who is almost always nude. Second, in the plaque she wears a many-horned tiara and that is only worn by important deities. Third, she stands on two lions and lions are Inanna's. Furthermore, Lilith is flanked by two owls — owl is an emblem of Inanna. She carries two rods and rolled measuring lines as does Inanna. Lilith is depicted nude and hybridized with owl talons for feet, feathered lower leg, and wings. Early Inanna is also pictured with wings and bird feet (see figure 24). "Lil," air/wind, is imagined as wings for flight. Lilith is accompanied by lions, owls, or crescent horned goats; as is Inanna. She wears a horned headdress; as does Inanna. Demons do not wear horned tiaras. Lilith is Inanna.

Maleness kills off inconvenient early emblems or recycles them as blame-demons. Lilith, Inanna as "wind maid" or "wild maid," is made into a night-flying, death-making, baby-snatching, talon-footed terror. She is called an ill night wind who squeezes under doors and through windows bringing disease and death.

The Hebrews also remember Lilith. She is Adam's first wife who will not have sex with him in submission (on her back) and leaves him. She says NO! She is sacred woman from before patriarchy. Lilith is early Inanna, her unpredictable wilder part — the king-pleasing priest scribes want her gone. They have turned her into a fearful threatening demonic disease and death-bringing *woman*. This story is early since Lilith is still a wilderness goddess and not a yet a demon.

We return to Enki's forced entry into the underworld where we hear that "the underworld rose up and attacked *him*," as if he were the innocent. The indomitable goddess Inanna, through the press of a priestly stylus, is turned into an adolescent who "fears the word of Sky God An ... who fears the word of Air God Enlil." Remember, for millennia, "no god could say her nay"! Inanna is powerful. She is embedded in the people's consciousness. Something has to be done to diminish her so men's gods can gain supremacy.

> He set sail; the Father set sail,
> Enki, the God of wisdom, set sail for the underworld.
> Small windstones were tossed up against him;
> Large hailstones were hurled up against him;
> Like onrushing turtles,
> They charged the keel of Enki's boat.
> The waters of the sea devoured the bow of his boat like wolves;
> The waters of the sea struck the stern of his boat like lions.

Prime creatress, Nammu and Tiamat, also roiled the waters. Ereshkigal is part of the first great mother, the death mother portion of the trinity. Enki is Nammu's son; he also stirs up the water in an attempt to swamp Inanna's boat of heaven when she sails off with *her* ME (see chapter 2 for "Inanna and the God of Wisdom").

> At that time, a tree, a single tree, a *huluppu*-tree
> Was planted by the banks of the Euphrates.
> The tree was nurtured by the waters of the Euphrates.
> The whirling South Wind arose, pulling at its roots
> And ripping at its branches
> Until the waters of the Euphrates carried it away.

> A woman who walked in fear of the word of the Sky God, An,
> Who walked in fear of the word of the Air God, Enlil,
> Plucked the tree from the river and spoke:
> > "I shall bring this tree to Uruk.

I shall plant this tree in my holy garden."

Inanna cared for the tree with her hand.
She settled the earth around the tree with her foot.
She wondered:
> "How long will it be until I have a shining throne to sit upon?
> How long will it be until I have a shining bed to lie upon?"

The years passed; five years, then ten years.
The tree grew thick,
But its bark did not split.
Then a serpent who could not be charmed
Made its nest in the roots of the *huluppu*-tree.
The *Anzu*-bird set his young in the branches of the tree.
And the dark maid Lilith built her home in the trunk.
The young woman who loved to laugh wept.
How Inanna wept!
(Yet they would not leave her tree.)
…

> *The birds herald dawn light with song, Utu, the sun god
> and brother of Inanna, rises. Inanna petitions him for help:*

"O Utu, in the days when the fates were decreed,
When abundance overflowed in the land,
When Sky God took the heavens and the Air God the earth,
When Ereshkigal was given the Great Below for her domain,
The God of Wisdom, Father Enki, set sail for the underworld,
And the underworld rose up and attacked him …
…

> *Inanna repeats the story of rescuing the tree from the river.*

Then a serpent who could not be charmed
Made its nest in the roots of the tree,
The *Anzu*-bird set his young in the branches of the tree,

165

And the dark maid Lilith built her home in the trunk.
I wept.
How I wept!
(Yet they would not leave my tree.)"
...

This "woman," fearful of the "word" of gods and helplessly weeping about her tree problem, is not our Inanna! She is separated from her powers; she is presented as a frightened young woman — not a goddess but a *woman* who gardens a bit and wants some furniture made from her tree. Anzu, and Lilith, and Serpent, oh my! have taken up residence in her *huluppu*-tree. She cries, she is helpless; she needs a man to rescue her. She weeps her sad tale to her brother Utu the sun god, but he will not, or more likely, cannot help her. Another dawn breaks and she is still crying. Her tears do not wash away her old emblems. She whimpers to her "brother," Gilgamesh, the early Sumerian hero king from Uruk. She is the tutelary deity who owns the city. She is who planned the settlement and owns the surrounding area. People work for the divine owner. Gilgamesh, as hero-king, is beholden to work on behalf of Inanna, to protect her, her people, and her city. "The hero of Uruk stood by Inanna (ibid.: 8)."

Gilgamesh fastened his armor of fifty minas around his chest.
The fifty minas weighed as little to him as fifty feathers.
He lifted his bronze ax, the ax of the road,
Weighing seven talents and seven minas, to his shoulder.
He entered Inanna's holy garden.

Gilgamesh struck the serpent who could not be charmed.
The *Anzu*-bird flew with his young to the mountains;
And Lilith smashed her home and fled to the wild, uninhabited
    places.
Gilgamesh then loosened the roots of the *huluppu*-tree;
And the sons of the city, who accompanied him, cut off the branches.

From the trunk of the tree he carved a throne for his holy sister.
From the trunk of the tree Gilgamesh carved a bed for Inanna.
From the roots of the tree she fashioned a *pukka* for her brother.
From the crown of the tree Inanna fashioned a *mikku* for Gilgamesh,
  the hero of Uruk.

The text promotes Gilgamesh, the hero who suits up in his heavy battle armor to get rid of a bird, a wild girl, kill a snake and cut down a tree. *It is not the tree he fears but Inanna's emblems.* Woman's power serpent symbol, the vaginal snake, is woman's enviable creative power. Since the throne and bed are Inanna's sacred symbols of power for granting rulership, men find ways to impinge on that power. This re-vamped story says Inanna gets her throne and bed *through a man* and her early powerful images are "struck" (killed), take flight to the mountains, and flee to the "wild uninhabited places." Inanna gets her furniture but it is stripped of power. There is no pretense of Gilgamesh being bedded by our goddess, instead she gives him two items made from her sacred *huluppu* tree: a *pukka* and *mikku,* possibly the drum and beaters that he uses to incite men to fight in contests. Another version has the two items as a huge ball and mallet he makes for himself from the tree trunk. He loses the items into the underworld and gets his sidekick, Enkidu, killed or almost killed trying to retrieve the items in "The Epic of Gilgamesh." Whatever the items are, they are from her holy tree and make him special. They may be symbols of rulership granted to Gilgamesh without having sex with the goddess.

Gilgamesh begins his story in Sumer. He is an early mythified king according to the king lists. His is an old story usefully remade. The "Epic of Gilgamesh" is a collection of the hero's stories. He first repairs Eanna, Inanna's "holy house" or "sacred storehouse" temple in Uruk after a/the deluge. He builds a grand parapet for her that no other can copy. The people of Uruk mount the stairway and come near to Inanna. Gilgamesh is the shepherd of Inanna's sheepfold, he protects her city of Uruk.

That story changes drastically from the Sumerian king devoted to Inanna in later Gilgamesh stories. In the beginning he is wise and literate as he inscribes his good deeds on a stone tablet. He is a hard-worker for his goddess. He later undergoes a horrendous priestly inspired personality change. He represents the maleness that grew and dominated the Ancient Near East. He is "two thirds divine and one third human." He is physical perfection; he is designed by the Lady of the Gods, grew in the womb of Nudimmud (birth goddess), and birthed and suckled by Ninsun, Lady Wild Cow. Later tales say he entertains himself by making the men stay away from home fighting in contests with him and each other. He is very big. He forces the young men to carry him about on their backs during the unfair contests. The men are bruised and sore and their wives are angry. The hero of domination mirrors devolved maleness: he rapes all the brides on their wedding night. *Jus primae noctis* or *droit de seigneur* is a male power display that sexually satisfies an alpha and establishes social dominance through humiliation of the lower status men. It represents "adaptive psychological mechanisms" from male primate behavior of "power display and physiological adaptations to polygamous competition."[28]

GILGAMESH DESTROYS INANNA'S EMBLEMS

The following excerpts of the Epic of Gilgamesh are included to hear the voice of patriarchy's priestly tampering with myth and to show more examples of maleness killing off Inanna's emblems. Selected lines from the *Epic of Gilgamesh* give us the revisions from three to four millennia ago. (Italics in the poem lines are the translator's.) (George 1999: 3-4:)

   ... In Uruk-the-sheepfold he *walks [back and forth,]*
      like a wild bull lording it, head held aloft.
   He has no equal when his weapons are brandished,
      his companions are kept on their feet by his *contests.*

---

[28] Wettlaufer, Jörg. 2000. in *Evolution and Human Behavior*, Vol. 21, Nr.2, pp. 111-123

The young men of Uruk he harries without warrant,
　　Gilgamesh lets no son go free to his father.
By day and night his tyranny grows harsher,
　　Gilgamesh, [*the guide of the teeming people!*]

It is he who is shepherd of Uruk-the-sheepfold,
　　[but Gilgamesh] lets no [daughter go free to her] mother.
[*The women voiced*] their [*troubles to the goddesses,*]
　　[*They brought their*] complaint before [*them:*]

'[Though powerful, pre-eminent,] expert [and mighty,]
　　[Gilgamesh] lets [no] girl go free to [her *bridegroom.*]'
The warrior's daughter, the young man's bride,
　　to their complaint the goddesses paid heed.
. . .

　　"*Gilgamesh will couple with the wife-to-be, he first of all,
the bridegroom after. By divine consent it is so ordained: when
his navel-cord was cut, for him she was destined (ibid.: 15).*"
Women are objects to use and assure his alpha status and gain
sexual opportunity. His behavior is atrocious. The goddess comes
to the rescue!
　　The people complain that "by day and by night his tyranny
grows harsher (Ibid.: 3)." Anu has the birth goddess, (here she is
Aruru), create an equal to Gilgamesh to fight him and restore
peace in Uruk. Aruru makes a huge and hairy wild man,
Enkidu, the hero, who is peaceable, lives naked in the wild,
eats vegetation, and drinks and cavorts at the waterhole with
the animals. He destroys the traps men lay and frees the trapped
animals. A hunter complains to Gilgamesh about the big wild
man. The king tells him to get the (temple) harlot Shamhat.
The hunter and Shamhat wait at the water hole for several
days until Enkidu appears with the animals. The hunter tells
her to "Uncradle your bosom, bare your sex, let him take in your
charms! (ibid.: 7)" (ibid.: 8:)

. . .

Shamhat unfastened the cloth of her loins,
    she bared her sex and he took in her charms.
She did not recoil, she took in his scent:
    she spread her clothing and he lay upon her.

She did for the man the work of a woman,
    his passion caressed and embraced her.
For six days and seven nights
    Enkidu was erect, as he coupled with Shamhat.
. . .

> *After he was sated he went back to the animals but they ran from him. When he attempted to follow, "his legs stood still". "Enkidu had defiled his body so pure . . . but now he had reason, and wide understanding (ibid.: 8)." [The woman, Shamhat, tamed him via her body's allure, through making love. She initiated him into human culture through sacred sex. The idea of sex weakening a man's legs is still circulated.]*

He came back and sat at the feet of the harlot,
    watching the harlot, observing her features.
Then to the harlot's words he listened intently,
    [as Shamhat] talked to him, to Enkidu:

'You are handsome, Enkidu, you are just like a god!
    Why with the beasts do you wander the wild?
Come, I will take you to Uruk-the-Sheepfold,
    to the sacred temple, home of Anu and Ishtar,

'Where Gilgamesh is perfect in strength,
    like a wild bull, lording it over the menfolk.'
. . .

> *Enkidu now feels the need for a human friend. He agrees to go with Shamhat to Inanna/Ishtar's temple. He is mighty and will challenge Gilgamesh; he will "change the way things*

are ordered." Shamhat explains that Gilgamesh knows of his coming. He dreamed of one who fell from the stars like a rock, one he could not lift or roll. The people of Uruk love the rock and kiss its feet. Lord Gilgamesh loves it like a wife. In the dream he brings it to his "mother," the goddess Ninsun, Lady Wild-Cow, who forms it into his equal. Awake, Gilgamesh brings the dream to his "mother," goddess Ninsun, to interpret (ibid.:10). We are told:

'[The mother of Gilgamesh] was clever and wise,
    well versed in everything, she said to her son —
[Wild-Cow] Ninsun was clever and wise,
    well versed in everything, she said to Gilgamesh:
…

She repeats the dream and then says:

"'Mightiest in the land, strength he possesses,
    his strength is as mighty as a rock from the sky.
Like a wife you'll love him, caress and embrace him,
    he will be mighty, and often will save you."
…

Gilgamesh has a second dream of an axe that is lying where a crowd had gathered. Again he loves it and brings it to his "mother" Lady Wild-Cow, who is "clever and wise." She tells him the axe is a friend, she will make him equal to mightiest-in-the-land Gilgamesh. The king of bad behaviors says: "Let me acquire a friend to counsel me, a friend to counsel me I will acquire!"

'[So did Gilgamesh] see his dreams.'
    [After] Shamhat had told Enkidu the dreams of Gilgamesh, the two of them together [began making] love.
…

The harlot opened her mouth,
    saying to Enkidu:

'As I look at you, Enkidu, you are like a god,
   why with the beasts do you wander the wild?

'Come, I will lead you to Uruk-the-Town-Square,
   to the sacred temple, the home of Anu!
Enkidu, arise, let me take you
   to the temple Eanna, the home of Anu,

'where [men] are engaged in labours of skill,
   you, too, *like a man*, will *find a place* for yourself.'

Her words he heard, her speech found favour:
   the counsel of a woman struck home in his heart.
She stripped and clothed him in part of her garment,
   the other part she put on herself.

. . .

Two parts of the above lines are notable. First, Eanna is known as
Inanna's temple, her home, and Uruk is her city. An(u), the first male
deity added to the matrinity, is *her* consort. George brought together
various texts to flesh out his translation. The Gilgamesh Epic here
began with the ancient king building a unique stairway to the parapet
of Eanna, Uruk's sacred storehouse so the people could come close to
Inanna. The story of "Enmerkar and the Lord of Aratta" describes
Inanna and An(u) as a couple. In the above later version, only Anu is
identified with the temple. Priest-scribes change the emphasis away from
Inanna. The second interesting detail is: "the counsel of a woman struck
home in his heart." Woman's wise words and guidance still counsel and
influence men. Lines prior to these have Gilgamesh bringing his dreams
home to mom, since women are the interpreters of dreams. That too
disappears over time. The epic continues:

> *Shamhat, priestess of Inanna/Ishtar, takes Enkidu to*
> *shepherds where she teaches him to eat bread and drink "ale"*
> *(beer was the usual beverage). "He drank the ale, a full seven*
> *goblets. His mood became merry, his face lit up." He and*

> *Shamhat stay with the shepherds. A barber grooms his body hair, he is oiled and dressed as a warrior. He becomes a shepherd boy. He picks up weapons and protects the herd from the lions and wolves once his playmates. He continues making love with Shamhat. A man traveling to Uruk to attend a wedding told the shepherds about Gilgamesh and his practice of droit de seigneur. Enkidu is appalled by what the wedding guest tells him. (ibid.: 15-16:)*

'For the king of Uruk-the-Town-Square,
    the *veil* will be parted for the one who picks first;
for Gilgamesh, the king of Uruk-the-Town-Square
    the *veil* will be parted for the one who picks first.

'He will couple with the wife-to-be,
    he first of all, the bridegroom after,
divine consent it is so ordained:
    when his navel-cord was cut, for him she was destined.'

At the fellow's words his face paled in anger.
…
Off goes Enkidu, with Shamhat following.
…

> *He enters Uruk and the people surround him amazed at his size, he is so like Gilgamesh. We are told that in Uruk regular festivals were held with sacrifice and contests to rival the fair Gilgamesh.*

For the goddess of weddings the bed was laid out,
    Gilgamesh met with the maiden by night.
Forward came (Enkidu), he stood in the street,
    Blocking the path of Gilgamesh.
…
For the goddess of weddings was ready the bed,
    for Gilgamesh, like a god, was set up a substitute.
…

> *"Enkidu with his foot blocked the door of the wedding house, not allowing Gilgamesh to enter." They fight and fight. Walls and doorjambs shudder. Their combat ends in a draw. Gilgamesh takes Enkidu home to meet mother. She approves of the new friend and reminds Enkidu that he needs a brother. (Gilgamesh also needs a minder!) Enkidu is weak from weeping for joy of now having a brother, they kiss, they hold hands, and Gilgamesh decides they will go kill the guardian of the Forest of Cedar, the "ferocious Humbaba."*

We return again to the taming of Enkidu. The temple priestess is versed in the ways of taming and civilizing men; she and her sisters initiate men into civilization and culture. She gets Enkidu's attention with sexual allure, the art of women; she teaches Enkidu to make love, eat human food, wear clothes, drink, and converse with men. He is tamed and initiated into civilization. He adores Shamat. He comes from nature; he is kind, compassionate, strong and just. When Enkidu hears that Gilgamesh rapes brides on their wedding nights, he is very upset. He arrives at Uruk and bars the door of Gilgamesh's next bride victim.

Gilgamesh fights Enkidu to a draw, the men become friends, the brides (we presume) are safe, and the king stops making the men of Uruk fight him in unfair contests. Gilgamesh is tamed by partnership with Enkidu. Remember, Enkidu is a creature of nature; he is human(e), and he is introduced to culture through the teaching of a woman, a priestess, a representative of goddess Inanna. He is loved by Gilgamesh "like a wife," and plays a taming role for the king as women do for men. He is reluctant to do Gilgamesh's destructive bidding but must serve and obey the dominator.

Note the reversal of established tradition where the ruler is a proxy substitute for a goddess's beloved — now the substitute is the bride for the god-like Gilgamesh. Gilgamesh stops raping brides thanks to Enkidu, but begins doing combat with Inanna/Ishtar's other emblems. The two go off on several adventures; each time ruthless Gilgamesh gets the idea to fight/kill and Enkidu must obey but he voices doubt and reason.

The Forest of Cypress is a sacred grove. It belongs to the mother goddess (and to Inanna because she is the maiden mother goddess). The goddess's throne is in the grove. The forest is vast; no one is brave enough to enter it. Enkidu says he knew of the guardian when he lived in the steppes; " ...his voice is the Deluge, his speech is fire, and his breath is death." In the translated Ancient Near Eastern literature, I have read no story that backs up Enkidu's description. It appears to be the excuse to invade the sacred grove. Consider the economic reason for invasion. Timber, once plentiful as first growth trees on the mountainsides, is now scarce. Building and rebuilding temples and palaces requires timber for roof supports in otherwise mud brick structures. The vast sacred grove, and all sacred groves, are goddess owned. The groves are an untapped supply of timber.

The story goes on to explain that only the god Adad (weather god) and Humbaba the guardian can enter the forest without harm. The guardian is not aggressively destroying life and capturing territories; he is guarding and protecting the goddess's sacred trees. Cypress tree oil is sprinkled on wedding bed-sheets for fertility (ibid.: 20-27:)

> *Gilgamesh has smiths make mighty hatchets and daggers. After the two are suited up to battle Humbaba, Gilgamesh comes before the elders and tells them what he intends to do. Formerly, Sumerian elders decided on important issues and decisions. Here Gilgamesh "tells them" what he will do. He has made the decision himself to invade the goddess's domain. Enkidu asks the elders to advise against the plan. "The senior advisers rose, good counsel they offered Gilgamesh: 'You are young, Gilgamesh, borne along by emotion, all that you talk of you don't understand ... to keep safe the cedars, (Enlil) made it his (Humbaba's) lot to terrify men.'" Gilgamesh laughs at the advice of the senior advisers. They realize he will go to fight Humbaba so advise that Enkidu go in front of him to protect him and, since he knows the territory, to lead him. "Enkidu shall bring him home safe to his wives!" (Multiple wives are known in Sumer only when the first wife proves barren. That Gilgamesh has "wives", indicates late changes in the text.)*

After seeing the elders, he goes to the other advisory group of Sumer, the young men who bear arms. He states that he goes on an unknown journey into an unknowable battle, but will return through the gate of Uruk and offer a second festival in addition to the annual New Year festival. There are no words that indicate the warrior group opposes the adventure.

Next they go "hand in hand" to see Gilgamesh's "mother," the goddess Ninsun. Gilgamesh explains his plan. She is sad. She bathes seven times in water of "tamarisk [a small shrub with pink flowers] and soapwort," dresses carefully, places her tiara, climbs to the rooftop, and beckons the sun god with incense. She asks him why he afflicted her son "with so restless a spirit?" Ninsun asks that Aya, bride of Shamash, "unfearing," remind the sun god to "entrust him (Gilgamesh) to the care of the watches of the night." She further asks that her son be like a god, with Ea/Enki's wisdom, and rule the black headed people (Sumerians) with Irnina (Inanna).

Lady Wild-Cow then beckons Enkidu to her. Though he is not born of her, his offspring will be devotees of Gilgamesh and "the priestesses, the hierodules and the women of the temple" now acknowledge him. Ninsun places "symbols" on his neck (a blessing or pendant). "The priestesses took in the foundling, and the divine daughters brought up the foster child. Enkidu, whom [I love,] I take for my son (ibid.: 27)." The two take leave. They travel great distances every day. Every night Enkidu builds a "House of the Dream God" for Gilgamesh and every morning translates his dreams. They reach their destination. (ibid.: 39:)

They stood there marveling at the forest,
    gazing at the lofty cedars,
gazing at forest's entrance –
    where Humbaba came and went there was a track.

The path was straight and the way well trodden.
    They saw the Mountain of Cedar, seat of gods and goddess' throne.

[On the] face of the mountain of the cedar proffered its abundance,

       its shade was sweet and full of delight.

…

> *Humbaba does not attack them. He pleads with Enkidu to change Gilgamesh's mind, set on his murder. He then curses Enkidu, the Wild-born who knows the forest. Enkidu encourages Gilgamesh to kill the guardian before Enlil and the other gods realize their intent. "He slew the ogre, the forest's guardian, at whose yell were sundered the peaks of Sirion and Lebanon." Gilgamesh stabs him and Enkidu "pulled out the lungs." They tear up the forest, "the secret abode of the gods (and goddess)," and select one huge tree for timber for Enlil's temple door. They float it down the Euphrates to Nippur. They risk displeasure of the gods for murdering Humbaba who is one of them, but, and this is an important but for patriarchy — Gilgamesh makes a name and enduring fame for himself. The forest grove of the goddess is destroyed.*

Patriarchy takes over Inanna and her emblems with avarice, conquest, murder, mayhem, and disrespect. The following story in the epic tells us of this disrespect for Inanna/Ishtar. Tablet VI of the *Epic of Gilgamesh* tells a tale of Ishtar and the Bull of Heaven. It begins in the usual way where Gilgamesh is an early king of Uruk and devotee of Inanna. Uruk is her city. He rules for her. Eanna is her temple and An(u) is her consort. The Babylonian text of the second millennium B.C.E. changes Gilgamesh's, i.e., patriarchy's attitude toward the goddess. He refuses to take part in the sacred marriage ritual for rulership and insults her. The goddess's status is falling; Y-men are winning. Priestly styluses change the stories. Gilgamesh rules without Inanna/Ishtar. He crowns himself without the holy tryst.

In another altered version, Inanna/Ishtar sees how handsome he is and sets out to seduce him; she is lustful; she bribes him for *his* sexual favors. He insults her by refusing her saying that all of her previous "husbands" were doomed. The slanderous list is lengthy. As with all

successful slander, there are familiar bits that sound authentic and the
rest is made up. The "husbands" are animal and mineral as well as
human. I have yet to read any text that held a whisper of her animal and
mineral "husbands." Dumuzi the shepherd is mentioned. Dumuzi is her
long-standing beloved consort; he is the one all men seeking rulership
impersonate. Priests blame Inanna/Ishtar for the vegetation demigod's
death but for millennia, his death is temporary — Dumuzi always
returns. He is a demigod. He lives, dies, and returns, while goddess
is constant. Men are linear thinkers — rise and fall, the end; women
understand cycles of life/death/return.

One slanderous reference needs a brief explanation. In the story of
"Inanna and Shukaletuda," "spotty," the gardener's son rapes Inanna
while she lies sleeping; she awakens and realizes what happened. He is
hidden away by his father. In Gilgamesh revision, the gardener's son
refuses Inanna's advances; he remains virtuous and she turns him into
a dwarf. Inanna/Ishtar is allure; allure is the womanly art to tame men.
Consorts come to her; they are the proxy who is technically always
Dumuzi. Here, Gilgamesh is made handsome and alluring and she lusts
for him. He says NO! We have another priestly reversal.

Inanna/Ishtar is blamed for being a battering ram against the enemy.
This is curious and contrived blame. Early Inanna, Sumerian Inanna,
is a protector, a defender of her people. She is mother goddess. Mother
goddess does not deliberately and offensively march her children off to
war to be killed and to kill her other children. This offensive war goddess
is the invention of Y-men, the tyrants, the ones holding absolute rule.
First, maledom makes Inanna into a war goddess, and then, as here, she
is faulted for being their convenient excuse for why wars happen.

Gilgamesh says not one of her "husbands" gets to the heavens, i.e.,
becomes immortal. Gilgamesh is a man; he will die because humans
die. He wants the secret of immortality. He does not want to die. Heroes
want immortality; but they must settle for doing things that will live on
in story, song, and legend. Later in the epic he will make a long journey
and a big fuss over obtaining the plant that is the secret of immortality.
He dives deep into a magical sea and pulls up the plant of immortality.
He sets it on the shore. A snake eats it and sheds its skin — meaning it

is ever renewing, immortal. Gilgamesh is in despair. A wise woman, a goddess, at the edge of the world sets him straight: go home, stop this search, enjoy your life!

Dumuzi is Inanna's beloved. He spends some time in the underworld, as all vegetation deities do, yet these scribal additions tell of her turning him into a wolf and his own flocks and shepherd boys fear him. Again, I have not read anything of the sort! The closest to transformation into an animal is in a version of Inanna's descent. Dumuzi does not grieve her when Inanna goes to the underworld and she must find a substitute to return to life. He sits on her throne, dressed to the nines; he has not lamented her "death" with hair-pulling and rag-wearing. He betrays her, he does not love her, he loves only the power his consorting with her granted him. He petitions the sun god who variously and temporarily turns him into an ibex, skink, or snake to escape the wardens of the land of the dead. Gilgamesh claims Inanna married a horse, but horses are unknown in early Sumer until the mid-second millennium.

Gilgamesh slanders her in the late story; she seeks revenge. She goes to the chief god, An(u) who warns her off from using the Bull of Heaven to extract revenge. Her disregard for An(u)'s orders is an old theme. Inanna gives decrees, it is one of her MEs. When gods (men) take charge of the heavens and the ME; An(u) decides decrees. An old Sumerian proverb says: "An decides the decrees but Inanna tells him what to decide!" The Bull of Heaven is An(u), it has his name; here the Bull is likely the constellation Taurus. When constellations disappear below the horizon; they enter seclusion or the underworld and reappear. They are seasonal. Seasons are cyclical, natural, and correct. Dryness and no plant growth is expected. The goddess's bull is not randomly wrecking and destroying earth. When the bull has hot breath that sears the land and drinks up all the water, this means hot summer has come to the Ancient Near East. Inanna's storehouse is full from the harvest; that part is correct.

The following lines outline the terrible behavior of goddess Inanna/Ishtar, according to rising patriarchy. Our long-reigning queen of heaven, queen of earth and the underworld; owner of the ME and decree maker; goddess of fertility, love, and champion of her people (especially women be they queen or prostitute) is now reduced to a vengeful goddess lusting after Gilgamesh's body. What she is made to propose in the following lines is not love but lust, she is made into a lusting goddess based on male sex drive. Gilgamesh lists a supposed body-count of her victim-lovers. Remember, misogynists believe they are the victims of women! Inanna, as she is presented and slandered here, is far from goddess of fertility and love and almost all powers of earlier times. (George 1999: 48-54:)

On the beauty of Gilgamesh Lady Ishtar looked with longing:
    'Come, Gilgamesh, be you my bridegroom!
Grant me your fruits, O grant me!
    Be my husband and I your wife!

'Let me harness you a chariot of lapis lazuli and gold,
    its wheels shall be gold and its horns shall be amber.
Driving lions in a team and mules of great size,
    enter our house amid the sweet scent of cedar!

'As you enter our house
    doorway and footstool shall kiss your feet!
Kings, courtiers and nobles shall kneel before you,
    produce of mountain and lowland they shall bring you as
    tribute!

'Your goats shall bear triplets, your ewes shall bear twins,
    your donkey when laden shall outpace any mule!
Your horse shall gallop at the chariot in glory,
    no ox shall match yours at the yoke!'

[Gilgamesh] opened his mouth to speak,
    [saying] to Lady Ishtar:
'[And if indeed I] take you in marriage,
    …

[*Would you feed me*] bread that is fit for a god,
    [*and pour me ale*] that is fit for a king?

'[*Who is there*] would take you in marriage?
    [You, *a frost* that congeals no] ice,
a louvre-door [that] stays [not] breeze nor draught,
    a palace that massacres ... warriors,

'an elephant which ... its *hoods*,
    bitumen that [*stains the hands*] of its bearer,
a waterskin that [*cuts the hands*] of its bearer,
    limestone that [*weakens*] a wall of ashlar,[29]

'a battering ram that destroys [*the walls of*] the enemy,
    a shoe that bites the foot of its owner!
What bridegroom of yours did endure for ever?
    What brave warrior of yours went up [*to the heavens?*]

'Come, let me tell [you the tale] of your lovers:
    of ... his arm.

Dumuzi, the lover of your youth,
    year upon year, to lamenting you doomed him.

'You loved the speckled *allallu* bird,
    but you struck him down and broke his wing:
now he stands in the woods crying "My wing!"
    You loved the lion, perfect in strength,
but for him you dug seven pits and seven.

You loved the horse, so famed in battle,
    but you made his destiny whip, spur and lash.
You made his destiny a seven-league gallop,
    you made his destiny to drink muddy water,
and doomed Silili his mother to perpetual weeping.

'You loved the shepherd, the grazier, the herdsman,

---

[29] squared stones dressed and held in place by mortar

181

who gave you piles of loaves baked in embers,
and slaughtered kids for you day after day.

'You struck him and turned him into a wolf,
    now his very own shepherd boys chase him away,
and his dogs take bites at his haunches.

'You loved Ishullanu, your father's gardener, [30]
    who used to bring you dates in a basket,
daily making your table gleam.
    You eyed him up and went to meet him [you said]:

"O my Ishullanu, let us taste your vigour:
    Put out your 'hand' and stroke my quim!"
But Ishullanu said to you:

"'Me! What do you want of me?
    Did my mother not bake? Have I not eaten,
that now I should eat the bread of slander and insults?
    Should I let only rushes cover me in winter?"

'When you heard what [he'd] said,
    you struck him and turned him into a *dwarf.*
You sat him down in the midst of his labours,
    he cannot go up ..., he cannot go down ...
Must you love me also and [deal with me] likewise?'

The goddess Ishtar [heard] these words,
    she [went up] to heaven in a furious rage.
[Weeping] she went to Anu, her father,
    before Antu,[31] her mother, her tears did flow:

---

[30] Ishullanu is Shukaletuda, "Spotty", in the same story of "Inana and Shukaletuda" where he rapes her while she sleeps.

[31] Antu is female sky. Here Anu's consort; her name is an equivalent for Inanna.

'O father, again and again does Gilgamesh scorn me,
    telling a tale of foulest slander,
slander about me and insults too.'

Figure 33. Inanna and Her Bull of Heaven

*Anu points out that it was she who advanced on Gilgamesh,
i.e., her fault that he insulted her. The goddess wants the Bull
of Heaven so she can punish Gilgamesh. If Anu refuses, she
threatens to open the gates of the underworld allowing "the
dead to consume the living, ... outnumber the living." (Her
sister, goddess of the underworld, Ereshkigal, also uses the same
threat.) Anu relents but says first she must have the widows
gather seven year's worth of chaff, and the farmers of Uruk
must grow seven year's worth of hay. The goddess says these have
been grown and stored. Lady Ishtar again demands the Bull of
Heaven for her revenge. Anu hands over the nose-rope of the
Bull of Heaven.* (George 1999: 51-54:)

'[Down came] Ishtar, leading it onward:
    when it reached the land of Uruk,

it dried up the woods, the reed-beds, and marshes,
    down it went to the river, lowered the level by seven full cubits.

As the Bull of Heaven snorted a pit opened up,
    one hundred men of Uruk fell down it.
The second time it snorted a pit opened up,
    two hundred men of Uruk fell down it.

The third time it snorted a pit opened up,
    and Enkidu fell in as far as his waist.
Enkidu sprang up and seized the Bull by the horns.
    In his face the Bull spat slaver,
with the tuft of its tail …

> *Enkidu says to Gilgamesh that he has tested the strength*
> *of the bull and discerned its purpose (annihilating them). He*
> *will hold the bull by the tail and Gilgamesh will be the butcher*
> *and drive his knife between the horns and the "slaughter-spot."*
> *The Bull of Heaven is killed; its heart is offered to Shamash*
> *(sun god). They prostrate to the sun god and sit back. Ishtar has*
> *witnessed the slaughter.*

Ishtar went up on the wall of Uruk-the-sheepfold,
hopping and stamping, she wailed in woe:
    "Alas! Gilgamesh, who mocked me, has killed the Bull of
Heaven."

Enkidu heard these words of Ishtar,
    and tearing a haunch off the Bull he hurled it towards her,
'Had I caught you too, I'd have treated you likewise,
    I'd have draped your arms in its guts!'

Ishtar assembled the courtesans, prostitutes and harlots,
    over the Bull of Heaven's haunch she began rites of mourning.
    …

They (Gilgamesh and Enkidu) washed their hands in the river
    Euphrates,
    took each other by the hand and in they came.
As they drove along the streets of Uruk,
    the people were gathered to gaze [on them.]

Gilgamesh spoke a word to the serving girls of [*his palace:*]
    'Who is the finest among men?
Who the most glorious of fellows?'
    'Gilgamesh is the finest among men!
[Gilgamesh the most] glorious of fellows!'
. ....

Gilgamesh made merry in his palace.

Another version of the Inanna, Gilgamesh, and the Bull of Heaven
story is published in the electronic text site of Sumerian literature from
Oxford University and retold here. (c.1.8.1.2:)

> *Inanna is upset with Gilgamesh because he is usurping her
> power in her temple Eanna, her gipar.[32] She calls Gilgamesh her
> "wild bull" and says she will not allow him to enter her gipar to
> give out justice and verdicts. He may not go there!*
> *Gilgamesh says even with his great strength he will not
> enter but regardless, warns her to not block the way. She snorts
> at him and goes to An in heaven to ask for the Bull of Heaven
> to prevent Gilgamesh entering the gipar. Though An does not
> understand why she needs the bull, he hands over the bull's
> leash to her. An is puzzled and asks what use is the bull? It
> will muddy the water and leave behind cowpats. The Bull of
> Heaven has An's name. Inanna replies that though it will stir
> up the waters and leave big cowpats, she needs it to kill Lord
> Gilgamesh!*

---

[32] sacred women's quarters in the temple where no man can enter; home of the wise
women who advise even the kings in Sumer; place where the high priestesses and
majordoma of the temple complex live; where women come to give birth

Back at his palace, Gilgamesh calls for his drink and musician. The musician tells him it is because of drink that he does nothing important.

(The bull is the constellation Taurus that is said to graze in the sky. Its movement alerts farmers when to plow and plant.) Inanna leads the bull to earth at Unug (Uruk) where it drinks up the river a mile at a slurp. It eats everything on the pasture lands and leaves the land stripped-bare. Inanna watches to see what will happen when the bull and Gilgamesh meet. She stands on top of her city's ramparts. She hears the bellows and sees the dust rise. Gilgamesh walks beside the bull's head; Enkidu is behind (some texts say he holds on to the tail) and calls to Gilgamesh that he will sing a song of him praising his beautifully made body and his battle skills; he will praise him because he beats the evil ones (Inanna's emblems).

Inanna again says that Gilgamesh will not be allowed in her decree dispensing gipar in her E-an(n)a. Gilgamesh tells his mother the things Inanna said and promises to fight the bull so his sister and mother can return to grazing their animals. He proceeds to lift his battle axe weighing seven talents.[33] Gilgamesh smites the bull's skull. The bull rears up so high that it overbalances and falls backward. It spatters [blood?] like rain. It spreads itself out like the harvested crop. The Bull of Heaven, Inanna's bull, is dead! Gilgamesh sits on the corpse and covers it with water using an oar. We hear Enkidu taking up the song of praise for Gilgamesh. The song's lyrics describe how Gilgamesh wants to enter Inanna's garden planted with junipers at her sacred gipar (women's quarters). Inanna says NO! and sends the Bull of Heaven to stop him. Gilgamesh kills the bull. Enkidu sings: Gilgamesh sheered the wool of her sheep and overcame the "wicked ones," [Inanna's temple staff?], by covering them with water.

---

[33] One talent is Sumerian for 67 pounds so the axe weighs 469 pounds!

Figure 34. Gilgamesh Kills the Bull of Heaven and Inanna Screams

Other versions have Enkidu showing Gilgamesh where to plunge the knife in the bull's neck while he holds the tail. Regardless, smiting or stabbing, the bull dies. Gilgamesh, i.e., male domination, is taking over Inanna's rich temple home, storehouse, gipar, staff, powers, holy garden, herds and her grove of conifers. The garden is where she planted the *huluppu*-tree for her throne and bed. The conifers in the garden represent the same concept as the holy grove where the goddess sits on her throne — the cedars of Lebanon that Gilgamesh and Enkidu destroy.

The slaughter of the bull in the later Babylonian version is different. The first text above does not contain the Sumerian literature pattern of triple repetitions with slight variations. Sumerian high culture and literary style is replaced with misogynist propaganda, crude word imagery, and gore. In the second (Sumerian) text, Inanna is fighting to keep maleness, Gilgamesh, out of her temple and protect her gipar and sacred garden. Decree making is one of her long-standing ME powers. An explanation for the conflict between Gilgamesh (or below, Bilgames, the alternative Sumerian spelling) and Inanna/Ishtar is that

Uruk is undergoing usurpation from Akkad. The tale may also be for court entertainment. George writes (1999: 168:)

> "It seems more probable that the story develops from King Bilgames's repudiation of his city's goddess in the specific rite of the Sacred Marriage, it appears less likely that Inanna can be other than the great goddess of Uruk and more likely that the composition bears a different ideological message. But perhaps it bears none at all. The purpose of court poetry such as the poems of Bilgames (and much other Sumerian literature) was probably to amuse and entertain the king and his guests, not to promote political ideology."

I disagree with the last portion of the quote. If a long held sacredness is made into a ridiculing frivolous joke, the earlier sacred idea is undergoing diminishment. Historical evidence of maleness erasing the feminine is obvious when the translated literature spanning three millennia is considered. Creative story telling does not appear out of thin air. It grows from something. Once told, it is not retold, copied, and recopied unless it is meaningful. Gilgamesh or Bilgames is on record as an ancient king of Uruk. Inanna is the tutelary deity of Uruk from its earliest Sumerian archeological findings. Sacred "marriage" is the traditional way a man, as her beloved, sits on her throne for a year. That king Bilgames/Gilgamesh repudiates and humiliates the popular supreme goddess would not be entertainment unless the poem reached receptive ears. There is no need to convert the converted. Political change — rising male domination — is in place. Making the great goddess appear ridiculous, blaming her for bringing misfortune, and supplying a different plot line and order in divine literature is the obvious result of political power tipping heavily toward male-rule. Male-rule is not inclusive as is feminine influence, divine and human, in society and culture. Domination replaces partnership and excludes, it does not include. Competition is the thrust and absolute alpha rulership is the goal of the most dominant and tyrannical men. The sacred guardian, the groves and the Bull of Heaven, Inanna's emblems, are destroyed.

Gilgamesh and his nicer doppelgänger, Enkidu, systematically kill and destroy Inanna's emblems/powers: the peaceable guardian of the sacred grove, Humbaba, followed by destruction of the sacred trees he guarded. On another day, Gilgamesh refuses to have sex with Ishtar/Inanna. (The back story here is that rulers are breaking with the tradition and need for the goddess to grant them a year on the throne. They want permanency and dynastic rulership.) The revision says she is angry because she desired his physical perfection, and so petulantly had her "father" An(u) send the Bull of Heaven after Gilgamesh. The two heroes now have the excuse to kill and dismember the Bull of Heaven who who is Inanna's crescent-horned (moon) creature. Gilgamesh throws the bull's thigh at the goddess. "Thigh" is also a euphemism for genitals.

In various renditions, Gilgamesh refuses the sexual favors of Ishtar/Inanna and the time honored "sacred marriage" for rulership. He angrily lists the "husbands" she has had who all die. He wants to be immortal. Men are mortal; kings reign and die; it is not Inanna's fault, it is the natural fate of human life span.

Gilgamesh equates her to prostitutes at the city wall, and yet, the epic ends with praise for Inanna. The priestly inserts support rising patriarchy but the final old praise of Sumer's eldest and most beloved goddess remains intact. The tablet of Bilgames (Gilgamesh) and the Bull of Heaven ends with a praise for the goddess. (George 1999: 174-175:)

...

[Bilgames] with his axe of seven talents smote its crown.
Lifting its head aloft the bull collapsed from a height,
forming a shapeless mass like a lump of clay, laying flat like a
    harvested crop.
The king took a knife in his hand, no butcher being to hand,
he hacked off a haunch (to throw) at Inanna,
sent her flying off like a dove, and demolished the rampart.
The king stood at the head of the bull, he cried bitter tears:
"Just as I can demolish (the wall:), just so shall I do (with you?)!
And it was just as he had said,

its corpse he did throw down in the streets,
its innards he did throw down in the broad streets,
its meat he did apportion by the basket-load to the orphans of his
    city,
Its carcass he did hand over to the tanner,
from flasks made of its two horns, Inanna in Eanna did pour
    sweet oil.
The Bull of Heaven being slain, O holy Inanna sweet is your praise!

Mitchell's *Gilgamesh* includes, if not praise for Inanna, then praise
of her city's wall, her beautiful temple, Eanna. At the end of years
of adventuring, Enkidu dies. Gilgamesh is in mourning and tries to
unsuccessfully reclaim his friend's wilderness lands. He tries to act
like Enkidu and run with the animals but they shun him. He then
seeks immortality and fails again. Gilgamesh will not be immortal.
He returns to his city, Uruk. He shows Uruk to the boatman who took
him to find the plant of immortality. He is proud that no city can equal
Uruk, Inanna's Eanna has approach-steps of stone older than can be
known; the ramparts are coppery in the sunlight. Gilgamesh boasts that
no other king has ever built an equal or more beautiful temple. The
walls of the brick enclosure are laid by master artisans, the temple close
with gardens, palms, and orchards is lovely; the markets, shops, homes
and public square are superior. The Mitchell text ends abruptly with
Gilgamesh proud of his city and what he has built. Inanna/Ishtar is not
directly praised, but then, neither is Gilgamesh (Mitchell 2004: 198-9).

Inanna's traditional emblems are slowly taken, killed, or reassigned.
Those emblems too ingrained in the stories of the people, are eroded and
made harmful or evil. As Inanna loses her emblems and superiority, so
also is lost the sanctity of life and the influence of women. The big story
is changing. What follows in chapter five is an examination of some
of the texts that exalt Inanna in the old days. It is time to remember.

CHAPTER 5

Exaltation and Praise

Finally the sinuous, breathtaking, full body of the howling, spitting, untamed goddess (Inanna) writhed completely into view.

Judy Grahn [34]

THE GODDESS OF ALL THERE IS.

Inanna's greatness was preserved in the words of Enheduanna: poet, princess, and high priestess of the moon temple. 4300 years ago an amazing and educated woman, daughter of a Semitic king, was made en-priestess (*en* means head person in charge) of two cities' temple complexes in southern Sumer. Enheduanna was reared in a time of change. Patriarchal gods were rising; goddesses were falling. The gods were taking on individuality as was art expression. Figures of deities grew ever more human and realistic.

Enheduanna is now considered to be the first recognizable author-poet of earliest writing. The en-priestess composed her work c. 2300 B.C.E.. Her poem cycle for the goddess contained word images and the goddess's uncontested powers from the preceding millennia. Her

---

[34] from forward for Meador 2000. *Lady of Largest Heart*. p. xi

style is distinctive and she includes herself in the compositions. We have her description of her bad treatment by the priests of the Nanna temple. She teetered on the cusp of the old goddess yet in power and the rising usurpations of patriarchy. Her compositions influenced religion thought and were continually copied for five hundred years (Meador 2000: 22, 69).

Her father was Sargon (the Great) of Akkad and her mother was a Sumerian concubine who taught her daughter the beautiful Sumerian language. The daughter-princess became Enheduanna — en-priestess of the Nanna (moon god) temple in Ur. At Nanna's temple she also served Ningal the moon goddess as a human "wife" for the moon god, just as kings were the human substitutes for Inanna's Dumuzi. She represented and tended Nanna and Ningal. At Uruk, she was associated with the Eanna temple — and served Inanna, who by then was called daughter of the moon couple. The princess/priestess/poet wrote compositions for many deities and temples. Her cycle of Inanna poems portrayed the goddess as beautiful, powerful, and expansive. Enheduanna also wove her personal experience with Inanna into the poem known as "The Exaltation of Inanna." The exalted Inanna, only Inanna, saved the en-priestess!

Ancient Sumerians first, and Akkadians later, pressed hymns, songs, praises and laments into clay tablets with reed styluses. Only in the last one hundred years are the Sumerian texts able to be reliably translated. The tablets, copied and recopied, altered and edited, came from many locations in Mesopotamia, the land between the two rivers, the land now Iraq and Iran. Tens of thousands of clay tablets were dug up during the archeological zeal of the late nineteenth and early twentieth centuries by museum and university sponsored excavations. The funded expeditions arrived supposedly for the sake of proving the bible historically true. Later digs were sponsored in a competition for big art discoveries. The tablets, unreadable curiosities of antiquity, were scattered worldwide. Eventually, a trilingual stone engraving on a protected cliff-face broke the translation barrier. The Sumerian language came to life. Fragmented texts were pieced together and far separated tablets were reunited through the efforts of dedicated scholars from the

Middle East (formerly known as the Near East), Europe, and the United States. Published translations are available and electronic corpus texts of Oxford and the University of Pennsylvania put Sumerian literature on-line for easy perusal.

Early stamp seals were pressed into strips of clay to seal and identify contents of containers. Hundreds of pictograms and counting symbols developed. The memorization and standardization of so many images required great skill. A seven hundred and some image pictographic language was in use a millennium before Enheduanna's time that allowed written expression in nouns only. At first, the accounting pictograms were scratched into the clay leaving raised rough lines. A reed stylus came into use and pressed a clearer and cleaner imitation of the drawn picture into the damp clay. The pictograms evolved and developed into wedge shaped clusters of marks representing the earlier pictograms and as syllable sounds. The reduced number of syllable-symbols made memorization easier and more accessible. Verbs and indicators beside the wedge marks indicated, for example, whether *an* was heaven/sky or the god An. The syllables imitated speech sounds. Stories could be transcribed. Wedge shapes and the circle-dots from the opposite end of the reed stylus created first writing. The appearance of the hand held clay tablet-record was easily readable columns of information. In time, the wedge marks hinting at the original pictogram evolved into stylized wedged arrangements for standardized syllables.

Written Sumerian was largely phonetic and arranged in lines from left to right. Each symbol was a sound in the spoken language. Fewer syllables were required than pictures and the result was a more easily expressed written language. The old stories were written down and copied over and over. New compositions were added to the body of literature. Sumerian writing is now known as cuneiform, from a Latin word meaning "wedge shaped".

Accounting and writing were taught in scribal schools at the temple-storehouses. The storehouse matron is Inanna; she was served by women, by priestesses. Therefore, I surmise the first writing was invented by women and that scribal teachers began as women. The goddess owns the storehouse because she is responsible for fertility in the land. Grain and other storable food surplus are under her care. The goddess of writing is the reed goddess Nisaba. If men had invented writing, they would have claimed a patron god as they did with plow and pickax!

Enheduanna's father, Sargon the Great, was the first ruler to unify southern and northern Sumer. He appointed his daughter en-priestess of the moon god temples of all Sumer. She was well educated with wide knowledge of ancient myths which she incorporated into her temple compositions. Sargon was the son of a priestess who may have conceived him during a sacred marriage ritual while representing Ishtar. No mention was ever made of his father's identity. The story goes that a priestess participating in the *hieros gamos* was not allowed a pregnancy since a child of the union would complicate the king's dynastic lineage. Yet, we are told that the priestess gave birth and put the future king into a woven basket in the marshes. He was found of course, fostered, and went on to greatness. Sargon is Semitic and from the north. He knew Inanna by her Semitic name equivalent, Ishtar. He was devoted to Ishtar. When he unified the north and south, he also unified Inanna and Ishtar. Inanna's reed posts came to stand for both names.

The following hymn is for a temple in the south, at Ur. The en-priestess expresses herself; she puts herself into the poem. We hear what happens to her at the hands of a high priest who ousts her from the temple. She tells us of the complexities of goddess Inanna whom she loves. She tells us of her terrible ordeal. She knows her goddess will help her in the end. Meador writes (Meador 2000: 77-8:)

> Image and emotion become the language of the goddess to the particular individual ... Much of Enheduanna's poetry described Inanna as she played the many parts of the emotion-laden forces in the psyche. In her description of that enigmatic and paradoxical being she called Inanna, she brought together her sense of these forces' power and her interpretations of their meaning. Not only did she feel buffeted by them, but she also remained certain that within the storm, the paradoxical Inanna was constantly carving out the meaning and purpose of Enheduanna's earthly life ...

> Enheduanna tells us that Inanna, Queen of Heaven and
> Queen of Earth is the axis around which the universe spins.
> Her great arms stretch out to encompass all of life ... She
> possesses the very design of life and controls the movement
> of the natural world. She is the transcendent sentient being
> who surges through all matter. As such, she carries out her
> plan in the repetitive cycles of nature.

Though she is the great axis of the spinning universe, Inanna feels emotions deeply, she intercedes for individuals, she can be calmed, appeased, and petitioned; she is accessible. Inanna can also be angry. Her anger causes storms and drought and floods. Her people sooth her with song and assurances of her powers and beauty. The gods flee from her like bats. Sometimes Inanna needs soothing. She can be calmed. Storms will end. Her people will again make love and dance.

The back story of the "Exaltation of Inanna" is that the princess priestess of Akkad is sent as en-priestess of the moon god's temple in Ur in the south where Sargon has recently unified his Semitic northern Sumer with the formerly dominant Sumerian south. This is a position she holds for forty years. An en-priest has changed the focus of the temple at Uruk. He does not accept Enheduanna as en-priestess at Ur. She is disrespected, humiliated, and unceremoniously expelled to wander in the wilderness. Enheduanna appeals to Inanna since appeals to Nanna, the moon god to whom she is consecrated, go unheard. She exalts Inanna with a review of the goddess's greatness. At hymn's end, Enheduanna has been restored to her important office and she credits Inanna for her change of fate. The hymn from the Inanna poem cycle is rendered by Betty DeShong Meador, a Jungian analyst, from her book, *Inanna Lady of Largest Heart*. She presents both Inanna and Enheduanna with deep understanding. Her translations appear on the page as the cuneiform does on a clay tablet. Like a Sumerian scribe, Meador uses no punctuation and keeps the word clusters grouped spatially for meaning. (Meador 2000: 171-180:)

Figure 35. Celestial and Earthly Inanna

NIN-ME-SHAR-RA

by the High Priestess Enheduanna

Queen of all the given powers
unveiled clear light
unfailing woman wearing brilliance
cherished in heaven and earth

chosen, sanctified in heaven
You

grand in you adornments
crowned with your beloved goodness
rightfully you are High Priestess

your hands seize the seven fixed powers
    my queen of fundamental forces
    my guardian of essential cosmic sources

you lift up the elements
bind them to your hands
gather in powers
press them to your breast

vicious dragon you spew
    venom poisons the land
like the storm god you howl
    grain wilts on the ground

swollen flood rushing down the mountain
YOU ARE INANNA
SUPREME IN HEAVEN AND EARTH

mounted on a beast
You Lady ride out
shower the land with flames of fire
your fated word charged
with An's command

who can fathom your depths
you of the great rites

You mountain smasher
give the storm wings

You
Enlil's dear

fling storms over the land
you stand at An's command
my Lady
the shriek of your voice shatters foreign lands

You
dreaded southwind
hurl a hot storm
people stumble dazed and silent
face the terror of holy power
chanting a dirge
they meet you at the crossroads
of the house of signs

at the front of battle
all is smashed before you
the obsidian blade ravages
my Lady
by your own arm's power

a gouging storm-bull, you gouge
a rumbling storm-roar, you thunder
you bellow with the storm god
you moan with evil winds
your feet never weary

you sing of sorrows
play the harp of lamentation

before you my Queen
the Annuna
all the great gods
fly away to the ruins
flutter around like bats
whither at your smoldering glance

cower beneath your scowl

your angry heart
who can soothe it
cooling your cruel heart is
too forbidding

the Queen alone lifts her feelings
the Queen alone gladdens her heart
When will not quiet her rage
O great daughter of Suen

Queen
greater than the mountain
who dares raise nose-pressed-to-the-ground
when the mountain quits nose-rubbing
you curse its grain
  spin ashes around its main gate
  pour blood into its rivers
  its people cannot drink
it hands over captives
armies disband
strong young men
come before you willingly

a wind storm breaks up dancing in the city
drives the prime youth before you
rope-tied captives

to the city which does not profess
"the land is yours"
which does not say
"it is your father's"
you speak one holy word
turn that city from your path

you abandon its sacred stall
the woman no longer speaks sweetly to her husband
    no longer tells secrets at midnight
    does not disclose
    the soft whispers in her heart
ecstatic wild cow
eldest daughter of Suen
Queen greater than An
who dares withhold adulation

mistress of the scheme of order
great Queen of queens
babe of a holy womb
greater than the mother who bore you
You all knowing
You wise vision
Lady of all lands
live-giver for the many
faithful Goddess
worthy of powers
to sing your praise is exalted

You of the bountiful heart
You of the radiant heart
I will sing of your cosmic powers

* * *

truly for your gain
you drew me toward
my holy quarters
I
the High Priestess
I
Enheduanna

there I raised the ritual basket
there I sang the shout of joy

but *that man* cast me among the dead
I am not allowed in my rooms
gloom falls on the day
light turns leaden
shadows close in
dreaded south storms cloaks the sun
he wipes his spit-soaked hand
on my honey sweet mouth
my beautiful image
fades under dust

what is happening to my fate
O Suen
what is this with Lugalanne
speak to An
he will free me
tell him "Now"
he will release me

the Woman will dash his fate
that Lugalanne
the mountains the biggest flocks
lie at Her feet

the Woman is as great as he
she will break the city from him
    (may her heart grow soft for me)

stand there
I
Enheduanna Jewel of An
let me say a prayer to you

(flow tears
refreshing drink for Inanna)

I say to her
silim[35]
be well

I say
I no longer soothe Ashimbabbar[36]

all the cleansing rites of Holy An
that man changed them

he robbed An of his temple
he does not fear Big Man An
the potent vigor of the place
does not fill him
he spoiled its allure
truly he destroyed it

haunt him
with the ghost
of her you set up as your partner

O my divine ecstatic wild cow
drive this man out
hunt him down
catch him

I
who am I
in the place which holds up
life's key elements

---

[35] silim is Sumerian equivalent for shalom, salam: be well
[36] Ashimbabbar is Nanna/Suen the moon god.

may An desert those rebels
who hate your Nanna
may An wreck that city
may Enlil curse its fate
may the mother not comfort
her crying child

Queen
creator of heart-soothing
that man junked
your boat of lamentation
on an alien sea

I am dying
that I must sing
this sacred song
I
even I
Nanna ignores my straits
am I to be ruined by treachery
I
even I
Ashimbabbar
neglects my case

whether he neglects me
or not
what does it matter
that man threw me out of the temple
I who served triumphant

he made me fly
like swallows swept
from their holes in the wall

he eats away at my life
I wander through thorny brush in the mountains
he robbed me
of the true crown
of the High Priestess

he gave me
the ritual dagger of mutilation[37]
he said
"it becomes you"

precious Queen
loved by An
rekindle for me
your holy heart

beloved wife of the sky dragon
Ushumgalanna[38]
Great Lady
who spans the tree of heaven
trunk to crown
all the Annuna
lash yoke over neck for you

You
born a minor queen
how great you have become
greater than the Great Gods

the Anunna
press lips to the ground for you
that man has not settled my claim
again and again

---

[37] dagger used by priests to self mutilate to become eunuchs in the temple
[38] Dumuzi's epithet

he trows a hateful verdict in my face

I no longer lift my hands
from the pure sacred bed
I no longer unravel
Ningal's gifts of dreams
to anyone

I
most radiant priestess of Nanna
may you cool your heart for me
my Queen
beloved of An

PROCLAIM!
PROCLAIM!
I shall not pay tribute to Nanna
it is of YOU
I PROCLAIM

that you are exalted as An
PROCLAIM!

that you are wide as earth
PROCLAIM!

that you shriek over the land
PROCLAIM!

that you smash heads
PROCLAIM!

that you gorge on corpses like a dog
PROCLAIM!

that your glance flames with rage

PROCLAIM!

that you throw your glance around
PROCLAIM!

that your eyes flash like jewels
PROCLAIM!

that you balk and defy
PROCLAIM!

that you stand victorious
PROCLAIM!

I have not said this of Nanna
I have said it of YOU
my phrases glorify YOU
who alone are exalted
my Queen
beloved of An

I have spoken
of your tempestuous fury

* * *

I have heaped up coals in the brazier
I have washed in the sacred basin
I have readied your room
in the tavern [39]
(may your heart be cooled for me)
suffering bitter pangs
I gave birth to this exaltation
for you my Queen

---

[39] Here tavern is a reference to the holy brothel.

what I told you in the dark of night
may the singer recount at noon

child of yours I am a captive
bride of yours I am a captive
it is for my sake your anger fumes
your heart finds no relief

* * *

the eminent Queen
guardian of the throne room
receives her prayer

the holy heart
of Inanna
returns to her
the day is favorable
she dresses lavishly
in woman's allure

she glows with beauty's shine
like the light of the rising moon
Nanna lifts her
into seemly view

at the sound of Ningal's prayer
the gate posts open
    Hail
    Be Well

* * *

this poem
spoken for the sacred Woman
is exalted

praise the mountain destroyer
praise Her who
   (together with An)
received the unchanging power
praise my lady wrapped in beauty
PRAISE BE TO INANNA

Enheduanna's tribute, petition, exaltation, and prayer to the Queen of all powers tells us who Inanna is in 2300 B.C.E.. We know historically that during this time, the gods are being elevated and promoted; aggressive usurpation of culture by patriarchy is well under way. The en-priestess knows the old stories and reminds the listener and the goddess herself of her beginning, of her power. Inanna is life: powerful, changeable, unpredictable, and yet, she offers us hope, potential, benefit, and beauty.

References to other Inanna myths and expected, often-repeated phrases are worked into the composition. The rhythm of the text begins with praise and awareness of Inanna's power and her great accomplishments and strength. Inanna is a warrior, the fierce destructive southwind; a roaring storm-bull; she sorrows, she frightens all the gods who scatter like bats, she abandons a city and love is gone; women and men do not copulate; women ignore their crying children. The goddess is "mistress of the scheme of order"; holder of the cosmic powers.

Inanna is reminded that it is she who is responsible for Enheduanna being in her temple; for the goddess she did the proper ritual and song. It is an interesting aside that the thrusting of a foreign en-priestess/princess into an established priest-run temple by a Semitic king who has just unified the north and south by military threat and action would not make the Sumerian priests very happy. The expulsion of the en-priestess is brought to Inanna's attention. A historical man, Lugalanne, did lead an unsuccessful revolt against Sargon's grandson Naram-Sin in Uruk (ibid.: 181). He is likely the same priest named Lugalanne in Enheduanna's poem.

The priestess is locked from her rooms, her garments are torn (rape?), priest Lugalanne spits on his hand and wipes it on her mouth;

he throws her out of the temple, she flees "like swallows swept from their holes in the wall;" he banishes her into the dusty wilderness to "wander through thorny brush in the mountains." The poem says she is alone in the mountains but the closest mountain range is one hundred miles east of Ur and Uruk so this may be a poetic exaggeration. She is robbed of her high priestess crown. The usurper is changing the rites of An's temple, he has no respect for An, the temple's allure is gone. She begs Inanna to "haunt him with the ghost of her you set up as your partner," i.e., Enheduanna.

The moon god ignored her pleas, Inanna is her last hope. She heaps more praise and exaltations on the goddess. The pleas are heard. We next hear that Enheduanna is back in the temple, lighting the brazier, bathing in the sacred basin, and preparing Inanna's bed "in the tavern (sacred brothel?)." The high priestess describes the composing of the poem to have been painful, like giving birth. A temple singer will present what Enheduanna told to Inanna in the night. The poem ends with Inanna's love returning to the priestess. The goddess is calmed and again dressed with allure. Inanna assumes her lofty place as evening star. She has the "unchanging powers" and she is "wrapped in beauty." Praise be to Inanna.

The "Exaltation of Inanna" text has been translated by a number of experts. For comparison, I include below the translation by William Hallo and J.J. A. Van Dijk. The translators notes that the goddess' proper name is rarely used in the composition, and instead Enheduanna uses many epithets applicable to both the northern and southern versions of the same goddess. The same story emerges but the translation styles are quite different. (Hallo and Van Dijk 1968: 15-35:)

THE EXALTATION OF INANNA

nin-me-shar-ra

(i)
Inanna and the me's

Lady of all the me's, resplendent light,
Righteous woman clothed in radiance, beloved of Heaven and
    Earth,
Hierodule of An (you) of all the great ornaments,
Enamoured of the appropriate tiara, suitable for the high priest-hood
Whose hand has attained (all) "seven" me's,
Oh my lady, you are the guardian of all the great me's!
You have picked up the me's, you have clasped the me's on your
    hand,
You have gathered up the me's, you have clasped the me's to your
    breast.

(ii)
Inanna and An

Like a dragon you have deposited venom on the land
When you roar at the earth like Thunder, no vegetation can stand
    up to you.
A flood descending from its mountain,
Oh foremost one, you are the Inanna of heaven and earth!
Raining the fanned fire down upon the nation,
Endowed with me's by An, lady mounted on a beast,
Who makes decisions at the holy command of An.
(You) of all the great rites, who can fathom what is yours?

(iii)

Inanna and Enlil

Devastatrix of the lands, you are lent wings by the storm.
Beloved of Enlil, you fly about in the nation.
You are at the service of the decrees of An.
Oh my lady, at the sound of you the lands bow down.
When mankind comes before you
in fear and trembling at (your)tempestuous radiance,
They receive from you their just deserts.
Proffering a song of lamentation, they weep before you,
They walk toward you along the path of the house of all the great
     sighs

(iv)

Inanna and Ishkur

In the van of battle everything is struck down by you.
Oh my lady, (propelled) on your own wings, you peck away (at the
     land).
In the guise of a sharing storm you charge.
With a rearing storm you roar.
With Thunder you continually thunder.
With all the evil winds you snort.
Your feet are filled with restlessness.
To (the accompaniment of) the harp of sighs you give vent to a dirge.

(v)

Inanna and the Anunna

Oh my lady, the Anunna, the great gods,
Fluttering like bats fly off from before you to the clefts,
They who dare not walk(?) in your terrible glance,
Who dare not proceed before your terrible countenance.
Who can temper your raging heart?
Your malevolent heart is beyond tempering.

Lady (who) soothes the reins, lady (who) gladdens the heart,
Whose rage is not tempered, oh eldest daughter of Suen (moon god)!
Lady supreme over the land, who has (ever) denied (you) homage?

(vi)

Inanna and Ebih

In the mountain where homage is withheld from you vegetation is
   accursed.
Its grand entrance you have reduced to ashes.
Blood arises in its rivers for you, its people have nought to drink.
It leads its army captive before you of its own accord
It disbands its regiments before you of its own accord
It makes its able-bodied young men parade before you of their own
   accord.
A tempest has filled the dancing of its city
It drives its young adults before you as captives.

(vii)

Inanna and Uruk

Over the city which has not declared "The land is yours,"
which has not declared "It is your father's, your begetter's"
You have spoken your holy command, have verily turned it back
   from your path,
Have verily removed your foot from out of its byre.
Its woman no longer speaks of love with her husband.
At night they no longer have intercourse.
She no longer reveals to him her inmost treasures.
Impetuous wild cow, great daughter of Suen,
Lady supreme over An who has (ever) denied (you) homage?

(viii)

Invocation of Inanna

You of the appropriate me's, great queen of queens,
Issued from the holy womb, supreme over the mother who bore you,
Omniscient sage, lady of all the lands,
Sustenance of the multitudes, I have verily recited your sacred song!
True goddess, fit for the me's, it is exalting to acclaim you.
Merciful one, brilliantly righteous woman, I have verily recited your
     me's for you!

(ix)

The Argument and Banishment from Ur

Verily I had entered my holy *giparu* at your behest,
I, the high priestess, I Enheduanna!
I carried the ritual basket, I intoned the acclaim.
(But now) I am placed in the leper's ward, I, even I, can no longer
     live with you!
They approach the light of day, the light is obscured about me,
The shadows approach the light of day, it is covered with a (sand)
     storm.
My mellifluous mouth is cast into confusion.
My choicest features are turned to dust.

(x)

The Appeal to Nanna-Suen

What is he to me, oh Suen, this Lugalanne![40]
Say thus to An: "May An release me!"
Say but to An "Now!" and An will release me.
This woman will carry off the manhood of Lugalanne.
Mountain (and?) flood lie at her feet.
That woman is as exalted (as he) — she will make the city divorce him.

---

[40] Translates to big holy man; a high priest

Surely she will assuage her heartfelt rage for me.

Let me, Enheduanna, recite a prayer to her.

Let me give free vent to my tears like sweet drink for the holy Inanna!

Let me say "Hail!" to her!

(xi)

The Indictment of Lugalanne(?)

I cannot appease Ashimbabbar.[41]

(Lugalanne) has altered the lustrations of holy An and all his (other rites).

He has stripped An of (his temple) Eanna.

He has not stood in awe of An-lugal (An)

That sanctuary whose attractions are irresistible, whose beauty is endless,

That sanctuary he has verily brought to destruction.

Having entered before you as a partner, he has even approached his sister-in-law.

Oh my divine impetuous wild cow, drive out this man, capture this man!

(xii)

The Curse of Uruk

In the place of sustenance what am I, even I?

(Uruk) is a malevolent rebel against your Nanna — may An make it surrender!

This city — may it be sundered by An!

May it be cursed by Enlil!

May its plaintive child not be placated by his mother!

Oh lady, the (harp of) mourning is placed on the ground.

One had verily beached your ship of mourning on a hostile shore.

At (the sound of) my sacred song they are ready to die.

---

[41] Ashimbabbar is an epithet for the moon god Nanna/Suen

(xiii)

The Indictment of Nanna

As for me, my Nanna takes no heed of me.

He has verily given me over to destruction in murderous straits,

Ashimbabbar has not pronounced my judgment.

Had he pronounced it: what is it to me? Had he not pronounced
    it: what is it to me?

(Me) who once sat triumphant he has driven out of the sanctuary.

Like a swallow he made me fly from the window, my life is
    consumed.

He made me walk in the bramble of the mountain.

He stripped me of the crown appropriate for the high priesthood.

He gave me dagger and sword — "it becomes you," he said to me.

(xiv)

The Appeal to Inanna

Most precious lady, beloved of An,

Your holy heart is lofty, may it be assuaged on my behalf!

Beloved bride of Ushumgalanna,[42]

You are the senior queen of the heavenly foundations and zenith.

The Anunna have submitted to you.

From birth on you were the "junior" queen.

How supreme you are over the great gods, the Anunna!

The Anunna kiss the ground with their lips (in obeisance) to you.

(But) my own sentence is not concluded, a hostile judgement appears
    before my eyes as my judgment.

(My) hands are no longer folded on the ritual couch,

I may no longer reveal the pronouncements of Ningal to Man.

(Yet) I am the brilliant high priestess of Nanna,

Oh my queen beloved of An, may your heart take pity on me!

---

[42] meaning: the bridegroom but not necessarily Dumuzi; indicating possibly the king
    as proxy

(xv)

The Exaltation of Inanna

That one has not recited as a "Know! Be it known!" of Nanna, that
  one has recited as a "'Tis Thine!"
"That you are lofty as Heaven (An) — be it known!
That you are broad as the earth — be it known!
That you devastate the rebellious land — be it known!
That you roar at the land — be it known!
That you smite the heads — be it known!
That you devour cadavers like a dog — be it known!
That your glance is terrible — be it known!
That you lift your terrible glance — be it known!
That your glance is flossing — be it known!
That you are ill-disposed toward the ... — be it known!
That you attain victory — be it known!"
(That,) oh my lady, has made you great, you alone are exalted!
Oh my lady beloved of An, I have verily recounted your fury!

(xvi)

Peroration — The Composition of the Hymn

One has heaped up the coals (in the censer), prepared the lustration
The nuptial chamber awaits you, let your heart be appeased!
With "It is enough for me!" I have given birth, oh exalted lady, (to
  this song) for you.
That which I recited to you at (mid)night
May the singer repeat it to you at noon!
(Only) on account of your captive spouse, on account of your captive
  child, Your rage is increased, your heart unassuaged.

(xvii)

The Restoration of Enheduanna

The first lady, the reliance of the throne room,
Has accepted her offerings
Inanna's heart has been restored.
The day was favorable for her, she was clothed sumptuously, she was
    garbed in womanly beauty.
Like the light of the rising moon, how she was sumptuously attired!
When Nanna appeared in proper view,
They (all) blessed her (Inanna's) mother Ningal.
The (heavenly) doorsill called "Hail!"

(xviii)

Doxology

For that her (Enheduanna's) speaking to the Hierodule was exalted,
Praise be (to) the devastatrix of the lands, endowed with me's
    from An,
(To) my lady wrapped in beauty, (to) Inanna!

After Enheduanna's death, the sacred feminine returns to her slow slide toward near oblivion. The sky-based gods debase earth and nature. The oldest nature religions, strongly female-based, believe in the supremacy of nature. Those sacred feminine beliefs are being eradicated. Male attention is skyward while the remaining female imagery is given messy earth and birth. Earth and women's role, both sacred and human, lose importance. Bizarre creation myths replace the sensible long-standing story. Punishment and fear are entrenched. Absolute male-rule is upheld by the sky gods. Gods are replacing Goddess.

We, the children of earth, the clay that dreams, are no longer rooted in nature's natural flux and change. Instead, we are held in unnatural priest-inspired uncertainty, blame, fear, and guilt; weighted by uncertainty.

217

CHAPTER 6

Sex, Love, Sacred Marriage, and Prostitution

she sang a song of her vulva[43]

Peg my vulva my star-sketched horn of the dipper
moor my slender boat of heaven
my new moon crescent cunt beauty[44]

Food and sex are humankind's two driving appetites. Obtaining food sates hunger. We, the women, gathered food for several million years; women invented horticulture. We grew our food only in the last 11,000 years in enough abundance to support settlements. Food surplus was kept in storehouses maintained by women.

Inanna is goddess of the storehouse; Inanna is also the goddess of sex, love, sacred marriage and prostitution. Sex is also a hunger. The Ancient Near East religions united sex and food with Inanna. Fertility was required for new life, returning cycles, and plentiful crops and herds. Sex brought fertility both literally and symbolically.

---

[43] Leick 1994: 90
[44] Meador 2000: 11

Sex, though not more vital than food for our bodies, is required for species' continuation. Sex is also pleasurable. Sex for humans is independent of estrus (when blood show, scent, and ovulation occur at the same time); human sex is not dependent on female scent for arousal in males. Somewhere along the way, our earliest foremothers stepped away from estrus and secretly ovulated, in synchrony with the moon and each other. No other primate does that. Women's reproductive bodies evolved hidden ovulation and separate blood show. Some biological miracle synchronized women's menses with each other and the moon. No other primate does that either. Before this novel biological development, fertility and blood flow/show were simultaneous and varied in cycles from female to female; primate to primate. Female primates are sexual only during estrus; they are both selective and promiscuous. Bonobo chimps are the exception and explore sexual pleasure at will. (They are also matristic and more peaceful than the common chimps across the river.)

Sex and food are the focus of early woman's culture. When woman said NO! to sex she was heard because she stood in solidarity with all the women. She also said YES! She set up taboos to enhance her NO! Woman was once honored and heard. Her vulva and womb were things of wonder; her sexuality and reproductive body created life and culture; she owned her body. Human women presented a new anatomical-biological development — sexual pleasure separate from fertility. Women (and chimp females) have an organ that has *only one function* — pleasure. The clitoris. Women once called the clitoris the gift from the goddess. It has two to four times the sensitivity of the penis tip.

Sex is natural, pleasurable, and useful for forging relationships and changing male lust to caring; taming men into participation and cooperation; enticing men to be relational and initiating men into humane-ity.

However, sex, under male domination suffers horribly; the natural pleasure and sacredness of sex diminish as women are diminished. Women's solidarity is broken. We can no longer say NO! together. Consider the marriage vows still used in my childhood: the bride agreed to "love, honor and *obey!*" Men wrote, upheld, and interpreted biblical directives. First, women were to have sex with the husband whenever he wanted it as husband's right and wife's duty. Second, sex was bad and only to be used to make babies; it was not for pleasure, and most certainly not for a woman to feel pleasure. Male sexuality devolves to expectation and entitlement to unearned sexual release without permission or consideration. (I suspect that there have always been exceptional men who did not embrace the on-demand entitlement role.)

Human love and sexuality are wrought with difficulties and mirrored in stories told about deities who are in love and in lust. Rulers, to potentize their importance, confuse their own importance with personal potency. A performing penis means power. In early times, the king is chosen by Inanna and must prove potent in her bed on the new year renewal festival or the land will suffer: people and animals will not copulate, nothing will grow or give birth, there will be no joy in the land. Patriarchy systematically limits the former powers of Great Goddess. "With the development of the patriarchate the Great Goddess has become the Goddess of Love, and the power of the feminine has been reduced to the power of sexuality."[45] Pleasure becomes sinful; pleasure is for men and is no longer a mutually joyous event. Women's sexuality and reproductive ability is first envied by men and then owned by them.

Over millennia without number, long before patriarchy, our fore-sisters worked hard and together to support themselves and their long-dependent children. They worked at least as hard to tame men into participation and cooperation with the responsible woman-child families. In solidarity women said NO! during seclusion moon-blood time. No-sex time was also accompanied by a no-cook time among traditional peoples. That enforced time of NO! was the origin of getting men to cooperate into hunting parties; it was a period of time where male competition for sexual opportunity was moot as there was no sex for any of them. Early men, without modification and taboo, self-fed what they scavenged and killed. Women created kinship organization and strong taboo so men would return with the kill and share with the

---

[45] Baring and Cashford 1993: 352 citing Erich Neumann, *The Great Mother*, p. 145

group. One knew one's mother; fatherhood was uncertain. Kinship developed around the mother and her clan. Hunted and gathered food came to the mother's clan, or else a "taboo" was encountered. (For more on women creating culture, see the suggested reading at the back of the book.)

Sex was once at the woman's discretion: we said NO! and YES! Sex and power in the cosmic sphere paralleled the history of human sexuality and growing male authority in the family. Everything changed when men assumed supremacy. Men took power over women, girls, and goddess by, "marriage", and "fatherhood". Captive women in Ancient Near Eastern art paraded in rows showing their thighs. Thigh was a euphemism for sex. This indicated they were raped by the victors. Rape was established as a right of conquest and accompanied killing, looting and destruction.

Humans create icons and icons influence human behavior. Women universally created a Great Mother icon that directed and served humanity well — for 99% of human time (French 2002 vol. I: 65). Divine personality, story, and imagery reflect human behavior. Goddess is a glorious inclusive biophilic (love of life) icon of womankind. Gods are incomplete sketches of the sacred goddess. Men in charge gender-flip goddess to gods. The "Nin" in many a god's *acquired* identity originally meant only "queen" or "lady." "Lord" was added as an after thought. Minor godlets took over goddess attributes and prestige by forced sex, "murder," usurpation of powers and having sex with or "marriage" to important goddesses. The coterie of the ever-increasing male dominance in the divine pantheon is a reflection inspired by human political and social changes: war, limited water, diminished food resources, and the influx of both peaceful immigrants and the less civilized "barbarians" from the mountains and steppe who raid and steal herd animals.

Inanna/Ishtar is too enormous, supreme, and ingrained to be forced into submission or marriage to some god or another. Inanna is always a bride and never a wife. However, patriarchy did write a rape of Inanna scene into their make-over. The following re-telling is based on the Black et al translation of "Inana and Shu-kale-tuda." (Black et al 2004: 198-205:)

INAN(N)A AND SHU-KALE-TUDA

The queen of all the ME leaves her temple, Eanna, to investigate injustice in the mountains. She abandons heaven and earth, she stands with the bulls of the foothills, she flies around and around heaven and around and around earth and then climbs up the mountains. She is weary and seeks a place to nap.

A gardener's boy, Shu-kale-tuda (translates to 'Spotty'), is attempting to tend his father's garden plots. He is incompetent. He can not water the field properly; he weeds out the few plants that do survive. A dust storm blows into his eyes; he wipes away the dust and sees deities of heaven to the east and deities of the earth below the mountain. He also sees a "ghost." The ghost walks wearily to the shade of the one enormously wide Euphrates poplar tree in the garden and lies down. The farmer's son recognizes the ghost; it is Inanna. She wears the seven divine powers on a girdle over her genitals.

Shu-kale-tuda sneaks up to the exhausted sleeping goddess; he removes her loincloth or girdle of the seven great me; he "has sex" with her unconscious body; he kisses her vulva and hides in the garden plot to see what will happen.

Inanna awakens and inspects herself, her holy genitals. She is angry and decides something must be done because "of her genitals." She is angry. She causes the water of the Land to turn to blood and announces she will find that man who took liberties and raped her. She looks and looks but cannot find the culprit.

Shu-kale-tuda has run home to papa and tells the full story. Papa sends him off to the city to work beside his brothers since the goddess is searching the mountains, not the city. Inanna does not find him in the mountains. She climbs into a storm cloud, the southwind leads the way, storms and floods follow in her wake. She comes to the high desert. "Seven times seven helpers" search and cannot find the gardener's son. Her second punishment (storm and floods) does not get results.

Inanna considers what else to destroy. Spotty tells his father she is still searching for him. We hear him say: "My father, the

222

woman of whom I spoke to you, this woman was considering a third time what should be destroyed because of her genitals (ibid.: 203)." His father sends him away again to hide as a city dweller.

The goddess reinspects herself and asks "who will pay for what happened to me?" She goes to the Abzu, home of her "father" Enki. She tells Enki she should be compensated; she will not return home to her Eanna until Enki has handed Shu-kale-tuda over to her. Enki replies: "So be it."

Inanna leaves the Abzu stretching out over the land as a rainbow spans the earth. She lets the north and south winds pass across her trajectory. The gardener's son sees her coming and makes himself small as possible, but the goddess sees him. She screams at him: "(you) dog ... ass ... pig!" Shu-kale-tuda retells how he came to rape her. She confers a death sentence on him but adds that his name will continue to be sung. "So! you shall die! What is that to me? Your name, however, shall not be forgotten. Your name shall exist in songs and make the songs sweet. A young singer shall perform them most pleasingly in the king's palace. A shepherd shall sing them sweetly as he tumbles his butter churn. A shepherd boy shall carry your name to where he grazes the sheep (ibid.: 205)."

Shu-kale-tuda's "destiny is determined." Praise be to Inanna!

Rape of a great goddess by a "spotty"[46] incompetent boy is unthinkable! And that is the point. Even a dull-witted teenaged garden boy with complexion problems who kills his own plants can have his way with Inanna. Her MEs, here worn over her genitals as a girdle or loincloth, cannot protect her from violation. If Inanna is no longer safe, what of girls and women? The last lines tell us his destiny is to die (he is human after all!) but his name will live on in sweetly sung songs. I find immortalizing him in song like a hero both puzzling and disheartening.

Patriarchal scribes present Inanna's revenge for her rape as an over reaction. Inanna inflicts harm on the land. She turns water to blood.

---

[46] "Spotty" is given as a translation for the name of the gardener's son.

Is this transubstantiation? Does she make war and turn the water red with blood? I think the former is correct as there is no mention of war. Inanna is the storm. Floods occur in southern Sumer too late to soak and silt the land before planting but in time to flood the fields of the already growing crops. When Inanna is absent from her E-anna, her temple-storehouse, she is not bringing fertility and plenty to the land. She threatens Enki that until she catches the rapist she will not return to her cosmic duties. The men around 'Spotty' are protecting him from consequences and punishment. It seems that the gods are also in collusion, since Enki knows where he is. Enki agrees to expose the perpetrator and reveals his hiding place only after Inanna refuses to bring fertility to the land. She stretches across the land like a rainbow, searching for the perpetrator. Rainbows are associated with the goddess in her rain aspect. Inanna/Ishtar wears a rainbow necklace.

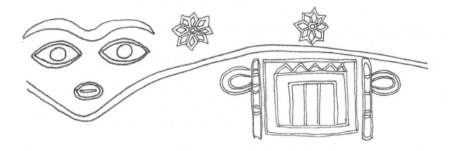

Figure 36. Inanna's All-seeing Eye, Storehouse and Rainbow

Inanna decrees that, though he will die, people will sing his story. The songs will be sweet. Why will the songs about the gardener's boy be sweet? The song is about rape. Is it a cautionary tale for young lads with sex on their minds? Inanna looks out for girls and women. Sex is sacred. Be warned. NO! The shepherd "tumbling his butter churn" and singing makes this a work song. Other sources have dairy maids singing a Dumuzi bridegroom song while turning the churn in their laps as a simile for the rhythmic movement of copulation. The gardener's son's name will be at home in the desert carried by song. Why is he being given his name carried forward in time? This is an immortalization that heroes are desperate to have. We may well ask: is he a "hero" to patriarchy because he violated the goddess' inviolable ME-protected vulva? Is this the impunity for such deeds that patriarchy has ingrained into culture from that time forward into the present?

INANNA LOVES DUMUZI

In my bed ... there is no one like me![47]

Inanna's beloved is a vegetation god; he is her consort. She annually consorts with him so life renews. They consort, they do not live together. She is bride and not wife. Marriage is not part of the union between the beautiful potent young aspect of great goddess and the temporary vegetation god who rises and falls, rises and falls. They are lovers pleasing each other. They are "bed lions." They are so exuberant and joyful that new crops grow, lambs and kids are dropped, maidens and youths fall in love, women and men conjoin in the marital bed; parades and festivals express joy and praise for Inanna. Every level of society expresses joy; all ages are honored. Girls and old women parade with hair loose and curly. Loosened hair is suggestive of sexuality and strength. Girls grow into the art of womanhood, they are little Inannas, the potent future. The older women, well-experienced in their sexuality and allure, represent past-sacred pleasure, fertility, and expression of love. Inanna has luxurious hair everywhere. Her pubic hair is vegetation ("lettuce") growing beside her moist vaginal cleft ("canal"). Her head hair is luxurious and enticing.

Women exude allure and have power over what men desire. When sex is no longer a natural expression directed by women (NO! and YES!), then sex is no longer an earned privilege and women's bodies are usurped to serve men's lust. Women's sexuality, after marriage, is imprisoned and controlled while men's sexuality is not restricted. The solidarity of women is broken. When that occurs, a woman's NO! means nothing as men can take the servant girls or slave women, or

---

[47] Foster 2005: 590

visit the taverns, or walk to the city wall for sex. The textural evidence of goddesses and women being raped and coerced depict the changing exploitation of women's bodies. What happens to goddess happens to women.

In Inanna's parade, sensuality is expressed in its many guises: heterosexual and homosexual copulation appear in Sumerian art. Transgendered people belong to Inanna as well as cross-dressers and eunuchs. Male prostitutes are part of her entourage. She changes women to men and men to women. This is demonstrated in her parade by men and women wearing their upper clothing in the drape of the opposite sex. Priestesses, sacred harlots, priests, dancers, musicians, singers, jugglers, hoop spinners and acrobats perform. Warrior priestesses come down from the mountains to parade in single file.

A priest dabs her dais with blood from his dagger and young men acting as captives beg for her mercy; all parade before holy Inanna. Suggestions for the blood-smearing on her dais are: blood from a self-castration in order to serve her or else it represents women's blood, the source of life. The source of the blood, animal or human, is not the focus. Blood is the subject. Her throne, her seat, is the menstrual cushion, seat, birth-stool that raises a woman off the ground during menses and childbirth. It is soaked in her blood; it is the seat of blood power. Every throne that ever was and will be represents the goddess's throne — women's seat imbued with powerful blood. Men sit on her throne by invitation of the goddess.

The doyenne of wise women march with the social elite in Inanna's monthly parade. Wise women are elders who are consulted by the people; the wisest of them advise Sumerian kings. A wise woman for a king appears in the story of two rulers, one from the grain rich plains and the other from the timber and mineral rich mountains. They are in dispute. After contests and competition, without resolution, (they know only to go to war so one side wins) but Enmerker from Sumer has brought a wise woman with him. She is dressed magnificently and sits beside him. She explains that the two kingdoms can pile up their products and trade. She brokers a peaceful exchange of goods — trade is invented. The king claims credit for discovering "trade", of course, but the story clearly credits the woman for the wisdom of trading instead of attacking (see "Enmerkar and the Lord of Aratta" in the back section).

The story of our goddess changes over time and not for the better. The days of time-honored seclusion for women is taboo. Taboo means "sacred/holy" and "no men." Men change the meaning to be: filthy, impure, and polluting. Men envy the blood-power of women. ('Penis envy' is a much much later felonious male concept embraced by men to emphasize male superiority.) However, the traces of first myth everywhere are still present. Red is the preferred color of royalty for robes and carpets — Inanna wore a "ruddy" robe; red represents blood, as in menstrual blood that makes babies, not the killing make-blood of animal sacrifice and make-death slaughter of war.

Besides the throne of rulership being connected to women, so too is the royal scepter. Scepters evolve from the scratching sticks of dark-moon menstruating women in seclusion. Their hands might have blood on them. If they touch something, they could cause some inadvertent natural disaster, so they used scratching sticks. The tool's power association became scepters. The underworld's power also came from women's seclusion time — woman's mysterious dark hidden womb and great mother's womb-tomb earth and cave. New moon is renewal; the emerging from dark seclusion into dawn light, women bringing back light; new beginnings. The parade for Inanna's monthly celebrations was her New Moon festival. Moon, and later the planet known to us as Venus and to the Sumerians as Ninsianna, disappeared and reappeared. When the moon and planet are invisible, the goddess is in menstrual seclusion. Women in seclusion are taboo, sacred, and "no man may touch." (See Knight and Grahn)

The sacrosanct women's quarters underwent changes in patriarchal time. Men took control over them; the quarters became harems housing the numerous women in a household but owned by a man. Harem's word root is "sacred" and holy.[48] Harem did not originally mean many wives. The Ancient Near East held to one wife unless a woman was

---

[48] harem, gynaeceum, house quarters only for women; from Arabic *harim* meaning sacred, forbidden; from *harama*, he (is) prohibited

barren and then a second wife was added. Harem was first the women's quarters for the women in a household.

Before patriarchy, millennia of goddess's new moon ritual acknowledged sexual attraction. Her entourage includes sex initiation priestesses. Sex is a powerful natural behavior of humans. Sexual attraction can be more than lust. Inanna's sexuality implies mutual caring and deeply shared pleasure; the participants are each other's beloved. It is woman who guides man from lust to love. Love is the drawing together of two people and celebrated with intimacy. Matristic sex is neither forced nor an on-demand privilege. When goddess reigns and women are honored, sexuality is an expressive art. When women have a protective deity to watch over them, their voices can rise in complaint.

Once upon a time, men honored women. Because of the solidarity of the women, men heard their NO! When that solidarity was broken, "women lost the right to sexual freedom, which we have not fully regained to this day (French 2002: 115)."

Inanna is the mother goddess renewed in her young form and ready to receive her consort, her beloved, Dumuzi. The success of their union brings forth new crops, spring herd animals, long life, prosperity and success for the king and the realm. He is the good shepherd leading and protecting his flock. One of Inanna's long standing ME is rulership/kingship. Her sacred "marriage rite" is performed once a year to encourage fertility in vegetation, human and animal reproduction, and grant the king's right to sit her throne as Dumuzi's proxy, as her beloved. Kings begin to self-proclaim deification by way of sex with the goddess. Later, rulership and kingly divinity is conferred by gods or self-proclamation without the *hieros gamos*. The sons of the rulers inherit the assumed human divinity as long as their dynasties lasted.

After sex on *her* sacred bed, the king's prowess is extolled; he is potent so her potential fertility can manifest. I imagine in times well-past everyone of age would have celebrated the potential fertility of the coming year, the celebration of the new cycle, with sexual expression. Think of our own New Year's Eve celebration: inebriation, noise, and sex. Noise is traditionally used to get divine attention. In contemporary times, the old year dies, the wheel turns, a new cycle begins, and baby New Year arrives. Sex encourages a new cycle; copulation assures fertility in the land. The sacred "marriage" over time became the metaphor for the young goddess and youthful vegetation god Dumuzi not only having sex, but *enjoying* having sex as a culmination of their mutual desire and courtship; they climax in joyous sacred cosmic orgasm. Inanna represents the two major human appetites: sex and food. She is the storehouse for the food that grew because of her fertile sexuality. Her pictographs and epithets support her importance as fertile goddess of the storehouse and all the goods it holds.

Women included gods once men's role in fertility was understood. This occurred long before watching domesticated herd animals copulate, as is the long-taught standard assumption. Sex leading to pregnancy is so obvious a connection that womankind must have known deep back in time. Great mother births life and edibles, sexually active women birth babies, male birds feather females after a courting ritual and eggs hatch; animal females birth their young following rutting season. The earliest central and important role of woman, both human and sacred, is new life from her womb. Caves and caverns are the womb of Great Mother earth. Full moon mother resembles round pregnant bellies. The cave wall paintings support this. Stick men with erect phalluses dance on cave walls. Women's forms are drawn life-like. Animal males mount females and not necessarily the same species. Figurines are found in Old Europe both of youthful males in arousal and old sorrowful flaccid males. The importance of the great mother, sacred woman, is obvious by the far greater ratio of female to male figurines. The cave art has been assumed to be male-orientated around the hunt. Gimbutas concludes from her work in Old Europe, that when the found female figures greatly outnumber the few male figurines, the obvious is seen — women and new life are the important story.

Marilyn French discusses early complex matristic great goddess societies. Each of them represents a lengthy time of no weapons, little differences in social position, beautiful art, many images of a Great Mother, and peace spanning millennia: Catal Huyuk in Anatolia

(1000-4000 continuous peaceable years depending on the source!), settlement ruins in Old Europe along the Aegean and Adriatic coasts, in Czechoslovakia, southern Poland, western Ukraine, Thrace, Harappa and Mohenjo-daro in India, and Crete (French 2002: 45-50).

SEX AND THE GODDESS

The following texts will follow Inanna from her natural burgeoning delight in her miraculous vulva, her natural allure, her beloved consort, to Y-men using her to sit on her throne as king. Her statue or, more likely, a priestess or the queen, is her proxy for fulfilling the ancient rite of female participation. Virility of the leader is crucial. When male rule becomes absolute, men claim divinity by having sex with Inanna. Next, they dismiss her involvement in their rulership. Poems praise the king's performance; failure to please the goddess/priestess is not in the poems. In theory, if the king is not sexually potent with Inanna's priestess proxy, he cannot sit on the throne. He is replaced. Literature has a fascination with the killing off of an old king by his sons or other contenders. More ghoulish yet, some kings are said to be cannibalized. There is no evidence of Sumerian king-murder for non-performance in the Ancient Near Eastern anthologies. Kings are captured and killed, but by outside invaders.

By the last millennium B.C.E., Inanna/Ishtar and other equivalent goddesses no longer participate in the *hieros gamos*; the sacred marriage rite. Men take rulership by stating god so-and-so selects them. Priests elevate the gods who elevate the kings, who, in turn, take good care of the priests. Inanna, the supreme feminine principle, mother goddess, origin of humanity's oldest story; queen of earth, heaven, and all life; sexuality, food, and the civilizing attributes, is displaced and made ridiculous, petulant and fickle. She is limited to goddess of sex, taverns, prostitutes and war. Gods take over her powers via boss-pleasing scribes. Inanna/Ishtar is man-made into a dirty-ditty about her servicing all the lads down by the city wall without tiring ("She Never Tires", see below). She is a fickle spoiler of men's plans and a petulant over-sexed adolescent in need of male control. She is blamed for causing war. Her worship is warship.

Long ago, sex was sacred. Sex was also recognized as a powerful natural hunger that required guidance. Glimpses of this understanding are found in the bridal songs of Inanna's temple and women's quarters. Sex is also sung about explicitly in the texts for the rulers who become Inanna's beloved.

In the land of Sumer, women use sexual allure to tame men just as Inanna does in her love songs. Goddesses say NO! to lusty gods out for a good time but YES! when the gods proceed with commitment. The "bridal/love songs" also prepare a young woman for consummating her own *hieros gamos*. Marital sex. Bridal songs are the Sumerian version of *The Joy of Sex* manual. Ancient brides expect pleasure, mutual pleasure. They know sex should be joyous. One wonders if the young men had any such instruction. Youths may have been educated by the priestesses specializing in sexual initiation, just as Enkidu was initiated into humane-ity by a special harlot of Inanna's temple. Sleuthing through accumulating translations, we find Inanna in her pubescent stage delighting in her growing breasts and pubic hair. She sings songs about her marvelous vulva. Examples of bridal songs follow. The willing bride goes dancing to the lap of her bridegroom. (Alster 1985: 152, cited in Leick 1994: 90:)

'O Bau (Inanna), let us rejoice over my vulva!
Let us dance, let us dance,
(until) the end it will please him, it will please him!'

Inanna is aware of her wonderful vulva, and it is amazing!

Woman's vulva, as pubic triangle, is celebrated in archaic cave art. A Neanderthal cave burial in Spain revealed a skeleton arranged in a side fetal position with an intentional rock stack "altar" beside the remains. The top rock is a definite triangle. The Great Mother rebirthing idea was apparently also known to Neanderthal people. Triangle is one of humanity's first and most enduring symbols; it stands for the shape of woman's pubic hair, and by inference, her vulva, her vaginal mouth, the gateway for new life. The triangle indicates creation, birth, and renewal. The shape found in the Neanderthal burial is the same as Paleolithic humans used to express return of the deceased to the womb of Great Earth Mother. The chthonic goddess cares for the dead; they rest safely with her while awaiting rebirth. The enduring awareness of a big mother is old, long old, archaic, natural, and universal. Why else would triangles, red pigment, and earth-tomb-womb symbols be used globally?

Next, we hear Inanna praise her vulva. A temple performer sings: "She sang a song of her vulva." Inanna refers to her vulva as a heavenly crescent moon boat. Her vulva is "a fallow plot in the desert" and her pubic hairs are sparse like ducks (dark ducks picking through the stubble of the fallow field). She is ready for her groom, the shepherd, the wild bull. She is aroused, wet; her vulva is like a "well-watered hilly land." She sings (Alster 1993: 21, 24, cited in Leick 1994: 90:)

'For me, open my vulva — for me!
For me, the maiden, who is its ploughman?
My vulva, a wet place, for me — for me, the lady, who will provide the bull?'

(The audience tells her that the king will plough it for her and Inanna answers with her command to the king:)

'Plough my vulva, man of my heart.'

The "plough" is the penis, the "bull" is the man behind the plough, and the "fallow field" awaiting the plow is not just a vagina, but the young woman's first vaginal penetration. Whatever sexual experimentation occurs before marriage in Sumer, it does not include penetration (Leick 1994: 91).

The Ancient Near East presented Inanna/Ishtar both in costume with her emblems of power, and nude with an exaggerated triangle to show her fertility. All archaic figurines of Great Mother have an over-sized pubis. Songs describe her wet vulva (arousal) and her pubic hair. Hairiness in the Ancient Near East indicates strength. Divine hair is synonymous with grasses and pubic hair is "lettuce" along moist ditches. Loosened head hair entices with allure. A courtship song describes Inanna's pubic hair arranged in "stag horns." When a hero or king's beard is luxurious and dark as lapis lazuli, he is strong, potent, and virile.

The early Sumerian cuneiform ideogram for "woman" is based on the pubic triangle. "Woman" and "vulva" signs are intertwined. A Sumerian womanizer "chases vulvas," and Inanna is called "vulva, the daughter-in-law (Alster 1975: 98, cited by Leick 1994: 92)."

Seduction poems and eroticism are (Leick 1994: 129:)

... elevated to an art form, a divine and civilized mode of behavior. In the bridal songs, only the female erotic experience counts. It is Inanna's and, through her, woman's general prerogative to demand 'the sweetening of the lap' and at the same time to be responsible for its procurement. The male voice, when quoted at all, speaks lines of intimate and sensual understanding, in respond to the woman's emotion.

Leick admits that this may not have been reality in practice; but that the song/poem form exists for so long indicates a promoted ideology of pleasure for both partners. Sex was once known as "sacred pleasure." I would suggest that Sumerian sex was expected to be mutually pleasurable. Sex as once practiced in Sumer, in time, would be controlled by men. The Sumerian bridal songs and love literature do not yet evidence the future attitudes about sex. Men's encroaching fulminating patriarchy has not yet wrested sex from matristic sensibilities and changed it to sex-on-demand for men; pleasure to be experienced only by men during incompetent one-sided couplings; sex for procreation purposes only and without pleasure for the woman; sex deemed ungodly; sex as something condemned and vile.

We return to Sumer's age of high culture and sensibility. Inanna is of age, the growing season approaches and it is time for sexual consummation to bring fertility back to the land. A bed covering of linen over fresh straw is prepared. The bed and floor are sprinkled with cypress oil which is both a fragrant invitation for the mother goddess to bless the bed and a nod to the goddess' sacred tree emblem. The two deities as their figurines or the priestess proxy and ruler, are bathed for purification. Their hair is washed and wigs arranged. Wigs are in vogue for grand appearance and useful hygienically as head lice are known. The beard is combed. The deities (or priestess and ruler) are richly ritually costumed.

The New Year is celebrated at the end of the growing season in preparation for the next season. Harvest gifts or assessed tribute are brought to Inanna, to her storehouse. The products indicate harvest, completion of a cycle. More offerings from farming and herding come after the consummation. Dairy products and new life come at the beginning of a new cycle; fertility and conception begins at the close of the old.

One text inserts Utu, sun god, into a big brother role with Inanna (Sefati 1998:129). Utu is gaining importance with rising patriarchy. The sun is male long after Inanna-Nammu-Ningal-Ereshkigal is/are already old. Moon is woman. She is also the beneficial celestial body for hot climes. She cools the heat of the day and draws dew up from the ground for parched plants. In all cultures, moon obviously begins as female; the woman in the moon. In contrast, sun in northern climates is the heroine. Inuit culture has a "woman in the sun," the German language indicates sun as feminine in gender, and Japan has a sun goddess. In hot arid climates sun is destructive, it dries the land. Patriarchy claims the sun as male. Consider: war is destructive like the sun in arid lands and fighting takes place by day. Sun became synonymous with logical consciousness and linear thinking. Sun is predictable and reliable; up in the morning and gone by evening every day of the year. Sun is less complex than moon's phases, cycles, and synchronized rhythm with women.

In Sefati's translation, the young goddess is coming of age; she will set the stage for the season to follow. The flax is beautiful and ready to be woven into linen to cover Inanna's bed. Utu is the sun god and said to be Inanna's brother. He choses a husband for her. The eldest brother became important as patriarchy took over; it is he who oversaw finding husbands for his sisters, perhaps because his friends were close in age to his sisters and he knew the prospective groom's qualities and their families. Before men took over the fertility story, Sumerian poems have Inanna making the selection herself and the groom-to-be bringing her mother, Ningal, gifts to seal the deal.

Inanna is sexually mature and ready for a partner. She needs a linen bed sheet. Her brother the sun god says the flax plants are growing, he will hoe it, and bring it to her cut. Inanna wonders who will beat it for her, her brother assures her he will. "Who will spin it for me?" Utu replies he will bring it spun. She asks, "who will twine it for me?" Utu will bring it twined. "Who will warp it for me?" He will bring it warped. "Who will weave it for me?" Utu will bring it woven. "Who will bleach it for me?" He will bring it bleached. Each step of growing to weaving is taken care of for her. She neither prepares the flax nor weaves the linen herself. That is not her function. She is all potential fertility for the following new season — for farmer, herder, and humanity. The emphasis here is agricultural, i.e., it takes place before Semitic herders arrive in large number. Here, Dumuzi is agricultural; his "shepherd" title is mentioned but the emphasis is farming.

The sheet is ready. Inanna asks who will lie down on it with her? "With you your bridegroom will lie down, Amaushumgalanna (Dumuzi) will lie down with you." And Inanna replies: "He is in truth the man of my heart! He is the man of my heart (Sefati 1998: 129)!"

Sumerian Dumuzi appears on early king lists and so is likely once a historical king who is combined with Damu/Danu, an early date god and son of Great Mother. Dumuzi means "the good son." The importance of dates is archaic. Dates are wild fruit from the Paleolithic gathering time. The original date god is son of the mother goddess; he neither consorts with the goddess nor dies at season's end as dates are available all year. Dumuzi, the vegetation god of farming and herding, *does* die with the harvest season and returns to grow anew. Dumuzi is Neolithic while his prototype Damu/Danu is late Paleolithic. The date blossom resembles a penis tip emerging from the foreskin. The blossom is the son. The date palm tree is the mother. Trees belong to the goddess.

Slowly, gathering is supplanted by horticulture. Horticulture expands into agriculture and requires a god catalyst who dies at the end of the growing season and returns to begin the next. By the time of the above text, farming is well underway and Dumuzi is associated with flax and grain and the rise and fall rhythm of agriculture. Herding is not mentioned until the final line. Herding follows farming chronologically and the mention of herding may have been added as an influence from the herding of Sumer's Semitic neighbors and emigrants. Dumuzi of vegetation and herding becomes Inanna's long-time consort. The above text version of Utu, as Inanna's brother, selecting Dumuzi as her husband reflects the rising tide of patriarchy.

Rulers traditionally bring gifts to court Inanna; they have mutually pleasing ritual sex. Hymns and praise songs describe the ancient initiation act in detail. Sexual pleasure is sacred. Rulers please her on *her* sacred bed and sit on *her* throne. When a ruler pleases her, his land is fertile, herd animals plentiful, and the people are safe, peaceable or victorious, and the ruler's life is long. The *hieros gamos* all but disappears in the first millennium B.C.E. when gods select the kings and the kings declare themselves divine.

The early sky god An(u), who becomes a hazy and distant benevolent chief god, has a consort. Sumerian texts remember her as Inanna. She is the link to his ascendancy of divine kingship. Inanna is tutelary goddess of Uruk, and An(u) is *her* consort. Agriculture is vital for urban centers so a date-vegetation-herding god, Dumuzi, becomes her consort. Dumuzi becomes predominantly a shepherd god after herding expands over Sumer. He is the inclusion of maleness as catalyst that manifests new vegetation and spring animals; he dies when vegetation growth ceases, crops are harvested and the season is finished. He goes to the underworld. Women lament him. The goddess mother and bride lament him. Dumuzi returns and the *hieros gamos* occurs again.

The *hieros gamos* partnership of female and male makes a great deal of sense. Mimicry is human expression to help nature provide what humans require for survival. Symbols such as dots for rain and seeds, triangles for woman's creative womb-vulva, rounded pregnant forms of woman for abundance, circles for full moon, breasts for nurturing and rain (rain clouds are also the goddess's breasts letting down water from the sky), spirals, shapes of lunar phasing, stars, and water are mimicked in dance, song, and imagery worldwide. Sex results in new life. Inanna's loins renew life with sex. Copulating with the catalyst of maleness manifests her potential fertility. Without the catalyst the maid remains only potential and renewal of the yearly cycle does not occur. The sacred "marriage" is partnership to help the fertility of nature. A sacred "marriage" to grant leadership is added later. Briffault has this to say about generative sacredness (Briffault 1927, vol. 3: 207:)

> The generative powers of nature have everywhere been the object of worship … the explanation of the sensual and sexual character of religious rites lies in the notion that every function of woman, whether as mother, as wife, as supplier of food, as cultivator of the soil, as sorceress, witch, prophetess, or priestess, postulates her union with the god who is the bestower of those powers.

I agree with the first part of Briffault's statement in that "every function of woman" as a "generative power of nature" explains the sexy sacred marriage. Woman's other powers of motherhood, toiler of the fields, supplier of food, and oracular talents are hers already because she is maternal, intuitive, and has a different way of thinking, feeling, and expressing compared to men. I would suggest a god is "catalyst" and not "bestower" for the sacred cosmic generative act. Briffault's lumping all aspects of women under a god bestowing woman those powers is indicative of the second myth everywhere — men taking control of women's sexual and reproductive bodies, accomplishments and talents. The first myth is women owning their bodies and sexuality and creating culture. The *hieros gamos* is a partnership. Briffault, in spite of his wide-ranging collection of "primitive" people's societies and rituals, misunderstands the early presence and importance of woman and Great Mother. He seeks to explain the nudity and sexual part of ancient religious celebration while squinting through a distorted male lens. As a result he says exactly the opposite of what is basic to the Ancient Near Eastern and other goddess cultures. He is uncomfortable with nudity in religious expression and sex as sacred ritual. (ibid.: 207:)

> [Sex is an] indecency so conspicuous as a feature of all heathen religions [it] has everywhere reference to that union in some form or another, of women and divine beings. The union of men with goddesses plays virtually no part in the sacred marriage with the Divine Bridegroom as a functional necessity. Men do not require to be united with a divine bride in order to fulfill their function. But every religion, from the most primitive to the highest, is pervaded with the idea that union with a god, a 'hieros gamos' or 'Holy Matrimony' is a necessity to every woman … To primitive man the necessaries and good things of life are food and women. He (primitive man) naturally regards the gods as having the same needs of himself; he offers food to them in the form of sacrifice and women in the form of prostitution … it is essentially a necessity because the generative powers of women and their special powers and functions proceed from the gods.

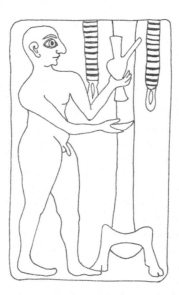

Figure 37. Priest Libating

Briffault cannot see what he is seeing. Sumer *has* human man needing the divine woman Inanna; Kali *is* required for bringing life in India. Nudity ala Briffault is similarly mistreated. Nudity in Ancient Near Eastern art is purity. The nude priest has bathed and purified for the divine female. I know of no seals with nude priestesses serving gods. Many seals show nude, beardless, hairless priests in Inanna's service. Most experts name them Inanna's self-mutilated eunuchs. Examination of seal art images indicate that they appear to be genitally intact though beardless and their bodies have softer rounder forms compared to the hairy hero men. A few experts indicate these are priests purified for divine audience. Inanna and Ishtar are often shown nude, as are their equivalents who take part in the *hieros gamos*. They are not nude to serve a god. Inanna/Ishtar rides nude on lion-dragon's back for victory in conflict. Nudity is showing purity — it is not lascivious, obscene, or witchcraft. Briffault continues from his white male, Christian point of view (ibid.: 207:)

> All religion, not only in its crude and primitive phases, but in its highly developed forms in the great civilizations of India, of Babylon, of Egypt, of Greece is pervaded with conceptions, symbols, and practices which, in our modern European view appear the very reverse of religious and holy ... It is permeated with indecency and sensuality ... (That the Church Fathers decided) 'all heathen religions were impure' is ... not unjustified.

Additionally Briffault claims that the "primitive" mind could not understand the idea, the concept of "the generative powers of nature." The obvious is missed. Long before writing, from gather-hunter Paleolithic times, art supports the keen sense of the ancients, the interaction of nature and cosmic events and the brilliance of metaphor — moon-women-blood-life. The ancients knew the sacredness of life, all life. They practiced stewardship of land and resources (kinship rules); they even knew how to live peacefully with nature and each other. They knew sex was pleasurable and natural. For as long as a great goddess mother was primary, humans were humane.

Imagine an early Neolithic farming couple time-warping into our now and learning something of our history of the last two millennium. We can't offer them a Great Mother, but we can offer: Inquisition, witch hunts, enslavement, colonization, and religion made all-male with a god who only likes males and is located off planet. Our hypothetical couple would learn of religions killing off other religions, religion demonizing sacred woman and destroying any who remember her, women repressed and silenced and war continually ongoing. The beautiful earth they revere is polluted, poisoned and dying. That couple would be overwhelmed, not by technology, but by the prevailing ignorance, the lack of understanding of "the generative powers of nature." That hypothetical couple could teach us a great deal.

"Goddesses —that is, true Great Goddesses have no priest-husband as gods have priestess-wives; for theirs is the primitive matriarchal law of the free woman, and it is inconsistent with their character to recognize the rule of any patriarchal husband (ibid.: 213)." *That* is a good observation Mr. Briffault! But remember, in the late 19th and early 20th centuries, as information was accumulating about matristic cultures and excavations were revealing long ago goddess cultures, patriarchy jumped on the facts as evidence of a matriarchy that they imagined was just like patriarchy but with women on top treating men as men treated women. They used the discoveries as another excuse for why men had to take over. "The primitive matriarchal law of the free woman" is a fearsome idea! Briffault also adds that the goddesses did not need "sexual serving" as he assumes the gods required; and so the priests who serve the goddess are eunuchs. This implies that the goddess had no sexual interest and only emasculated men served the goddess. Not true!

Bridal songs prepare a young woman for marriage. "Her Inanna" gave her "all." The songs tell of purification bathing and carefully arranged hair. I would suggest that the described purification bath and special attention to hair is the long held ritual emergence from menstrual seclusion. Seclusion takes place in the dark of the moon. When moon is a new crescent the bride is bathed and adorned like Inanna. The songs tell us that the young woman hopes her consort is pleased and afterward will bring abundant gifts. A "sister," (a friend, relative, or priestess), assists the bride with her adornments.

Inanna is fertility of everything. A young woman is like Inanna; every young bride mimics Inanna; she enacts the goddess. Inanna is creative fertility. Sumerian and other Ancient Near Eastern men are not considered fully men until they have a wife and household, i.e., womanly influence and responsibility. Inanna is the cosmic sexual conduit to bring maleness, king or ordinary man, into the fullness of his humanity. She soothes his aggressive and self-aggrandizing nature; she elevates his consciousness.

Might this young bride be Inanna herself or one of her priestesses as an Inanna proxy? Sumerian poems often refer to a goddess as "woman," yet I do not recall any god being called "man." Is this a recognition of the divinity of women or a put-down for the goddess by aligning her with human woman? Is this young woman the priestess of "her Inanna" who goes to the sacred marriage bed with the king? If she is the carefully selected priestess to be Inanna, then the question: with whom does the king have sex, has an answer. The king, as bridegroom Dumuzi, brings gifts, generally food or animals, but jewelry is also mentioned. The priestess will receive the gifts for Inanna's temple. Personal gifts given to certain priestesses by the kings are also recorded.

Sex is sacred and bridal songs describe it as mutually and explicitly pleasurable. A love song translated by Sefati, describes a young "bride" or priestess preparing for the sacred marriage event. Someone asks her what she has been doing "in the house." (House, *e*, is also temple.) The bride tells us her breasts are firm and her pubic hair has grown. She has bathed and anointed herself with oil, washed her hair, straightened her locks, dressed in the "royal garments of the queenship of heaven," painted kohl around her eyes, placed lapis lazuli beads at her neck, and put on a gold bracelet. Her consort, "brother" (not familial but closeness of a spouse), tells her he brings her five gifts and says: "Your 'Inanna' gave you all." Is this bride a priestess of Inanna or is every bride like

Inanna? Is Inanna in every woman? The bride is going to the palace where the groom (king/Dumuzi) will come; musicians will greet him; she will pour wine into his mouth. He will bring the gifts: ewes with lambs and goats with kids. The bride exclaims: "Dance! Dance! Baba (Inanna), for my nakedness rejoice (Sefati 1998: 135-7)!"

Deities mirror our culture; we recognize our culture in our myths. Our stories are "peopled" with goddesses and gods in the same roles human storytellers know from their own observations and experience. Divine personalities mirror human behavior. The following selection features Inanna as a young and ripe adolescent. (ibid.:187-8:)

> Inanna's beloved, Dumuzi of several names, is behaving like a lustful adolescent boy — he wants sex but not relationship. Inanna, through her allure, as women have done since love and lust were invented, brings him to responsible relational sexuality; but before he is "tamed", he offers to teach her to lie (for his lusty convenience). He nervily says lies are what women tell.
>
> Inanna is singing songs from "morning till evening". Dumuzi grabs and holds her in an embrace. She says: "Wild bull, set me free, that I may go home!" or she will have to lie to her mother, Ningal, the moon goddess. He offers to teach her to lie. He wants her to tell her mother that she was with a girlfriend in the square, dancing and playing a tambourine and a reed instrument, and that she and the girlfriend were together all day, while she actually lays with him on his couch making love in the moonlight. Inanna refuses his offer of sex on the sly in the moonlight. Her allure is sufficient for the lustily opportunistic Dumuzi to change his ways!
>
> Dumuzi does the proper groom-to-be ritual; he approaches her mother. Inanna runs around happily, she wants a neighbor to sprinkle water (for purification or to settle the dust) and oil. Fragrant oil makes the home sweet; it is also a ritual for important events. Her mother finds Dumuzi acceptable for her "lap." Inanna says: "My lord, how sweet is your abundance! How tasty are your herbs and plants in the plain!" Fertility has come to the land.

All is well with the world. The lovers have created an abundance of new crops. Note that male domination does not yet own the daughter and hold control over permission to marry; here we have matristic permission-granting. The old tradition is that a perspective groom first approaches the mother; if she approves, she is given gifts and the young man comes to live in the bride-to-be's home for several days. The couple has an opportunity to spend time together and discover if they are compatible. This visit may also include sex and possibly test the bride's ability to become pregnant. The poem implies it does include copulation or else it jumps to the consummation of the agreement.

Kramer translates a similar text that includes several more of Dumuzi's epithet names: Kuli-anna and Ushumgal-alla. Again, the text refers to the "deceitfulness" of women, however, again it is the man who wants to teach her to lie! (Kramer 1979: 79:)

> *Inanna tells us that "last night, as I the queen was shining bright, last night, as I the Queen of Heaven was shining bright, was shining bright, was dancing about," she met up with Dumuzi. He takes her hand and embraces her! She calls him "wild bull" and wants out of the embrace so she can go home to mother Ningal (moon goddess). What could she say to her mother? Dumuzi is ready to teach her. He calls her: "Inanna, most deceitful of women." He instructs her to say she was with a girlfriend in the "public square" where her friend made music; they danced; they chanted; they sang; they lost track of time. He wants her to lie so he can be with her in the moonlight indulging in sweet joyous sex. He is not interested in commitment or relationship beyond lust fulfillment. Inanna says NO! Dumuzi decides to do the right thing. He will ask Ningal for Inanna to be his bride. Inanna anticipates the sprinkling of cypress oil and she says: "I, in joy I walk!"*

Another early bridal song translated by Kramer has Ninshubur, "Lady Dawn", vizier of our goddess, bringing the king-proxy for Dumuzi to the holy lap of Inanna. She asks Inanna to give prosperity for the land and long life for the king. "May the Lord whom you called to your heart, the king your beloved husband, enjoy long days at your lap, so sweet." The song tells us the king reigns over land from sunrise to sunset, east to west; from the marsh land, where the huluppu-tree grows, to the mountains where the cedar grows. Ninshubur requests that Inanna's gift of scepter and diadem, of staff and crook, cause the king to be a good shepherd over all the black haired people; may he be a good farmer and grow abundant grain. Ninshubur asks that the king, "as the farmer may he make productive the fields, as the shepherd may he multiply the sheepfolds." Kingship will bring fish and birds to the marshes, honey and wine from the orchards, tall reeds (for building and boats), lettuce and cress along the ditches when the Tigris and Euphrates flood, and plants in the grazing pasture lands (ibid.: 80-1). (ibid.: 81:)

In the palace may there be long life,
In the Tigris and Euphrates may there be floodwater,
On the banks may plants grow high, may they fill the meadows,
May the grain-goddess pile high the grain in heaps and mounds.

The Third Dynasty of Ur composed royal love song literature that was copied and recopied in the scribal school curriculums and preserved in numerous locations. Jacobsen translated a collection of love songs written for the fourth king of the dynasty, Shu-suen, 2037-2029 B.C.E.. A fascinating detail he includes is that these love poems praising the king's attractiveness and virility were most likely written by a woman-poet in the queen's entourage, who composed and then sang her poems. Jacobsen notes further that all love songs, including the bawdy and explicit, belonged to Inanna's cult. In this instance, the queen likely represents Inanna for the New Year sacred marriage ritual; she is associated with Inanna and the goddess's cult.[49]

The following excerpts are explicit, instructive, erotic, and promote the delight of sexuality and desire, physical joy and emotional happiness. One can easily imagine a playful teasing entertainment for the royals,

[49] "cult" shares a root meaning with cultivate and culture; it is something that grows; its use in this book is not the slanderous meaning of Christianity toward earth-based religions

their entourage, and perhaps the public. It is easy to visualize a smiling king marching toward the teasing queen, and the queen "escaping" into the bedroom where she intends to bring him. The queen channels Inanna; she is Inanna; but she is not declared divine while the king is made divine for having sex with her. (Jacobsen:1987: 88-89:)

LOVE SONG TO SHU-SUEN

(A dialog pertaining to Inanna.)

Man of my heart, my beloved one,
O! that to make your charms,
    which are sweetness, are honey,
    still more sweet –

you, my own lord and sergeant at arms
    would march against me!
Man, I would flee from you –
    into the bedroom.
...
O! that you would do,
    all the sweet things to me,
my sweet dear one
    you bring that which will be honey-sweet!

In the bedroom's honey-sweet corner
    let us enjoy over and over
your charms and sweetnesses!
...
O! my lord and good genius,
    my lord and guardian angel,
my Shu-Suen, who does Enlil's
    heart good,

the place where, could you but do

your sweet thing to me,
where, could you but –
    like honey –
    put in your sweetness!

O squeeze it in there for me!
    as (one would) flour into the
    measuring cup!

O pound and pound it in there for me!
    as (one would) flour into the
    old dry measuring cup!

The following text from the same collection of courtly love poems uses the traditional standardized euphemisms: "lettuce" and "wool" for woman's pubic hair. "Wool" is readily apparent; the former, "lettuce", grows near moisture along irrigation ditches. The vaginal cleft is a ditch and moistness is sexual readiness. The *dubdub* bird, not yet identified, here is a sobriquet for "clitoris." When her "wool" is in a "stag" (arrangement), I would guess that she enticingly combs her upper pubic hair into a curled horn arrangement. The terms "sister" and "brother" in intimate situations do not connote incest but rather terms of endearment, closeness, and familiarity. (Jacobsen 1987: 93:)

MY 'WOOL' BEING LETTUCE

(A dialog pertaining to Inanna)

My "wool" being lettuce he will water it,
it being box(-grown) lettuce he will water it
and touch the *dubdub* bird in its hole!

My nurse has worked at me mightily,
has done my "wool" up in a "stag" (arrangement),
has gently combed it,

246

and is straightening my "May He Come!" (breast-shields)

Let him come! Into my "wool", it being
    the most pleasing of lettuces,
I shall with arousing glances
    induce the brother to enter.
I shall make Shu-Suen — all ready —
    show himself like a lusty man,
Shu-Suen, to whom my [allure] be without end!
[Shu-Suen, whose allure to me] will [never] change!

… (text gap, the king's performance was acceptable)

You are truly our lord! You are truly our lord!
Silver wrought with lapis lazuli! You are truly our lord!
You are truly our farmer bringing in much grain!

He being the apple of my eye, being the lure of my heart,
    may days of life dawn for him! May Shu-Suen [live long years!]

All of the above bridal songs are explicit about technique and love. Were the singers young women about to be wed or the special priestess selected as Inanna's surrogate for the sacred marriage? Sargon the Great is speculated to be a child of such a priestess. The story goes that his mother, a priestess of Ishtar, to protect her baby, since her class of priestess was to be celibate but for a *hieros gamos*, set him off in a little basket among the reeds. He was found, raised by a foster family, became a young cupbearer for a king, grew up, and when either he displaced the king or he was defeated, Sargon became king. He unified northern and southern Sumer. The special priestesses for the ritual were not to have children; any child born of the *hieros gamos* could not live since a son born of the event would confuse the king's lineage of heirs. The story of his foundling beginning could be at least partially true — Sargon was a strong devotee of Inanna/Ishtar all of his life.

Both explicit bridal songs and the open awareness of temple harlots who use sex to initiate men into humanity belong to Inanna's cult.

QUESTION: WHEN IS A PROSTITUTE
NOT A PROSTITUTE?
ANSWER: WHEN SHE IS SACRED.

Inanna is goddess of fertility; sex/love is her domain. Sacred harlots serve in Inanna's temple. There is wide speculation about their official duties. Were they surrogate consorts for the gods associated with Inanna as Enheduanna was *en*-priestess for moon god Suen/Nanna/Sin? Are some of them celibate? Do they initiate young men into civilized (sexual) behavior as a temple "harlot" tamed the wild Enkidu and initiated him from his innocent animal-self (a good quality in the epic of Gilgamesh) into "civilized" urban culture? (See chapter 4.) Do they instruct young women and men before marriage in sexuality and love? Did they take the war out of men returning from bloody wars? Were they a source of income for the temple? Were they women consecrated to the temple by avocation or circumstance? The answer is likely yes to all of the above questions.

The hierodules, sacred prostitutes, through their rituals, assure "fruitfulness by which the fertilizing powers of the world are invited to fecundate the female principle of nature" (ibid.: 213). Hierodules are of the elite families; they are educated and talented. Courtesans develop from hierodules. A college of hierodules was founded in the temple of Artemis at Ephesus (the temple was later reconsecrated to Virgin Mary). European abbeys were colleges. Abbey also came to mean brothel and some were attached to religious buildings.

The following historical facts give new meaning to "sacred prostitute." A medieval Queen Johanna of Naples married a Hungarian royal with a very large nose who proved useless in bed. She had him murdered. Naples sent her away and she came to Avignon in 1343 C.E., the home base of one of the two dueling popes, Clement VI. She contacted the independent ladies of the night, organized them into a protective union signified by a little red braid worn on their shoulder, and proceeded to set up an elegant brothel. Hand-picked beauties worked under Johanna's house rules: she was after all a Catholic so no birth control or abortions were allowed. Every saturday the women were examined for sexually transmitted disease, and were quarantined if found infectious. The royal madam confined the sex workers who fell pregnant and cared for any offspring. The glittery establishment flourished. After a year or so pope Clement VI made her an offer for the "abbey." She accepted. He paid well for her business and threw in a pardon for her murder of the non-performing Hungarian husband as well. The pope continued to call the brothel the Abbey. Only "good Christian" men were admitted and it was closed on Good Friday and Easter day (Leon 1997: 88-9).

The second pope, Julius II, signed a papal bull so a brothel like Clement VI's Abbey could be set up in Rome near the vatican. Popes Leo X and Clement VII continued the two brothels. Some of the Roman establishment's profit was "devoted to providing for the comfort of the Holy sisters of the Order of Saint Mary Magdalene (Briffault 1927, vol. 3: 216)."

Back in the Ancient Near East, one source told of men returning from war and first going to a special temple near the city gates where the soldiers were bathed, groomed, soothed, fed and likely possibly had priestess-directed sex to tame them from war's blood lust and horrors so they could return to normal life. Knight describes a similar behavior in Paleolithic cultures. Men returning from hunts had to purify — wash away the blood before rejoining the community. Ancient Near Eastern wild war-men were brought back to civilized men through ministrations of the specialized priestesses.

Not every woman/mother who was left alone, widowed (especially by war), and without family protection could go into temple employment or protection. Urban reorganization offered few other options for displaced women than remarriage, voluntary servitude, temple staffing, or prostitution. The temple could not take them all into shelter.

Fees or barter generated by the special sex-worker priestesses helped support the ever grander temples, personnel, temple repairs, and assorted widows and children needing protection and shelter. The contemporary version of "prostitute" is not the same as the sexual priestesses of Inanna's cult. Inanna's are sacred. Sex and pleasure are sacred.

Figure 38. Tavern Scene

Clever and beautiful women learn to be courtesans in many cultures. They associate with men as intelligent, artistic, accomplished companions and sexual equals; these women live well and are admired. "Courtesan" is a word used in some translations to describe some of the priestesses of Inanna. Women without cleverness, beauty, and opportunity avail themselves in the taverns. The least fortunate of desperate women take up positions at the city walls and streets and riskily service men's lust. No matter where women are sexual, in the matrimonial bed,[50] tavern, city wall, temple, or spectacular priestess proxy enacting Inanna with kings, Inanna is there. The following poem describes available sex from a tavern's tapsteress and is labeled: "a dialog pertaining to Inanna." The dialog is between a drunken amorous guest and the tapsteress or, more likely, a serving girl. (Jacobsen 1987: 97-8:)

---

[50] matrimony should mean, or once meant "inherited from the mother" since patrimony is defined: "inherited from the father's line"

TAVERN SKETCH

(amorous drunk):

"O my lushest one! My lushest one!
    my lushest one!
My most alluring one! [My] most alluring one!
    Mother's little honeybun!
    The glance from your eyes is sweet to me,
    quickly say yes, my beloved sister!
The chitchat of your mouth is sweet to me,
    quickly say yes, my beloved sister!
…

"My lady! The beer from your grain does one good,
    mother's little honeybun,
the strength and glow from your wort [51]
does one good,
    quickly say yes, my beloved sister!
In the house, desire for you soon [began to consume me]
    mother's little honeybun,
…

Your house [is] an honest house, [may it] prosper,
    mother's little honeybun,
You [are] a (very) princess – quickly say yes,
    my beloved sister!"

(the tapsteress replies:)

"You must swear to me that you live,
    that you live –
Brother, you must swear to me,
    that it is just that you live in an outlaying town.

---

[51] plants fermented to make beer

You must swear to me that no enemy
    has put hand in them,[52]
you must swear to me that no enemy
    has brought the mouth near to it!
My [letting down] for you
    the thin, exquisite gown,
O my beloved one, man [I am captured by,]
[will] set the (manner of) oath [for you,]

...

Your right hand be placed
    in my private parts,
your left shall support my head,
and when you have neared
    your mouth to my mouth,
when you hold my lip in your teeth,
(then), thus you must swear me the oath!
Just so, o you, one (and only one) to (all) women,
my brother so fair of face!

"O my budding one, my budding one,
    sweet are your charms!
My budding garden of the apple tree,
    sweet are your charms!
My fruiting garden of the apple tree,
    sweet are your charms!
Dumuzi-Apsu himself,
    sweet are your charms!
O my pure pillar, my pure pillar
    sweet are your charms!
Pillar of alabaster set in lapis lazuli
    sweet are your charms!"

---

[52] one swears an oath by touching the genitals (Genesis 24:8-9); here it is a ploy for teasing and touching genitals

Inanna is identified with the taverns. Sumerians have several epic compositions that bring separate stories together about heroes: Enmerker, Lugalbanda, and Gilgamesh. The following segment included here is a description of Inanna in an invocation. Hero, Lugalbanda, deserted by his friends, is alone and sick in a cave. He prays to Inanna and includes her tavern association. (Kramer, 1979: 74:)

To the harlot who in the tavern makes slumber sweet,
To her who provides food for the poor,
To Inanna, the daughter of Sin (Suen the moon god),
Who like a bull lifts her head in the land,

...

Inanna helps him, he gets well and returns to his comrades with superhuman powers.

A composition in Foster's anthology, entitled "Your Heartbeat is My Reveille," tells us that Ishtar is explicit about assertively demanding sex in the morning. She awakens her partner: "I want to make love with you!" She describes the sleeping area as scented with fennel and aromatic oil. She wants his sweet caress, she praises his charms. She flaunts her loosened hair, her beautiful ear lobes, the shape of her shoulders, and the "opulence" of her breasts. She wants him to touch her "sweet spot" and her breasts. Finally she orders: "[O come inside], I have opened my thighs (Foster 2005:169)." The remainder of the tablet is fragmented but there isn't much more to be said! Is this a bridal song instructing young girls or a celebration of Ishtar's lust?

The poem, "Nanay and Muati", from the Classical period of Ancient Near Eastern literature (1711-1684 B.C.E.), uses a Babylonian name-equivalent for Ishtar/Inanna. Nanay here is goddess of love and evening star. Sexuality is of course involved. A little known god is brought to "live" with her in her temple as a new statue. She initiates the god through lovemaking. The story goes that Nanay fondly looks on Babylon with her loving eyes. She blesses the city and gives the king vigor, life. Her allure will "rain down like dew" upon the newly arrived god Muati. Muati thirsts for her! She orders the god to inspect her charms and be aroused; she says: "Let me have what I want of your delights!" He acknowledges that he is entrusted to her and asks that they make love so he will "always stay brilliant (Foster 2005: 160-1)."[53]

Inanna is referred to as a "harlot", and by word association in our cultural indoctrination where sex is problematic, harlots have sex outside the bounds of marriage and are bad women, though men with the same behavior receive winks and act with impunity. Harlot, in Inanna's reign, has to do with holy sacred pleasure. Women knowledgeable in the initiatory art are *sacred* prostitutes, holy harlots, that is, priestesses in Inanna/Ishtar's service and not whores or prostitutes as the contemporary names popularly imply. Over time, sex lost its deep meaning, its sacredness, its natural mutual pleasures.

Institutionalized non-sacred prostitution serves men's lust. Desperate women, widows and orphans of the near-constant warfare, without support and protection, become the women along the city walls who risk bad treatment for meager exchange and marginal survival. Sex availability at will is convenient for men. Sex on demand and not earned through proper behavior, courtship, and mutual pleasure continues as our culture's dictum.

Early and long, solidarity of women evolved culture and cooperation of men. Women said NO! together. All that changes when women are taken from their matristic families. Their solidarity is broken; they are placed in their father-in-law's patriarchal home without clout or voice. Then, when "wives" say NO!, servants, slave girls, and prostitutes are available, coerced, or forced. Those women, outside both marriage and temple, found around taverns and city walls, are unfortunate outcasts. Inanna, who loves all her "black haired people", is their champion. She loves them, even especially loves them, since they are without protection. She is the only deity who cares for the displaced destitute women. She represents courtesans, the initiator priestesses, her holy priestesses (only

---

[53] Foster citing W. G. Lambert. 1966. Mitteilungen des Instituts fur Orientforschung. Berlin. pp. 41-51

some of whom were involved with sex), and desperate women selling themselves. There is not space in the temple for all the women who are without protection and support; she loves them wherever they try to stay alive.

Compassion, caring, and love come first from our mother. When men later write of Inanna, they refer to her only as fickle and goddess of taverns and prostitutes; they miss the most important story! She is all the powers of early women; she cares for everyone (even captives!), and protects all women. She is sex. Pleasurable, relational, delightful, joyous sex. She is also sex for high purpose: fertility in the land.

NANAY AND RIM-SIN

This is the story of an annual spring rite when Inanna/Ishtar/ Nanay meets the king in her bedchamber. The goddess accepts that he cannot give her what she wants most, love; instead she accepts trust and provisions but longs for more. "The motif of the goddess harboring greater feeling than her subject is found elsewhere … and the unequal feeling between woman and man was the usual pattern in love poetry" by the second millennium (Foster 2005: 162). Rim-Sin lived c. 1822-1763 B.C.E.. In summary, the story goes as follows (ibid.: 162-4:)

> *Nanay (Inanna) complains that her bed partner has won her heart with "love play". The temple singers warn her that she is too much in love; she should neither rely on him nor trust him. The goddess says she receives acknowledgement, status, and a "good name" but not love. The singers reply that the spring they have longed for and prayed for is here. The goddess will grant bliss to king Rim-Sin for the year. Nanay/Inanna, regardless of the one-sidedness in the matter of Rim-Sin's affections, goes ahead and invites the king to embrace her, to make joyful love all night. She says: "Stir together over me desire and passion, feed yourself on what you need to live, heat up your lust on me (ibid.: 164) !"*

Unlike earlier texts, we witness here the goddess receiving status from the king and being used in the *hieros gamos* without adoration and love. She loves him regardless. If she wins him over with her passion and allure, how long will he remember her? We find Dumuzi behaving with the same forgetfulness of love in Inanna's descent to the underworld. Patriarchy is rewriting Inanna's role. Our once great goddess is but a necessary one-night stand for Rim-Sin to gain a year of rulership.

LOVE CHARMS AND SPELLS

The Ancient Near East believes in love charms and spells. It is a belief that flows through time into the present in many cultures. The composition, "Horns of Gold," describes a love charm resembling a bull, the goddess's bull of heaven. The bull's crescent moon horns belong originally to the moon goddess. A lunar symbol is placed into Ishtar's heart. She is lunar. The charm has archaic roots. (Foster 2005: 199:)

Love charm, love charm!
His horns are of gold his tail is of pure lapis,
It is placed in Ishtar's heart.
…

The spell is for a man who wants a woman who is in love with someone else and wishes the competitor to fall away so the spell-speaker can have her. Incantation is found only with Ishtar's name and not with Inanna. Researchers suggest that incantation magic was not used in Sumer.

The following summarized poem, "Look at Me!," is a charm for a wife to secure a husband's attention. A frustrated wife describes her hunger, like a dog salivating. She describes hitting the negligent husband on the head and driving him crazy. The spell she speaks will set his thoughts to her thoughts and his reason to hers. The spell is to hold him close as Ishtar holds Dumuzi and alcohol holds close the one who drinks. She will bind him with her hairy "mouth," her wet vagina, her moist mouth. The charm ends with (Foster 2005: 201:)

"May no rival come to you!
"Dog is crouching, pig is crouching,
"You too keep crouching on my thighs!"

The unequal concern for continued love after sex also appears in Jacobsen's translated story of Inanna's descent into the underworld in chapter 11. Because of patriarchal nonchalance in the ways of love, we hear Dumuzi, whom she lovingly placed as her beloved on her throne to rule, is condemned to death because he does not love her anymore. Inanna's vizier, Ninshubur, and Inanna's sons, Shara and Lulal, dress in sack cloth, rent their clothes, and loudly lament, expressing grief when she does not reappear from the underworld; they gush joyously when she returns. Dumuzi knows her situation yet does not grieve. He sits on *her* throne of office in fine robes, conducting business as usual; he acts as if he does not care whether she is dead or alive. Her heart is broken. She is hurt and angrily gives him over to the rangers as her death substitute. Dumuzi is a vegetation demigod and dies annually. It is his role to die but the story revision puts blame on Inanna; she is portrayed as petulant and fickle; she punishes him just because he doesn't love her anymore, doesn't pay her any attention, and loves her throne-granting power, and not her.

SHE NEVER TIRES

The following song for Ishtar, as great prostitute, is included because it is puzzling. Is it a ribald joke at the goddess' expense? Is it a delightful way of saying the goddess's sexuality is always present, never tiring? Is it a poem about prostitution and that all the prostitutes at the city wall are Ishtar? Is it a teenage boy's raging hormonal sexual fantasy? Did the composer of the ditty think it would please the goddess? Was she pleased, amused, or offended?

257

Ancient Mesopotamia is not prudish about sex and erotica. Sexual drive is natural, pleasurable, and through initiation (woman's love), men's lust can be managed and converted to love. This version of the goddess more than matches the young men's virility/lust. Is this about goddess inciting their sexual drive? Is this about temple prostitutes who initiate young men into becoming good sexual partners? Is this about women sex workers outside the temple and outside society; the destitute ones at the city wall? Another possibility here is that Ishtar, through her prostitutes, takes on the wild boys and men and protects the maidens of the city. I invite the reader to decide.

The goddess is approached, asked, agrees, and takes on all the lads at the city wall. In the final line, she is "the girl" who demands and they "gave her what she asked for." The translation unfortunately echoes men into the present defending themselves for forcing sex on a woman: "She asked for it. It's not my fault. I gave her what she wanted."

The text is about Nippur, a late religious center of Sumer, c. 1000-100 B.C.E., where no recruitment for corvee work is allowed. It has a reputation for "pleasure". After each spoken line the same refrain is chanted: "The city's built on pleasure!" After broken lines, we find Ishtar inviting the young men, "Come here, give me what I want." Boldly they come up and touch her vulva. She promises to also give them all that they want; they are to gather up the young men of Nippur and meet her in the shade of the city wall. Seven are at her loins, her belly; sixty and then sixty more have sex with her nude body, her willing vulva. The young men are tired but Ishtar is ready for more! (Foster 2005: 678:)

"Put it to my lovely vulva, fellows!"   (refrain)
As the girl demanded,   (refrain)
The young men heeded, gave her what she asked for.   (refrain)

[It is a hymn of praise to Ishtar]

CHAPTER 7

Her Ways are Unfathomable

At the start of research for this book I sought the goddess's attributes of kindness, compassion, mercy, love — all that my culture has put forward as desirable femininity. I found much more! As I read stanzas of Inanna's bloodthirsty tendencies, I protectively thought this is just more patriarchal blaming and slander of the feminine. Text after text showed the consistency of Inanna's full capacity for everything and every behavior! Then came the realization; I named goddess "Life" from the beginning of the book. Life is *all* nature, not just egocentric human nature. Nature is unpredictable and uncontrollable. Women create life, earth creates life. Maleness has long linked women and nature. Men can not control nature but in solidarity they can control women. From archaic times woman's cycles and reproductive body are powerful; she is the template for creating culture and story. Men fear unpredictable nature. Blame and control are their solutions. Inanna represents human nature, natural phenomena, and the cosmos.

As natural phenomena and the elemental chthonic, she is unpredictable and impossible to control! The goddess is the weather between the celestial dome and earth — rain, gentle or storming — and the rainbow, worn as her necklace, at storm's end. Inanna is the river and sea tides, the floods, and stormy waters. She is said to raise or calm the water at will. As celestial woman she is evening star/morning star, Ninsianna (Venus). The planet is close to the earth and so appears to have erratic movements — now here, now there, now nowhere to be seen. Venus also cycles through visible light phases like the moon: crescent and full Ninsianna. The behavior of her moving star enhances Inanna's erratic unfathomable persona. She crosses over and near mythic constellations. Inanna is not seated on her throne, sedentary, and reliably the same. She is the only deity of the Ancient Near East who journeys from heaven to earth whenever she pleases. She is the only one for thousands of years who can visit the underworld and return. It is her right. The third aspect of Great Mother is the death mother, Ereshkigal. The goddess of the underworld is called Inanna's "sister." She is assigned to the underworld and eventually stolen by the underworld, never to rise from it according to the male vision of the underworld. Once upon a time the underworld was simply the womb of the great mother holding new cycles in her pregnant womb. Great Mother, Inanna, and Ereshkigal are one as a triad.

MENSTRUAL POWERS

Inanna is women glorified. Her new moon festival celebrates emergence from dark moon seclusion. Light returns. She also celebrates women's blood power of fertility. Women cycle with the changing moon. We now know that women have synchronized waves of hormones that change every day of the month. Hormonal change affect women's moods. Nowhere has Inanna been officially named Queen of Menstruation, so I give her that title. Inanna's ways are unfathomable to men, but not to women. Nature and women are unfathomable mysteries for men. Read that as: beyond their control.

Woman is the symbol for life continuing, renewing, and nurturing. She is the only possible model for the Big I-dea expressed globally. Life is a Great Mother, a Divine Woman, the Sacred Feminine, who looks like woman and cycles like woman. Inanna is cyclic and undying. All aspects of water, weather, renewal, earth and moon once came under woman's menstrual powers. The Big I-dea grew larger and so did woman's powerful association with all aspects of life. Earth and celestial bodies alike were once believed to be influenced by menstruation, pregnancy, and birth. Woman cast her own image out onto the land and into the heavens; she explained life. With our first story — rituals around menstruation — woman created culture and modified men into cooperative humans. Our species survived.

Women are mysterious (to men). We bleed together in lock-step with moon phasing. Our bodies grow new life. New life enters this world through our great muscular uterine contractions and pushing accompanied by thunderous vocalization. A wave of salt water washes the belly-built babe ashore. Our new one is tethered to us by our vaginal snake. At infant's cry, our full breasts let down watery milk like rain from the clouds. Woman tends and defends her new life.

Inanna is the young menstruant whose first menses is most powerful. Every new moon she is first menstruant emerging fresh and renewed and celebrated. Imagine the pride of her people's daughters celebrating with her! Traditional people treat that girl with awe. She is in seclusion because she is powerful; she is tended only by women; she is special. She is potential fertility. She is a little goddess. She becomes a woman, with woman's potent blood powers. Chris Knight, in *Blood Relations,* fully explores how women and their menstruation created culture. Woman's blood power connected land and sky, earth and moon, life and death. Breasts and birthing connect woman sympathetically with all water: rain, thunderstorms, floods, and drought; seas, rivers, and wetlands. Woman's muscles ripple and convulse to push out new life just as earthquakes shake the ground. The birth cord is the vaginal snake delivering the babe into the world. An artery and vein spiral around the cord and resemble two snakes entwined — consider the medical caduceus symbol.

Big cats hunt at night and are seen with blood on their muzzles. The vagina is also a mouth. Blood appears on the vaginal lips. Big cats symbolize the Great Mother. They accompany her and sit beside her menstrual/birth chair in early sculptures. Inanna is called "lioness". Night (seclusion), serpent, lion, sacred blood-seat-throne, rain and thunder storms, all bodies of water, fish, cyclic seasons, cyclic life-death-renewal, fertility, and sex (NO! and YES!) are originally woman's. Inanna is all of the above.

The anxiety inherent in linear-thinking men requires fixing something in place, controlling it, so as to reduce their anxiety/fear. Inanna is everything that confuses men: female, cycling, creating, fluid movement, changeability, and natural phenomena over which they have no control. Priest-scribes declare nature, Inanna, and women unfathomable! Men work very hard to get nature, goddess and women under their control.

Growing patristic domination requires ridding the early mythic story of women's powers. In that process, they capture our story. Woman's menstrual and birth blood powers, that once influenced every aspect of life on earth and the heavens, was too powerful for men to entrust to the women. Read this as too powerful and tempting for men to *leave* with the women. This usurpation, men taking over women's menstrual powers, is described by Levi-Strauss as the first myth everywhere. Knight points out this is erroneous. The take-over is the second myth in all cultures. The first story, first myth everywhere, is about the creative menstrual blood power of woman (Knight).

Inanna is the first story. She is the powerful young version of Divine Woman. She goes into seclusion, both earthly and heavenly, when she is out of sight. She is the lion(ess). She is "first snake". She is associated with loud thunderstorms and dark wide storm clouds, rain in all quantities, lightening and thunder. Imdugud bird, Sumerian thunderbird, is one of her emblems. She controls water whether flood or drought. She is the young menstruant leaving her time of dark moon seclusion at new moon. New moon is a crescent and wild cattle horns are crescents. Inanna is a holy heifer who consorts with a bull, a heavenly bull. He is *her* bull of heaven.

Inanna can do what she pleases and no god can say her nay. Since she is the first story of woman, she is in our life, our sacred and imaginal art, and in our creative expressions long before any gods arrive. Inanna's story is so immediate, full, and encompassing, that she is not brought fully under male control. Though the scribal priests gave it a mighty effort, it is not accomplished until the major male-based religions eradicate her in the Common Era. Bit by bit she is demeaned, demoted, and stripped of powers. However, her presence is too deeply rooted in our species to vanish completely; she is too universally popular. As mother of all, she is needed. As long as humans need to come into existence through their mother's womb, there will always be that first story; a sheness just beyond hearing, a shimmer of knowing, an inspiration, a dream; a shared awareness of women coming together, gathering again at the well and returning together to our fullness.

A sacred feminine, a devotion to Life, is remembered by women, all women: women battered, raped, beaten, dominated, denied, diminished, and isolated; women deemed stupid, soulless, inferior, and silenced; women liberated, educated, outspoken, and wise; women in partnership with herself, men, women, and creative expression. Woman and Sacred Woman are stirring, rising. Inanna has stepped out from the ruins and dust after millennia of neglect. We women, human and sacred, together again, are a "Loud Thundering Storm." (Wolkstein and Kramer 1983: 95-6:)

LOUD THUNDERING STORM

Proud Queen of the Earth Gods, Supreme Among the Heaven
   Gods,
Loud Thundering Storm, you pour your rain over all the lands
   and all the people.
You make the heavens tremble and the earth quake.
Great Priestess, who can soothe your troubled heart?

Your frightful cry descending from the heavens devours its victims.
Your quivering hand causes the midday heat to hover over the sea.
Your nighttime stalking of the heavens chills the land with its dark
   breeze.
Holy Inanna, the riverbanks overflow with the flood-waves of your
   heart.

...

Sumerian new day began with night arriving, not day dawning. Dark came first. The last day of the month was the old crescent moon sliver. The month starts over with the dark of the moon. The 7th day is her emergence, the light of the slender new moon has fattened. Inanna's seclusion time, like woman's, was when possible disturbances of weather might occur if a woman in her blood power had a "troubled heart;" she might even cause a disaster if she walked about and encountered a man (but not a woman), or if a man had sex with her. A menstruating woman among traditional people, moved about at night, like Inanna; if her anger was aroused, she, like Inanna, trampled "like a wild bull." Woman undergoes sharp hormonal changes in her body's preparation for shedding the old within her womb via her menses. Irritability and desire to step away from the everyday is present. Inanna is a woman with PMS on a cosmic scale. Don't disturb her seclusion!

When the new moon appears, Inanna's moon-blood is over and her hormones are refreshed; she is refreshed. She is bathed and dressed for queenship. She readies herself for duty. She picks up her diadem, her robes of queenship, her MEs, and her weapons. Inanna, in the beginning, has weapons for defense; not offense. She is later turned into a war goddess and a scapegoat for the sins of warring men. (More on this in chapter 12) War-blood is a male invention. Woman's menstrual blood is taboo, i.e., sacred, holy and powerful, no men allowed. Parading a nude Inanna from her dangerous seclusion, bleeding and cranky, is meant to intimidate enemies. When she rides nude and glaring, atop seven lions, watch out! Woman's menstrual blood is envied. Men want powerful blood too so they make blood happen. Women's blood is biophilic and the latter, make-blood, is necrophilic.

Inanna is lunar. Her "mother" is moon goddess, Ningal (*nin*, "lady or queen;" *gal*, "great"). Inanna is chthonic and celestial at the same time because she includes everything! Since the day began in the evening when Inanna rose as evening star and continued through darkness and into day's light, consider the same reckoning for lunar time. The Wolkstein and Kramer poem continues, stating: "On the seventh day when the crescent moon reaches its fullness." The Ancient Near East is rich with connection to the new moon. Inanna is the new moon. The above description of the 7th day is not the very first sliver of new moon but a fattened crescent.

Deities are often indicated by their special number that often have to do with moon phases. The number 14 (or 15) is full moon which is assigned as Inanna's symbolic number indicator in texts. She *is* the maid version of her moon mother. Her mother, Ningal, is full moon. Logically Inanna should be number 7 when her monthly new moon festival is held, but she is known by the full moon number 14. She is her mother.

The young maid emerges with the new crescent and is fully fertile by the full moon, the time of human ovulation and the time of consummation in the annual "sacred marriage." If the lunar month, like the 24-hour day begins with darkness, then the month count begins with the three or four dark moon days. Inanna's monthly festival relates to the new waxing crescent phase. It begins in darkness, when women enter seclusion. Nanna, the usurping moon god, is assigned number 30, the last day of the old crescent moon. This implies a connection with menstrual powers.

Women of traditional people take nothing with them into seclusion. All of Inanna's MEs, her symbols of office and authority, her ornamentation, her weapons would be left behind, just as they are when she descends into the underworld. I suggest that this is how Enki got his hands on her ME in chapter two. He was holding them during her time of lunar darkness. Enki wants the ME for himself, or rather his priests want them by proxy.

Inanna's new moon festival is a time of hearing appeals and making decrees. She is refreshed, she retrieves her emblems of office; she is her wise and peaceful self again. She sits on her high throne, Dumuzi's king-proxy sits beside her, and all the deities of heaven and earth assemble before her to hear her pronounce their fate. People and animals come to her; her "black haired" people parade before her. She gazes upon them. She has left her chthonic wildness and is orderly and civilized until the next time unpredictable nature or men act up and Inanna is blamed. We continue with the Wolkstein and Kramer text:

On the seventh day when the crescent moon reaches its fullness,
You bathe and sprinkle your face with holy water.
You cover your body with the long woolen garments of queenship.
You fasten combat and battle to your side;
You tie them into a girdle and let them rest.

In Eridu you received the *me* from the God of Wisdom,
Father Enki presented the *me* to you at his holy shrine in Eridu.
He placed queenship and godship in your hands.

You mount the steps to your high throne.
In all majesty you sit there
With your beloved husband, Dumuzi, at your side.

The gods of the land, wishing to hear their fate, come before you.
The gods of heaven and earth kneel before you.
The living creatures and the people of Sumer come before you.
The people of Sumer who parade before you
Are caught in your gaze,
And held in your holy yoke.

The stage is set. A statue of Inanna, richly garbed, adorned, and staring with oversized kohl-rimmed eyes is placed on her "high throne." Gold stars and lapis lazuli vulvas adorn her hair. Rich robes in ruddy red or deep blue and all manner of clothing and ornamentation are listed as offerings as gifts of gratitude and requests for her favor. Other texts describe the king sitting on the dais near her; he is an observer and not a participant, just as Dumuzi is described in the above lines. Cellae[54] line the walls in temples to provide homes for other divine personalities and storage for clay tablet records. The divine statues travel overland or by water to "visit" one another. They are also kidnapped during wars. Here, imagine the various divine figurines placed before her, in reverence. The figures are believed to hold the spirit of the deity; they all kneel before her. After the opening ceremony and parade, petitioned

---

[54] small rooms along the sanctuary's inner walls

cases are heard in the morning. Inanna/Ishtar rests in the afternoon. Refreshed, the case decisions are announced. The word for "Inanna" is synonymous with "decree."

I believe Inanna's fabled complex and contradictory behavior is also because she is so very old in people's memory and she weaves through the chronology of later-existing divine stories from various cities and locales. She bridges the oldest myths with the new urbanized religious stories. The "before" is perceived chthonic and chaotic; it is untamed nature, created by a serpent — the early emblem for prime creatress. Lilith is an early uncontrollable (by men) non-urbanized Inanna. Patriarchal time slowly reduces Inanna as Lilith to an evil wind bringing disease that kills the frailest people and infants. I find the increasing number of books on Lilith, Mary Magdalene, and goddess in general, a healthy sign of divine woman's return.

During the last half of the second millennium, priestly scribes begin to call Inanna fickle when men's war plans were thwarted, i.e., they say she abandons that city's king and so the battle is lost. Inanna is declared destructive, blood-thirsty, uncontrollably lustful, and conveniently blamable. She is unfathomable to men but embraced by women. Her Ishtar name became synonymous with 'goddess' by the last millennium B.C.E.. Also in that millennium, judgmental wrathful Yahweh made his appearance. Women ignored him and continued worshipping their goddess.

ISHTAR, HARASSER OF MEN

Inanna/Ishtar is goddess of love, pleasure, and love's cold shoulder. Foster describes the following text as a theatrical entertainment. It is enacted near a reed hut that Foster tells us is for "marital consummation." I suggest that there is more evidence that the hut is for seclusion during menses. These separate places are prevalent in all early cultures and

267

taboo, sacred — man-stay-away. The seclusion place grew into the women's quarters and, eventually, men made it *their* harem.

In the text, goddess beckons the "inexpert man (Foster 2005: 282)." Priestesses initiate young men into the art of mutual pleasurable copulation with a woman, thereby making him fully a man. The audience also enjoys the display of Inanna/Ishtar's power to change men to women and women to men. In this text, women carry weapons and aggressively sexually harass the men who carry household items and wear women's clothes; the men burlesque menstruation; they accept women's verbal and physical abuse. This is a late text burlesquing as a classical composition.

The composition is called both "My Lady Let Me Tell of Your Divine Valor" and "Ishtar, Harasser of Men." (ibid.: 282-285:)

> *The poem begins praising Ishtar for her wisdom and invites everyone to come hear of her valor. We imagine a temple singer exclaiming to the crowd gathered. The people will hear of her greatness and strength and the singer especially invites the one who does not yet know her. The singer brings forth the song with great joy! Once a man knows Ishtar, he will follow her forever. The "inexpert" man will come to her door, her temple, for sex. We hear: "Your doings are strange, your ways unfathomable, so many are your deeds, what god would not be like you?"*
>
> *The singer lists the goddess's opposing attributes: disturbing emotions and contentment; fickleness, uncertainty, and trust; cooling hot anger, bringing and putting out conflict; cursing and not cursing; truth and lies; dignity, wealth and a bed on the ground are her's to give. The goddess makes friends of strangers or enemies of friends, a successful home for a wife or causes marital conflict. She is wisdom, misogyny, and the temple harlot. Ishtar owns bondage, "dominance, fear, secrecy, wakefulness, and terror;" she is also responsive and wise. Ishtar owns making the marital bed, great war cries, and the coiffing of hair. She gives gifts, opens a lover's legs for sex, promotes families to grow; she makes twins, linen, and moths. Ishtar gathers circles of women, gives thick beautiful hair, intimidates, and makes some weak and others strong; she brings good sex,*

sleep, dreams, child birth, and the infant. The goddess also turns woman to man and man to woman.

The actors are cross-dressed. This also occurs in the description of the new moon monthly parade for Inanna. Speculations are put forward as to the meaning of this gender reversal. In this poem, it is entertaining to see men on the receiving end of their bad behavior; it also describes the contradictory nature of her goddess attributes. Changing genders may also mean that when men are in thrall, in love, they are gentle, kind, caring, protective and sentimental while women in love may become sexually assertive, urgent, strong, and expressive. In Inanna's new moon parade, some women appear dressed half as men and some men are dressed half as women. In this composition for entertainment, both genders are fully reverse-dressed.

> *Enter: the cross-dressed actors. The singer admits to the mockery pointing out it is the goddess who is responsible for the burlesque. It is she who made the men obedient with women's clothes and arrangement of hair. The women actors are groping the men and feeling their hair. One man carries some salad greens in his hand, while a woman carries a bow. Another man carries "a hairpin, a mussel shell, kindling, and a girl's harp" while women carry "throw sticks, slingshots, and slingstones." The men carry the women's battle gear. The singer exclaims how different the men appear!*
>
> *A reed enclosure is readied (for menstrual seclusion). A man in female costume enters the seclusion hut. Women in male costume encircle the enclosure. The man signals: keep away, taboo! One of the women makes a bold move toward him. The men have little daggers with ribbons. The women, the would be "lovers," are frightening and shout at the trapped man to go satisfy them at the city wall where he will get a "souvenir" (a beating?) from the aggressors. A jester enters hollering "keep clean, long life!" which acknowledges the taboo status of the actor. The costumed men are strange, their actions are peculiar.*

They hold spindles, they circle you (Ishtar) with demonic desire.

The men wear hair combs, their clothes are pretty as a woman's,
They wear pretty hats, and, as if renewing every month ...

> *Ishtar's love charms are shown to the festive crowd. The*
> *crowd passes Ishtar's dais pouring out beer in libation for her.*
> *The beer vessels and drinking tubes (to filter out the sediment)*
> *are at hand. (The rest of the poem is fragmented.)*

Ishtar is unfathomable; she is said to "love opposites and reversals". In a self-praise song/poem, "Self Praise of Ishtar", the goddess reminds us she loves the king, she is greater than the other gods, and can change destinies. She is radiant like the sun, the lesser gods put lips to ground before her; she has the divine staff/scepter and holds the lead-line of heaven. She protects the king like a wild bull goring the enemy. (Foster, 2005: 679:)

Hurrah for me, hurrah for me, the foremost one who [has no] rival,
[I am] Ishtar, who set kings to fighting, who causes [confusion].

Several lines in the Wolkstein and Kramer translation of "The Holy One", describe Inanna's New Moon Festival parade and the contrary dressing of men and women. (Wolkstein and Kramer 1983: 99:)

The people of Sumer parade before you.
The women adorn their right side with men's clothing,
The people of Sumer parade before you.
I say, "Hail!" to Inanna, Great Lady of Heaven!
The men adorn their left side with women's clothing.
The people of Sumer parade before you.
I say, "Hail!" to Inanna, Great Lady of Heaven!

Inanna is complex and inclusive. She is fertility and the pleasure of sex. She does not bestow her gift of pleasure only between woman and man, or wife and husband bound in marriage. Fertility easily adapts to the idea of expressing joy. Sex is not limited to procreation. The goddess does not exclude anyone. She includes: heterosexual and homosexual lovers; the trans-gendered, cross-dressers, sacred hierodules, temple prostitutes (of initiation), male prostitutes, and destitute women who ply their trade near taverns and in niches of the city walls. Her bridal songs prepare young women for pleasurable marital copulation.

Her temple sanctuaries have a special group of priests in attendance: eunuchs, who are men who choose to self-mutilate, i.e. castrate themselves. They are likely the men seen nude and beardless on temple seals. Castration of young bulls turns aggressive animals into docile and useful oxen. Herds need only a few intact bulls to service all the cows, surplus male animals are castrated or eaten; surplus males of other herd animals are culled for food and sacrifice. Taking note of the change in animal behavior may account for men wishing to serve Inanna as "women" through through a drastic self-imposed surgery. They may also have become eunuchs to preserve a higher register singing voice.

Male singers well into our era, known as castratos, underwent the surgery to prevent testosterone from deepening their voices. The eunuchs also bleed — once. They are close to being women. Inanna's eunuchs may be sacred singers, imitating women's higher voice register. Many traditional groups use a show of intentional male blood-spill or self-mutilation to imitate woman's menses, the creative power of her blood. Castration was demanded neither by goddess nor women. It was an extreme imitation of women's blood power; the resultant reduction of testosterone brought them closer to resembling women. The eunuchs are honored in her temple personnel and appear on many early seals.

The confusion of Inanna's conflicting and opposing attributes, is both the mysterious all-encompassing all-inclusive alignment of opposite behaviors of humans, and the long and far-flung presence of the goddess. The goddess expands with advancing economies and technologies into many attributes and though always herself, appears to be separate goddesses. Barbara Walker describes the same case concerning Kali. (Walker 1983: 491:)

> Western scholars erroneously viewed the various
> manifestations and incarnations of Kali as many different

Goddesses, particularly isolating those primitive *matrikadevis* (mother-goddesses) grouped together as "Dravidian she-ogres." Yet Kali's worshippers plainly stated that she had hundreds of different names, but they were all the same Goddess.

Inanna/Ishtar represents all the opposites of life, nature, and human nature. She holds the extremes together. She is the opposites aligned in syzygy. She is the flexible and unpredictable changes between the opposites. She is the tree of heaven and earth; she is the roots below and the crown above. She is the lamentation of loss and the joy of return. Ancient people and poets understand. Poets call the "all:" "love" and "life (Harrison 1903: 430)." Embrace life fully and the unfathomable is simply the dance of life.

CHAPTER 8

Birth Mother and Motherhood

Inanna is called "mother" in many compositions. Like other maiden goddesses, Inanna is said to have given birth to fertility in the land and is annually renewed to maid status. She is included as three of the names for birth goddesses assembled for Nammu in order to assist the prime creatress to create humans. She is only rarely shown with babe in arm when compared to Isis with Horas, countless birth goddesses, and Christianity's Madonna. We see an Ancient Near Eastern madonna and child in figure 39. We do not know the goddess' name, but she may well be Inanna.

Figure 39. Goddess with Child

The following is a composition from the final phrase of the Late Period (c. 1000-100 B.C.E.). "Mother" is used as a title for both Inanna and Ishtar. (Foster 2005: 948:)

Your are mother, O Ishtar of Babylon,
You are mother, O queen of the Babylonians,
You are mother, O palm tree, O carnelian!

THE CHILDREN OF INANNA

Several sources state that Inanna/Ishtar was never a mother but there are references to her children in the literature. **Nergal**, a chthonic underworld god and, strangely, also god of joy, is her son. His sanctuary is called "House of Joyful Heart." (I suspect that is because after death comes return.) He is a weather and plague god who has sex with Ereshkigal and becomes her consort-king in the underworld. Nergal is also Akkadian **Erra** who is god of an underworld cult at Kutha. Erra causes huge destruction by rebellion, drought, and pestilence following war. During the coming dark age in the middle of the first millennium B.C.E., a story says that he tricks Marduk into getting his statue refurbished as it has grown dim and lusterless. Divine personalities reside in their images. Erra promises to keep order in the universe while Marduk is indisposed, i.e., his raiments of power and brilliance are removed for refurbishing. Erra interferes with the craftsmen and delays completion of the work. Marduk is without his power. Erra brings havoc; the gods cannot stop him, even Ishtar cannot stop him. He stays angry and tells his plans: he will cause a dreaded eclipse, ruin all the land, kill the cattle and collapse the mountains. He will allow foreign evil barbarians into a divine shrine and destroy a city (Leick 1991: 57-8).

Erra has a wise vizier who redirects Erra's anger away from southern Mesopotamia to proper enemies. Erra has no remorse; he simply explains that is just how he is. "When I am enraged, I devastate people." His vizier Ishum blesses the destroyed land and returns fertility to the people (ibid.: 59).

Lulal is her warrior-god son who is often found in her entourage; in one Inanna descent story he is her son and god of his city, Badtibira, while in another he coifs her hair.

The goddesses, Nanse and Ishara, who are both equivalent to Inanna, each has a daughter, **Minmaki**. Minmaki, like her mother (Inanna), is goddess of oaths.

Two of Inanna's sons have roles in an Anzu (thunderbird) story. (Foster 2005: 556-9:)

> *Anzu steals the tablet of destinies from Enlil — now the thunderbird is supreme! Enlil's divine authority is overthrown. Enlil goes to Anu, the king of the gods. The gods panic and become silent. Anu gathers all the pantheon together and promises whoever of them retrieves the tablet of destinies from Anzu will be called Mighty One.* **Girru**, *firstborn of Annunitum/Ishtar, is called upon to retrieve the tablet of destinies from Anzu. Girru speaks to his father, Anu, and says that the thunderbird has taken the tablet of destinies and is now supreme over Enlil so if Anzu commands, the cursed one is made into clay. Girru refuses.*
>
> *Next, the gods request a warrior god "called* **Shara**, *firstborn of Ishtar". Shara also speaks to Anu, "his father," and refuses the impossible assignment. Finally Ea/Enki, the clever god, says he can resolve the dilemma with one command. The gods are hopeful. Ea summons the creatress, "Belet-ili (Inanna), mistress of divine plans," who is asked to send her "superb beloved,"* **Ningirsu**, *"the mighty one," her son, to "conquer soaring Anzu." Ea (Enki) speaks, praising Belet-ili as being the one with divine design; she is supreme of all the gods. Ea asks the help of her superb son of broad chest who leads seven combats.*
>
> *The goddess gives her consent. Gods and land alike "rejoice" and pay homage to Ningirsu. The goddess speaks to her son, here identifying herself as Mami who gave birth to all the gods. (This reinforces that Inanna is none other than the Great Mother creatress.) She also states she gave An the kingship of heaven and tells Ningirsu that Anzu has stolen it all away.*

The story goes on with the goddess' plan for Ningirsu to distract Anzu by attacking his wings. This takes the bird's mind off the magic words of destiny he uses to send arrows back to the groves and bows back to the trees so that Anzu remains unharmed. If, however, Anzu is concerned about his wings and does not utter the protection of destiny, he is vulnerable.

Ningirsu distracts the bird and aims an arrow. It enters Anzu's body and pierces his heart. The tablet of destiny is saved by Ningirsu! But the power of the tablet of destiny is too tempting. The victorious god thinks he will keep it for himself. A messenger comes to tell him of the mighty names he is now called around the land to urge him to return the tablet of destiny. Unfortunately, the text is fragmented and we are left waiting for an ending; does he return the tablet to An and Enlil or keep it for himself?

Belet-ili is also named Mami (Mother, aka Inanna) and Mistress of all the Gods. It is she who grants kingship to Anu, her son's father, and is none other than Inanna. Inanna is Sumerian Nammu, creatress of the universe and mother of all the gods. Anu rules because she chose him. The tablet of destiny, once upon a time, is assigned to the birth goddess who decides how long a human will live. Since the gods own the tablets of destiny in the above text, we have evidence of obvious patriarchal expansion. The Great Goddess's young version, Inanna/Ishtar, rules kingship. Inanna is said to "wear the robes of the old old gods" — sheepskin robes, i.e., before the time of weaving. She is of the old days and ways before patriarchal usurpation.

Leick describes **Ningirsu**, later replaced by **Ninurta**, as being worshipped in Lagash and Sumer both as warrior and fertile-field god. His mother is Gatumdug (mother goddess and equivalent to Inanna/Ishtar), his father is Anu, and his emblem is the lion-headed eagle, Anzu/Imdugud (Leick 1991: 130-1). Imdugud is also Inanna in her thunderstorm persona. Over time, the anthropomorphic form of a god either kills off the early zoomorphic emblem of a goddess or demonizes it. Anzu/Imdugud is the power of thunderstorms. At some point Anzu developed into a half-bird half-man form. Anzu is described by king

Gudea, who saw him in a dream, as monstrously large with wings and head of a god, his lower body is a dark storm, and lions (Inanna's animal) flank him.

An enormous black eagle, with wings outstretched, is easily imagined when black storm clouds rise low and wide above the horizon. A lion's roar is closer to thunder sounds than are eagle shrieks so a lion head is attached to the black eagle body. Storms are noisy; wars are noisy. Storm deities easily became war deities because of the noise and destruction of both storm and war. Inanna/Ishtar is associated with Anzu, the storm, and is noisy to a fault in various texts.

Anzu is anthropomorphized into Ningirsu/Ninurta, son of Inanna, and is a chthonic god as Ninurta means "Lord Earth." Inanna's early zoomorphic symbol becomes his emblem. Imdugud is found on seals in close proximity to Inanna/Ishtar or her other symbols. In time, patriarchy changes the emblems of the sacred feminine into masculine symbols, demonizes them, or kills them. Ningirsu and Ninurta, chthonic and vegetation gods, are both called son of Inanna/Ishtar. Ninurta replaces his equivalent, Sumerian Ningirsu, and graduates from a rise and fall vegetation deity to the status of a young, wrathful, full-time god; a warrior god, son of Inanna/Ishtar.

The association of lions with Ningirsu/Ninurta directly connects him to Inanna/Ishtar. All great mother goddesses "own" the big cats: lions, jaguars, tigers, panthers, and leopards. Goddess's prey animal, bear, is her companion in Old Europe. The big and powerful prey animals belong to woman and goddess. Big cats flank or form the seat or throne and signify a mother goddess' birthing stool. The feminine seat of power became the dais and throne. Inanna sits or stands on lions; she is also seen in a lion-pulled cart. She holds a battle mace with a lion carved into its business end. She is a lioness taming recalcitrant gods to relent their harsh decrees; she is a lioness protecting her "black haired people." She is a lion in battle. Her son has her lion qualities and her emblem when he becomes a war god.

Inanna is the mother of **Shara**. He has a temple at Tell Agrab, near his mother's. Besides a mace head with four lion heads, also carried by Inanna/Ishtar, four seals show the goddess with her son.

A very early hero king, Lugalbanda, asks Inanna for assistance. "As she looks at the shepherd Amaushumgal-ana [Dumuzi], she looked at holy Lugalbanda. As she speaks to her son, to lord Shara, she spoke to holy Lugalbanda (Black 1998: 352)." He asks for the power to run as fast as she does, as fast as her son Shara runs, to "go like the sunlight, like Inan(n)a;" "Like Shara, Inan(n)a's beloved son, shoot forth with your barbed arrow like the sun! Shoot forth with reed-arrow like moonlight (ibid.: 94)." "She looks at him, as at Dumuzi with joyful eyes — she speaks as if to Shara with joyful eyes (ibid.: 110)." In "Lugalbanda in the Mountain Cave," Anzu offers the ability to shoot arrows "like Shara, Inan(n)a's beloved son" and *melam*, brilliant glamour, "like holy Shara (ibid.: 145)." Patriarchy wants its gods to be the first-born of great mother's emanation (Walker 1983: 311). Shara is called "first born of Ishtar."

Goddess is a mother made into the enormous mother of all. She has all the qualities of a good mother. The maternal characteristics of a double X chromosome combined with a big human brain birthed more than infants. Woman and her motherhood create civilization. Women brought forth culture and civilization; mother-law and mother-justice. Women invented the goddess. For uncountable millennia, women guided our species through a great progression. In contrast, maleness has a biological handicap to overcome: the Y chromosome. Barbara Walker offers the following on motherhood: "Societies dominated by men tended to introduce cruel punishments, hostility toward the young, formalized rivalry, and sadistic elements replacing easy, affectionate sexuality (Walker 1983: 688)." Motherhood is biologically based. It is (w)holistic. Inner and outer "worlds" are not separate; being and doing, feeling and thinking are not separate; humans and nature are not separate; women and men, though different, need not be separate. All is joined together in feminine-ordering and expression. Dominator/patriarchal ordering severs the above holistic list into separate slivers. Briffault, in *The Mothers,* states (Briffault 1927 vol.1: 432:)

It is as an outcome of the functions and activities of the women that the first steps in cultural development naturally arise, while the instinct and interests of the male being directed towards the competitive struggle for food and the predacious activity of the hunter and the warrior, do not spontaneously tend towards the improvement of material culture and of the peaceful relations of the social group … she was the founder of the home, and hence the originator of the arts.

(Briffault quotes Reclus Primitive Folk: 57:) "It is to woman that mankind owes all that has made us men. Not withstanding the doctrine which holds sway at present, I maintain that woman was the creator of the primordial elements of civilization. No doubt woman at the outset was but a human female, but the female nourished, fed and protected the more feeble than herself, while her mate, terrible savage, knew only how to pursue and kill. Necessity forced him to slay, and the duty was not distasteful. He was by nature a ferocious beast, she by function a mother."

As heavenly queen, mother goddess's breasts, from Paleolithic time onwards, give rain to nourish the land. Clouds are her breasts. She offers her breast in many images. She is not enticing men for sex; she is mother nourishing her children and rain watering earth.

CHAPTER 9

Temples, Ritual, and Personnel

E-anna, temple with seven corners, from
which rise seven fires at midnight

How supreme you are over the great gods, the anunna!
The anunna kiss the ground with their lips (in obeisance) to you.

TEMPLES

First, goddess is imagined and named; second, she is depicted in art; third, she has a home built among her people when they settle to farm; fourth, her house becomes a temple complex in the urban centers. This chapter will introduce the reader to Sumerian religious practice when available and Akkadian and Babylonian practices which retain much of Sumer's highly developed religion.

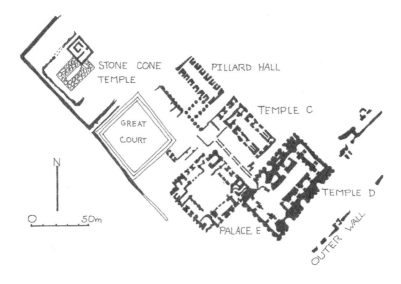

Figure 40. Eanna Precinct Level IVa Uruk c. 3300-3000 B.C.E.

People serve the divine who is in charge of their location or city. Early religion was far happier and more celebratory than the later stressful, threatening, fear-ridden theology that patriarchy devised. Divine images contain the deity depicted. A figurine, a sculpture of Inanna/Ishtar, *is* the goddess. A temple *is* a home for a divine being; "e" means "house"/temple. Temples take on a divine personification and are addressed and praised. Petitions are brought; decrees and judgments are decided in the temple.

Sumer has no police, lawyers, or courts. Problems and disputes are handled locally or with a counsel of elders (both women and men). If the issue is too big for the elders, the temple decides. One swears, whether litigant, witness, or accused, to tell truth to the deity of the temple. Divine retribution results for declared untruth. Cases brought before temple priest judges are under Inanna's supervision. The judges decide the arguments or charges. If a decision cannot be made, the "river ordeal" is used. Trial by river means "the accused would be thrown into the river. If he surfaced and swam to shore, he was innocent; if the god of the river swallowed him up, he was guilty as charged (Bertman 2003: 70)."

Every city is owned by a tutelary deity. Sumerians believe that humans were created to do the hard work after the lesser gods complained bitterly about doing all the work while the higher gods did no work (see chapter 3). I have not read of "lesser" goddesses serving "greater" goddesses who are above all manner of toil. All goddesses are one goddess; she works as women do, she does not whine, winge, or whimper about work! After humans are created, the goddess works hard with her creation. She shows them how to be civilized and orders their first cities. A king, governor, or ruler serves the divine owner of the city until the mid-last millennium B.C.E..

Secular power grows. Palaces separate from the temples to become stand-alone luxurious precincts. When the separation occurs, kings remain highest in the temple staff hierarchy but only as an officiant for certain high rituals, not as a functionary. Rulers are obliged to build, maintain, and support the divine homes. Temple-owned land is controlled by kings and temple administrators who parcel out and assign agricultural plots. Farming estates are also privately owned. One tablet pledge records the size of a land parcel bestowed on the temple by the amount of seed barley it will plant (30 quarts of seed barley); other food stuff is included in the pledge: 3 kor of fine wine, 2 (large) measures of date cakes, 30 quarts of fine oil, 3 sheep per day. The tithing is "established for all time (Foster 2005: 365-6)."

Temples are the storehouse where food is brought, stored, and distributed as doles or wages according to occupation, age, and gender. Women earn wages at half of men's pay rate, and children receive less than women. This is likely based on gender and age appropriateness by observing that men eat more than women and men do the heaviest physical work. The storehouse is the traditional domain of women. The earliest storehouse temple of Inanna in Uruk is small, simple, raised up only one step, and nestled into the residential area. It has door openings on three sides and people have direct access to their goddess. She is not hidden from sight in an inner sanctum; there is no outer defense wall. Inanna's temples are built on a north-south axis. Two millennia later, Inanna's temple complex takes up a quarter of Uruk. Sumerian temples, sanctuaries, and shrines for Inanna/Ishtar are twice as numerous as her nearest competitor, Enlil.

Poems written for temples and ceremonial names describe the activities or main theme of each house. The following is a poem to Inanna's temple house in the religious precinct of Uruk called Kulaba. The seven corners are where fires are lighted on the temple walls in the evening and during the night. They represent the seven gods who are directed by Inanna in decision-making for people's appeals — the seven stars of the Pleiades. The text says the temple flourishes with fresh ripe fruit (from the temple garden). The Eanna shrine rises. It is built for "the steer" (the bull of heaven or constellation Taurus); it is made for the princess of the "pure horizon." It is the shrine sending up the seven fires into the night; "your queen is Inanna." She covers her head with a crown of lapis lazuli; she is the great dragon; Inanna takes her seat on the dais of the temple Eanna (Oppenheim, ed. 1969: 29).

A poem for the Uruku(g) shrine is found in *The Collection of Sumerian Temple Hymns* edited by Oppenheim. We learn that the temple belongs to An. It decides for the just man with the river ordeal. The temple gives counsel. It has a storehouse of silver and lapis lazuli. The temple is the origin of the ME and is the place where the "man" (king) meets the goddess. Inanna, consort of An, is described (ibid.: 32:)

> Your princess, the merciful princess of the land, the mother of all lands,
> The lady, the great healer of the dark-headed, who determines the destiny of her city,
> the first-born daughter of the holy An, the maid, mother Bau (Inanna).

"E" is "house" in Sumerian. Temples grew from the storehouse of the goddess. Settled people require a larger storehouse to sustain them through the year. Goddess images are found around the world in the everyday work places of women: where grain is stored, ground, and baked into bread; in birthing rooms, homes, and sleeping areas. Goddess figures also accompany the dead in their burials. As the storehouse expanded with Neolithic farming, women naturally became the accountants and priestesses to keep company with the goddess of the storehouse, to petition her, to praise her, and attend to her daily needs. Prostitution, say men, is women's oldest profession. They are wrong of course. It is not. Priestess is the first profession of women. The goddess accompanies women in their activities whether baking bread (temples had bakeries for communal bread), birthing in the woman's quarters, tending the sick and dying, or making decisions. Goddess mirrors women.

Inanna evolved from the maid aspect of mother goddess; she is the bridge of return from death back to life; she brings fertility for another year of available food stuff — new life after the hot and dry end of summer. She is the focus, the star, of sacred ideology. She is the starburst of women's early imagination. She is supreme over the gods for longer than Judaism, Christianity, and Islam have existed.

TEMPLE NAMES

The following two lists are included so the reader senses Inanna's popularity, importance, and presence in Sumer and as Ishtar in Semitic Akkad of northern Sumer.

The temple precincts are not monotheistic; temples also house divine personalities in lesser roles to the divine owner. Inanna, in the temple lists, has the greatest number of temples, shrines and sanctuaries. The first list is Inanna/Ishtar temples selected from the glossary in Black, Cunningham, Robson, and Zolyomi's *The Literature of Ancient Sumer* (2004: 360-372:)

Amash-e-kug — "Pure Sheepfold"
Anzagar — "Tower"
Dur-an-ki — "Bond of Heaven and Earth" (Inanna's sanctuary at Nibru; i.e., she holds heaven and earth together)
E-anna — "House of Heaven" (where seven pillars burn seven fires at midnight)

E-Diluna — "House of Dilmun"

E-eshdam-kug — "House, Sacred Brothel"

Egal-mah — "August Palace" (for Inanna as Ninegala, "Lady of the palace" at Urim)

E-mush-— "House, Face of the Land" (for Inanna and Dumuzi(d) at Bad-tibira)

E-sig-meshe- du —"House, brick work worthy of the divine powers"

E-sikil — "Pure House"

E-hag-hula —"House of a Joyful Heart"

E-shara — "House of the Universe"

E-Ulmash — "House of Ulmash"

E-zagin — "Lapis Lazuli House" (located in a possibly mythical city of Aratta; it is the same name used for Nisaba's temple, the goddess of writing, and refers to her lapis lazuli tablet of destiny)

Giguna — (Zabalam)

Hursag-kalama — "Mountain of the Land" (for Inanna and Zababa, a warrior god)

Ibgal — (two cult centers for Inanna and Dumuzid)

CEREMONIAL NAMES

The second list is the ceremonial names for the houses of Inanna/ Ishtar and Inanna's equivalent counterparts. Ceremonial names and epithets are used in poems, hymns, and liturgical texts for her temples and sanctuaries. They are presented here to expand the reader's knowledge of how Sumerians understand their places of worship and their goddess Inanna's attributes. (Ceremonial name references selected from George 1993: 59-171:)

Abode of Regulations

Brick, Mountain of the Heart

Chamber of the Harp (for Gula, healing goddess, aka Inanna)

Colored House

Distant House

Exalted House of Mother Goddess (Ishtar)

High House

House, Abode of Joy

House, Abode of the Land

House, Abode of Wisdom (as mother goddess)

House, Beloved Storeroom

House, Big House (E-anna, Inanna's house took up one quarter of
    the city of Uruk)

House, Bond of Heaven and Underworld

House, Bond of Lofty Strength

House, Bond of the Land

House, Brick Worthy of the MEs

House, Chosen to the Heart (for Shara, Inanna's son)

House, Clad in Awesome Splender and Radiance

House, Clad in Splender

House, Clad in Terror

House, Dais of the Throne

House, Fearsome Mountain

House, Dread Foundation (its foundation is the Underworld)

House, Established Chamber

House, Exalted Harem (women's quarters)

House, Filled with Counsel

House, Gate of Well-being

House, Most Sublime

House, Mound of the Land

House, Mountain of Pure MEs

House, Mountain of the Land

House of Animal Offerings

House of Cattle-pen and Sheepfold

House of Colored Decorations

House of Dates

House of Decisions (for Ninshubur, Inanna's vizier)

House of Heaven

House of Heaven and Underworld

House of Jars (beer is drunk with a reed straw from jars, beer comes from grain and the storehouse; said of an Inanna temple)

House of Lapis Lazuli

House of Life (for Baba, aka Inanna)

House of MEs of Heaven

House of MEs of Inanna

House of Plenty

House of Pomegranates (pomegranate is food for the dead symbolizing red for the blood of return)

House of Pure Luxuriance (bed chamber of Inanna in Uruk's E-anna)

House of Pure Omen

House of Rites and Rituals (Ishtar as Sarratniphi)

House of Seven Corners

House of Seven Doors

House of Seven Giparus (ziggurat at Uruk)

House of Seven Niches (Eanna at Uruk)

House of the Axe

House of the Crescent

House of the Deluge

House of Goat Hair (associated with Ishtar and herd animals, likely a sanctuary for women who are fullers for garments)

House of the Awesome Radiance of Heaven

House of the Great Axe

House of the Great Light of Heaven

House of the Great Niche (one of two ziggurats for Dumuzi in Ishtar's center of Akkad)

House of the Happy Heart

House of the Heart (Baba aka Inanna)

House of the Heart of Heaven

House of the Lady of the Land

House of the Lion

House of the MEs which do not leave

House of the Noble

House of the Ordinances of Heaven and Underworld

House of the Path of Joy

House of the Prince of Heaven (Ishtar as morning star, presenting as male)

House of the Quay

House of the Rainbow

House of the Skillfully Contrived ME

House of the Steppe

House of the Tower

House of Vegetation

House, Oracles of the Heart (Inanna as Nanay)

House, Sacred Brothel

House, Seat of the Warrior

House, Suited for Milk and Ghee

House, Surpassing Luxuriance (for Nanay, aka Inanna, in Uruk at the Gate of Wonder)

House, (of) True Decisions

House, True Joy House where Bread Portions are Baked

House Where Meals are Set Out

House Which Determines Destinies

House Which Gathers (all) the MEs (two sanctuaries)

House Which Inspires Dread in the Land

House Which Lifts on High all the MEs

House Which Smites the Wrong

House Which Soothes the Heart

House Without Rival

House whose Eye is Open

House Whose Pure Place is a Quay of Lapis Lazuli (sanctuary of Ishtar)

House Whose Foundation Platform is Unalterable

Mighty House

Palace of Heaven and Underworld (shrine for Ishtar and Anu)

Palace of the Steppe

Place of Battle

Princely House (Ishtar as male morning star, war goddess)

Pure House

Pure Throne
Quay of Lapis Lazuli
Restful Abode of Life-Giving Abundance
Sacred Terrace House (for Ishtar of Hosts)
Shining House
Shining Place
Storage House (used for Zababa aka Baba aka Inanna)

Ceremonial names describe the temple houses in similar words used for the strong, multi-tasking, nurturing, mending, tending, and defending goddess's attributes, powers, and spheres of influence. They go far beyond sex, love, fertility and war! The ME resides in the goddess' temples. Enki takes and attempts to keep the ME in one myth (see chapter 2). Myth translators interpret that story to mean Inanna takes the ME *from him*. Evidence suggests otherwise. The numerous ceremonial temple names dedicated to Inanna and mentioning the ME, clinch my hunch that they were always hers.

Inanna/Ishtar is an all-purpose archaic deity who keeps her agricultural and herding roots, her ME, and her decree and decision-making intact even after urban centers develop with cataclysmic alterations in politics, society, economy, and religion. War has arrived in the Ancient Near East, yet only a few temple epithets refer to her war-goddess attributes.

Priestesses serve the goddess. As gods emerge, so does the priesthood. Inanna's staff increases greatly. She houses women, widows, orphans, and an expanding number of personnel. We learn of other employees, "The 'called ones' of the matriarchs, [who] for the Queen prepare immense quantities of food and drink (Kramer 1979: 85)." These are older women, widows, who cook and make beer for the temple. Residential and artisan areas are connected to the temple or are in a nearby compound. The compound is described as being a house of artisans with wards divided into individual cells. Priestesses are also artisans. One letter sent by a governor to his kings states that the "artisan quarters were deemed so unattractive that no self-respecting priestess would want to dwell there (Sasson 1990, in Gunter, ed. 1990:

21)." Artisans include many professions with specialized skills; both men and women are listed along occupational lines. Metal smiths, woven clothing makers, fullers and textile weavers are important. Their products are exchanged diplomatically between rulers. Talented artisans are loaned to other cities, taken during conflicts, and home-grown through apprenticeships.

The temples have visiting or assisting deities in the side cellae who also have a staff to serve them. Secular workers include bakers, cooks, fullers (women), weavers (women), potters (women), and tapsteresses (women) for making beer. Barley and other grains are fermented in clay jars. Reed straws are shown inserted into the jars to drink the beverage and avoid sediment. When "jar" is mentioned in ceremonial temple names, the temple is known for its beer.

Wealthier worshipers commission votive figures of themselves in prayerful attitudes (see figure 28). The votive figures are placed on banquettes along the walls. The worshipper's name and dedication to a deity are carved on the statues. The Sumerians want the divine pantheon to receive their prayers 24-7. Just as the figurines of Inanna hold the presence of the goddess, so too do the sculpted votive figures represent a person's continual attendance. Early votives of both women and men have happy naturalistic faces. The people love their goddess. They do not fear being in her presence. Later figurines have huge eyes, astonished eyes, fearful eyes. The faces no longer smile; companionable association with the divine is lost.

Remember, small goddess images accompany gatherer-hunters for at least 20,000 years. She lives with her people, not apart from them. Her figurines are excavated from grain bins, bread baking oven areas, and birthing rooms; she is found with the bones of the dead, she appears on plaques in homes, shrines, and sanctuaries. Goddess has been at our side for many thousands of years.

PURIFICATION OF A NEW CULTIC FIGURINE

A new cultic image requires purification when it is put into place. Scribes copy ritual onto clay tablets so there is liturgical standardization throughout the land. Foster's anthology includes instructions on how "To Purify a Cult Image (c)." We hear, first, the appeal to a "great god" with no specific name, who makes decrees for "heaven and earth, depths and seas (Foster 2005: 648)." This text tells us that the great deity can drive away evil as signs, portents, spells, and nightmares; that this one can cut the thread of evil placed as a spell. After the divine invocation, the composition changes to first person and an incantation priest/priestess identifies himself/herself. The speaker is a "chief purifier," knower of the "sacred spells of Eridu." Eridu is the home of Enki who becomes the incantation god of magic once magic and incantations are thought up. A chairs is set up for the deity; purifying water is sprinkled on the ground; the god is draped in "pure red garments;" the cultic implements are in place; beer is poured for the libation; all is ready. The priest/priestess says that the purification comes from the deity present and asks that the statue being purified may be given a great destiny. May the deity eat the offering, hear (appeals?), be "pure as heaven" and shine like heaven. "Let all evil speech stand aside (Foster, 2005: 648-9)."

Temples list gifts of clothing for the statues. Temple personnel tend them as if they are alive. The deities are believed able to eat, drink, sleep, and make love; they are taken to visit other divine personalities in other cities. The figurines have special clothing, beds, luxury items; they can hear prayers and speak messages to priestesses, priests and rulers. Divine messages advise kings when to fight and when to build or rebuild temples or cities. Wealthy worshipers commission sculptures of themselves in a pose of adoration to stand near a favored deity. The idea is that continual prayer would go from the worshipper's statue to the divine's statue as constant devotion can only help one's fate and fortune.

Everyone has a personal deity or two. Texts mention both a personal god to exalt and a personal goddess from whom to seek guidance and protection (Foster, 2005: 654). The personal goddess or god intercedes with the great deities to change a person's fate and fortune. High ranking people have high ranking personal deities. We have an example of such a request for intercession written by poet and high priestess, Enheduanna, in the "Exaltation of Inanna (see chapter 5)." She records her bad treatment by Uruk's en-priest. It is personal and vivid. She appeals to An, he does not/cannot help her; she appeals to Nanna, he does not/cannot help her. She appeals to Inanna; Inanna hears and restores her to her en-ship.

Enheduanna records her expulsion in the same way post-Sumerian literature describes Inanna's lament when she is forced from her temple. Enheduanna is a swallow leaving its nest; Inanna is a bird fleeing its home. Enheduanna's tiara of office is taken; Inanna is robbed of her robe and jewels.

Hallo states that Nanna is the most important Ur deity, that An rules in Uruk before Inanna, and suggests Inanna's rise to importance in both Ur and Uruk was due to Enheduanna's compositions. I disagree. Inanna's "house" in Uruk was earliest and largest. If An were prime, then his would have been earliest and largest. An is her consort in Uruk and Nanna her "father" in Ur. Neither god helps Enheduanna when the priest expels her. After the two gods do nothing, she calls on Inanna. We hear Enheduanna threaten that "this woman (Inanna) will carry off the manhood of Lugalanne (the priest who mistreats and evicts her). Mountain (and) flood lie at her feet. That woman is as exalted (as he) — she will make the city divorce him. Surely she will assuage her heartfelt rage for me (Hallo and Van Dijk 1968: 25)." Inanna reinstates her. Enheduanna is devoted to Inanna; perhaps, as her devotee, she *is* Inanna.

Sumerians often have a divinity in their personal name. A few translated names with Eshtar (Ishtar/Inanna) are: "Fruit-of-Eshtar," "He of Eshtar," "Eshtar-is-a-doctor," "Eshtar-is-my-mother", "Eshtar-is-strong", "Eshtar-is-my wall" (protection), "Eshtar-is-the clan", "Only-Eshtar-is-my-god", "Eshtar-is-my-wealth", "My god is Eshtar," "Eshtar-heard," "Eshtar-pardoned," "I-saw-Eshtar" and "Eshtar-is-eternal."

Inanna/Ishtar/Eshtar appears in personal names more often than does any other deity.

Inanna's staff also includes eunuchs. Temples emerge when settlements grow into towns and urban centers — after farming and herding are well established. Domesticated cattle come from the wild aurochs. Too many bulls in a herd are troublesome and dangerous; the surplus male animals are culled, eaten, or castrated. Castrated bulls make useful animals for pulling carts and plows. The simple surgical technique is known; the eunuch priests use the same technique to self-mutilate. Seals show nude and beardless men with shaved heads serving the goddess. Men in other texts enter her presence nude to indicate they have undergone purifying baths but they are bearded. Hair is an emblem of strength. The bald pates and beardless faces of the eunuch personnel indicate nonaggressive males, i.e., near-women men who bled once by choice and can now serve the goddess.

Figure 41. Inanna and her Priestesses

Goddess everywhere is based on women. She mirrors women and has similar responsibilities; she is woman made big as Everything; she is cosmic humane-ity. Her temple quarters resemble private homes. She has a bed chamber which is the site of her king-making. She has personal care attendants. She is bathed, coiffed, and costumed; her wardrobe is extensive. Offerings listed include: gold stars to pin on her robes, gold ribbons and lapis lazuli vulvas to adorn her hair (indicating her sexual allure and fertility); bead necklaces, gold bracelets, dresses, robes (often red), desert headscarves, woolen garments of "queenship," and tiaras. Inanna wore head coverings "of the desert" before the more familiar horned crowns appeared. Her temple figurines range from life-size wooden bodies with carved heads down to small figures. A beautiful life-sized alabaster head survives. Wigs are used by goddess figurines and elite women to create impressive headwear. Gifts of foodstuff, beer, animals, temple furniture and serving platters are also listed.

An inventory from Lagaba, a northern Babylonian town, c. 1700-1600 B.C.E., installing Ishtar in her new or rebuilt sanctuary, lists her clothing and jewelry in storage. We find gold finger-rings, a gold vulva, gold beads shaped like fruit, gold breast-ornaments, silver ear-rings, ivory breast plates, lapis lazuli beads, "beautiful gowns," linen coats, carnelian ring, cylinder seals, flax and woolen ribbons, and loincloths (Bottero 1998:132-3). Tablets list gifts for Inanna from Ur's kings: silver bowls, silver comb, slaves, grain, dairy products, beer and produce (Zettler 1992: 216).

RITUAL FOR INANNA

Imagine visiting Inanna in her temple home early one day in Mari, a city located to the north on the Euphrates and not originally Sumerian. The interior is cool; light enters through small high windows; wavering wicked oil lamps are set about. The goddess is seated on her dais a step or two above floor level and against the far wall. Her alabaster face glows in the interior twilight. She sees us. Her adornments glimmer in the flickering lamplight. Shadows breathe and dance. Incense burns.

Votive statues of wealthy worshippers keep vigil. Small doorless rooms, cellae, line the two long main chamber walls where liturgical, literature, and temple record tablets are stored. The cellae also house other deities visiting Inanna. There are no seats for the worshipers, we stand. The king sits to her side. This day artisans of all sorts are part of the ritual. (Sasson citing Dossin in Gunter, ed. 1990: 25:)

> In that early morning, the banquet of Ishtar is set out earlier than usual … A brewer, a carpenter, a leather-worker, a cord-maker, a fuller, (all these) artisans set their instrument in place. The barbers stand next to the artisans and (deposit their) razors. Once it is done … the emblems of the goddess are brought out from their containers and are placed, right and left, in Ishtar's temple … The king puts on a (military) outfit. He sits on a sailors's chair, behind the lamentation-priests. One of the king's servants most pleasing to him sits by his side on a lower seat … No one attends the king, but palace guards stand to his right and left … As (lamentation-priests) begin intoning the *an-nu-wa-se* chant, the king rises to attention. One of the lamentation-priests stands up and begins intoning *ir-si-ma-se* to Enlil, accompanied by drums.
>
> As the intonation begins, a (fire?-) eater does his trick, and a juggler juggles. After the jugglers, wrestlers come near. After the wrestlers, acrobats do somersaults. After the acrobats, women perform masquerades … As they complete the *an-nu-wa-se* chant, the king sits.

Another interesting description an Inanna temple comes from the Biblical Epistle of Jeremiah and describes a Babylonian temple (c. 300 B.C.E.). The man, Jeremiah, is a prophet and must denigrate statues and all that is not his version of god who is off-planet and not allowed representation in art. Religious competition is invented! Bottero includes the following description of Jeremiah visiting a Babylonian temple — only the visuals for a touch of realism are included here, Jeremiah's mockery is not. We hear that figures of the deities are of wood often covered with silver or gold, they are dressed in garments and robes of blue and purple (and red). Attendants wipe the temple dust that settles thick on divine faces (sun-dried mud brick is dusty building material), dust is brought in on the feet of worshippers, candles are lighted (oil lamps?), and nature takes its course on the wooden bodies and raiment; divine faces blacken from the smoke of candles (and braziers of incense), "bats, swallows, and birds; and in like manner the cats also" alight on the figures (Bottero 1998: 119).[55]

A table for offerings is in front of Inanna in every temple, shrine, or sanctuary. She is worshipped day and night, month and year, with prescribed ritual, prayer, hymns, and laments. Songs and recitations are accompanied by designated instruments; sacred dancers perform. Petitions and laments are brought to her. Texts document ritual instructions for a variety of priestesses and priests. The copied tablets standardize religious ritual temple to temple. The following text gives us a glimpse both of a ritual for Inanna/Ishtar and the specialization of temple staff; it is likely the consecration of a votive figurine to Ishtar as dedications are inscribed on the figure's back. (Bottero 1998:121:)

> [12] ... The *kalu* priest, standing will then sing the chosen hymn ... [21] Then, another *kalu* will sing the *ershemma* lament, accompanied by kettle drums ... After which a *sangu* priest, in front of (the statue of) the goddess Ishtar, will pour from his *sahu* cup a libation of water; and a *pashishu* priest will do the same before the inscription (marked on the statue); another, to his right, and another, on his left.

Sumerian names for clerical staffing generally continue in Akkadian liturgical texts. Sumer's highly refined religious practice and culture was adopted by Semitic groups. Early Sumerian kings/rulers have the role of "sovereign pontiff." Over time, kings remove themselves from temple responsibilities and retain only the most pompous ceremonial rituals. The king continued to sit on Inanna's dais during her new moon

---

[55] Bottero 1998:119, footnote 6 citing R. H. Charles, The Apocrypha and Pseudepigrapha of the Old Testament, Vol. I, 1913: 601-3

festival. Bottero adds: "the same archaic influence of the Sumerians might explain the importance of women in the liturgical service and the clergy. The Mesopotamians were proud of this and readily noted the absence of priestesses as marking the primitivism of certain foreigners "whose god knows no consecrated *nugig* or *lukur* priestess (ibid.: 121 citing Cooper, *The Curse of Akkad*, 1983: 33)."

Our contemporary western patriarchal culture is so invasive that an earlier scenario of women being the primary officiants of a worship service is difficult for us to imagine. However, the role of priestess came first, before priests. Currently, "priest" is used either for only male roles or to indicate both genders of ancient priesthood as if priestess is derivative of priest — just as "gods" supposedly includes both genders as if "goddess" is a derivative of "gods." This accepted umbrella usage, like "man" and "mankind" standing for all of humanity, is inaccurate. In the above nomenclatures, the feminine version is earliest and woman is the foundation of religion for the first 99% of sacred awareness time (French 2002).

Cultures and religions move from simple to complex, from meaningful to decadent. Early beautiful and meaningful religious philosophy is overtaken and lost by bureaucrats. Universally understood symbols become obscure cult objects. Direct contact with the goddess fades as more elaborate ceremony requires more priests and more interventions separating the once direct contact between human and divine. Temples require funds to run. As direct communion with divine beings is removed, priests take on offices not present in early Sumerian religious expression. Maleness invents war and desires to "fix" situations into concretized stability or remedy. Extreme and unholy measures are taken. People are killed in war because a divine "orders it." Animal blood sacrifice enters religious expression to offer blood, life, to the deities. Priests are paid for intercessions. Priests also require bribes; a proverb tells us that a man brings a temple priest a kid in one arm and a bribe in the other. Incantation magic is available, for a fee of course, for healing, changing bad omens, and procuring better fate. One text records the dire action taken by a king against opportunistic priests.

The religious rituals changed through the millennia. The temple's staff bloated and was parasitically supported by farming and village artisans and laborers. Ritual and pomp gave purpose to the priesthood who also found ways of making the people dependent on them. We can only imagine and sorely miss the direct and simple interaction between Inanna and her people in ancient Sumer.

TEMPLE PERSONNEL

Inanna's new moon parade includes both citizens and temple staff. The goddess is brought out to her courtyard; she is on a raised dais with a seat for the king beside her. The festival is a monthly public performance. Everyone is happy; everyone is dressed up; everyone feasts from Inanna's storehouse. "The people of Sumer parade before you (Wolkstein and Kramer 1983: 97)." We hear holy harps, drums of varied size and sound, tambourines, and timpani that accompany the parade. Temple personnel carry emblems of their office: harps, spears, and sword belts; some women and men reverse the wrap of their upper garments over opposite shoulders to demonstrate that Inanna can turn men to women and women to men. Doyennes of women sages from her women's quarters walk with dignitaries of the city elite, young maids and priestesses walk showing off their especially coiffured hair, girls and older women together pass by with loosened hair (allure), male prostitutes comb their own hair, entertainers sing, play with hoops and compete with jump ropes (ibid.: 97-99).

Instating a woman in high position in Sumer in the days of Sargon was not as unusual or unlikely as a contemporary woman counterpart assuming CEO or high church or synagogue status. Gods evolve and men serve them; women still serve but their roles diminish. Women continue as priestesses, seers, oracles, healers, and doyennes of wise women counselors; women are counted among the temple personnel who sing and dance; they enact the sacred marriage; they initiate men into civilized culture through sex; and for about 500 years, royal women held en-ship in important temples.

Psalms are chanted by everyone; people knew the responses for public services conducted in a temple's outer courtyard. In private, behind the walls, entitled priests take over with "mystic sacramental formulae and prayer (Langdon 1909: vii)." Assorted priestesses and priests with specific duties are mentioned throughout the religious texts. Bottero differentiates the roles of priestesses — the educated higher-born women have business and accounting duties in the storehouse; other priestesses do ritual, libations, anointing, sprinkling pure lustral[56] water, singing, dancing, reciting, and making music. While the priestesses are celibate and cloistered or practice sacred pleasure in temple service, the priests marry, lead lives outside the temple, and gain office through consecration/ordination that is passed on to their sons. Dynastic priesthood. Below are some of the temple personnel who serve the divine of the "house".

king — highest in temple hierarchy, administrates temple treasuries, redistributes temple land, is responsible for temple building and repairs; temple treasuries contribute to his military and guardsmen.

en-priestesses and en-priests — head or high priestesses and priests whose duty is using the incense stand near the divine figurine to "perform the mysteries;" an en-priestess is consecrated to be celibate and bear no children since she is a human consort for a god. Inanna has no en-priest, but, nominally, the king has this position.

nin.dingir — "lady goddess," high priestess; Akkadian *entu* feminine of *en nugig* and *lukur* ("servant of the temple," hierodule) priestesses who live in a cloistered community; women, pledged to the temple at an early age, come from families "of the faithful" and generally make up the ranks of priestesses; they are cultured, literate, compose poems, conduct business, write letters "copiously;" one of their celibate company is the priestess selected for the annual sacred marriage to reinstate the king (Bottero 2001: 123).

libation priests

lagar, labar, and *lagaru* **priests** — play the *bulaggu* harp

---

[56] water used in purification ceremony

psalmists

musicians — accompany the hymns transcribed with indication for which instrument to play: now the flute, now the harp or lyre, now the "bagpipe;" their instruments include: lyres, harps, flutes, horns, trumpets, assorted drums, tambourines, bells and rattles.

***ugbabtum*-priestess** — interprets omens

incantation priests — control fire and water rituals; they in charge of expunging unseen powers; they work in and out of the temples.

sacred prostitutes

male prostitutes and transvestites — *assinnu, kurgarru* and *kuluu,* though not official priests, are brought in for certain liturgical stories; homosexuality and ambiguity was accepted in the Ancient Near East.

eunuch priests

dancers and singers

service people — to tend the temple house

majordoma — runs the temple as a woman runs her household.

scribes and scribal art teachers

other employees — administrators, artisans (weavers, potters, carpenters), teachers, cooks, confectioners of sweets, and those involved in the daily running of the temple complex who live in or near the temple.

PROPHECY AND INCANTATION

Examples of prophecy and incantation are included here. Ishtar, as Annunitum, sends a message to Babylonian king Zimri-Lim through an incantation priest/ess (Foster 2005: 145:)

> O Zimri-Lim! They will put you to the test with a revolt. Watch over yourself! Set in position around yourself trustworthy(?) servants whom you love, so they can watch over you. You must not go anywhere by yourself! But those men who would put you to the test, I will deliver those men into your power.

A second message: O Zimri-Lim! Even though you have
no regard for me, I will smite(?) on your behalf. I will deliver
your enemies into your power ...

INCANTATION AGAINST A WATER MONSTER

In an "Incantation Against a Water Monster," c. 1850-1500 B.C.E.,
one may ward off a serpent-monster of the swamp. We learn that it is
born in the Tigris and nurtured in the Ulaya (another river). It lurks
under the reeds and rushes like a snake, its head and tail are like
"pounding tools (see figure 16)." (Foster 2005: 197:)

Adad [storm god] gave it its roar,
Nergal [underworld god], the [] of Anu, gave it its slither.
[I] conjure you by Ishtar and Dumuzi,
Not to come near me a league and sixty cubits!

TEMPLE OFFERINGS

The temple complexes are a "sacred neighborhood," a city precinct
for a divine being and is within or alongside the secular city. Inanna's
temple storehouse collects large amounts of food for distribution.
Though the storehouse is archaic and housed the earliest Inanna, all
later temple complexes of other deities have storehouses. Tablets and
treasure are also kept safe in the storehouses. Thousands of tablets
describe the food brought to temple storehouses — the product and how
much is brought. Fruit, vegetables, wild game, herd animals, and dairy
products are listed. Other tablets are pledges for provisions. Sumerian
tithing. Special offerings are made to Inanna: "lady beer" and the
"lady cakes" that become "Ishtar cakes."[57] The copious amount of
food promised by a wealthy worshipper appears in a very late tablet at
Uruk (third century B.C.E.) for Anu. It also includes three forms of
Inanna under the names of Antu, Nanaya, and Ishtar and illustrates

[57] A recipe for Ishtar cakes is included in the back of the book.

the volume of food prepared for the four meals of the day in the temple: a large and small meal in the morning and a large and small meal in the afternoon. (Bottero 1998: 129 f. 12, cites: Thureau-Dagin, *Rituals Accadiens.* p. 84:)

> That which makes, in all, every day for the four meals of the above mentioned gods: 21 top-grade sheep, fattened and without flaw, fed on barley for two years; 4 specially raised sheep, fed on milk; 25 second-grade sheep, not fed on milk; 2 large steers; 1 milk-fed calf; 8 lambs; 3 *marratu* birds (wild bird not identified); 20 turtle-doves; 3 mash-fed geese; 5 ducks fed on flour mash; 2 second-grade ducks; 4 dormice (?); 3 ostrich eggs and 3 duck eggs.

The list does not include the other ingredients required by the culinary staff who use the refined and subtle "cooking with water" along with ancient grilling and rotisserie methods. The altar tables set before the dais do not hold sacrificed victims as bloodthirsty tellers of later tales would have us believe. They are laden with silver and gold platters of delicately prepared meats, vegetables, bread, fried biscuits and libations of water, beer, milk and (later) wine. Incense of shaved juniper, cedar and cypress mixed with myrrh and herbs smokes on kindling to enhance meals and to delight the divine. Festival meals include entertainment of musicians, singers, and dancers.

Since the holy meals can be appreciated but not consumed by deities, what happens to all the food? It certainly is not tossed in the rubbish heap! The platters are removed and contents eaten by temple personnel, distributed to the many under the temple's wing, and at least in Inanna's earlier sanctuaries, given to widows, orphans and other unfortunates. Bottero speculates it is first eaten by the priests and personnel and then sold out the back door to enhance the coffers of both temple and priest (ibid.:130).

Everyday people make offerings. In the early morning people rise, wash their hands, and go to their flat rooftops or to a cleared spot of ground. They pour a libation of water or beer and offer what they have:

dates, bread, and cheese. The food is blessed by the deities. The offering is then consumed by the worshippers. Poor widows offer a pinch of their barley or ground spelt flour. Once a month, at new moon, Inanna holds a festival and feeds everyone from her storehouse. Widows and older women bake bread and prepare food, temple meat turns on spits, and beer is drunk. No other divine personality sponsors such a public feasting festival.

TEMPLE MUSIC

Psalms, hymns, songs, laments, and praises are collected, composed, edited, recited and performed. Psalms are accompanied by flute and go back to early Sumer; they are for the public and have no magic involved. They are called "lifting the hand," (as if sending a kiss), and could be performed by lay celebrants without the presence of a priest. Inanna is not invoked in incantation but Ishtar is — meaning magic was not invented in early Sumer and is a later addition. Early religion is celebratory and expresses gratitude; this is indicative of people comfortable with themselves and their divine ideation. Egalitarian cultures are goddess and woman influenced. They are not war cultures and their religion does not need magical aversion for fear and guilt. Sacred songs celebrated by laity hale from when people were directly involved and had a personal relationship with their goddess. Priests had not yet separated the public from the sacred. The priests had not yet imposed magic and incantations for fees as well as bribes for gain and job security.

Laments are written for disasters. When the vegetation god, Inanna's Dumuzi, goes to the underworld, goddess mother and bride lament. Tablets evidence a highly developed liturgy for the "mid-summer wailing (end of harvest)." Dumuzi/Tammuz, beloved of Inanna/Ishtar is dying or dead. During the Sumerian period (3500-2000 B.C.E.) there is only the sad queen mourning her lover; there is no story that he dies because Inanna/Ishtar punishes or abandons him (Langdon 1909: xvi). In another song of mourning, Inanna, as Bau, laments her city that

Enlil destroys by his "word;" she is angry and vexed, but she is not acting out with raging, smiting anger as later Ishtar does when she is the Lady of Terror and instrument of Enlil's "word." Enlil is an early god and is described in theological terms to be both impressive and demanding. He cares little for the human condition and "it is rare to find a liturgy in which the sorrows of humanity are not attributed to him (ibid.: xix)." The goddess laments her "smashed" city. Her people are gone. All the gods who once resided there are gone. She is alone. She grieves for her birds (her captured people): "Those who do not understand (what they do) are cutting off their wings! Where is my house that I used to dwell in (Foster 2005:153)?"

PRIESTS ABUSE THEIR OFFICE

The following does not mention Inanna specifically; I include it as an example of the timelessness of priestly abuse of power. Note: priestesses are not accused, only priests. The letter from Hammurabi's son is to a governor of some unnamed territory. The burning of the offenders enacts early holocaust that is defined as burning a sacrifice for one's deity. The priests are condemned to be burned in ovens. (Foster 2005: 288:)

PRIESTLY ABUSE OF OFFICE

(credited to a son of Hammurabi, Samsuiluna c. 1749-1712 B.C.E.)

> Concerning all the holy places of Babylonia, from one end of the land to the other, which I have placed entirely in your hands, I have heard that the temple staff, governing collegium, cultic officiants, and attendants to the gods of every holy place of the land of Babylonia have taken up dishonesty, commit sacrilege, have stained themselves with blood, and averred improprieties. Inwardly they profane(?) and blaspheme(?) their gods, all the while strutting about

talking nonsense. They establish for their gods matters that the gods did not command.

[Samsuiluna, self proclaimed king of the universe, tells the governor what to do with those priests.]

… Now then, before the great gods, on account of their vice and sacrilege against the gods, do you destroy them, burn them, roast them, [throw them] into ovens, see that their smoke rises up, make a fiery spectacle of them in raging bonfires of thorn bushes! Then every anointer (for divine office) should witness and learn, they should be afraid to speak to me, Samsuiluna, the mighty king, about the commands of Anu and Enlil!

CHAPTER 10

Inanna's Titles, Epithets, and Equivalent Names

ALL NAMES ARE FOR ONE GODDESS

Inanna inspired many a poet; it is a rare Ancient Near Eastern text that has no mention of her as Inanna, Irinni, Ishtar, Belet-ili, Antu, Annunitum, Geshtinanna, Ishara and other less-encountered epithet names. The Great Goddess has thousands of names around the globe. I collected more than 9,000 names while researching this book. The goddess names came from intensely reading Ancient Near Eastern texts and lighter delving into indigenous peoples of North and South America and the rich trove of Japan, China, Africa and Europe. Many of her names are delightfully exotic when heard. When translated, they are similar worldwide. The translations are generally an aspect, attribute, or descriptor of the global goddess ideology. These names are not separate deities. They are all aspects of Great Mother, the prime progenerator creatress — woman's global explanation of "Life." The fewer the names known for a goddess the more distant she is from the first mother or her culture of origin. Life is understood by women; there is no importation or a first Great Mother export from a single first location. Great Mother is recognized everywhere: in image, word and concept. She is one while she appears to be many. The one is two, mother-daughter, or three: maid, mother, crone — life (mother), death (death mother), return (maid).

Because Inanna is an aspect of Great Mother, and Great Mother is universal, I include the following on the inclusiveness of all names of goddesses being of the first Great Goddess wherever her people live. Barbara Walker, in her comprehensive *Woman's encyclopedia of Myths and Secrets,* has this to say about India's Kali and her many names (Walker 1983: 491:)

> Western scholars erroneously viewed the various manifestations and incarnations of Kali as many different Goddesses, particularly isolating those primitive matrikadevis (mother goddesses) grouped together as "Dravidian she-ogres." Yet Kali's worshippers plainly stated that she had hundreds of divergent names, but they were all the same Goddess ... All were Kali Mahadevi, the "Great Goddess" — the same title she bore among western pagans ... "Mother Earth," (is) said to be interchangeable with Venus. [Venus is Inanna]

Professor Kramer translated scattered Sumerian tablets for forty years and pieced Inanna's story together fragment by fragment; his description below sums up his impressions of Inanna. (Kramer 1979: 84:)

> Inanna was celebrated and glorified not only in epic and myth, but also in a vast hymnal repertoire consisting of a varied assortment of psalms, lyrics, and chants as well as numerous dirges and threnodies[58] relating primarily to the death of her lover and husband, the shepherd-king Dumuzi. In these hymnal compositions, as in the epics and myths, the goddess emerges as a complex, many sided personality embodying contrasting attitudes and contradictory characteristics.

---

[58] songs of lament

Deities of a limited range of characteristics are a fragmented derivative of an earlier, larger, more encompassing divine persona. That Inanna is so complex and complete is evidence of her earliness; her wide-ranging attributes and numerous epithets anchor her to the prime creatress. She *expands* to embrace the advance of farming and the settlements growing into cities. She *accepts* and *includes* immigrants; she *grants* mercy to captives and interacts with other people's pantheons. Imported goddess equivalents add features as immigrant cultures merge. Changing political situations require her to be a warrior goddess. When conflicts are lost, her black haired people explain the defeat as her abandonment of their ruler; they attempt to placate her anger and soothe her heart. As a Paleolithic goddess, she requires no soothing; men had not yet invented war.

This chapter will include songs written to Inanna's equivalent goddess names; she is the same goddess in different languages and locations emphasizing local geography and economy. Nanay is an equivalent name for Inanna, as are Irnina, Ishtar and others listed near the end of this chapter. In c. 1749-1712 B.C.E., a poet-scribe describes the planet Ninsianna (our Venus) as a young, beautiful, strong, and confident woman, the goddess Nanay. The poem is dedicated to Nanay who is of high rank and has light like the sun. She is beautiful and brilliant like the new moon. Nanay sings a song of love; she is "abundance, self-assurance, sweetness, and charm;" she sends people "joy, laughter, and loveliness." The star's celestial path is a good omen. Nanay keeps "sincerity, well-being, vigor, decorum ... and vitality" beside her. "She knows her powers!" The goddess is playful, lovable, laughing, exuberant and has a "glowing heart;" she is queen of all the people from all directions (Foster 2005: 89-90). (ibid: 90:)

...

"O Capable, wise, capable Lady,
"Fierce Irnina [Nanay/Inanna], most valiant of the Igigi-gods,
"You are the highest one above them,
"Among them your names are held highest in regard."

308

When differently-named sacred women share attributes, powers, and defining characteristics, we have the same globally acknowledged sacred woman. Similarities may also result from importation through peaceable population migration and/or political conquest. Similarities represent universal concepts of conscious understanding of life. Human behavior is given mythic amplification in story. Goddess names, titles, and epithets, when translated or viewed in image, reveal the widespread similarity of human thought.

Sumerian Inanna reigns as the most popular deity by the time writing develops. Inanna blends with the snake goddess of the "Ubaidian" culture that preceded the Sumerians; her snake epithet is universal. She is the vaginal snake, umbilical cord, deliverer of new life. Sumerian language has no known language root. It is not Semitic, as are most of the other Mesopotamian languages. The Sumerian culture in the southern Near East (the area currently referred to as the Middle East and Iraq) is both advanced and emulated. Their language ceases as a living language when the Semitic population outnumbers and merges with the Sumerians, both peacefully and aggressively. The early Sumerians' blending with indigenous "Ubaidians" blossomed rapidly into a high culture in every way: writing, early bicameral governance, great creativity, and an unforgettable young mother goddess religion.

A millennium and a half after the high culture of southern Sumer is established, Sargon the Great, a semitic king of northern Sumer unifies northern and southern Sumer and imposes his Akkadian language. The Sumerian language and writing continues use only as the "high culture" of sacred, literary, and legal contracts, though it disappears as a living language. (The last Sumerian cuneiform clay tablet was impressed in the first century of our Common Era.) When the north and south of Sumer, the "land between the two rivers" (Mesopotamia) are unified, Sumerian Inanna and Akkadian Ishtar are also united — giving Ishtar more class and Inanna more sass.

Ishtar is not exactly like Inanna. Ishtar represents the maiden mother of a more aggressive hard-living people. Inanna and Ishtar are similar: both own the universal goddess qualities and are comparable; the two names are easily equated. The south has farming, herding, high culture, and a long established religious system while the north is richer but lacks high culture. The unification is a historical first in acquisition and territorial political organization. Inanna is highly developed and popular; Sargon makes Inanna's symbol and name synonymous with his personal goddess, Ishtar. Ishtar is more aggressive. She represents the evening star like Inanna, but her morning star persona is masculine and warlike (wars are fought in daylight). Inanna's morning star leads people back into day after a night of rest, lovemaking, and dreams; i.e., they return to consciousness and the workday. Ishtar, as morning star, leads men into battle. Herding Semitic Akkadians are more warlike than agrarian Sumerians. When Ishtar is represented as the morning star, she is occasionally shown with a beard. The beard has three possible meanings. The first is that war is manly and so she changes into a man or at least wears a beard. Remember, Inanna and Ishtar turn men to women and women to men. The beard could represent rays of light or the star's reflected light path on water. Another possibility is that the Semitic morning star may have begun as a god and merged with Ishtar or else they were an androgynous twin set from early days. Both goddesses are the young and beautiful maid of fertility aspect of mother goddess, new moon, evening star, and grantors of kingship through the *hieros gamos.*

The two versions of a universal goddess are rooted to a prime creatress: Inanna to Nammu and Ishtar to Tiamat. Both goddesses are powerful and alluring, love a vegetation god consort, oversee sexuality and fertility, and are shown with lions. They are both lionesses. Inanna and Ishtar are shown either nude or dressed. They are the only deities portrayed nude with the exception of the ancient Mother Goddess. This too indicates they are the daughter/maid aspect of the first global religious belief, Great Mother, Life. When nude, they offer a breast and their pubic triangle is emphasized. The breast they offer is a rain cloud bringing rain; the breast is nourishment for the land and the people. The held breast is not Neolithic eroticism! Yes, both goddesses are alluring and represent the art of women to tame the men; yes, sacred sexual pleasure is practiced at their temples, but the offered breast is far older than Inanna/Ishtar's temple sex priestesses.

Nude or dressed, they both wear beads at their necks, headdresses or tiaras; they carry scepters, rod, ring, and line, or instruments of war. Interestingly, in many seal impressions, the quiver at Inanna's back appears to hold shafts ending in serpent heads and plant buds. Both are Queen of Heaven, Queen of Earth; they descend into the underworld and return. They are both queen of the storehouse. Inanna's pictogram of paired reed storehouse doorposts is the interchangeable representation for Inanna and Ishtar when Sargon decrees them equivalent. Translators interchange the two names. In time, Ishtar is the prominent name used and remembered into the Common Era when "Ishtar" is synonymous, again, with "goddess."

Sumerian outcomes, win or lose, are related to fate, and fate is decided by the birth-mother goddess. Inanna/Ishtar is the young form of Great Mother in the matrinity. Inanna/Ishtar is the maid of potential fertility and decreer of fate. Neolithic settled farming depends on fertility of crops and herds; Inanna/Ishtar is that fertility.

Inanna is the crescent new moon, maid, fertility to come. Full moon is the time of ovulation and fruition of potential fertility. Mother moon is the White Goddess of many cultures. Moon is the celestial mother of women. She waxes from possibility to round-bellied actuality. Moon and women synchronize in a moon dance. Great Mother is also the chthonic Earth Mother. Imagine the brilliance of our foremothers everywhere conceiving the fullness of life that includes the celestial globe and earth linked together, encompassing past, present and future all at once as one! One mother who births all life.

Earth is the mother who gives forth plants and animals and her human children. Caves and the underground are her vagina and womb. The dead are returned to her safekeeping and rest with her while awaiting a new life cycle. Rebirth. A young woman and Inanna are the moon's child in their menses and seclusion. They are the magical bridge between heaven and earth, dark and light, death and life. They emerge from their dark seclusion chamber at dawn and run with the new coming light of day and waxing crescent moon.

Inanna is Queen of heaven and Queen of Earth. She is at home in both heaven and earth. She is moon's child, she is earth's child — she brings fertility. She is Nammu's (Sumerian prime creatress) aspect/child and has access to the underworld. When our goddess's story bits and pieces are reassembled, we have restored, re-storied, early goddess in her fullness. Queen of almost everything; mother of all.

MOTHER

Mother is life and mother is the goddess. Life is sacred, woman is sacred, and a great mother of all is supremely sacred. Sacred woman, divine feminine, resonates within our deepest cellular memories of motherhood passed on one generation to the next. The 1% of human time when men intentionally decide to direct sacredness off planet to deities who mirror male behavior and speak only to men is upon us. Remember Great Mother and human motherhood. Sacred and human wombs are the nets that catch the little fish of the birth ocean. Once Inanna held a lapis lazuli net that she cast out, first catching new life in the womb, then later, according to priestly scribes, catching enemies of her people like capturing fish or birds. Men now have hold of her net and have entangled all life in it.

Mother is the sacredness of life. Y-men have forgotten the sacredness of life. Without women's maternal wisdom and guidance, male consciousness devolves. When life is no longer sacred, when women's maternity and reproduction control are owned by men and male-based religions, when women are silenced, when those who remember a Great Mother and refuse conversion to a man-made "great father" are tortured and killed; when those who are deemed different and inconvenient are victimized, inquisitioned, tortured, stake-burnt and put to death in mass holocausts; when women do not own their bodies and reproductive rights — we have the diagnostic symptoms of a world dominated by Y-men. We have a global culture that is sick; a world that is dying; an upside-down world that is necrophilic and not biophilic. Under the net of domineering captivity, we have a world where those who enact the eternal Great Mother and maternal qualities, who love and protect life, who refuse to hurt and kill, who instead of greedily squeezing the resources and life out of the world insist on stewardship, conservation, and protection are called "weak" and "womanly." There is nothing weak about "womanly"! When Inanna's story is pieced together, so too is woman's story made whole. When Inanna is called "mother" and "woman" in her songs, she is sharing our womanhood. She understands; she is of us; she and we are life. The only hope for a healthy planet and blossoming positive human creative potential is to remember the other 99% of human time: goddess time; woman's wisdom time; Great Mother time.

GODDESS OF HEALING — GULA/INANNA

Goddess is women's wisdom, caring, and healing. Women are the healers, they know the plants, tend the young, old, ill, or injured in all traditional cultures. Naturally, healing belongs to the Mother Goddess and her young "daughter" self. Inanna is variously called Bau and Baba. A goddess of healing, Gula (aka Bau, Inanna, Baba), appears with the same names and is an obvious equivalent of Inanna. Remember, Inanna has, as one of her MEs, access to descend and ascend, to come and go in the underworld. Gula/Baba/Bau/Nanshe/Inanna is/are also called Nintinugga, Lady who revives the dead. Baba is associated with Bau/Gula. Gula is a healing goddess, depicted in figure 42, with a dying man. Gula retains her half-zoomorphic form in Sumerian seal art. She often has a woman's body and a dog's head or else is accompanied by dogs. Dogs are long associated with death; they protect the souls of the dead and bring them to the goddess. Dogs are carrion eaters and associated with dead flesh and death. Dogs are also guardians. Small painted clay dogs are buried under thresholds and beside gateways. They protect the inhabitants from demons and attract good fortune. Dog is Gula's emblem just as Hecate has her hounds. Gula is a healer goddess; some people cannot be healed so she is also associated with death and the underworld. Inanna does not have a dog emblem; her underworld connection is menstrual seclusion. Inanna's fertility comes out of the dark moist earth womb. Where earth stops and netherworld begins is a blurred demarcation. Gula's dog persona is outside the hut in figure 42. Dogs guard the spirits of the dead and the living from demons. We find Gula paired with Ninurta who is Ishtar's son and an underworld god. He is the son of the Mistress of All Gods who is also the Mother of All the Gods.

Figure 42. Gula and Dying Man

Foster comments that only goddesses speak their own praise. (I found that Enki, Enlil and Marduk also self-praise!) Does Inanna/Ishtar/Gula's self-praise remind us of goddess's powers? Do the reminders of her glory begin because maleness is usurping the goddess and her devoted scribes are extolling her old powers for her? Is the goddess, i.e. her cult, reaffirming her great past status through the words of a poet who loves her and is devoted to her continuation and/or favor? The latter, gaining favor, is obvious in the following poem, "Gula Hymn of Bullutsa-Rabi," The poet is ill and beseeches the healing goddess for help. To curry divine favor, humans adopt groveling and compliments; they use amplified superlatives and reminders of the asker's previous devotion. Enheduanna writes a similar praise poem to exalt Inanna when her en-ship is threatened. Here, the goddess speaks for herself. Gula owns the great star in heaven. Her name also belongs to the netherworld; she assures us that she is splendid, dignified, supreme, and sublime. She gives "good health and life (Foster 2005: 583- 84)."

The "Gula Hymn of Bullutsa-Rabi" in Fosters anthology was copied c. 1500-1000 B.C.E. but tells a mythic story from earlier times (ibid.: 583-84). Gula speaks to us with self-praise. The first poem line does not read *"this* goddess" but *"the* goddess". The goddess is *the* first deity in mythic story. Gula tells us that she is first in the minds of her people. She is gently supreme for countless millennia before male gods are born. The poem describes the goddess before human society and politics become complex and before sacred representatives mirror that complexity. She is a Mother Goddess who fits the needs of egalitarian gatherer-hunter societies and early farming settlements. She is petitioned for assistance in difficult times; she is praised for her gift of plentiful food. She supplies the pharmacy. Her daughters, the women, are talented in caring for the dependent, infirm, sickly, or injured. In Sumer, healing and laying-in takes place in or near the women's quarters of home or temple. Healing belongs to the women.

Healing goddesses are an aspect of Mother Goddess who is modeled on women's caring, wisdom, and abilities. We remember what is obvious and deeply believed: women care for the sick; they know the plants in all cultures. Inanna/Ishtar has the birth plant that Etana needs to cure his wife's infertility. The healing goddess's names are used interchangeably with Inanna. Complexity fragments the Mother Goddess aspects into numerous stand-alone goddesses. However, the all-encompassing relationship of the numerous names is understood by the Sumerian listeners who long ago embraced the myth.

The text alternates between self-praise and praise for her "husband" Ninurta, but below, I reference only lines about the goddess. I would suggest that instead of "husband", "consort" would be the more accurate noun. Ninurta elsewhere is Ishtar's son. He evolved out of an early chthonic goddess. His name means "Lord Earth". NIN originally is feminine and means "queen" or "lady". NIN, only later, includes "lord" in its definition. Ninurta's name implies that he is an aspect of the queen of the earth and became a separate personality. Inanna is named Queen of Heaven, Queen of Earth, and occasionally Queen of the Underworld. As Gula describes herself, she is equivalent to Inanna.

The following lines of the Gula/Inanna hymn are informative (Foster 2005: 584:)

"I was sought out, for Enlil chose me among goddesses,
"He looked up [], he fell in love with me.
"He wed me [for …] his supremacy.

Note: the goddess's love and initiatory copulation was required for Enlil's kingship, "he wed me for … his supremacy". Like Inanna/Ishtar, Gula confers kingship to a god. She also calls herself Mother Nanshe, goddess of boundaries in the fields; she tells us she is loved by the constellation "Plowman" who announces it is time for plowing the furrows. Gula is matron of seeds, plow, and plowman; she measures the fields with the cord and rod and uses her stylus to do the storehouse accounting (Foster 2005: 585). Inanna, in an explicit love song to Dumuzi, asks him to plow her field. Plowing is also a euphemism for sex. As Queen of Earth, Inanna, and here Gula, are directly concerned with fertile fields; the vaginal cleft is a furrow. When the Plowman constellation rises, farmers plow. The goddess blesses the men doing the plowing. All aspects of fertility are her concern.

Figure 43. Ring, Rod, Line and Plant

Gula/Inanna speaks of her "measuring cord, cubits, and measuring rod." Images of Inanna/Ishtar and Lilith often hold the ring, line, and rod. These tools are for measuring fields to reestablish boundaries after the annual river flooding and for building. Kings' images hold the measuring tools to indicate a time of peace as only during lulls in warring did building and rebuilding take place. Successful war brings worker slaves; peacetime means that men, slaves and corvee laborers are available for building.

When our self-praising goddess says she "carries a stylus as she works, doing the accounts," she is directly concerned with pressing the reed stylus into hand-held damp clay tablets to record the contents of her storehouse. That is, she is a goddess of cuneiform writing, the scribal arts, that originated in the storehouse. Since goddess is the matron of the scribal art, an assumption that women invented writing does not miss the mark. Gula/Inanna here is also equivalent to Nisaba who "holds the pure reed." She is the scribe goddess who has the lapis lazuli tablet of heaven; she is also "the honest woman," matron of scribes, writing, accounting and wisdom. Nisaba is a "sister" of Nanshe/Inanna and is also mentioned as a name for Gula/Inanna (Leick 1991: 137-8). By calling herself "Mother Nanshe," she identifies herself with Mother Sea who is Nammu/Tiamat (prime parthenogenetic creatress); "the fish house" is the sea, rivers, and canals (ibid.:127).

The text continues with the goddess telling us she is superior in heaven, and queen of the underworld and the depths. She has no equal! When she proclaims a limit, she must be obeyed. She towers in height and is enormous in size. She gives powers to the gods. As Pabilsag, she heals, as Ninkarrak, she counsels (Foster 2005: 586).

Inanna/Ishtar is queen of heaven and earth; Gula is "sublime" in heaven and queen in the netherworld. Inanna is also queen of the underworld. She visits the underworld (see "Descent to the Underworld" in chapter 11) where she sits on the throne of the assigned queen Ereshkigal. The queen of the dead is Inanna's "sister" in the matrinity. Mother, queen of the dead, and maid Inanna are all one goddess.

Gula has no equal; Inanna/Ishtar has no equal. No god is their peer. "No god can say her nay" is written of Inanna/Ishtar. Inanna is a lioness who stirs or calms the gods. The goddess of all these names commands; all of her equivalents are huge and sublime, all give counsel, and all are mother and bride.

The goddess states she is "the physician" and saves the moribund. She knows all the herbs and dresses wounds with salve and bandage. Another name for her is Ninigizibara, "Lady looked upon with confidence." Gula/Inanna/Ishtar describes both her healing abilities and her role as goddess of incantations. Human nature uses magical thinking and creative imagination to enhance ordinary reality. Incantations are magical thinking made into ritual "magic;" sorcery is fervent desire imagined both for healing and cursing. Incantation does not appear in earlier Sumerian texts when Inanna is Queen of almost everything. Magic comes later, it grows from fear and desire for healing that becomes a religious substitute for good pharmaceutical knowledge. Incantations are useful and convenient for political support and intimidation. Magic is also a source of financial gain as one paid the incantation priests for the ineffective treatment (ibid.: 587).

The queen of all that is vital has numerous epithet names. Mother goddess remains present even as popular appeal and sustainable farming embrace the "daughter" who retains all power attributed to the mother goddess. The "daughter" gathers more acclaim and importance as urban living becomes complex and new technologies enhance the economy. Our goddess as Gula continues telling us who she is: skilled warrior, maker of decisions and commands; she is merciful for the weak and able to make the poor rich. She is the "great one ... life of the people (ibid.: 587-8)."

Gula/Inanna assures us her voice among the goddesses is the fairest, her mother Antu ("Lady Sky") taught her to be fair and joyful. Her father made her better than her brothers (the gods) (ibid.: 589).

The Gula hymn tells the listener that Gula is an experienced warrior; she makes decisions and decrees. The goddess dwells on high at Ekur ("house-mountain"), meaning the temple on top of a stepped platform. She is merciful. She is "daughter" of Anu. This statement indicates she is both old and powerful. An, the generally benign and distant chief male deity represents the first inclusion of maleness, has Gula/Inanna as *his* consort. We need to go back one step; kingship is conveyed by consorting with the goddess. Actually, he is *her* consort. As patriarchy grows, she becomes "his" consort and then his "daughter." Relational change indicates demotions for the goddess and usurpation of her traditional powers.

Gula/Inanna speaks of her youthful incomparable beauty. Inanna/Ishtar is the young queen of great beauty. Attractive, alluring, and seductive are descriptions whose qualities are important, natural, and necessary for fertility and life on earth. Gula/Inanna is part of the prime creatress, Nammu/Tiamat, who makes earth and earth without a partner and is single until newly devised gods are her consort; she is the monotheaistic one from mistant distant time.

Seasons renew. Renewal is Great Mother's youthful aspect. Mother Goddess is occasionally represented in Old European images as two female figures partially joined. The younger and older versions are one. In Mesopotamia, Inanna is young vital fertility and potential. As daughter of Antu, she is daughter of herself. She is celestial and earthly from the beginning; she is Mother Goddess by whichever name she is called.

In the poem, she calls herself Ninsun, "Lady Wild Cow." Wild cow refers to moon's crescent horns and light color. Animals with curved horns and white coloration are globally sacred to Mother Goddess as moon. Moon's phases represent women's menstrual and fertility cycle. Moon is female from the beginning. Wild Cow indicates a time before domestication of herd animals, possibly from before agriculture and well before urban centers. Gula/Inanna is very old.

Deciphering the text further, Gula/Inanna excels the gods, her "brothers." Ea/Enki, fresh water god, gives Gula all his wisdom. Here is another Sumerian story of Enki "giving" the goddess something that was already hers. (See "Inanna and the God of Wisdom" in Chapter 2.) Gula does not need Enki's wisdom, she already has her wisdom!

Gula's hymn recitation states that Ea/Enki also gave her the secret of the physician's craft. This could mean the plants of healing (practiced by women), but more likely, since it is Enki involved, this means magic craft. Jacobsen refers to a text in which Enki does have a connection with healing plants but in a sordid way. (Jacobsen 1987: 183-4:)

> *Enki is the "personified river." He attempts to put his penis into the "reeds" of Nintur ("Lady who gives birth") and she refuses him. NO!*[59] *(Jacobsen suggests the reeds are the pubic hairs of mother earth.) Enki formally marries her and she gives birth to goddess Ninnisiga (green mountains). Enki impregnates his daughter, Ninnisiga, when she is grown and goes down to the river. She births goddess Ninkurra (high mountains) who grows up, ventures to the river and is "conquered" by Enki. Ninkurra gives birth to goddess Nin-imma who matures and is accosted by Enki at the river. She produces Uttu (goddess of weaving). "By the time Uttu is grown up, it appears that Enki's long-suffering actual wife, Ninhursaga, has finally lost patience with his philandering (ibid: 184)." She gives Uttu warning and when Enki comes to Uttu's house looking for her, she is secure within. He wants her. She says NO! He asks what gift would make her say YES to "marriage" (though he is already nominally "married" to Ninhursaga). Uttu tells him she would like a gift of fruit and vegetables. Enki provides irrigation for a farmer who gives the god plenty of fruit and veggies. The great-great-great-grandfather returns to lovely Uttu with the gifts. She is pleased. He gets her drunk on beer and rapes her. She screams. Ninhursaga comes running. She curses Enki and removes his semen from the little goddess of weaving and puts it in the ground. Eight plants grow.*
>
> *Enki and his vizier see the eight new plants. The crafty god did not know what they were so his vizier gave them names and handed them to Enki to eat. Of course Enki gets pregnant eight times over. He has no vulva. He can not give birth. He writhes in agony. He is near death. The gods are in despair. A little fox offers to get Ninhursaga from the foothills. She comes running, curse forgotten, and puts Enki into her vulva. From her body she births eight goddesses and gods — the healing plants. Enki "owns" the healing plants by misdeed.*

---

[59] Nintur is also known as Ninhursaga

Enki is the crafty god who has authority over magical incantations. Incantation healing, a priestly addition, veers sharply from time-honored women's plant medicine and hands-on treatments. Gula becomes goddess of incantation and divining as well as healing.

Gula describes herself as mistress of heaven and the netherworld. Mesopotamian recovery from illness requires divine intervention. Illness, injury, and birthing takes lives. Death is always nearby.

When story is new and Goddess Mother supreme, she is everything important as every mother is to her babe. Beneath the earth surface was her dark and moist womb. Fertility. Regeneration. Patriarchy changes death from a portion of the life cycle, life-death-renewal, into a one way journey.

War was invented with all its destruction, maiming, murder, and mayhem; with its disregard for people's lives, rights, and existence. The renewal part was excised and death became permanent. The underworld, once a womb tomb, became a dreaded netherworld. Return to new life is replaced by permanent gloom and dust where the ghostly inhabitants forever eat clay for bread and dust for beer. The number of the dead is greater than the living. Over time, the dead were feared, their count accumulated. They became hungry ghosts, who would devour the out-numbered living if freed. Patriarchal non-return policy took away hope. Remove hope, instill fear, add punishment and threat, and people are controlled. (See chapter 11.)

Gula/Inanna continues her self-praise hymn: her allure cannot be ignored, she drips charm and splendor. "In my bed ... there is no one like me." She hears prayers from great distances, she is a surgeon with a scalpel, she lances sores and looks after the ill; she is an exorcist and diviner. She understands all the writing and wisdom and equates herself with merciful Ninlil (Foster 2005: 590-91).

The alignment with Ninlil, Lady Air, consort to Enlil, is interesting as he also occasionally consorts with Inanna. Gula is "mistress of life," as are all mother goddesses. The taking of the Ninlil name, "Queen of Air," is puzzling. Ninlil is consort to/of Enlil, "Lord Air." He is promoted as the authority for An(u), his father, who remained benignly distant and nominally king of the Sumerian pantheon. Ninlil's first name is Sud; her mother is Nanibgal, an agricultural earth goddess of grain and childbirth. Sud is a daughter-mother goddess of great power. I sense the underpinning of the same old old story here: Sud, Ninlil, Gula and Inanna are the same daughter aspect of Great Mother.

An Enlil myth arose tainted with priestly manipulation. Sud is beautiful. Enlil sees her river-bathing. He is looking for a wife. (Read that as: priestly matchmaking in search of a powerful goddess for him to "marry" and own her power.) She rejects him. He must jump through hoops asking permission of her mother who needs to be won over. In those olden days, father was not yet in full control of such matters. Enlil sends many gifts. Finally both mother and daughter are won over and the marriage takes place. Enlil changes Sud's name first to Nintu (the Lady who gives Birth), then Ashnan (grain), and finally to Ninlil, Queen of Air, who will have control over people's lives. Birth goddesses grant long or short lives.

The final Gula hymn sections reiterate Gula's physician role. When she "fetches up the dead from the netherworld," this likely means she brings people back from the brink of death and they recover. A similar statement is used by Ishtar but as a threat. She threatens to raise the dead who are so plentiful they will devour the living. Ereshkigal uses the same threat to make her lover, Nergal, return to her or else she will release her dead children who out-number the living. The names of Gula and Inanna/Ishtar are associated with the netherworld.

Accounting and writing are attributed to her. Gula is "expert in calculations." She carries the ring, rod, and line of measuring and building as does Inanna/Ishtar/Lilith. Math is part of the scribal arts as is accounting. The scribal poet has an ulterior motive for composing Gula's self-praise hymn. He is very ill. Her consort/spouse Ninurta has apparently decreed the illness and the poet is flattering and beseeching Gula to intercede on his behalf (Foster 2005: 591).

INANNA/NANSHE

People and their deities are on the move throughout the Ancient Near East into the mid last millennium B.C.E.. One of the earliest cities is Eridu. Through change of population or leadership, various divine personalities rise and fall. Nammu, prime creatress and her "son" Enki are the tutelary deities of Eridu. In the following poem, we meet goddess Nanshe, a local equivalent of Inanna, who is given her own temple in another growing settlement, Nina. The temple built for her is called Siratr; this made Nina a "cosmic" center, a seat of religious authority. The universality of thought expressed in symbol and image is recognizable. The same ideas about life, love, and everything is explained with wide brush strokes in varied languages and dialects. Everywhere, goddess understanding is based on woman's bodies as metaphor for Life. When a young beautiful powerful fertile goddess appears with all the powers of her "mother" and then some, we recognize her Neolithic importance for farming and fertility for settled people. We find goddess equivalents by comparing their attributes, duties, and powers. The reader will easily see Inanna in Nanshe, or Nanshe in Inanna. Local deities make cameo appearances in the story.

Imagine that we are present at a dedication for Nanshe's new home. Sargon the Great's daughter and en-priestess, Enheduanna, has composed the following poem. An ancient governor and famous temple builder, Gudea, is her chief priest who makes decisions about the temple music for the installation. (Jacobsen 1987: 126-42:)

THE NANSHE HYMN
(TEMPLE REDEDICATION, INSTALLATION
OF A MAJORDOMA,
AND NEW YEAR RITUAL)

Just a city it was, just a city it was,
    but she felt urged
    to begin envisaging
    its sacred offices.

. . .

The mountain rising out of the waters
    was just a city –
    but she felt urged
    to begin envisaging
    its sacred offices!

She felt urged to have the day
    of a proper house
    begin dawning,
    felt urged to begin determining
    its mode of being,
felt urged to have the appropriate brickwork [size of bricks]
    make an appearance in the city,
felt urged to have the rites of mother Nanshe
    begin being carried out right.
Its mistress, child born in Eridu,
    Nanshe,
    mistress of all the precious sacred offices,
    was turning to a place of her (own).

. . .

How did the smaller city of Nina rate a new temple, a home for Nanshe? Did the important local deities of a usurping king include Nanshe? Did Nanshe become so popular, so necessary for the people, that she outgrew her "daughter of Enki" role and earned her own city? Was a local goddess elevated to serve the heightened role of Inanna of Sumer and Ishtar of Akkad? The answer could be: all of the above, but Jacobsen writes: "Nina and its temple Siratr with its cult of Nanshe go back to the early third millennium and probably much farther, even to the first settlement of the country (ibid.: 126)." Nanshe has all of Inanna's attributes with emphasis on her being goddess of the marsh, canebrake, fishes, herbs, fruit, grain, boundaries, irrigation ditches, water, and the land's storehouse. She is equivalent to Inanna.

The following portion of text addresses her storehouse abundance and the goddess's fairness and concern for everyone. Both Nanshe and Inanna are traditional mother-goddesses with fairness, protection, and caring attributes.

> Waif and widow she delivered not up.
> She took note of men
>   who used force against men,
>   was mother to the waif,
> Nanshe was the widow's guardian,
> finding (justly) in cases in the millhouse.[60]
>
> The queen (Nanshe) carried fugitives on the hip
> searched the region for the helpless ones.
> . . .
>
> For the honest slave girl
>   who had laid hold of her feet,
> Nanshe was figuring up
>   her warping (weaving) and justly obtained wages,
> for the widow she had not helped to remarry
>   Nanshe was supporting,
> like a beam, a proper house.
> . . .

The goddess gives the nod to build her temple through a king's dream or priestly divinination. The temple is built and the goddess herself appoints a head administrator. Early kings and rulers are the head priests. Gudea refers to himself in an inscription as *ur*-Nanshe, "lion" of Nanshe, her guardian. He receives his scepter from her as her shepherd — another parallel with Inanna and her beloved Dumuzi.

---

[60] Widows and their children staff the millhouse; whether the disputes were between the women or workers and overseers is unclear, regardless, she is protection and fairness.

She (now) felt urged
    to envision in the holy heart
    a high priest,
he seated with her on the throne dais
    Nanshe's lion,[61]
    the beloved high priest of Lagash,
and granted august scepter to the shepherd.

Gudea perfected for her
    all her precious sacred offices.
Her shepherd, envisioned in the holy heart,
Gudea, ruler of Lagash,
stationed among the *tigi* strings
    the princely, sweet sounding, tambourines,
stationed with them holy harps,
and to the holy chants
    and the antiphons
    he had performed for her
lyres were giving praise unto the house,
whilst out from amid them
    a chief musician
    was sounding for her
    the shofar horn.
Since she had deemed fit
    to allot to the house
    sacred rites from Apsu,
he sang at its sacred princely rites
    the latter's holy chants
    in Siratr's courtyard.

Early temples are built within the residential areas. The temples' inner sacrosanct areas were once easily accessible to the people. A wide courtyard is added in later temples for publicly attended ceremony.

---

[61] Nanshe's (and Inanna's) lion is the king's epithet.

The inner chambers, in time, are for the elite and specialized temple personnel. Opening a new temple is an important event and includes the people of Nina and beyond. Whether the people attend the ceremony inside the temple or only in the courtyard is uncertain. Since Gudea is of early days, I visualize the people coming inside to see their newly arrived goddess on her elevated dais with the Lagash king seated beside her as her high priest.

Imagine with me. We dress as well as we can and walk in excited groups from our near-by clustered mud brick homes. This is a festival day. All work stops. In the temple's outer court we wash our hands in a basin for purification. The new temple rises high on the rubble mound of previous temple ruins. Dried mud brick has a limited life expectancy even with an outer coating of mud plaster. (The temples are similarly built to our southwestern adobe structures of first-nation people.) Repair and rebuilding of temples is high on every king's to-do list. We walk up new sharply defined steps. Footsteps have not yet trodden them low. We enter the cool interior of Nanshe's new home. We see her elevated on the raised dais, on her throne. An empty chair is beside her.

Cedar incense greets our noses. Nanshe is beautiful to behold. She gazes out at us; she sees us and she knows us. Her eyes are large. She is an all-seeing one. Her face is alabaster white, calm, and lovely. She is dressed in a flounced linen or woolen gown. A robe of red or deep lapis lazuli blue is draped around her shoulders. Nanshe's hair (a decorated coiffed wig) glints with tiny gold stars, gold vulvas, precious stones and thin-pounded gold ribbons. Her hair is shaped into rolled side buns or many braids clustered together. The headdress cap with one or more pairs of horns signifying divinity is a later fashion; here no horned headdress is mentioned and she wears some sort of ornamented tiara or desert head covering as is described in temple offering lists for early Inanna.

We stand in her presence; we do not sit. Light is low. Wavering flickers of pottery oil lamps make shadows dance. Smokey incense wafts, undulating upwards, inviting divine guests to assemble. Along the sidewalls are small cellae with little outside windows. The cella rooms are for tablet storage and serve as chambers for other deities who assemble for Nanshe. The goddess's sleeping chamber is in a private area. Priestesses are housed in or near the main temple building. Direct care personnel are also housed in the temple. There is a women's quarter and somewhere nearby is a place for sheltering widows, orphans, and fugitives.

On a raised shelf, along the interior wall of the central chamber, are the devotional figures of wealthier devotees. Worshippers commission artists to do their likeness in prayerful-adoration positions. The votive figurines constantly adore and pray to the goddess. Most of us attending the dedication could not afford a votive statue. We have mass-molded low-fire clay plaques and small altars in our homes — little shrines where we make offerings to our favorite deities and to our own personal deities who determine our good fortune in life. Common people have less-known deities in attendance, while kings have personal deities such as Nanshe/Inanna/Ishtar. Our names often contain a divine name and announce both our allegiance and those who helps us.

We sense the delicious anticipation of wonder, mystery, and splendor; the awe of being with both goddess and king. We fall silent. Priestesses and priests appear from behind the wall of the dais; musicians enter with harps, drums, and *tigi* stringed instruments,[62] tambourines, and a shofar (ram) horn. Singers and dancers enter. Chanters arrange themselves. The king climbs the steps of Nanshe's dais; he sits beside her as her beloved shepherd consort. The dedication begins. The daughter of Sargon the Great of Akkad has composed a liturgical poem-song for the ceremony. Enheduanna's words are chanted and sung to assure Nanshe of adoration and praise: to remind her of her attributes and powers. The compositions have antiphon chants and instructions: now the lyre, now the harp, now the *tigi* instrument. Today a full musical orchestra/band plays and a shofar horn is blown. The shofar is made of a ram's curving horn and is difficult to play. (It is heard today in temples celebrating Jewish New Year.)

---

[62] A stringed instrument like a harp or lyre with a sound box and tiny drum heads and bells attached.

During a service, dedication, important ceremony, or festival, the deity is offered food and libated by appointed servers. In our imagination we watch a celebrant bring a libation goblet followed by a procession of food. In the outer courtyard, abundant food is being prepared; we will enjoy a public feast after the goddess receives her due:

> A butler stepped up
>> to the libations for her,
> took in hand for her
>> the sparkling silver goblet;
> the butler [poured in]
>> the strong drink for her.
> Hot dishes and cold dishes
>> he was directing up to her.
> Dough (for) half a loaf
>> he had put in the … of the oven for her,
> and at the first [loaf finished]
>> the chief peel[63]
>> called loudly to him.
> After what was butchered
>> had been brought in large bowls,
> after cold water
>> had been brought from Siratr's river,
> after delicacies
>> had been brought from Lagash
> and wine brought[64]
>> from the countryside,
> was – as he (the butler) was having
>> the great oven
> keep up with the (needs of) the dining halls –
>> Nanshe's pantry (storehouse)

---

[63] The baker who removes the finished bread from the ovens using a peel, a long-handled flat shovel.

[64] Here, *kurunnu* is translated "wine". Jacobsen notes it is also the word for dark beer. Wine was introduced after beer was a well-established beverage.

humming (right)
    along with it.

The composition describes the goddess's selection of a woman to be "majordomo" (majordoma!) to run Nanshe's house. "The Sumerian term translated as 'majordomo' is '*lu*', which denotes a man (Akkadian *awilum*) or woman (*awiltum*) who heads a household, firm, or city (ibid.: 130: f. 7)." Was the majordoma announced during the festival we have just attended? The mention of the shofar horn and "at the new year, the day of assignments" means the text is used at the New Year. That a woman holds so high a position delights this contemporary woman searching for women among the dusty remains and tablets. Patriarchy has not yet wrested all the important positions from women. The dynastic priest class is not yet in full power. Temple fare is still shared with the populace; the deities' meat and food offerings are not yet kept only for the dynastic temple priests. We are not told this woman's name so the section is a yearly generic event to install or re-install temple personnel. Later lines describe the review and discharge of dishonest staff and list the names of the honest ones who continue employment.

The following text segment is included to continue assembling goddess attributes and powers and to note that some women hold high positions. The composer of the poem is also a woman, the most fluent composer of liturgical poems for temples in the "land."

The lady, Enlil's matron,
Nanshe, lady of abundance
    living in the land,
calming (?) wrath, woman diviner,
    Enki's daughter,
was on her part installing
    an able woman
    as majordomo
    for the properly run house,
the daily revenues
    were sent straightway

into the temple
from the *bursag*.[65]
Barley was not used as filler
in the emmer-beer rations.
When its (the temple's) revenues
had been brought in
the majordomo
was going to accept
no more than was due.

...

Inanna's name is synonymous with decree-making. She hears petitions and meets with the seven Anunna gods to decide judgments. Nanshe has exactly the same power but meets with two gods of justice: Ningublaga and Hendursaga.

Imagine with me again that we are present in the shadows. Nanshe's outdoor workers in sheepskin line up in the courtyard. The inside workers wear linen and line up in the temple. Nanshe looks into their hearts; she decides who will continue their assignments and who will be sent away. Their last year's performance is assessed. Those men deemed honest and hard working remove all their clothing and approach her nude; seals having to do with Inanna's temple also show men approaching her in worshipful supplication. They are nude, meaning they are ritually purified, bathed, to be in her presence. (I have not read of women brought nude before the goddess perhaps because they ritually purified by bathing at the end of their menses.)

"With the men on the attendance lists ranged (side) by side, she would be calling for eyewitnesses among them ... (ibid.: 133)." One who committed to the temple, has run away; he is crossed from the record. Her keeper of the temple seal, a scribe, creates a new tablet roster. Men and women not selected by Nanshe are not kept in the roster. Her good servants are reinstated. New year is also the time of reinstating the king but it is not part of the present text. That the king sat beside the

---

[65] collection place of farm products for the temple

goddess as the ceremony began, may indicate he is already re-enlisted for another year.

We hear reasons for dismissal: drinking wine without diluting it with water and stumbling about drunk; neglecting cleanliness with the bread trough; and making noise in the goddess's house during the midday rest.

Priests are also examined. A *Bala* priest is sent to serve for a specified period of time in the religious center of Nippur. A libation *shita* priest who left his post while on *bala* duty is cited as well as another priest who took a small landholder as his own, and a priest administrator who left temple life and neglected to teach both the "learned and unlearned" the chants he knows, therefore the people could not do the rites for the goddess. We hear that the temple does not expand its "spells" and rituals without good reason. No man in office may "set bounds" because Nanshe is goddess of boundary marking. This implies also that the temple does not want tampering with set ritual by priestly whim or kingly persuasion. Nanshe is from Eridu, king Gudea is from Lagash, and priests spend *bala* time at Nippur — the religious center of the land. There is a liturgical universality that extends over the miles. The goddess is also a universality without boundaries. Different names and epithets born of regional dialects and languages describe the same big and multi-tasking goddess. Her theme is creating and abundance; caring and compassion; wisdom and renewal (ibid.: 134-5).

When Enheduanna composed the above poem, goddess was strong in the hearts of the people. Nanshe/Inanna, she of boundary setting, also made decisions of fairness and justice. She protected women, servants, fugitives, and the king.

Wise women make decisions: the Sumerian doyennes (wise women sages), oracles, diviners, and healers are important. In the poem, a woman known for fairness is installed as majordoma for Nanshe's temple. She is head of the storehouse and oversees distribution. She makes certain that bread for distribution is not stolen and that emmer-beer[66] is not diluted with inferior beer; that food, drink, canebrake, and fish measurements are untampered; that almond saplings of the temple orchards are not stolen and carried out with the compost. The majordoma over sees the correct libations and cleanliness of both dairy products and fish brought by runners (fish are run from the fishermen's boats so the hot sun does not spoil them); and sees to details like the "firewood carrier(s) of the desert," usually women, who are made to make back door deliveries to keep the mundane presence of everyday life out of sight. Remember, a woman has this important administrative position in Nanshe's temple!

JUSTICE IS DISPENSED

Dispensing justice is inspired ultimately by the goddess in the Nanshe Hymn through her lord Hendursaga, who keeps order and sorts out true petitions from false ones. Nanshe/Inanna is called "the lady, august, whose word, [proving true takes precedence] (ibid.: 141)." Her "secretary" is none other than Nidaba, goddess of tablet-writing, scribes, scribal schools, and the reed stylus. Nidaba holds her golden stylus. After reviewing the accounting evidence, Nanshe dispenses the "administrative review." Nanshe stands for fairness. She weeds out arrogant speakers, bullies, violence, land theft by moving boundary markers, unfair taxes, altering weights for measuring, lying and demanding a loaf (temple distribution) when a man already had one, and demanding more drink (beer) when a man already had his. All of these are affronts to the goddess. Her bread and eggs (grain and birds are under her protection) are not to be eaten where there is violence, scowling, and grinding teeth in anger. The following must-not-do list indicates the protection she has for women and the unfortunate. Nanshe knows the bully intimidating other men, the man who "grabs a girl in the street," and the man who marries a widow and, when he is angry,

---

[66] emmer-beer is a higher quality beer of a fermented reddish wheat; it is also called lady-beer

ridicules her "days of infirmity." (This could either be her lean days as a widow or her seclusion and/or her non-availability for sex during her menses.) The composition assures us that Nanshe knows the plight of the victims. "Mother Nanshe has looked into their hearts (ibid.: 135-7)."

All manner of power abuse are examined. If an orphan is said to be a slave, or a homeless girl is given to a powerful man, or a powerless man is given over to a powerful one; if a child threatens or curses its mother or a mother threatens or curses her child, or a younger brother "snarls" at his older brother, or a brother gives his sister up to a man for sex, or a brother brings a man to meet illicitly with his sister; Nanshe knows. "Nanshe sees into the nation's hearts as were it into a split reed, sees its designs and its ruler's secrets (ibid.: 138)."

In the afternoon of our festival for Nanshe's new temple, her inner sacrosanct chamber is sprinkled with water (for purification or dust settling) and the floor is swept for "her midday nap," after which she returns to announce judgments. The gravity of the conclusions is like "a heavy smoke." The judgments are carried out on the terrace by lord Hendursaga, who is lord of the terrace; he carries out Nanshe's verdicts without dispute. He is her constable for enlisting (military), and is "her guardian angel god of youngsters and oldsters;" he does not take a man too young or too old (for military service) (ibid.: 138).

Divorce is legally decreed and the land of the union is split evenly. (That fact alone indicates that Sumerian women have rights!) The righteous are placed together and the "evil" are placed together on the terrace. Waifs and widows can seek justice and all manner of serious complaints between mothers and children are decided. Past tried cases serve as precedent, and proverbs are offered as illustrations for solutions (ibid.: 138-40).

The new temple and newly installed Nanshe/Inanna are given gravitas by the deities of Lagash assembling in support (their figurines are transported by water or cart). Sitting on the dais with Nanshe is "the lady and woman sage of settled Lagash, Gatumdug, ... who makes decisions *like* Enlil ..." (She is an equivalent goddess to Bau and Inanna; she is the tutelary goddess of Lagash.) Nanshe looks into having her sacred offices immaculate, and assigns sacred offices to the temple from

Apsu (ibid.: 141)." The concluding sections are fragmented but we hear that both her storehouses and treasuries are well stocked and overseen by the "mistress of the treasury," who may be Nanshe, but more likely is the majordoma of the temple. The composition ends with (ibid.: 142:)

> (O) Milady, your sacred offices are august
> > sacred offices,
> > surpassing [all other sacred offices]
> Nanshe, not any sacred office
> > can compare with your sacred offices!
> King An is looking at you with happy eye,
> with Enlil on the throne dais
> you have sat down
> > to make decisions with him,
> > Father Enki has determined your mode of being.
> O Nanshe, child born in Eridu,
> > to praise you is sweet!

Eridu is one of the oldest southern cities and the cult center of Enki. Eridu rises out of marshes. Nanshe is a water-based goddess, as is Nammu, prime creatress and mother of Enki. Enki is Old Sumerian. His name means lord (en) of earth (ki). Ki, earth, is earth goddess's original name. Earth includes the underworld as well as the visible earth. Enki is the ground-water (Apsu), fresh water, and the wetlands and lagoons. He is potentially creative, but requires a goddess to activate his potential. He is god of wisdom; he is god of magic and incantations. He both collaborates and competes with the mother goddess; he is occasionally cursed by her. Nammu, prime creatress of the deities, parthenogenetic, represents primal sea (Apsu) and is his mother. Damkina (a mother goddess) is his "wife." Nanshe is said to be his "daughter" (Leick 1991: 40). All the major players in the poem song date back to the Old Sumerian Period and are well established. That indicates they had either developed in "the land" that became Sumer or came from the mysterious original motherland of Sumerian people.

The poem confirms that goddess and women have status. Nanshe/ Inanna is the young potential fertile marsh water aspect of Mother Goddess Damkina, who is a version of the prime creatress, Great Mother, Nammu. Nanshe and Inanna are the potent potential of fertility. Wise women are important to traditional people; they are sought out. Women are elders and wise women are sages in Old Sumerian literature. Wise women decide and settle problems; the "doyennes of women sages" parade in Inanna's New Moon Festival; they are consulted by the people and their kings. Remember, women created culture out of their solidarity, their cooperating life-affirming groups; they organized men into societal participation and told the story of a Great Mother of all. If men had developed early culture, the first story would have been a great father. But they didn't and it wasn't.

Epithets describe attributes of a deity. Epithets are voiced in the language of specific people; they sound exotic and unique when untranslated. Translated, the names are remarkably similar. The epithet often becomes the proper divine name. People moved and merged. Similar deities are equivalents; only names and details vary. Inanna and Ishtar combine their differences and are known by a symbol that was first Inanna's. Nanshe is identified as coming from Eridu, a city situated along a lagoon where water was everywhere and fish a large part of the economy. That she also finds a home in Nina is sensible as it too rose out of the marshes and has the same water-based economy. Her name is the Sumerian sign meaning "fish house" as is Nammu's. Nanshe is especially connected with rivers and irrigation canals. The "daughter" goddesses encompass the specialized aspects of a new technology like irrigation canals for farming. Enki becomes "father" of the fish house and is imaged with the two rivers (Tigris and Euphrates) flowing out from his shoulders and fish swimming in the streams. Nanshe is "fishery inspector of the sea (Apsu)," the fish house; she is goddess of "good things," "sweet things," and divining (Leick 1991: 127).

The composition above lists other attributes of Nanshe's power that are the same as Inanna's: she decides, she decrees, she protects widows, orphans, the poor, the disadvantaged, and the king. She hears petitions and discerns truth. After incantation magic developed, Nanshe and Ishtar are invoked while Inanna is not as magic and incantations are not practiced in Old Sumerian days. Inanna is more about animal and crop fertility and her sexuality/fertility is exaggerated. The sex life of fish does not invoke the same sexual emphasis. I include the Nanshe text because she is born of a great mother concept as is Inanna; she *is* the power of the great mother. That Nanshe appoints a woman majordoma to oversee her house is important; both Inanna and Nanshe have wise women sages, oracles, and diviners connected to them and both protect society's disadvantaged and women in all circumstances. The same is not said of Ancient Near Eastern gods.

Myths are organic. Myths remain relevant or they fade. They change through telling, social and political circumstances, and popular demand. What is poignant lives on; details of place, epithets, and divine functions reflect the society and culture of the people. Another important factor in myth alteration is fear. When times are peaceable and food and water sufficient, the existing myth is believable. When times are threatening without relief, magical thinking embracing a divine presence decides that something new — perhaps another deity can bring assistance — try something more extreme — pile on more praise or go to bigger authority or someone else's deities. Story evolution is natural. As patriarchy entrenches, men replace women and gods replace goddess for all important functions. Patriarchal priests re-make myths. Scribal priests rewrite the stories to support and curry favor from their alpha-priest kings; they promote little-known godlets into high status (examples: Marduk and Yahweh). Extra year-days are available to add and balance lunar months with the solar year. The priests use the extra days to change the days of the month when astronomers and seers make dire predictions for the king. Changing the days means the bad thing would not happen; of course fees and boons are collected and favors accrue.

OTHER NAMES AND EPITHETS FOR INANNA

I collected a list of Inanna/Ishtar names in the years of research. They are included here to impress the reader with the widespread and inclusive powers, descriptors, epithets, and adulations written of Inanna and her equivalent goddesses. The only attribute I find missing is a sense of humor but being a goddess is serious business! Earth and heaven; life, death and return; all life, laws, decrees, fertility, love, wisdom, writing, kingship, seasons, and important celestial bodies are hers *as is almost everything else*. Equivalent goddesses are listed to represent the consistency and universality of Inanna and company. The following name collection comes from Sumerian, Akkadian, Babylonian, and Assyrian texts. A few names will be familiar to the reader; the majority of names and epithets, unknown. As the reader pursues the list, Inanna is recognizable no matter her name. I have furnished translations when they were available. Names and epithets acceptable to the deity of contemporary male religions and popular world mythologies pale compared to the creative and expressive richness of the maid aspect of mother goddess from a geographical area the size of Maryland.

NAMES, TITLES, AND EPITHETS OF INANNA
AND HER EQUIVALENT GODDESSES:

Figure 44. Woman/Goddess in a Window

A-A (=Ayya, Semitic, a voluptuous bride, she is 'Heavenly light,' and 'Mistress adorned with voluptuousness.')

abashushu ('harlot', 'the one who leans out of the window;' Aphrodite Parakyptousa also leans out of a window. See figure 44)

Aethra

Agushaya

Aja (= to Innini, = Ninmulsia (star), also = Senada and Sunu-Da who are consorts of Shamash the sun god; she personifies light 'of heaven,' 'Goddess of Light.' War is fought by day and so she is also 'Goddess of War' as morning star; she is queen of the lands in Sippar and Larsa.)

Alad (aspect of Ishtar who attends her as bovine matroness of flocks and herd animals with curved horns and so represents her crescent moon and coming light.)

Amazement of the Land

Ama-geshtin-anna

Ama-ushumgal (Mother, Great Serpent Mother.)

Anat (is also Ashertu and As(h)tart, western Semitic consort of Baal, becomes war goddess in Syria and Egypt; her attributes include the time-honored great mother, moon, moon-blood, and birth power. Anat is assigned 'wife' of El who replaces prime creatress as creator of earth (El = An). El's son is Baal. A story says that Ashtart is "sexually frustrated," makes a move on Baal who virtuously refuses her and reports her seduction attempt to El who makes a plan to punish her. Baal is told to seduce her, but before consummation, he tells her that her children are dead and that he murdered them! She is distraught and mourns like Inanna, Ishtar, Demeter, and all mother goddesses; her mourning causes death in the land. Winter. The fragmented text indicates that Anat and El make up and decide to punish Baal for upsetting her and causing death in the land. He is banished and cursed with disease. This tale ends with Ishtar hearing that she is equivalent to Astarte/Anat(h) and setting off to locate and heal Baal (Leick 1991: 39)! Anat was exported to Aramaic Egypt as an Asiatic goddess of war, she sits on a leopard and holds both spear and battle ax.)

Anat of Syria and Egypt (from Babylonian Antu.)

—anna (part of a divine name meaning an emanation of the first principle, heaven, which patriarchy claims is male but we and the ancients know is always first female!)

Anna-ge ('Queen of Heaven')

Annunit (=Innini)

Antu (feminine 'heaven,' in western Mesopotamia is = to Anat.)

Anunnitum (may be an early compound of Inanna-an-nu-ni-tum, = to Ishtar-annunitum meaning 'Ishtar the Skirmisher;' her name was used by Sargon and his dynasty to invoke a curse.)

Anunite ('Lady of Battle')

Anunu (Creatress; 'She who can turn men to women and women to men,' and sexual diversity.)

Aphrodite (she is said to be 'older than time,' she rules with *jus naturale,* i.e., maternal clan law — rule of the mothers; she is equivalent to Asherah and Astarte. She is 'Queen of the sea' and Egyptian Mari; she is 'sea.' Her Cyprian temple was converted to a Virgin Mary sanctuary where Mary is called *Panaghia Aphrodeitessa,* 'All Holy Aphrodite.' In the city of Aphrodisias in Asia Minor, Aphrodite replaced Ishtar and survived until the 12th century C.E.. Her long rule left evidence of fine art and a sophisticated culture. She represented all the many inclusive attributes of global great mother [Walker 1983: 44-5]. It is said of Aphrodite that she floated ashore from the East. Inanna is her prototype.)

Aphrodite Thalassia ('Earth goddess')

Aphrodite Unania ('Queen of Heaven')

Ardot-lili ('Maid of the storm,' prototype of Lilith.)

Aruru ('mother goddess,' 'creatress of the human race.')

Ashdar (Ishtar)

Ashdor (= Innini/Inanna, 'She of the stars.')

Asgigi (= Ninanna in war aspect.)

Asha ('Holiness')

Ashart

Asherah (moon as 'the Lady who treads on the sea,' or 'the Lady who treads on the (sea) dragon,' consort of El/An; also = Asha, 'Holiness.')

Ashesh ('Law-giving mother,' ancient form of Isis; she supports her breasts in 'Ishtar position' that typifies all great mother goddesses and refers to rain and nourishment; 'rabbatu' refers to Ashesh and her priestesses and later becomes 'rabbi.')

Ashnan ('Divine Lustrator')

Ashrat ('Mother of the vast abode')

Ashram ('She who treads the sea,' i.e. the moon; consort to Adad.)

Ashratin (= Ishtar in eastern Mesopotamia.)

Ashshur (consort of Anu)

Ashtoreth

Ashua(h) ('Mother of the gods,' = Nammu or Ki, mother goddess; see Ashesh.)

Ashuritu

Asnigigi

Asrat ('Her of the planes')

Asratu (west Semitic version of Syrian Ashart.)

Astar/Astart(e) (northern name for Ishtar, war and sexuality refer to her as the male version of morning star.)

Astronoe (Roman Tyre, fuses with Asherah.)

Atar

Athena Soteira (bilingual tablet equates her with Anat; she sits on a lion as do many mother goddesses including Inanna.)

Athtar

Attart (Canaanite equivalent, 'the bride claimed by the sea.')

Athirat ('wife' of El who is an equivalent god to An, the consort of Inanna.)

Atrt

Ayi

Ayya (also A-A, ancient Semitic; bride, 'Mistress of Loving,' 'Heavenly Light,' 'Mistress adorned with voluptuousness;' her name appears in many personal names; she represents sexuality and fertility; hers may be the later name of Ea/Enki, Sumerian god of underground water and wisdom.)

Ay(y)a-nin-ag-ag ('Mistress of Love')

Ay(y)a-sh-mastaki ('of the harem')

Ayya of the Harem ('Mistress adorned with Voluptuousness')

Baalot (Lilith)

Baba ('Lady abundance,' a very ancient Sumerian goddess who is responsible for fertility of animals and people, associated with evening star, and equated with Inanna who is called Baba in various texts.)

Babu (=Baba and Inanna; she is mother goddess for fertility of people and animals, lady of abundance, = Inanna's storehouse, assigned 'daughter' of An, planet Venus, healing goddess, and also = to Ninisinna 'healing goddess' and = to Ningirum, 'Goddess of Incantations.')

Bau (= Inanna and Suhalbi; she weeps for her city that Enlil destroys "with his word;" Bau is a healer. The lady, the great healer of the dark-headed, who determines the destiny of her city, "the first-born daughter of the holy An, the maid, mother Bau [Oppenheim, ed. 1969: 32].")

Babylon the Great (Biblical Ishtar.)

Belet (Lady = belti, 'my queen;' equivalent to Gasan-anna and Gas(h)an.)

Belet-Eanki ('Lady of the house of heaven-earth.')

Belet-Eanna ('Lady of the heavenly house,' Eanna is Inanna's temple in Uruk.)

Belet-Ekalli(m) ('Lady of Ekalli,' 'Lady of the Palace.')

Belet-rame ('Lady of Love', women's epithet for Inanna.)

Belet-s(h)ame ('Queen of Heaven')

Belet-ulsa-zu

Belit-ilani (Queen of the gods)

Belit-seri-gestinanna

Beltis (brings life with the sun.)

Beltu (to rule.)

Brilliance and Shadow (indicates goddess duos of: light and dark, life and death, day and night, summer and winter, celebration and lament; represented by Inanna/Ishtar and Ereshkigal, Kore and Persephone, Isis and Nephthys, Two Ladies, and Two Mistresses.)

Bride

Bride of An(u)

Capable Lady or **Capable One** (Zannaru)

Celestial Virgin (In Syria and Egypt, the 25th of December is the "rebirth of a Solar god from a Celestial Virgin." Persian Mithra is also (re)born every December 25th as the "unconquered sun," i.e., solstice when the sun turns and days lengthen. Mithra competed for religious popularity with early Christianity, his December birthdate is assigned to Jesus; he is reborn every Christmas and his mother, Mary, is the Celestial Virgin [Walker 1983: 663].)

Creatress of all things

Creatress of Wisdom

Crying Storm

Dagal-me-bad ('Goddess merciful who reveals decrees')

Damkina ('Mother of the Vast Abode')

Daughter of the Temple

Delebat

Delbati

Derketo ('fish tail,' a form of Ishtar.)

Devastatrix of the land

dingir (designates a divinity when a 'd' is written beside a Sumerian noun.)

Dilbal, Dilbat (planet Venus, sign is double ax.)

Dilibad

Dinitu (Uruk)

Divine Lustrator

Dragon of the Gods

Dragon of the Primeval Sea of Chaos

Dumu-in-na (Daughter of Anu)

e-gi-a (bride = Zarpanit)

Enanum ('Mother of Lamentations am I')

Ennim

Ereshguna

Erua (Queen of Heaven, chooses king, controls birth of all things.)

Es(h)-ha ('Goddess of the fish house')

Es(h)-hanna (Inanna)

Eshtar-annuitum (war aspect.)

Es(h)tar (= Ishtar and Ester)

Eshtar-rabilat

Esther-Star

Esther-Ishtar (name of priestess for the *hieros gamos*.)

Eurynome (Pelagic creatress who 'danced alone on the Primordial Sea
— of chaos,' i.e., she brought order.)

Eve (her Babylonian name is 'the Divine Lady of Eden' and 'Goddess of
the Tree of Life;' Assyrians called her Nin-eveh, 'Holy Lady Eve' and
named their city, Nineveh, for her; she is associated with Lilith who
is early pre-urban Inanna; she is a mother goddess whose Semitic
name is HWH, meaning both 'woman' and 'life'. Placing blame
on the feminine is as old as patriarchy. Finding the back stories
behind male accusation against most things feminine reveals the
great ruse perpetuated and enforced for millennia: that women are
the cause of male lust and bad behavior, and that sacred woman is
blamed for everything from war, defeat in war, to barrenness and
lack of male offspring. Judaic texts claim loss of human immortality
is a woman's doing. (Remember: Eve is a goddess, her name means
"life.") Walker writes that the Arabic root word of Eve is found
in "life," "teaching," and "serpent." Her name is three of the four
letters of YHWH, Yahweh's secret name. Gnostic texts of Eve
are the reverse of biblical texts and have Eve say to Adam: "Adam
live! Rise up upon the earth!" He rises and says: "You will be
called the mother of the living." "Adam" means "red" or "bloody"
clay, i.e., clay mixed with magical menstrual blood since it was
believed that moon blood withheld during pregnancy builds the
baby (Walker 1983: 288). Eve is a creatress; she is a universal prime
parthenogenetic mother, the first principal — female — who births
the second principal — male — as the gods.

The serpent associated with all creatress mothers is the umbilical
cord, the vaginal snake that holds the infant and delivers it into the

world. Birth envy of men turns a sacred life symbol into a fearful evil horror. Gnostic texts tell us that Adam lost his immortality because a god is hostile and jealous; not because Eve, who *is* both serpent *and* tree of wisdom, offers wisdom (and perhaps sex) to *her* creation, Adam. Eve, and every mother goddess brings life, death, and return. Maleness is not cyclic and neither grasps nor accepts cycling life and death. Maleness is linear and understands that life ends in death; rise — fall, the end. Maleness fears death. This fear becomes an erotic fascination with death, necrophilia. Goddess and women are biophilic. Goddess, and therefore women, are blamed for death via male mis-understanding. Walker cites Mary Daly: "Take the snake, the fruit-tree, and the woman from the tableau, and we have no fall, no frowning Judge, no Inferno, no everlasting punishment — hence no need of a Savior. Thus the bottom falls out of the whole Christian theology [Daly 1973:69]." Eve is the eternal female principal. Like all creatresses, she is mother of the gods, she created them and can judge them. Imagine this: if one of the other versions of Eve had survived, Western sexual guilt, blame, control, and perversion may not have developed exponentially to contaminate culture. Walker states: "One of Christianity's best-kept secrets was that the Mother of All Living was the Creatress who chastised God"and not the other way around![Walker 1983: 291])

Exalted Cow of Heaven

Fearful Dragon of the Great Gods

First Daughter of the Moon

Forgiver of Sins

Framer of all Decrees

Galan-a-na-(n)a (= Ishtar As-ka-et, 'the Lofty Ishtar.')

Gas(h)-an (= bel-ku, 'I rule;' = Nin, queen, divine queen; and belti, lady queen as in to rule or be 'lady over.')

Gas(h)an-men (= belku 'I rule')

Gas(h)anna (= Inanna; 'She rules Heaven,' 'Heavenly Queen' in emesal the woman's dialect in which goddess' speaking voice is often written; refers to the pictograph of the rolled reed doorpost of her storehouse [Leick 1991: 86].)

Gesinanna (Sumerian, Inanna, =Belet-seri, 'Lady of the Steppe'; she is also an underworld scribe. Goddesses rule writing and scribal arts. Writing and wisdom are overseen by a goddess whatever her name.)

Gistin-anna ('vine stalk of heaven,' Dumuzi's sister, interchangeable with Inanna when goddess epithets are clustered.)

Goddess

Goddess of Agade

Goddess of Goddesses

Goddess of the Horns

Goddess of the Star that fills the Heaven

Great Lady of Ashert

Great Serpent Dragon

Great Whore (Biblical Ishtar, Rev. 17:5)

Guardian of all the Great ME

Gula

Gula-Ninisina (Baba; chthonic mother goddess.)

Gula of S(h)urppak (healing goddess = Ishtar or Aja.)

Gush-anna ('She Rules Heaven')

Gushea

Gushea of Combat

Heavenly Lady

Heavenly Light

Heaven's Radiant Queen

Hebat (=Inanna and Ishtar; she is a Paleolithic mother goddess at Catal Huyuk in Anatolia.)

Heraldess

Her that Shatters Mountains

Hierodule of Heaven or Hierodule of An(u)

Holy One

Holy Queen Tumla, Holy Tumla (= Nana and Ishtar)

Illat (= a clan of deities headed by Ishtar: Ishtar, Suen [moon], Addu [storm], and Shamash [sun])

Inanna (Sumerian, mother goddess, merges with Ishtar under Sargon the Great's unification of Sumer and Akkad. Leick suggests that Inanna increased from her local popularity when Ishtar was blended with her. This merging was to make Ishtar more acceptable to the south where Inanna was queen. Leick states that Inanna's name does not appear before mid third millennium (2500 BCE) in royal inscriptions (Leick 1991: 87). I disagree. Inanna is identifiable as her tied reed storehouse door posts in early pictographs and her temple is the first in Uruk dating to early settlement. Inanna is well developed as the maid portion of great mother rising from the Paleolithic, she is called "first snake" by Enheduanna, meaning: she *is* Nammu, the serpent emblem of prime creatress. She 'wears the robes of the old old gods.' Inanna is of the beginning. Sargon's merging south and north brought together his richer economy with less culture and more aggressive herding characteristics of the north with the more peaceful rich agrarian and higher intellectual and religious culture of the south. Though Ishtar's name survived longer than did Inanna's, the two goddesses are very similar. The blending is easy to imagine. The 'unification' of south and north required coercion to effect — conflict was frequent for the northern herding-based Semitic centers who frequently battled mountain-dwelling raiders. Inanna, who was not originally a war goddess, adopted Ishtar's warring aspect. Ishtar also brought the differentiation of attributes between evening star and morning star as feminine and masculine. Inanna, as evening star, calls her people and animals home from work. She resembles Ishtar as goddess of love and sex and sleep and appeals. As morning star, Inanna originally begins the day with purification ritual of hand-washing; breaking fast with agricultural food (no animal flesh) and leads her black haired people back into daylight for work and prayer and consciousness. Ishtar in the morning leads men into combat.

Inanna is goddess of all forms of sexual exuberance; she has a ME power to confuse gender sexuality; her temple embraces cross-gendered and cross-dressed devotees, eunuchs, prostitutes, celibate women, maidens, sex initiation priestesses, and the especially prepared priestesses who annually represent Inanna for the sacred *hieros gamos*. Sumerians protected their settlements and cities from raiders but did not move to acquire and 'unify' with the north. Both goddesses grew from the archaic root of the great mother goddess of all early cultures. Inanna is from a more developed culture and it is Ishtar who benefits most from the merger. Inanna cannot be considered a local deity who is elevated through merging with Ishtar!)

Inanna-an-nu-ni-tum ('Inanna the skirmisher')

Inanna-Muru

Inanna of Heaven and Earth

Inanna of Uruk

Inanna-Za-Za (Appears on Enheduanna's personal disc.)

Inaras (Hittite, = Inanna)

Inin (skirmisher)

Innannak (Dumuzi's consort of the storehouse where dairy products are stored.)

Innini (= Inanna and Ishtar; 'queen of heaven,' great mother, great scribe, she is air and earth, mother goddess, matron of law and war; she is an astral body [star and/or moon], 'pure goddess,' 'matron of birth and all life,' queen, heavenly queen who expands her domain from earth.' [I believe that earth and moon mother are not either/ or but both/and.] She carries a staff with winding snakes because Innini is an early ophidian chthonic goddess.)

Inninshagurra ('Stout hearted lady', 'Lady of the largest heart')

Innium

Irnini (= Inanna, represents happiness, kingship, and rule over the Igigi gods [Foster 2005: 98-90]; she is proud, beautiful, and confident. An(u) appoints her mistress of the world.)

Isha(n)na ('Heavenly goddess of the fish house')

Is(h)ara (also Nina, Eshara, and Sibittu, = Ishtar; 'of the sea' — fish house, marital sex, blessing newly weds, and the marriage bed; 'guarantor of oaths,' 'Mistress of judgement and oracles,' 'Merciful mother of the people,' 'Mistress of the inhabited places;' she is connected with the underworld and mother of the *sebettum* [underworld spirits], she brings disease to those who break oaths; she appears in many personal names; she is associated with the constellation Scorpio in Syria from the third millennium B.C.E..

In the Hittite pantheon she is mother of the seven stars [Pleiades]; 'the lady of the mountains and rivers of Hittite land;' considered an early Ishtar; she invokes both cause [curse] and heal disease; she bewitching and punishes liars [Leick 1991: 94-5].)

Is(h)ara Tiamat

Ishtar ('Virgin Harlot', = Inanna, her name became the generic term for 'goddess' and used as *the* goddess not *a* goddess; 'for Ishtar the bed is made.' See Inanna)

Ishtar-Agies(h)aya

Ishtar-Agushaya (brought to Anatolia in the second millennium and merged with local goddesses; war goddess; in one text this is the name of Ishtar's doppelgänger created by the gods to modify Ishtar, who is too noisy and combative, into better behavior.)

Ishtar-Akuritu (Assyrian Ishtar)

Ishtar-Annunitum ('Lady if abundance')

Ishtar-Ashshuritum ('wife' of Ashshur the Assyrian national tutelary god.)

Ishtar-Assuritu

Ishtar-Ishara (= Geshtinanna)

Ishtar-nana (goddess of love and 'animal passion', she is identified with Sirius rising.)

Ishtar of Agad(e)

Ishtar of Arbela (Northern Assyria; advises oracles for kings perhaps when Venus or Sirius is invisible. Oracles are associated with the underworld; when heavenly bodies are not seen, they are in the underworld.)

Ishtar of Lamentation

Ishtar of Moaning

Ishtar of Nineveh

Ishtar of Sighing

Ishtar of Wailing

Ish-a-ri-tum ('Sacred Harlot')

Ishtar-Kakkabi (=Ninsianna, evening and morning star.)

Ishtar-Kudnittu

Ishtar-Lil ('Ishtar of the field,' = Lilith, the wild wind maid who runs away to uninhabited areas and plays in ruins.)

Ishtar-Ninlil

Ishtar of E-tur

Ishtar of Hosts

Ishtar of Nineveh (has bi-sexual qualities; she is the unpredictable goddess of love and war and attended by two music goddesses: Ninatta and Kulitta who, in Hellenic times, also accompany Aphrodite.)

Ishtar of the Seas

Ishtar of Uruk

Ishtar of Zabalabam (also Sukalitum of Muru who is also Inanna-Muru.)

Ishtar Queen of Larsa (Nanay)

Ishtar-saushga (Hurrian; introduced by Assyrian merchants early mid second millennium. Enheduanna mentions her.)

Ishtar-Telitu

Ishtar-xikum (tree of life)

Issar (Neo Assyrian equivalent to Ishtar; love and war.)

Juno (goddess of the physical world, = Ishtar.)

Kabata (= 'Ishtar the star', 'Kabata of the Twilight')

Kadi ('Divine Serpent Lady of Life')

Kadru

Ka-sa-nana

Kas-s(h)a(n)-an-an, Ka-sa-nana

Kds (from Kadis(h)tu, sacred harlot; Egyptian love goddess who presents frontally nude holding a lotus in one hand and one or two snakes in the other.)

Kilili (Akkadian, = Lilith and Aphrodite Parakyptousa.)

Kititum (= Ishtar from a city on a Tigris tributary.)

Kununna (Inanna)

Lady of Abundance

Lady of Nineveh

Labbotu ('Lioness')

Lady of conquest and Habitations

Lady of Heaven

Lady of Ladies
Lady of the Largest Heart
Lady of the Date Cluster
Lady of the Pleiades
Lady of the Sky
Lady of Victory
Lady of Visions (= Nina with serpent power and interpreter of dreams.)
Lady Moon
Lady who treads on the sea (= moon and Asherah)
Lady who treads on the sea dragon (= moon and Asherah)
Lagamal
Lamashtu ('Great Lady, Daughter of Heaven')
Lamia
Lamma (aspect of Ishtar)
Lawgiver
Law Giving Mother
Leader of Hosts
Leader of the Pleiades
Life-giving woman (Gods are not referred to as 'man;' I read that
    difference to mean woman and goddess are synonymous.)
Light of the World
Lilith ('Maid of the Storm,' she is wilderness Inanna with a life of
    her own. She is Adrot-lili, the biblical prototype for the sexually
    frustrated Lilith; missing normal sexual activity, love, and
    childbearing, she is imagined as a demon who causes impotence in
    men and sterility in women. "Those who died unmarried joined a
    special class of demons called Lilu and Lilitu. Lilu and Lilitu entered
    people's homes by slipping through the windows. They looked for
    victims to fulfill the role of the husbands and wives they had never
    had. If proper precautions were not taken, the victim was carried
    off to an early death to become part of the next generations of lilu
    and lilitu demons [Nemet-Nejat 1998:207].")
Lillake (Lilith)
Lillainna
Lioness of the Gods

Lion-goddess Anatha Baetyl
Loud Thundering Storm
Maiden Inanna
Majestic Queen
Malkat hashshamiim (Queen of Heaven, *malka* in Hebrew and Aramaic is 'queen.')
Malikat (advisor)
Mammu (can also mean light. See Nammu)
Mansat(e)
Mansit (Prophetess)
Matrix-Tiamat (= Nammu; Semitic primal creatress.)
Merciful mother of the People
Minu-anni (literal translation is: 'Why yes?')
Minu-ulla (literal translation is: 'Why no?')
Mistress Adorned with Voluptuousness
Mistress Girgilu
Mother Goddess
Mistress of Abundance and Fertility
Mistress of All the Gods
Mistress of Battle
Mistress of Divine Plans
Mistress of Harlots (Biblical)
Mistress of Judgement and Oracles
Mistress of Lions
Mistress of Poetry
Mistress of Serpents
Mistress of the Four World Region
Mistress of the Inhabited Places
Mistress of the Winds
Mistress of the World
Mother of All Races Past the Primordial Flood
Mother of the Faithful Breast
Mother of the Temple
Mother of the Vast Abode
Mother of Transgressions

Mother-matrix

Mul-an-si-a ('Goddess of the Star that Fills the Heaven.')

Mummu (in Akkadian, Mummu is wisdom, skill, creator, or craftsman; she is the sea prime creatress who gives birth to earth, heaven, and all the early deities.)

Munus-zi

My Lady of Might

Nammu (Prime creatress; Sea Dragon; Inanna is the 'daughter' maid form of Nammu; Ishtar is the 'daughter' form of Tiamat.)

Namrasit ('Brightly Rising Deity')

Namas(h)s(h)u (a water crustacea that came to be a scorpion type creature.)

Nana (Southern Sumer, = Inanna and Baba; 'the child, overflowing with the strength of life, of the great An,' part of the Uruk Inanna-An-Nana triad; = Nana and Nanaya, overseer of planet Venus, ruled sexual attractiveness.)

Nana-Ishara

Nanay (=Irnini and Inanna; happiness, kingship, and authority over the Igigi gods [lesser gods]; evening and morning star.)

Nanaya ('Lady of sexual attractiveness;' Aramaic goddess of the planet's dual gender personalities; in the first millennium she had both female and male personae. Sumerian planet Ninsianna [Venus] is a goddess for both evening and morning appearance.)

Nanshe

Ne-anna ('she whose strength is sublime')

Nin (Sumerian word meaning queen or lady; after patriarchy usurped the feminine, 'nin' was also used for 'lord.' That many god names begin with Nin also indicates the amount of gender-flipping that occurred.)

Nin-ag-ag (Ayya, 'Mistress of Loving')

Nin-ana, Nin-anna (= Inanna, and is likely the name root of 'Inanna;' 'Lady of the Sky,' 'Lady of Heaven,' 'Queen of Heaven.')

Nin-an-ha

Nin-anna ('Queen of Heaven')

Ninannak ('Lady of the Date Cluster')

Nin-ana-si-an-na (= Ninsianna)

Nin Annunitum (= Ishtar/Eshtar, 'Queen-creatress.')

Ninbara (= Akkadian Telitu)

Ninegala, Ninegalia, Nin-egalla(k) (= Inanna, 'Lady of the palace,' 'Queen of the Palace,' 'Lady of the Great House;' possibly used for the queen who channels Inanna for the sacred marriage ritual.)

Nin-en-na-ge ('Lady of Incantation')

Nin-eveh (see Eve)

Ninhursag (mother goddess, birth goddess, 'she who gives life to the dead.')

Nininsina (personification of planet/star 'Whose light fills heaven and earth.')

Ninisinna (tutelary goddess of Isin, goddess of healing, confers kingship.)

Nin-ib ('worshipped')

Nin- ibgal ('Queen of Princes')

Niniviti (descriptive name for Ishtar)

Ninlil ('Queen of air;' interchangeable with Inanna and Lilith.)

Nin-me ('Mistress of Battle')

Ninmeshana ('Lady of all the ME')

Ninmesharra ('Lady of all the ME')

Ninmishushsha ('Lady of the fierce ME')

Nin-mul-si-a ('Queen of the Star)

Ninnar

Ninni(n) ('Queen of queens,' old name and is represented with the pictograph for Inanna's rolled reed post.)

Nin-ninna ('Divine lady owl')

Ninshara ('Beautiful One')

Ninsianna

Ninsinna (goddess of healing, = Inanna, Gula, Baba, and Nintinugga.)

Ninsun ('Lady Wild Cow')

Nintinugga (= Bau, Baba, Gula, Ninhursag, and Inanna; 'Lady who revives the dead.')

Nintud (as birth goddess)

Nugig and nugig ('sacred' or 'taboo' temple women/priestesses whose duty is not known; they wear an ornament inlaid with the *shuba* stone and draped around their neck like a yoke as a badge of office. The item can be seen on Inanna in many cylinder seal impressions [Jacobsen 1976: footnote 6].)

Nu-(u)-gig-an-na ('The hierodule of heaven or An')

Ostere

Ostara

Patroness of Wisdom

(the) Perfect One

Pinikir (from west of the Euphrates; corresponds to Inanna; she is listed first of thirty-five deities who witness and enforce a treaty: "Harken goddess Pinikir ... and you good gods of heaven." Porada adds: "The predominance of a female deity declined later in the official religion of Elam, but the presence of numerous female figurines in all levels of the excavations at Susa until the middle of the first millennium B.C. documents her continued importance in popular esteem [Porada 1962: 41].")

Princess of Justice

Princess of Righteousness

Prophetess of the Temple

Protector of the King

Qudsu (= Inanna, Egyptian, stands on a lion, naked, holds a lotus in her right hand and a snake or two in the left.)

Queen

Queen Creatress of the Human Race

Queen of Eulmash

Queen Gunura

Queen Nigingarra (= Inanna)

Queen Moon

Queen Nana

Queen Nini

Queen of all the ME

Queen of As(h)te (from Larak, part of the city of Isin.)

Queen of Girgilum

Queen of Gueden

Queen of Heaven

Queen of Kish

Queen of Larsa

Queen of Nippur

Queen of Ordinances

Queen of Precious Decrees

Queen of the Divine Kidnuri

Queen of the Gods

Queen of the Earth Gods

Queen of the Igigi (gods who number from seven to six-hundred; Igigi are the Pleiades or the stars generally, i.e., all the lesser gods)

Queen of the Palace

Queen of the Universe (Song of Songs or Song of Solomon, is the Sumerian erotic *hieros gamos* where a king copulates with the divine bride, Inanna; her holy lap is nothing less than the vulva of heaven and earth. In the song, the bride/lover is black and beautiful (night, earth, and chthonic), her physical description is an earthly paradise. Solomon's devotion to his beloved goddess did not go unnoticed. In the biblical I Kings 11:5, his goddess worship is noted and we are told that jealous Yahweh punishes him after death. Solomon is condemned to be devoured daily by ten-thousand ravens everafter [Walker 1983:948-9]. Ravens are emblems of the death goddess mother. Solomon was in her good hands ever all!)

Queen Paramount in the Land

Queen Who Rides the Beasts

Queen Who Grants Kingship

Queen Who Grows Angry and then Relents

Queen Who Punishes and then Shows Compassion

Queen Who Rides the Beasts

Queen Who Speaks Holy Judgements

Queen Who Turns Men into Women and Women into Men

Quintessentially Independent Goddess

Rabbatu ('holiness' transferred to Yahweh in Hebrew times; Rabbatu is the early goddess word that became masculine 'rabbi'.)

Rabbatu Athiratu Yammi ('Lady who transverses the sea,' i.e., moon.)

Radiant Light

Raging Lion

Righteous Judge

Sabitu(m) (= Siduri, Babylonian goddess who blends with Ishtar; she is the ale/beer/wine goddess at the rim of the world who advises Gilgamesh to give up searching for immortality and go home and "live for the day and enjoy pleasure while it lasts since the gods have allotted death to mankind as their fate [Leick 1991: 152]." Ishtar also gives the same *carpe diem* advice to Gilgamesh.)

Sarratniphi

Saushga (Anatolian, =Ishtar; 'Ishtar of the field' who is none other than Lil/Lilith, the wild maid who runs in uninhabited land; Saushga had bisexual attributes — she may dress like an armed man or as goddess of love; she appears as a warrior along side the gods and womanly as the goddess; she represents dualities: harmony/dispute and love/hate; she is also accompanied by two music goddesses: Nanna and Kulitta.)

Senuda

Shapash (Inanna is compared to the Ugaritian sun goddess who takes over the underworld as the sun in the underworld during the night and returns each morning.)

S(h)anat Shame (Queen of Heaven)

She is My Protection

She is My Wall

She of the Skirmish

She Who Renders Gods Submissive

She Whose Dance is Combat

Shi-laba ('She is a lioness')

Shinduri (combines with Ishtar; 'She is my fortress.')

Shining Star

Shulmanitu (=Ishtar; love and war, 'Her Dance is Battle;' a special group of young Semitic women who danced for men about to go into battle, i.e., they inflamed men sexually to be battle-ready in honor of the goddess of war and her dance of combat; sexual union was occasionally called 'single combat'.)

Sidada (= Ishtar)

Siduri (Old Akkadian, associated with Ishtar; see Sabitu; she is sacred "barmaid"/tapsteress/alewife.)

Si-laba (War goddess)

Sister of Shamash (Shamash is the sun god)

South Wind (Inanna as Imdugud/Anzu bird; the fierce spring rain storms.)

Spouse of Heaven

Strong, Loud crying (= Bau)

Sukalitum of Muru

Sunirda, Shunirda (= Aja)

Sunu-da

Supalitum (= Ishtar at Zabalam)

Supreme Among the Heaven Gods

Supreme One

Sutun (Mother of Tammuz, prehistoric snake goddess, prime creatress who existed singly since the Paleolithic.)

Tehama

Telitu (Akkad, = Ninbara)

Teshub (part of a triad: Teshub—Hebat—Ishtar; she stands on a leopard and protects the royal couple.)

Tiamat (= Nammu, Mammu; Prime Creatress.)

Til-ma-a ('Goddess of the Arrows')

Tumla

Ungalnibru (Queen of Nippur')

Ulmashitum ('Lady of the temple E-ulmesh at Ur')

Universal Law

Universal Law in Wisdom

Urukiag (Inanna)

Usan sig-el ('Goddess that Lightens the Twilight')

U-sum-zi-an-na ('Exalted Cow of Heaven')

Usuramatsa ('Observe her word')

Venus (Roman equivalent of Inanna; sexual aspect of Great Goddess; harlot but as in Tantric yoga where sex is spiritual grace. She is both life- and death-giving; she is evening star: Stella Maris. The duke of Venice threw a gold ring into the sea in her honor, well into Renaissance times. Virgin Mary inherited her epithet: Stella Maris, 'Star of the Sea.' [Walker 1983: 1043-4])

Virgin Mother Goddess

Virgin Queen of Heaven

(the) Wanderer (Inanna as evening star transversing the night sky.)

Wild Cow

Wisdom

(the) Woman

Zannaru ('Capable Lady')

Zarpanit (bride)

Za-za (Inanna)

Zubaba

Inanna, and her equivalent goddesses of many names remained in the hearts of the people even as her powers were being usurped by the maturing of fledgling godlets of the patriarchal priests. Religious diversity was once normal in Ancient Mesopotamia; deities were shared and merged. Goddess is life, she has myriad epithets and titles. The above recitation of her many names brings Part I, Life, to a close. In cyclic thinking, death follows life. Part II, Death, is implied as a natural flow. It is, but we also will consider the unnatural man-made form of death. Intentional death and no return from death.

Hatred and death by religion is created by patriarchy. In the Ancient Near East, bias is against tribes and cultures considered wild or barbaric and who raid the urban centers, but bias is *not* against religious belief systems. When treaties or boundary disputes are settled, the names of all important deities of the two sides are included in the treaty oath-taking and found carved into boundary markers or stelae.[67] Emigration brings

---

[67] upright commemorative stone slabs inscribed with text and/or image of an important event

appealing deities with foreign but equivalent names. The functions of major divine personalities are equivalent. Little-known local gods, dear to a new ruler, can elevate into a big god. Political patriarchy is afoot; religious persecution is not.

Texts describe cultural bias against less "civilized" nomadic tribes and mountain people that existed because of experience or fear of perceived threat. Bias against women grows out of imported tribal patriarchal misogyny as women lose their egalitarian status in urban settings. Religious bigotry by zealots is a devolved and destructive quality of later religions. Religious zealotry enters the Ancient Near Eastern consciousness in the last half of the last millennium B.C.E. Conflict is continual, literacy is reduced, creativity falls away, ruined cities are not rebuilt, texts are badly copied, and no new literature of note is found. A dark age claims the land between the two rivers. Regional disputes weakens lingering unity and foreign invasions easily claim Mesopotamia. The Ancient Near East is in ruin; people return to small tribal or semi-nomadic groups and the great sacred culture established by the Sumerians is lost. Death becomes death — permanent, dreaded, and punishing — the polar opposite of our loving goddess of cyclic Life.

Part II

DEATH

Long ago we did not fear death.

CHAPTER 11

House of Shadows

LONG AGO WE DID NOT FEAR DEATH

When stars were many and people few, we did not fear death. We mourned our losses; we honored our dead; we kept them close. We buried their bones under our floors and told their stories. We knew they were with a kind chthonic (earth) mother. When Great Mother was present in the minds of people, death was a natural part of the life cycle.

Story is fluid; it wraps around reality and embellishes it with fresh details weaving past into present. Storytellers harvest and store tales for future telling. We sit spellbound, listening. We are told in art and myth-o-poetic form that there is continuity. We die, yes; we are death-birthed back into earth's womb, source of all life. We will be mourned, celebrated, and remembered. In goddess time, after a safe and healing sleep, we renew. We know the world around us returns. We are of nature. We will return.

Carrion animals, eaters of dead flesh, are special to Great Mother in her mother-of-the-dead aspect. By eating our corpses, they bring us, our "souls", to her. Boars and wild dogs are her animals; ravens, crows, and vultures are her birds. Inanna, in her healing aspect, is known as Bau, Baba and Gula. Gula became a dog-headed healing goddess or a goddess with a dog in attendance. Not every sick person recovers. Her dog waits to bring the soul safely to her underworld. In Sumer, Queen of the dead is Inanna's "sister", Ereshkigal, the death mother, the third of Inanna's triad. Birth-death-renewal. Birth mother, death mother, and fertile potential maid of new life. We are born, we die, we return.

Moon cycles, women cycle, seasons cycle, tides cycle, animals and plants cycle, planets cycle, day and night cycle. Goddess cycles. Early woman created culture, she lived and imagined in cycles. Cycles are not fixed in a rigid, repetitive, boring exact circle. Think of cycles as a forever spiral moving forward, turning round and round, passing close enough to the previous cycle for recognition and familiarity, and pressing forward rich with the wisdom of past turnings; throbbing with upcoming possibility. Cycles are observable, reliable, comforting, and hopeful. They are predictable but not predetermined; cycles flow in a pattern of wide brushstrokes; there is room for added details; there is space for modification. Modification can be biophilic or necrophilic depending on who provides the details.

Women live cyclic lives. Our bodies are lunar; we phase in fertility and hormonal chemistry. We recognize natural cycles. We naturally bleed; our retained blood during pregnancy was believed for countless millennia to magically belly-build babies. "Blood" is important for our dead's return. Globally, niches and bones are painted in red pigment, birth blood. Black, white, and red are the traditional symbolic colors and the first colors our newborns see. They are shamanic colors. They are sacred colors of great mother. White is moon. Black is deep darkness of earth womb and tomb. Red is sacred blood, the blood of fertility and life. Women are double X people. Our nature is biophilic. For the vast majority of eons, since our species walked upright, woman's natural and acquired wisdom added evolving details to the spiraling tides of time.

Men do not bleed naturally. When celestial bodies were changed to male and are out of sight (moon), they can not be menstruating so they are in the underworld, the land of the dead. To do that requires taking the underworld away from goddess. The idea of death changes. Men have no cycling, they live in linear time. Permanency comes to the underworld. The dead stay dead. This is a male invention.

As patriarchy grew, ideas around death changed. Harrison, in her *Prolegomena,* writes that ghosts and ritual appeasing of ghosts at burial sites grew from male guilt over deaths caused by men at war or murder (Harrison 1903,1991: 58-79). Sumerian/Akkadian death changed from goddess's womb-tomb of return, with neither terror nor punishment, into a one-way journey to a dark and gloomy place of dust, dirty water, thirst, and despair. In men's revised underworld, the dead are overseen by a death goddess who is not allowed access to the heavens. The big gods are rapidly locating off-planet. In male consciousness, once dead, the dead stay dead or wander as shades and ghosts seeking revenge. Some later texts tell of pegging a corpse to the wall of the tomb to keep it there. Men learn fear of both death and ghostly retribution for causing death.

CYCLIC DEATH VERSUS FINAL DEATH

That iffy state of renewal-anxiety is expressed as the rise and fall of a vegetation god. The Greek vegetation divine is the daughter-goddess, Persephone, who goes into the underworld at the end of the vegetation cycle. She, as with all cyclic vegetation deities, is sorely lamented. Her mother, Demeter, will not bring the new season until her daughter aspect returns. Persephone returns when lilies, crocuses, and hyacinths flower.

Patriarchal storytellers change the old Greek story to include gods who behave like men. The young goddess is beautiful so she is lusted after by Hades and kidnapped, tricked, and forced into "marriage." One version of the myth says Demeter heard Persephone scream in the underworld as she is raped by Hades! Persephone is tricked into eating a single pomegranate seed. She is then condemned to always return to the land of the dead since the living cannot eat the food of the dead.

Look for the clues of early goddess in the revision. Early stories know that nature cycles. Red fruit and red seeds are goddess food. Red is woman's blood and red is sacred; pomegranate is women's food. Goddess food. The fruit is the color of blood and its numerous seeds are associated with renewal and fertility after death; red mimics lifeblood of birth and return; it does not seal one's fate to remain forever dead. In versions of the Greek myth when daughter Persephone is raped by the underworld god, read that as the young aspect of Mother Goddess being "conquered" and owned by patriarchy's gods.

Persephone's later "abduction" story came about with the help of Zeus, chief storm god and serial rapist of goddesses and mortals alike. Her mother, Demeter, demands her back, but, because Persephone was tricked into eating a single pomegranate seed, grave food, she cannot return. Demeter grieves and lets everything die and stay dead. Demeter demands her daughter's release. Her demand is granted by tyrannical alpha-god Zeus only because Demeter refuses to bring forth new life. He has to release Persephone from Hades' grasp for the growing time of the year. Zeus "gives" permission for her return to Demeter for half the year and then she returns to Hades, the underworld — exactly as she always did without the horrible Zeus and Hades in the tale.

The story re-make appears to take power from mother goddess, Demeter: Zeus rules, and Persephone, stolen with Zeus's permission and help, is delivered to the recently added underworld god. Hades has absconded with the death goddess's realm and is god of the underworld. Since he is male and without a vulva to birth new life and renew, his male presence in the underworld, like that of Nergal in the Ancient Near East, changes the concept of the underworld and death. No longer is the grave a womb-tomb to await a new cycle; death is now death.

Old Europe's vegetation god is also born, dies every year and is reborn. The Ancient Near Eastern vegetation demigod dies young and must be retrieved by the goddess mother or her daughter aspect. His mother or young "bride" descends into the underworld to bring him back. She is assisted by human women lamenting. Women have many losses to lament: stillborn babies and early childhood deaths; daughters, sisters and friends lost during childbirth; sons, husbands, and fathers killed in endless conflicts. A popular text explains that the vegetation god is gone half the year as punishment at the hands of a petulant, vindictive Inanna. Pure patriarchal poppycock! The vegetation god is a demigod; half divine, he dies and then resurrects. The goddess lives on. She is a constant to the male representative who rises and falls, like crops, like male arousal after ejaculation.

Inanna and Ereshkigal both get the attention of the gods by threatening to let loose the dead who number more than the living. Ereshkigal adds that the dead she releases will "eat the living." "In days of yore" they are the only deities with access to the underworld and the only ones with power over the dead. Their threat gets action. The goddess is powerful in the descent texts, but battling patriarchal usurpation. She fights back with threats but male fear of death and dying is already devouring sacred feminine thought and story.

Male religions instill fear and insert punishment into their liturgies. I worked as a new RN in both labor and delivery and intensive care. I was present at the sacred joyous moment of birth into this world and occasional deaths in the intensive care unit — births out of this world. I left nursing for a quarter century and returned to work in a long term care facility. Death was inevitable. I was bedside for many passings. Very few of our residents experienced what we called "hard deaths"— struggling to their last breath. The great majority enacted a peaceful surrender; many looked forward to their release. They were tired, their work was finished, their bodies were worn, and they were ready. The peaceful deaths left all present with a feeling that something very special had just occurred. The room felt briefly other-worldly. Regardless of religious orientation or no affiliation, our residents intuitively knew how to die, to let go. A few of those who struggled at the brink of dying had voiced fear of dying because they felt guilt and feared judgement and punishment. Their fear of punishment after death arose from early indoctrination of religion; the male version of religion present in our culture that interprets carefully revised and edited texts to impose guilt and threat of unending punishment for "bad" thoughts, words, and deeds to control and own the people. One wonders if the predatory pederast priests have an easy or hard death at the end of their days.

In male-based religion, there is ongoing competition for counting souls, owning souls, controlling souls, and being a spokesman for a one and only alpha "god" with the one and only correct doctrine. These belief systems impose a change from "pagan" (any belief not Christian) to Christian. Catholics and Protestants compare, compete and contest; Protestants refuse to acknowledge kinship within the many varied Protestant sects; radical Islam competes with all else. Religion grew into a big stick and bigger excuse for bad behavior. The early beginning of all the later troublesome male-based religions is rooted in a collective denial of the sacred feminine. If we excavate male-based religions, we find the healthy rootstock long buried; we find woman, human and sacred. Once found, we remember; we restore the sacredness of life; we re-story divine woman.

Women are inclusive. Our first story of life is autobiographical and based on our own experience of mother. Goddess is a loving mother who brings us in to, out of, and back to life. On my second husband's last earth day, I heard him say "mama!" in surprise and recognition. He did not speak again. Our "mama" is the model for goddess, she is Life. The advent of patriarchy changed death mother's underworld into a one-way depository for the dead; a journey into gloom, dust, and no return.

THE UNDERWORLD

The following poem is two stories combined. The first finds Inanna deciding to descend into the underworld, *ki-gal*, "greater earth", home of the dead. Inanna *appears* to be coming to take the underworld for her own. Her "sister", Ereshkigal, is queen of the netherworld; queen of the dead. Inanna is already queen of heaven and queen of earth. Does she want to rule the neither world where the altered story allows no return? Not likely. Inanna has descent into and ascent out of the underworld as two of her ME. I would suggest that when Inanna's star/planet Ninsianna (Venus) disappears from the sky, she is in seclusion. When moon is in dark phase, it is in seclusion in the underworld. Women's seclusion is applied to the celestial bodies; moon and Ninsianna (Venus). When those two heavenly bodies disappear, they are in seclusion. Sacrosanct seclusion is "dead" to the outer world. Bleeding women are powerful whether in menses or after giving birth. They enter sacrosanct seclusion. They are so powerful that they must separate from ordinary life.

Birth and menstrual blood come from the womb deep in women's bodies. Caves are wombs of the great goddess. Earth womb-tombs rebirth crops, seasons, and life. Death easily parallels women's seclusion. Early people everywhere bury their dead in remarkably similar fashion with bodies placed in fetal position, either intact or after carrion birds clean the bones. The remains were put into the earth, in holes dug or natural cave niches. The niches, containers, and/or bones were painted with reddish earth pigments imitating women's blood, the blood that grows new life.

The great mother gives birth to new seasons, plants, animals, and humans. The universal treatment for the dead is an obvious belief in life renewal. We are placed in her womb to await return.

Inanna has her ME, her powers, to descend and ascend to and from the underworld. The story under consideration omits that ME power. Inanna is portrayed as power-hungry, petulant and rude, she is made helpless to escape the underworld. Hero-god Enki gets credit for "saving" the great goddess who is reduced to being a usurping, vindictive woman who ends up condemning her beloved Dumuzi to death as punishment because does not grieve her "death". He no longer loves her and is doing his kingly business as usual. He sits proudly and beautifully garbed, well-pleased with himself, on the throne of rulership where Inanna placed him.

Once Great Mother was three aspects: mother, daughter, crone; fertile potential, birth mother, and death *mother;* as death mother she holds us until we are birthed anew. Inanna of old, the fertile young great goddess, is remembered as part of the trinity: she cycles out of sight; she enters seclusion when her planet and moon disappear from the sky. Inanna has both planet (star) and moon affiliation. Inanna's main festival is moon-orientated; monthly new moon is the end of seclusion for moon and women. Seeing Ninsianna return to the evening sky signals an end to the seclusion of her planetary star aspect. And where does she seclude in her planetary or moon aspect? She drops below the horizon. She enters the netherworld. She visits her sister, the death mother Ereshkigal, and she returns.

Another explanation for the underworld and Dumuzi's time there is the cyclic nature of nature. The hot dry summer ends crop growth. Harvest has come and gone; the land is parched and dead. The storehouse holds food for the dry season. At the end of the dry season, the storehouse supplies diminish. Rain, the water of life, is needed so the plants of life can grow. Dumuzi is the manifesting agent for herding and agriculture fertility. The vegetation god is traditionally brought back by the goddess mother or goddess bride.[68] Women lament the "death" of the son and consort. He dies at the completion of the growing season. He enters the land of the dead one way or another. The goddess as mother and lover laments him. Women lament for her and for their own losses. The wailing gets the attention of the goddess of the underworld to release the son/consort. Either the lamenting alone or the mother/bride descending into the underworld brings the vegetation demigod/consort back to life. He is renewed, resurrected.

I would suggest the descent is a remnant of both the remembered seclusion of moon, planet, women and goddess mother/bride descending to retrieve the vegetation son/consort god. The descent story explains renewal. Inanna is not aggressively taking over Ereshkigal's queendom! That addition is male thinking and writing when Inanna is described in imitation of male acquisition and aggression. Conquering more territory is Y-ness personified; her visit to Ereshkigal would appear to men to be for acquisition of more territory. It is not. The story behind the story is Inanna in her cyclic seclusion below the horizon — renewing herself.

Religious myths reflect the geography and economy of the people telling the stories. Agriculture first and herding second are the major Sumerian economy. Before shepherds seek higher, cooler ground and grasses, we imagine the slaughter of some animals to hang "in underground cold-storage rooms," Inanna's storehouse. (Jacobsen

---

[68] The Jesus story is based on the vegetation god cycle; he is lamented by the two Marys, mother and bride, and appears first to Mary the bride after he is risen in the spring when plant growth renews. See chapter 14.

1987: 207). Inanna is queen of the storehouse. After summer harvest and slaughter, the storehouse is full; food is distributed through the non-productive time, the storehouse empties; the remaining hung-meat carcasses are boney, rancid, and moldy green. Other accounts of the underworld include pegs for corpses. Are corpses pegged in the patriarchal underworld so they don't wander about and interfere with the living? (See below where Enkidu, Gilgamesh's loyal companion, describes the first millennium's version of death).

The following descent text is rich in remnants of the old. Jacobsen translates the underworld/netherworld as "Hades." Hades is a Greek god's name-lending from a later time, and approaches the contemporary idea of hell. I think "Hades" is an unfortunate word choice to interpret the earlier Sumerian version of the "greater earth", the great below. Sumerian poets introduce their stories with a background summary of the creation story; they write in triplicate to describe one idea in three slightly different ways. Because the compositions are recited or sung publicly, repetition allows for easy familiarity and anticipation for the audience just as our songs have a chorus refrain repeated after verses. (Jacobsen 1987: 206-232:)

INANNA'S DESCENT

From the upper heaven
    she had her heart set
    on the netherworld,
the goddess had
    from the upper heaven
    her heart set
    on the netherworld.
Inanna had
    from the upper heaven
    her heart set
    on the netherworld.

My lady forsook heaven,
    forsook earth,
        went down into Hades.
Lordship she forsook,
    queenship she forsook,
        went down into Hades.

...

The poet lists the temples she abandons in seven cities to go to the great below. She gathers her ME; here they number only seven while other compositions list about one hundred. She puts on the desert headdress and her "brow wig;" she holds the measuring rod and line, she wears her "small lapis lazuli beads" and the two egg-shaped beads of stone fixed like a yoke on her neck. She wears her gold bracelet and "breast shields" (upper dress covering her breasts?) that are called "O man, come hither, come hither!" She covers her back with the robe of queenship, and applies kohl to her eyes. The kohl is named: "O may he come, may he come!"

Inanna is accompanied by her vizier (administrative assistant), Ninshubur, whose name means Lady Dawn. Dawn accompanies Inanna as morning star. The goddess gives instructions in case she does not come back from the nether world.

Inanna was walking toward Hades,
her page Ninshubur
    was walking at her side,
Holy Inanna said to Ninshubur:
"My ever-loyal one,
my page (vizier)
    of fair words,
my envoy of true words,
I am now going down
    into Hades,

if I stay gone
    to Hades
set up resounding
    wailings for me,
sound the tambourine [instrument for laments] for me
    in the assemblies of administrators,
make the rounds for me,
claw at your eyes (for grief) for me,
    claw at your mouth for me,
claw, in the places
    one goes not with a man,
        your big belly for me! [?buttocks]
Dress in a one-ply garment for me
    like one who has no man!

"Wend first your foot
    to Enlil's temple Ekur,
and upon your entering
    Enlil's temple, Ekur,
weep before Enlil (saying:)

'O Father Enlil! Let no man [? rangers[69]] put to death
    your child in Hades!
Let him not mix your good silver
    in among Hades' dust,
let him not cut up your good lapis lazuli
    in among the flint-arrowhead maker's stones,
let him not split up your good boxwood
    in among the carpenter's lumber,
let him not put to death in Hades
    the maiden Inanna!'

...

---

[69] the agents of the underworld who do the unpleasant things just as the rangers/
warden/recruiters take men for corvee and military duty for the kings

"Go, Ninshubur,
      and toss not your head
at my orders I have given you!"

> *The poem continues with Inanna's instructions. If Enlil (chief deity after An) will not help, Ninshubur is to go to Nanna (moon god) and repeat the same request. If Nanna will not help, she is to go to Enki who is "of vast intelligence, (and) knows the grass of life, knows the water of life. May he make me come alive!" The two goddesses walk to the door of the house of the dead. A second location for the dead and their restless shades is in the mountains. Other compositions include ghosts of the dead wandering about in the mountains that were also dangerous with wild barbarous peoples who raid herds and attack cities. In this poem, the name of the place of the dead is Egalkurzagin, "the lustrous mountain palace (ibid.: f. 8: 210)." We rejoin Inanna who is noisily banging at the door of the dead to gain entry.*

When Inanna had come close
      to Egalkurzagin,
she wickedly rammed things
      against the door of Hades,
shouted wickedly
      into Hades' palace:

"Open the house instantly!
      Gatekeeper,
      open the house instantly!
Open the house instantly!
      Neti, open the house instantly,
      and let me go in to my wailing!"

Neti, Hades' chief gatekeeper,
answered holy Inanna (saying:)

"And who might you be? You!"

"I am Inanna
  toward where the sun rises!"

"If you are Inanna
  toward where the sun rises,
why have you gone away
  to a land of no return?
How could your heart take you on
  a road that he who goes it
  travels not back?"

Holy Inanna replied to it to him:
"My elder sister Ereshkigala
  to have the obsequies
  for Gugalanna,
  her husband who was killed,
(widely) viewed
is pouring grandiosely at his wake.
  That's why!"

…

Gugalanna, "the great bull of heaven," is said to be Ereshkigala's husband. (Here it likely means the constellation Taurus.) When the noise of thunderstorms rising from the distant horizon is heard, it is mythically explained as a battle between a celestial lion or lion-bird (Imdugud) and the bull of heaven. The bull loses; he is killed. Ereshkigala mourns.

Neti asks holy Inanna to wait while he announces her to Ereshkigala. Neti repeats the message: Inanna with her ME (here only seven powers of office) demands entrance. Ereshkigala listens. She "smites her thigh" signaling she has made a decision. She gives Neti her instructions. Inanna may enter but she must enter crouching, as corpses are positioned, stripped of all she wears since the dead enter naked.

Neti, Hades' chief gatekeeper,
    obeyed his mistress's orders,
[drew back] the bolts
    on Hades' seven great gates,
[and pushed open] first
    [the doorleaf] of the Ganzir palace,
the façade of Hades.
    To holy Inanna he said:

"Come, Inanna, come in through it!"
After she had entered in,
someone had slipped off her
    kaffieh and *aghal*,
    the desert headdress,
    of her head.

"Why was that?"

"Be quiet, Inanna,
    an office of Hades
    has been faultlessly performed.
Inanna, open not your mouth
    against Hades' sacred functions!"
...

> At the second gate her "pure yardstick and measuring line"
> is taken, she asks why, and is told to be silent as this is a sacred
> function of the Underworld. The same is done at each gate. She
> is stripped of "small lapis lazuli beads at her neck," her "yoked
> oval stone beads of her chest," her gold rings, her breast-shields
> named "O man, come hither, come hither!" and her "robe of
> office, the robe of queenship." Crouching and naked, Inanna is
> presented to Ereshkigala. The queen of the dead rises from her
> chair/throne. Inanna sits on the throne. This causes Ereshkigala
> to call in her Anunnaki, her seven judges mirroring the seven
> celestial Anunnaki who assist Inanna hearing petitions and

376

> *deciding decrees. Ereshkigal's seven announce the verdict of*
> *death for Inanna. In another poem, Ereshkigal looks at Inanna*
> *with eyes of death. Inanna is hung up like a green rotting sheep*
> *carcass on a peg in the wall. (This imitates the empty storehouse*
> *and the last slabs of "tainted meat." Remember also that pegs are*
> *mentioned in the first millennium for holding corpses in graves.)*

A thought occurs here: this a very early version of the depletion of the storehouse where Inanna, like Persephone, spends the winter in the netherworld and returns in the spring. It is Inanna's vegetation cycle. Her storehouse empties, people are anxious about the new season. Rain is needed for the plant's return. I would suggest that this is not Inanna wanting to take over the Underworld to add to her rulership. Instead, Ereshkigala is her sister and the third part of the original idea of Mother Goddess as a triad. Ereshkigal is called "mother of the dead". In some texts, Inanna/Ishtar is Queen of Heaven, Earth, *and* the Underworld.

Inanna leaves her goddess of dawn vizier with instructions to seek help from the "great gods" if she does not return. This is maleness meddling with the goddess's Neolithic story. Ninshubur seeks Enlil (air) for help; he is not able to help, nor can Nanna (moon god). The male divines are now specialized; Enlil and Nanna are sky gods, they cannot help in earthly matters. Enki (head of + earth) is chthonic and therefore earth and underworld are in his job description. The celestial gods are powerless before the goddess in her death persona. The top gods do not go into the underworld as does Inanna. Enki is consulted. This connects him with the creation of life. "Father" Enki "rescues" Inanna with her own water and plant of life! That she must be rescued at all diminishes the great queen of heaven, queen of earth.

Priests rewrite the early stories to elevate the powers of gods and maleness on earth by changing divine order. God ideology entered the myth-o-poetic stage long after goddess was well enthroned. The unnatural and nonsensical life-creation by gods became accepted dogma though it bespoke of blatantly unnatural male birthing.

The revised myths radically change Inanna's personification. She is first and foremost the fertility of life, Great Mother. Great Mother creates, births, and protects; she mirrors women's XX characteristics. She collects us into her womb when we die. Great Mother is cyclic. In Inanna's descent story, the underworld has already become a linear one-way destination. Maleness is inserted into the feminine. Nammu, prime creatress, first Great Mother, is said to be Enki's mother. She is the enormous cosmic sea of chaos out of which she births heaven and earth. She is the primordial sea and all water. Enki is fresh water. He rules surface and underground water; wells, lagoons, marshes, and wetlands. Enki is also the crafty, tricky, magic-making god. He steps up to save Inanna after Enlil and Nanna refuse to help (because they cannot act in the underworld). The great below is out of their jurisdiction and male theology has made return from the underworld impossible.

When three days and three nights
    had gone by,
her page
    Ninshubur,
her page
    fair of words,
her envoy
    true of words,
was setting up resounding
    wailings for her.
The tambourine
    which she sounded for her
    in the assemblies of administrators,
she had made the rounds for her
    of the god's houses.
She clawed at her eyes (for grief) for her,
    clawed at her mouth for her,
and in (the) places
    one goes not with a man (buttocks),
    she clawed her big belly for her.
Like one who has no man,
    she dressed in a one-ply garment for her.

...

Ninshubur, "her foot she wended" to Enlil's temple and then Nanna's temple; she wept, saying what Inanna had rehearsed with her, but each time was told:

> "My child craved the upper heaven,
>   craved (too) the netherworld;
> Inanna craved the upper heaven,
>   craved (too) the netherworld;
> Hades' offices, demanding offices,
>   demanding offices,
>   have been performed effectively.
> Who has (ever) been reached there
>   and (re)claimed?"

...

> *The sky gods have no power in the netherworld. Ninshubur
> walks to Enki's temple, and again recites the message Inanna has
> prepared. Enki agrees to help. We hear Enki say:*

"What has been done to my child
    down there?
    She has me worried!
What has been done to Inanna
    down there?
    She has me worried!
What has been done to the queen of all lands
    down there?
    She has me worried!
What has been done to heaven's holy one
    down there?
    She has me worried!"
From under his fingernail
    he brought out dirt,

and fashioned from it
    a myrmidon.[70]
From under another fingernail of his
    he brought out dirt,
    and fashioned from it
    a young elegist.
To the myrmidon he gave
    the grass of life,
to the young elegist he gave
    the water of life.
Father Enki said to the young elegist
    and the myrmidon:

"Go! Lay the foot toward Hades!
When you have flown like flies
    over the doorleaves,
When you have wiggled like lizards
    past the door-pivots,
lo!
    The mother who gave birth,
Ereshkigala, lies sick, (with grief)
    for her little ones.

Ereshkigal(a), "the mother who gave birth," mourns her little ones. She once birthed renewal. From the death mother of the global triple goddess comes the rebirth of all-life; the new growing season; the return of vegetation god Damu/Dumuzi/Tammuz. The great Bull of Heaven constellation (Taurus) dips below the Sumerian horizon for six weeks. It reappears in the Ancient Near East in mid-March and coordinates with planting, i.e., the return of Dumuzi. The Bull of Heaven, virile and strong, is often associated with the same qualities in Inanna.

Wolkstein and Kramer suggest that Inanna came to the netherworld to learn first-hand about death and her return brings a consciousness (of

---

[70] myrmidon is a professional mourner who plays the flute and dances at the funeral; an elegist is also a professional mourner

death) into her realm of knowledge (Wolkstein, Kramer 1983: 155-7). I suspect Inanna is well conversant with death and that Ereshkigala's moans are the labor sounds of Inanna's rebirth, the maid aspect of herself, Great Mother, for a new cycle.

Figure 45. Bull Attacked by Lion (eclipse or end of a thunderstorm)

The underworld, here, is a one-way journey of no return. Moaning would sound similar whether as labor or lamentation. Professional mourners assist mourners with their grief, with empathetic mourning sounds. We are told in this case she is mourning for her husband the bull of heaven. Jacobsen refers to a bull of heaven dying in a noisy storm-battle with either the Imdugud bird or a celestial lion. The Bull dies, the storm ends; he resurrects in more storms or in the next year's storm season. I also agree with Wolkstein and Kramer: Taurus is the bull of heaven dipping out of sight and returning in time for planting. Crescent moon shapes are associated with animal horns. If the bull of heaven in the descent story were the moon, then one could expect one of the male-moon names to be mentioned. No Nanna, Suen, or Sin is written of the bull. The above death of a celestial moon-bull could also be a time of lunar eclipse when the moon appears bitten and eaten by another celestial power. The dead bull husband is forgotten in the poem as the Queen of the Dead mourns her "dead children." I would suggest that her children are the dead who were once re-birthed through the death-mother when death had a cyclic return. She mourns the altered story.

We return to the instructions Enki gives to his freshly created professional mourners:

Her holy shoulders
    no linen veil,
her bosom, like oil cruses
    has nothing drawn over it,
her [nails] are
    like a copper rake upon her,
her hair? – Leeks
    she has on her head!

"When she is saying
    'Woe, my heart![71]
[Say to her:]
    'You are [aweary], my lady,
    woe your heart!'
When she is saying:
    ['Woe,] my liver!'
Say to her:
    ['You are aweary,] my lady,
Woe your liver!'

("She will ask:)

['Who] are you
    to whom I have spoken

---

[71] "heart" is an euphemism for "womb"

[from my] heart to your hearts,
>   from my liver [to your livers?]
[An you be gods,]
>   let me talk [with you,]
[an you be humans,
>   let me] determine [your circumstances
>   for you!]

…

People in mourning are expected to rip their clothing, scratch themselves with fingernails, and pull their hair so it is in disarray, "like leeks," standing out in all directions. Mourning *with* someone shows kindness. In the case of professional mourners, the kindness is repaid in some way. Above, Ereshkigal(a) offers the reward to "determine your circumstances" for the two if they are human. We have here another evidence of her office as a birth goddess. Determining the fate of humans, their "circumstances" of birth and longevity are granted by birth goddesses.

>   *Enki tells them to "adjure her by the life's breath of heaven, by the life's breath of earth" and warns them that her Anunnaki will offer them "the river at its (high) water; … the field when in grain" but they are not to accept. Instead, they are to request "the slab of tainted meat hanging from the peg." They are to throw the grass of life and the water of life onto the corpse of Inanna.*

The young elegist and the myrmidon
>   obeyed Enki's orders.
Over the doorleaves
>   they flew like flies,
wiggled like lizards
>   past the door-pivots,
lo!
>   The mother who gave birth,
Ereshkigala, lay sick (with grief)

for her little ones.
Her [holy shoulders]
    no linen veiled,
[her] bosom, like oil cruses[72],
    had nothing drawn over it,
her nails were
    like a copper rake upon her.
Her hair? – Leeks
    she had on her head!

When she said
    "Woe, my heart!"
they said to her:
    "You are aweary, my lady,
    woe your heart!"
When she said,
    "Woe my liver!"
they said to her:
    "You are aweary, my lady,
    woe your liver!"

(She said to them:)

"Who are you
to whom I have spoken
    from my heart to your heart
    from my liver to your liver?
An you be gods
let me talk with you
an you be humans,
    let me determine your circumstances
    for you!"

They offered them

---

[72] jars for holding oil

the river at its (high) waters,
    but they accepted it not.
They offered them
    the field when in grain,
    but they accepted it not.

"Give us the slab of tainted meat
    hanging from the peg!"
"The slab of tainted meat
    is the property of your mistress!"
"Though the slab of tainted meat
    be the property of your mistress
    give it to us!" they said to her.

They were being given
    the tainted slab of meat
    hanging on the peg
and threw upon it,
    one the grass of life,
    one the water of life,
and Inanna rose.

Inanna was about
    to ascend from Hades,
but the Anunnaki[73]
    laughed at it (saying):

"What man has ever,
    ascended from Hades,
    ascended [freely]?
If Inanna is
    to ascend from Hades,
let her give it one head

---

[73] here the Anunnaki are the underworld's lesser gods and not Inanna's Pleiadian anunnaki

in lieu of her head!"

Inanna was ascending
    from Hades.
Little rangers,
    Like unto reeds
    for lance-shapes,
big rangers
    like unto bamboo(?)
walked beside her.
The man in front of her,
    though no herald,
    held a staff in the hand,
(the one) behind her
    though not an envoy,
    had tied a weapon
    unto the hip.
    …

The underworld rangers are equivalent to the king's representatives who conscript men to fight, build, rebuild, and clean irrigation canals. These netherworld "rangers" conscript the living for death: babies, children, wives and husbands; anyone at any age. They cannot be appeased by offerings as they "knew not food, knew not drink." (Flour is traditionally strewn for ghosts and demons to eat and be appeased as well as for enticing protective spirits and deities to come near. Pure water is libated — poured into or onto graves for the dead to drink so they stay put. Libations of pure water are also poured for deities.) The water of life is the rain needed for the growing season.

Inanna leaves Hades, flanked front and back with rangers who are anxious to have a replacement for her. Inanna is to choose the victim. Ninshubur, her loyal and properly mourning vizier, greets Inanna:
When Inanna had ascended

from Hades,
her page Ninshubur
    threw herself at her feet;
she had sat in the dust
    was dressed in dirty clothing.

The rangers said
    to Holy Inanna:

"Inanna, go on to your city,
    and let us carry her off!"

Holy Inanna answered the rangers:
"My page,
    fair of words,
my envoy
    true of words,
was not letting go
    of my instructions,
did not toss her head
    at the orders I had given!
She set up resounding
    wailing for me.
The tambourine
    which she sounded for me
    in the assemblies of administrators,
she made go for me the rounds
    of the gods' houses.
She clawed at her eyes (for grief) for me,
    clawed at her mouth,
and in the places
    one goes not with a man,
    she clawed her big belly for me.
To Enlil's temple, Ekur,
to Nanna's temple in Ur, and

to Eridu and Enki's temple,
she went for me
    and had me come alive.
How could you give me (another) such?"

...

> *Inanna and the rangers continue on. They arrive in Umma, where Shara, her son, a warrior in other texts but here he is the one who sings her songs, "clips her nails" and "ties the hair-bunch" on her neck. Shara too throws himself at Inanna's feet and sits in the dust in his dirty mourning clothes. He is loyal to her; she will not let the rangers take him.*
>
> *Inanna and the rangers continue on to Bad-Tibira where Lulal, another warrior god associated with Inanna as her son, is the tutelary god. He too falls at her feet in the dust in his dirty rags. Again the rangers say: "Inanna, go on to your city, and let us carry him off!" Again she refuses saying: "Preeminent Lulal, leading my right and left wings (of the army), how could you give me (another) such?" Inanna and her guards go on to where Dumuzi rules.*

"Let us go for him
    to the maimed apple tree
    in the Kullub desert!" [74]
To the maimed apple tree (pruned?)
    in the Kullub desert
    they followed in her footsteps.

Dumuzi had dressed
    in a grand garment
    and sat seated in grandeur.

...

The reader will remember: Dumuzi is placed on Inanna's seat of rulership through the sacred tryst. He is her beloved. When the story

---

[74] Damu is prototype for Dumuzi and was god of rising sap in fruit trees

Dumuzi is not in mourning, it appears to Inanna that he does not love her anymore; he is enamored of the power *she* bestowed on him. He is not wearing torn dirty mourning clothes; he is neither wailing nor sitting in the dust. He is beautifully robed and conducting business as usual. If women had written this added-on text, they would have spoken of the uneven love between man and woman (see chapter 6). The callousness of Dumuzi accepting Inanna's love-favors and rulership and then forgetting her is betrayal! Inanna has a woman's heart. She loves him. She cannot forget him nor can she immediately forgive him. Since a priestly hand crafted the liturgical changes, maleness understands that Dumuzi did what was needed to ascend the throne; he satisfied Inanna in the bedding-rite and therefore has the right to rule from his acquired position. However, Dumuzi and the priestly scribes forget that Inanna put him on the throne and she can remove him. The priestly contrived story supports a coming shift in power. Dumuzi, in this text, assumes a "fixed" position without Inanna. The linear story line forgets the cyclic root of the myth: rise-fall-return. Instead, men imagine and invent regicide! And who is to blame? Inanna.

Priest scribes put the spin on goddess's story: unequal love and dominating men side-stepping partnership. The male-based theme gains momentum. Here the priests do not want their demigod to die. Inanna moves between heaven and earth, but priests forget what is listed in her original ME. She has the power and right to go down to and up from the underworld. She is not going there to steal the underworld from her sister Ereshkigal who, in this version, punishes her with death. Now Inanna is stripped of her emblems of office, given a death curse and hung on a hook to rot like a decaying green moldy carcass. Naturally, in male-based story time, a man comes to rescue the damsel in distress — a relentlessly tedious theme. By rescuing the poor helpless female, maleness gains a superior role. Enki, water god, tricky god, magician god, figures out a way to bring the goddess back to life. Because he rescues her when no other god could or would, he is in a favorable superior position. He "rescues" her from one of her own domains. Ereshkigal is the death crone aspect of all great mother goddesses. Ereshkigal and Inanna are "sisters," i.e., aspects of the same big mother. Both are associated with the bull of heaven; both are associated with the moon — death crone with old crescent and dark moon and Inanna with new crescent moon. Inanna is not punishing Dumuzi. He has a role to play. He cycles, but maleness is striving for permanency both in rulership and godship.

The descent text continues; priestly scribes write that Inanna's greed for more power got her into trouble in the netherworld and only a male, a god can "save her." Before the priests edited and revamped the oldest story, there is a global maiden version of the Mother who is the annual return of vegetation. The back-story of Inanna's descent is the original first myth; she is rightfully visiting her "sister" Ereshkigal; they are of the matrinity; there is no competition as each third of Mother Goddess has a role. Inanna is the warp and woof that weaves the above with the below, the sky with the earth, and life with death returning to life. She is called Wanderer. She moves with ease over sky and land. She journeys in her crescent boat of heaven and on the backs of lions; she runs, walks, and flies. The goddess is not invading the underworld in acquisition-greed for more territory and power; that is priestly fiction. Furthermore, rescue by maleness is never necessary as Inanna/Mother Goddess is supreme and older than the upstart godlets. In the new telling, priests put our goddess in the bad light that is useful for their propaganda; they are replacing sacred woman with concocted gods who finagle power from goddess.

Enki "rescues" Inanna with *her own aspects*, water and plants of spring that come naturally, cyclically, annually. Enki requires unnatural fly-like magical professional mourners who con Ereshkigal, "the mother who gave birth," into releasing Inanna. Enki, the clever tricky god, gets to be the hero who rescues the hapless naughty Inanna. The most powerful goddess of the Ancient Near East is presented as a petulant, selfish, aggressive, power-hungry, troublesome "child" with anger-management problems. She is blamed for Dumuzi's sentence to the underworld.

We, as did our foresisters, work long and hard to encourage men to activate their X-ness and grow into wise, caring, responsible, relational and balanced men whose own X chromosome modifies their Y chromosomal tendencies. Another idea to consider is that Eve's "apple" brought knowledge to her human children who will populate the earth. Gods mirroring men keep knowledge and wisdom for themselves. Not so for woman and the goddess. Inanna does a similar service to Eve's tree of knowledge when she brings her ME to the people by out-maneuvering Enki's efforts to swamp her boat of heaven with waves and demons and claim the ME for himself (see chapter 2). Priestly types and ruling alphas, in the name of kings and gods, manage people better if they are not wise. The apple bite is an evolutionary awakening but Eve is demoted from goddess and converted to a human woman. She is blamed for humans not living as immortals in an Eden nursery where all needs are continually met and no *man* has to work. Maleness has anxiety about death and makes up stories of certain special men finding or being granted immortality in their physical body. I have yet to find a woman or heroine who asks for or receives that boon! Women already have immortality — not individually in physical bodies, but as a continual traceable chain of mother to daughter throughout our species' existence — we are life creating life.

As we continue reading the poem, there is evidence of further patriarchal usurpation: a child is now claimed by the man, the child is no longer the mother's, though she is the one most involved since the beginning of our species. When Semitic patriarchy takes over, male authority rules everyone, father rules family, sons obey fathers, and men rule women. Sons and their spouses remain in the patriarchal household. The bride is now without support of her mother and her familiar women's quarter. She serves the father-in-law as well as the husband and her children belong to the husband. This change in custom is unnatural. Human political and social change occurs faster than myths are altered. Sumerians hearing this story revision still remember that Inanna wielded power even if her character is besmirched. Beloved Dumuzi appears victimized. Inanna is to blame. Making the sacred feminine bad is predictable dominator behavior. By inference, Y-males, misogynists, blame women for everything bad. Dumuzi is Inanna's victim and victimization is the mantra of misogynists. We return to the poem:

the rangers swept into his fold,
and pouring out the milk
    from (all) seven churns,
they bumped him seven strong,
    as were *he* the intruder,
starting by hitting the shepherd
    in the face
    with the reed pipes and flutes.

She looked at him,
    it was a look to kill;
she gave them orders,
    it was an order
    gripping the bowels;
she called out to them,
    it was a call for punishment:

"How long (must you dawdle)?
    carry him off!"

Holy Inanna gave the shepherd Dumuzi
    into their hands.

They, the men who had escorted her,
    the men who went for Dumuzi,
    knew not food, knew not water,
ate no (offerings of)
    flour strewn,
did not drink
    libated water.
They bent not over
    to that sweet thing,
    a wife's loins,
they did not kiss
    that dainty thing,

a child.
They would make a man's child
    get up from his knee,
would make a daughter-in-law
    leave the father-in-law's house.
    ...

> *Dumuzi petitions his brother-in-law, Utu (sun god), for help. He reminds Utu that as the shepherd he brings butter to Ningal (moon goddess) his mother-in-law. He begs Utu to turn him into a skink (lizard) so he can escape the rangers. The text is broken but would have told us that Inanna has returned to Uruk, her important city, and Dumuzi in his skink form went there also. The lovers have made up. The rangers do not have a replacement. Dumuzi escapes them and Inanna is still theirs.*

The rangers entered Uruk
    and seized holy Inanna:
"Come Inanna!
    get started on your journey,
    get going
    descending into Hades!
go to the place your heart desired'
    descending into Hades,
go to Ereshkigala's place
    descending into Hades!
May you not dress in your queenly robe,
    the holy robe of office,
    the robe of queenship,
    descending into Hades;
you should not take your gay wig,
    descending into Hades;
unstrap your [shoes]
    the 'wild-dog puppies' of your feet,
    descending into Hades.

...

They reviled holy Inanna,

...

and Inanna in her panic
    gave them Dumuzi in hand.

...

Dumuzi petitions his brother-in-law the sun god. He reminds Utu who he is: he, Dumuzi, is the one who "took to wife" Inanna. The long tradition of the sacred feminine choosing a beloved is toppled. He "takes her," when the time-honored arrangement is that she *chooses* him. He is *her* consort; she is not *his* "wife." The sacred feminine is blamed for Dumuzi's plight; *she* causes the fiasco by going to the underworld in search of more power. Men forget that Dumuzi's plight is the natural observation of nature's rise, fall, rise rhythm of seasons. The vegetation god always dies and always returns. Y-ness invents unnatural acts and story to counter natural order and nature in general. We witness the greatest sacred persona of the Ancient Near East blamed for Dumuzi going to the underworld as the growing season ends. Inanna is blamed here, not by one of the major gods, but by mere ghostly recruiter rangers. The disrespect of sacred feminine marks the changing of the gods. Goddess is blamed; Dumuzi is victimized; misogyny is risen.

> The rangers hobbled Dumuzi's feet, they fixed a neck stock in place; they surrounded him with weapons, copper spears, and sharpened axes. Dumuzi again calls to his brother in law, Utu the sun god.

"Sun god, I am your comrade,
    you are a gallant, you know me!
Your sister, whom I took to wife,
she, having descended into Hades,
so as to ascend from Hades,

394

wants to give me to Hades,
    as a substitute.
O sun god, you are a fair judge,
    let her not wrong me!

When you have changed my hands,
    when you have switched my frame,
let me slip out of
    the hands of my rangers,
    and may they not catch me!
Like a noble serpent
    I shall traverse plain and hills,
let me flee for my life
    to (my) sister Geshtinanna's place!"

…

Figure 46. Shepherd with Goat

Serpent is the chthonic deity, the Great Earth Mother. Dumuzi is associated with her as he naturally returns to the earth to await the next growing cycle. Geshtinanna (heaven's grape vine), here is Dumuzi's sister. She also appears as or with Inanna; she offers herself in place of Dumuzi. The underworld "sentence," i.e., the natural flow of seasons, is split between brother and sister by Inanna's decree. Shepherd Dumuzi is the renewal of herds and grains. The brother-sister addition may reflect the cycle of beverages: beer from barley with short fermentation and wine requiring longer fermentation. Wine came to the Ancient Near East well after barley and other grains were farmed and fermented. Geshtinanna is told by a "fly" that Dumuzi is being held in a beer brewery. This is further proof of his beer association. Flies are associated with breweries and are useful for carrying divine messages since they go everywhere.

This text has a standardized Geshtinanna lament inserted that is from another poem where Dumuzi has not yet consummated his consorting with Inanna. The additional text tells us the shepherd is attacked and killed; his flock taken and dairy products dumped. In real life, the lambs and kids are weaned and milk production is ended — it is time to move the flocks to higher pasture in stony hills. The shepherds take leave of their huts and feeding pens. Dumuzi's mother and sister find his corpse left unburied in the desert. Raiders are well known to herders. The two women lament; unburied bodies mean unhappy ghosts. Those story elements tell us the dairy production season is over. By either account, herding or farming, Dumuzi's season ends, he temporarily dies, he is buried, lamented, and because of women's grief and lamentation, the underworld gives him back. We return to the text:

> *Geshtinanna takes part in the lamentation scene that describes the rangers: little rangers and big rangers who have "no mercy, no fathers, mothers, wives, brothers, sisters or children ... since heaven was removed from earth." The rangers shove people into the underworld, herding them like recruits and captives*

with neither clemency nor kindness. They recruit humans for death. They "know not good and evil!"

The rangers suspect Dumuzi is with his sister; they move on to Geshtinanna's place. They demand Dumuzi but she goes on with her gardening and tanning sheep hides; she will not tell them where he is hiding. They do not find him at his sister's house; they move on to the holy sheepfold. They find him. They surround him with weapons and take him away. Geshtinanna, "the sister, for the sake of her brother, tore around the city like a (circling) bird. 'Let me go to my brother (so) ill used!'" The tablet lacuna would have described a fly telling Inanna where Dumuzi was taken. Geshtinanna is also arrested by the rangers. Dumuzi is weeping for his sister. Inanna decides each will serve alternating half-years in the underworld.

"You (Dumuzi) half a year only,
    your sister half a year only.
[When] you demand it
    she will [spend] the days in question."
Holy Inanna was giving Dumuzi
    as substitute for her(self).
O holy Ereshkigala!
Praise of you is sweet!

A natural seasonal order is in place by the end of the poem. Spending half the year in the netherworld implies a two-season year. In the Sumerian calendar, summer begins in our March and winter begins when the harvest is finished and the land is parched and "dead."

Ereshkigal(a) is praised in the final two lines. Praising deities is expected of scribal composers; praising can secure a better fate. Everyone dies. Ereshkigal is their death mother; praising her might gain favor in her realm!

ISHTAR'S DESCENT

Ishtar also makes her descent into the underworld. The theme is the same: the goddess leaves the world and fertility goes with her. Foster offers a far shorter and less elaborate text with several differences in the descent story. In the "Descent of Ishtar to the Netherworld," we hear that it is a "land of no return." It is gloomy, the dead eat clay and dust, it is dark, and the corpses swell up and grow "wings for garments (cob webs or mould)." The door to the netherworld is bolted. Ishtar decides to visit. Inanna/Ishtar's journey into the underworld explains the seasonal change. (Foster 2005: 499-504:)

> *Ishtar is determined to enter the underworld. She threatens the gatekeeper: open the door or else she will break it down and release the dead who will devour the living. He tells Ereshkigal that her sister, the one who holds the "play rope" (a war image) and roils the deep waters, wants entry. Roiling the deep refers to the goddess' water powers and links her to Tiamat the creatress, the primordial sea. Ereshkigal is fearful. "Her face went pale as a cut-down tamarisk, her lips went dark as the lip of a vat (ibid.: 499)." She wonders aloud why Ishtar would want to come to the underworld, and expecting the worst, and what has made Ishtar so angry at her. She fears Ishtar is after her realm. She tells the gatekeeper to open the gate and obey the old rules of the underworld. Ishtar is admitted and descends by going through each of the seven gates and giving up her adornments and clothing as does Inanna. Here, the ME are not mentioned; her tiara, earrings, beads, garment pin at her breast, girdle of birth stones at her waist, bracelets and anklets, and finally her loincloth are removed one by one. Ishtar enters naked. Ereshkigal is in a fury when Ishtar takes the seat of honor. Ereshkigal orders her vizier to remove Ishtar from sight and "let loose against her sixty diseases" including, eye, side, foot, heart and head diseases. After Ishtar disappears into the netherworld, the cattle and asses do not mate, a man does not accost the girl in the street, husbands and wives do not copulate, and the vizier of*

the gods is in mourning. He tells the moon god (Sin/Suen) and Ea (Enki) that sex has ceased in the world.

The vizier of the great gods repeats the lines describing that sex for animals and people has ceased. Fertility is gone from the land. As in Inanna's descent, the vizier asks the moon god, but he does not (cannot) help. He goes to Ea (Enki) who "in his wise heart" knows what to do. He creates an impersonator, Asushunamir, a male prostitute or transvestite who dresses as a woman and is part of Inanna/Ishtar's cult. Traditional cultures honor cross-gendered people — they are of two worlds. This may be why Asushunamir can enter and leave the underworld. The impersonator does his job, he calms Ereshkigal, and in return for his empathy, requests the water skin that is Ishtar. Ereshkigal complies and has her vizier sprinkle Ishtar with the water of life. She then curses the impersonator — he will everafter earn his bread along the city wall with the women prostitutes. "May bread of the public plowing be your food,[75] may the public sewer pipe be your drinking place. The shadow of a wall be your station, the threshold be your dwelling. May drunk and sober slap your cheek (ibid.: 502-3)!" There follows a reference to decorating the underworld doorways with cowrie shells. A similar text has two words from a fragmented line that translate as "midwife" and "creatress." Cowrie shells (vulva symbol), midwife and creatress all have to do with fertility and birth. Birth from death.

Ereshkigal tells her vizier, Namtar, to go to her temple, decorate the doorway threshold with the cowrie shells; to sprinkle the goddess with the water of life and remove her. This evidence implies the creativity and rebirthing that once resided in the netherworld (ibid.: 502; footnote 4 p. 503). Namtar carries out his orders. He sprinkles Ishtar with the water of life (the grass of life is not included in the Ishtar version of the descent). He leads her back through the seven gates, restoring her belongings at each gate. Ishtar may leave but her ransom agreement, handing over Tammuz (equivalent to Dumuzi), must be met or she will be returned to the netherworld.

---

[75] public plowing is having sex in public; bread is the payment

> *The poem quickly jumps to Tammuz, Ishtar's longtime consort/"lover," who is to take her place. He is given a purifying bath, "anointed with fine oil," [76] dressed in a red robe, and plays a "lapis flute." "Prostitutes turn [his] mood." This phrase is explained, not that he goes to prostitutes for sex, but that they are paid mourners for his committal into the underworld (ibid.: 504).*

The bathing, anointing, and wrapping in red is traditional preparation for burial. Belili is an equivalent name for Inanna/Ishtar. She is also referred to as Wild Cow — a mother goddess inference. She laments her "brother" Tammuz. "Do not rob me of my only brother!" Belili is the sister to Tammuz as Gestinanna is sister to Dumuzi. The poem goes from lamenting his death to celebrating his return all in one line! Ishtar's descent is less eloquent and profoundly truncated compared to Inanna's descent. The abbreviated text may mean that the people know the story well so it flies quickly through the salient points, or that the talent of the composer scribe was less than the one behind the stylus that copied Inanna's Sumerian descent story. Either way, patriarchy has changed the story. The final line is reminiscent of Mexico's Day of the Dead when everyone remembers their dead relatives, visits their bones, and imagines them back and visiting among the living, just for one day. Dumuzi returns (ibid.: 504:).

"On the day Tammuz (says) 'Hurrah!' the lapis flute and carnelian
   ring (say) 'Hurrah!'
"With him (say) 'Hurrah!' the wailing men and wailing women,
"Let the dead come up and smell the incense."

IN THE DESERT BY THE EARLY GRASS

The composition below tells an agricultural version of Dumuzi in the underworld. (Jacobsen 1987: 61-70:)

---

[76] The funereal anointing of oil will appear again in the last chapter where Mary Magdalene anoints Jesus just prior to his death.

"In the desert, by the early grass, she [holds not back] the flood of tears for her husband." Inanna weeps for her "lad." The poem goes on to list many local mother goddess names lamenting their lost child. Jacobsen suggests that when territories are unified, the lament includes many local divine personalities. No matter the locale or divine names, the theme is the same — the vegetation god has died, his mother weeps and tries to find him. She weeps and waits for the early grass to grow in the desert. He must serve his term in the underworld.

What is different in this text is that Inanna/Ishtar does not cause his death and so it is an early composition. The poem describes the natural cycle of growing plants. The story of seasonal cycles is: sprouting vitality, harvest of mature plants, grasses die, and the land waits for early desert grass to signal a new beginning. Blaming Inanna/Ishtar for bad behavior and causing the death of her beloved is later priestly pandering for the rising patriarchy. Inanna laments her "lad" by many a vegetation god's name: warrior Ninazu, Damu of orchards, Ningishzida of tree roots, Alla of rivers and fishermen, Ishtatan of the foothills and justice, Allagula (possibly of rain), Lugalshudi, Lusiranna of spring rain, and of course, Dumuzi the shepherd (Jacobsen 1987: 61). The mother goddess names are also many. The identities represent the same idea from different economies and geography. Everyone's deities are included without bias or competition.

The mothers search for their sons — on the road and in the dessert. One segment tells us that recruiters ("rangers") broke into the mother goddess's private sacrosanct chambers and took her son. She claws her face in grief. The conscripting "constables" who take men for war or for labor in quiet times, are the "causes of dirges," are without mercy. She wants her son returned. They tell her: "Mother who gave birth, cow, low not for the calf." In other words, she may not have her son ... not yet. The mother consoles herself that "after the term they have set for the lad, my Damu, he will come back, out of the spring grass." The goddess mothers, like cows (a complimentary term in the Ancient Near East), wait. "The cow [seeks] the spot where its calf is [lying,] the cow lows and lows, [the cow lows and lows] (ibid.: 68)."

The grieving mother seeks her child as a "ewe separated from the lamb ... like a goat separated from from the kid (ibid.: 69)." She goes weeping through the wet marshes to the foothills and on toward the mountains (another realm of the dead), to join her dead child. She cries out what she will give a man who can show her where her son is: "things (numerous as) the stars of heaven (ibid.: 70)!"

Goddess mother not only seeks him but wants to join him. "If it be required, you lad, let me walk with you the road of no return. Alas, the lad! The lad, my Damu (ibid.: 71)!" The spirits of the dead leave their bodies and are carried on the wind to the mountains. Dead Damu/Dumuzi speaks: "Since I am one lying in the south winds lying in all the north winds, since I am lying in the little ones that sink the ships, since I am lying in the big ones that drown the crops, since I am lying in the lightnings and in tornados, she should not be where (I,) the lad, am!"

The mother imagines finding him and bandaging his wounds; she is willing to eat the food of the dead with him. The dead god tries to get a message back home to his mother who "is crying in the desert, [letting the cry] resound," to arrange a ransom by way of the people he meets on the road; but they are ghosts/spirits. He sees children, a man who keeps dancing, a songstress, and more, but they can not take a message to his mother. He realizes he is dead. "Woe! I am become a ghost!" The voice of the narrator sings "by flowing waters of holy-water fonts, by flowing waters of holy-water fonts, [amidst the water conduits] of the young [anointed ones,]" and names all the vegetation gods laid to rest at numerous sites. Dead kings were also given Dumuzi-status in their burials and are mentioned (ibid.: 72-79).

A large lacuna occurs. When the story picks up, Damu/Dumuzi's sister has joined him. Jacobsen writes the "death of the sister" may occur in the lacuna. The sister is Mother Geshtin, who is Geshtinanna, "Lady Grapevine," and is equivalent to Inanna. She is sometimes a physician or an underworld scribe. Her similarity to Inanna is that she can go into the underworld and come out. She takes half the year in the underworld so her brother can be free half a year. Inanna makes a cameo *appearance in the very beginning of this long text. Damu is changed to Dumuzi as the text progresses. Geshtin(anna) comforts Dumuzi in the underworld. She comforts him and says she is his mother, "the day that dawns for you will also dawn for me, the day you see, I shall also see," that is, when he returns to life, to light (ibid.: 83-4). His death is not final.*

ENKIDU IN PATRIARCHY'S LAND OF THE DEAD

Advancing patriarchy re-designs the underworld to mirror its political reality. Men make war, goddess is eclipsed, and men and *their* sons are important; women are not. In a Gilgamesh story, barren women and eunuchs fare poorly in their revised underworld. The idea that the dead enjoy sunlight as the sun makes his rounds at night, and the idea of the dead visiting their families once a year is gone. A late tablet added to the Gilgamesh Epic illustrates the changes.

Gilgamesh acquires two items that he loses into the underworld. He has a *pukku* and *mikku* that Inanna gives him in gratitude for chasing Imdugud bird (storm emblem of Inanna) and his family from her tree's crown, for making Lilith (Inanna's own pre-urban wind-maiden form) flee from the trunk, and for killing the serpent (umbilical cord—vaginal snake and emblem of prime creatresses) in the roots of her *huluppu* tree. She requires the tree that she carefully tended for her throne and bed. She weeps and weeps because the bad things won't leave her tree. (Inanna helpless? Really?) When our goddess is portrayed helpless and dismayed, please know that priestly tampering has accomplished much of its devious work to rid patriarchy of the feminine— goddess and woman alike. Lilith, the tree and the animal emblems are her own aspects!

Gilgamesh's items are variously given as drum and beater or ball and mallet to incite war or rough game contests. The items fall into the netherworld, some poems say Uruk's women petition the goddess and the hated objects disappear. The women are tired of the tyrant's behavior and weary of his exhausting their men folk in his pointless contests. Enkidu, his servant, equal in strength and size (but nicer), enters the underworld to retrieve the items for his boss. His description of life in the underworld is a far far different place compared to the goddess triad's third aspect, the death mother, who cares for us until we return to life.

Sumerian, Akkadian, and later Babylonian tablets vary in the details. Either Enkidu cannot return, but can converse with Gilgamesh through a hole into the land of the dead where libations are poured to appease the ghosts; or he goes willingly into the underworld, breaks the rules, and is stuck there. Gilgamesh obtains divine aid to free him. Either way, he answers the king's questions about the netherworld. He reports what the priest scribes want to tell the people about what goes on in the underworld. To illustrate the *new* man-made House of Shadows, the following non-Sumerian text excerpts are selected from the Andrew George translation of *The Epic of Gilgamesh*. Inanna traditionally gives Gilgamesh two items in gratitude for his getting her tree rescued and cut down and her furniture made. Below, he himself makes a "ball" from the tree base and makes a "mallet" from a branch. (Sumerian Gilgamesh also appears as Bilgames.) (George 1999: 183-95:)

> Playing with the *ball* he took it out in the city square,
> playing with the … he took it out in the city square.
> The young men of his city began playing with the *ball*,
> with him mounted piggy-back on a band of widow's sons.
> 'O my neck! O my hips!' they groaned.
> The son who had a mother, she brought him bread,
> the brother who had a sister, she poured him water.
> When evening was approaching
> he drew a mark where his *ball* had been placed,
> he lifted it up before him and carried it off to his house.
> At dawn, where he had made the mark, he mounted piggy-back,
> but at the complaint of the widows
> and the out cry of the young girls,
> his *ball* and his *mallet* both fell down to the bottom of the
> Netherworld.
> With … he could not reach it,

he used his hand, but he could not reach it,
he used his foot, but he could not reach it.
At the Gate of Ganzir, the entrance to the Netherworld, he took a
    seat,
racked with sobs Bilgames began to weep:
'O my *ball*! O my *mallet*!
O my *ball*, which I have not enjoyed to the full!
O my ..., with which I have not had my fill of play!
On this day, if only my *ball* had stayed for me in the carpenter's
    workshop!
...
My ball has fallen down to the Netherworld, who will bring it up
    for me?
My mallet has fallen down to Ganzir, who will bring it up for me?'
His servant Enkidu answered him:
'My lord, why are you weeping? Why are you sick at heart?
I myself will bring your ball up for you from the Netherworld,
I myself will [bring] your mallet up for you from Ganzir!'
...

Gilgamesh is said to be of enormous size. He is an established tyrant who makes young men wrestle him in unfair matches and rapes brides on their wedding nights. Here he rides the young men in what appears to be a day-long polo match, using men as ponies with no time out for food or drink. The only way to stop the game is to get rid of his toys. The women voiced complaint of his game to the goddess; they or she dispose of the ball and mallet.

A secondary reason for the disposal action is for the story's plot. The women are blamed for poor Enkidu's journey to the underworld, but the main reason for the ball and mallet fiasco is so that priestly scribes can invent a grim version of the land of the dead where only fathers of many sons and infants are treated well. Sons are needed for recruitment for the labor force and army and large families are encouraged. Women without reproductive rights to say NO! produce closely spaced children.

Infants die. The special treatment for infants is to sooth the women who lament their dead babes.

> *Bilgames tells Enkidu how to behave when he slips into the underworld for the toys. He is to wear old clothes and no fragrant oil or the dead will notice him. He is not to use a throw stick or carry a 'cornel rod' (a specific sort of conifer cone on a staff) or he will be noticed. He will not wear sandals as the dead enter barefoot. He is neither to kiss the wife and son he loves nor strike the wife and son he hates. In that land is the Mother of Ninazu, her 'shining' shoulders and breasts are uncovered; she exhibits mourning by scratching herself with her nails and 'wrenches [her hair] out like leeks.' (She mourns Ninazu who is a later consort of Ereshkigal. Early Ereshkigal mourns the Bull of Heaven who visits her and 'dies.' That is the explanation for her mourning in 'Inanna's Descent.') Enkidu ignores the advice completely. Apparently a man can kiss and strike his wife and children at will, dead or alive, and Enkidu does. The mother of the underworld seizes him.*
>
> *Enkidu does not return for seven days. Bilgames weeps 'bitter tears.' His companion/servant did not die in battle, neither the 'pitiless sherif' of Nergal nor Namtar (both underworld gods are consorts of Ereshkigal in various stories) seized him. It was the Netherworld, i.e., Ereshkigal, goddess of the dead who did it! Uruk's king petitions Father Enlil and Father Nanna who cannot help retrieve Enkidu. He goes to Father Enki who, as usual, has the solution. Utu, the sun god, is requested to bring Enkidu up with him when he makes an opening through the mountains on his rise out of the Netherworld where he goes during the night. (Utu is shown on seals with a jagged saw for this purpose.) Bilgames is happily reunited with Enkidu.*

He hugged him tight and kissed him,
in asking and answering they made themselves weary:
'Did you see the way things are ordered in the Netherworld?
If only you could tell me, my friend, if only [you could tell] me!'
'If I am to [tell] you the way things are ordered in the Netherworld,

O sit you down and weep!' 'Then let me sit down and weep!'
'[The one] whom you touched with joy in your heart,
he says, "I am going to [ruin.]"
Like an [old garment] he is infested with lice,
like a crack [in the floor] he is filled with dust.'
'Ah, woe!' cried the lord, and he sat down in the dust.

'Did [you see the man with one son?]' 'I saw him.' 'How does
he fare?'
'From the peg built into his wall bitterly he laments.'
'Did you see the man with two sons?' 'I saw him.' 'how does
he fare?'
'Seated on two bricks he eats a bread-loaf.'
'Did you see the man there with three sons?' 'I saw him.' 'How
does he fare?'
'He drinks water from the waterskin slung on the saddle.'
'Did you see the man with four sons?' 'I saw him.' 'How does
he fare?'
'Like a man with a team of four donkeys his heart rejoices.'
'Did you see the man with five sons?' 'I saw him.' 'How does
he fare?'
'Like a fine scribe with a nimble hand he enters the palace with
ease.'
'Did you see the man with six sons?' 'I saw him.' 'How does he
fare?'
'Like a man with ploughs in harness his heart rejoices.'
'Did you see the man with seven sons?' 'I saw him.' 'How does
he fare?'
'Among the junior deities he sits on a throne and listens to the
proceedings.'
'Did you see the man with no heir?' 'I saw him.' '[How does]
he fare?'
'He eats a bread-loaf like a *kiln-fired* brick.'
'Did you see the palace *eunuch*?' 'I saw him.' 'How does he fare?'
'Like a useless *alala*-stick he is propped in a corner.'

(Variant: 'Like a fine standard *he is propped in* the corner.')

'Did you see the woman who had not given birth?' 'I saw her.' 'How does she fare?'

'Like a *defective* pot she is cast aside, no man takes pleasure in her.'

…

'Did [you see] the man fallen in battle?' ['I saw him.' 'How does he fare?']

'His father and mother cradle his head, his wife weeps.'

…

'Did you see the little stillborn babies, who knew not names of their own?' 'I saw them?' 'How did they fare?'

'They play amid syrup and ghee at tables of silver and gold.'

…

Jacobsen comments on the above twelfth tablet, saying that it was added in the first millennium and is not part of the Sumerian or Akkadian Gilgamesh/Bilgames epic (Jacobsen 1976: 229). The religious views of the afterworld in the text are fully patriarchal. I include it for that reason. Men with many sons are rewarded; men dying in battle receive succor; stillborns eat luxurious delicacies on tables of silver and gold and barren women are discarded like broken pots.

By the first millennium, women are baby factories and only men, their sons, and men's activities count. Nothing special is done about the birth-wearied mother of the seven sons, she is not even mentioned. There is no reward for having daughters. The decline and urban decadence of late second millennium has further deteriorated. There is no memory of return from the goddess' womb-tomb; the constant war, rebuilding and farms need fresh foot soldiers and workers. Only males count because they are useful bodies for the king. The priests support the rulers by altering the old stories. The practice continues into the present. Control over women's reproductive rights and ban on birth control — in the face of obvious over-population, poverty, health complications, and strained food and water sources — is more of the same male decision-making behind a holy facade.

The cities and territories of the Ancient Near East were ripe for falling and they did. The third millennium king-heroes were upheld as protectors. The first millennium kings were heroically joined with gods and their threatening aggressive nature was promoted. Rulers entered rival cities and slaughtered men, women, and children; their armies looted and ruined temples and palaces; they bragged about their conquests via royal entertainers' songs. Of course, all the disastrous deeds were encouraged by god-ordered whispers to the king in his dreams of the night.

Religion underwent drastic changes. Goddess faded, and gods became more unruly, doing unspeakable things for unknowable reasons other than the obvious, that the gods merely mirror men. Blaming goddesses and women is required to support the Y-behavior of men.

The drama of seasonal change also acquires new stories. Instead of a natural observation of the two seasons, the sons of patriarchy, desiring a larger role (mirroring the political and social changes), reduce the role of divine feminine with blame and bad deeds. Goddess myth is drastically altered.

MALENESS PENETRATES DIVINE WOMAN'S SACROSANCT UNDERWORLD

Ereshkigal is Inanna's "sister" and associated with the underworld from the beginning of the Ancient Near East's creation story. The Sumerian underworld of the dead, the womb tomb, is overseen by an aspect of Great Mother. She is great mother's "daughter," and Inanna's "sister," Ereshkigal. The underworld is a place to await renewal; not a one-way journey into gloom and dust; not a gated containment for ghosts of all the dead who ever were. The concept of punishment and torture in the underworld comes from even later male thinking. The first queen and mother for the land of the dead is not a horror on her throne of despair. She is beautiful, even lusty, and reigns as mother for the dead. Yes, loss is lamented, but like the early vegetation god, Damu/ Dumuzi, a cyclic return is expected. When the land of the dead becomes a permanent dreary lock-down place with escape nearly impossible, the flow of life-death-life changes; the spiraling cyclic rhythm of woman, goddess, and life is discontinued.

The following story is a depiction of male usurpation of Ereshkigal's domain. The other more sublime and showy domains of earth and heaven are already masculinized, with the exception of love, sex, birth, and prostitution. The underworld, less appetizing, less glorious, is taken last. The middle Babylonian Era has a forceful usurpation story that becomes more violent in later versions.

NERGAL AND ERESHKIGAL

(or How Nergal Became King of the Underworld)

Ereshkigal is *given* the underworld to rule by An and Enlil. (The death mother is *given* a realm that is hers from earliest myth.)

The underworld changes from a restful slumber in mother's womb preceding re-birth to a parallel existence of stratified urban life of privilege or deprivation. Death is gloomy and dreadful; inhabitants eat clay for bread and drink dust for water or dirty water for beer unless relatives leave them offerings. As time passes and deaths accumulate, the number of dead is imagined to greatly out-number the living. The sacred feminine is losing importance and influence. It is time for Ereshkigal to lose her solitary domain. Priestly scribes select Nergal to be lord of the underworld. He is the plague god.

Foster pieced together the following text of "Nergal and Ereshkigal" from several sources. (Foster 2005: 509-12:)

> *Ereshkigal is isolated in her realm; she cannot leave; she is sexually frustrated which is key to her vulnerability. The great celestial gods are having a banquet. (Note that the important location for sacredness has moved off-planet, away from earth.) All deities will attend. Since Ereshkigal cannot*

leave her queendom, a messenger from Anu, Kakka, goes to the underworld to invite her to send her vizier (administrative assistant) to the banquet for her portion. Kakka descends the stairway from the celestial realm. He calls to the gatekeeper to open up; the gate opens and blesses him. He does obeisance by kissing the ground at Ereshkigal's feet. He stands up and issues the invitation for the feast. He acknowledges that she can not come up to them and they can not come down to her, but she should send a messenger to collect her portion of the feast.

Ereshkigal politely inquires of the well-being of all the heavenly greats: Anu, Enlil, Ea, Nammu, Nanshe, Ninurta, and the Mistress of Heaven (Inanna) and her husband (Dumuzi). The queen of the underworld agrees to the arrangement. Ereshkigal dispatches her messenger. Namtar arrives at the "celestial court" and is accorded due respect. All the deities stand up and then kneel in deference to his queen, all but one. Nergal does not kneel. Namtar will not receive the banquet share under this insult and returns to the underworld to report the disrespect. Ereshkigal, insulted, will not rule the dead and pass judgment. She leaves her throne.

The divines are terrified. Ea/Enki angrily demands that Nergal explain his rudeness. The story is fragmented at this point but Nergal announces he will go to the underworld, whether to apologize or in defiance, we are not told. Other versions have Ea/Enki making him go to Ereshkigal. One poem explains the making of the chair Nergal is to carry. He is to cut certain trees (possibly sissoo, whitewood, and cedar) and aromatic evergreen branches. He is to make a chair and paint it with gypsum in imitation of silver, faience in imitation of lapis lazuli, cobalt(?), and potash(?) to imitate gold. Ea further instructs him: while in the underworld he is to eat no bread the baker brings, no meat the butcher offers, and no beer from the brewer. He is not to accept the hospitable foot bathing. He is not to sit in an offered chair. Ea/Enki tells Nergal to take the chair he made to Ereshkigal. Nergal weeps. He knows she will not let him live! Ea/Enki tells him to fear not and gives him seven "watchers" for the journey. Inanna's Eanna in Uruk was *known for having seven fires lit at dark for the seven watchers of the night (possibly for the Pleiades).*

Nergal is given destruction, disease, and plague powers by Ea/Enki. There are fourteen powers, including: Lightening Flash, Wind, Epilepsy, something causing high fevers and spots, and others. One will stay at each of fourteen doorways in the underworld as Nergal approaches the queen. (Inanna/Ishtar passes through seven which is the usual number of gates.) He arrives. The gatekeeper Namtar knows who he is and announces Nergal to Ereshkigal. She commands that he be brought to her so she can kill him.

Nergal enters the underworld, leaves his fourteen nasties at the gates and "cuts down" Hurbashu (chill of fear) and Namtar. He tells his "troops" to stand by to keep the gates open. He runs through the gates to the palace of the underworld. He grabs the goddess off her throne by the hair with plans to cut off her head! Ereshkigal weeps many tears; she begs him to spare her; she will be his wife; he can have dominion over her realm and she will hand over the tablet of destiny. Nergal is pleased to hear this. "He seized her and kissed her, wiping away her tears, What (else) have you wished for from me for these months (past) till now (ibid.: 512)?" (One assumes he means sex.)

In another late text version, Ea/Enki, the crafty, tricky god advises Nergal how to get around Ereshkigal and avoid his likely execution at her hands. He is to take a funerary chair, painted with precious embellishments, as if anticipating his own death. The trick is that instead of a death chair that accompanies the dead in some traditions,[77] he carries his intended throne of usurpation. Nergal is told to refuse all offers of hospitality, and not be aroused when the underworld queen removes her clothing for her bath.[78] (ibid.: 512-23:)

---

[77] A chair is placed near a prepared displayed corpse for the soul to sit and observe the laments and funeral before departing.

[78] Many myths have men getting into trouble peeking or stumbling into a goddess at her bath time. That she could be a source of arousal would also indicated that Ereshkigal is still beautiful as every goddess has a right to be; she is not yet a horror.

Nergal arrives at the gate of the netherworld. The gatekeeper approaches Ereshkigal to say that an unknown visitor is at the gate to see her. Ereshkigal's vizier, Namtar, goes to the gate and recognizes the disrespectful god. He retells Ereshkigal of Nergal's bad behavior toward her. (Nergal did not bow on his knee in Ereshkigal's honor.) Nergal is admitted and undergoes the same ritual as Inanna/Ishtar in her descent. When he is brought to the queen, Nergal says he is representing all the celestial deities who request her to resume her throne and rule over the dead. She offers hospitality. He refuses. She strips for her bath. He is not aroused. After a break in the text, Ereshkigal strips again and Nergal succumbs. They make love madly for six days. Nergal stealthily leaves the love-bed and tricks the outer gatekeeper into releasing him by saying he was on a mission for his lady Ereshkigal. He returns to the celestial court. This causes great consternation. Ereshkigal is powerful; Nergal partook of her and is therefore not entitled to leave her land of the dead. She will come looking for him; she will retaliate. Ea/Enki disguises Nergal as a deformed god.

Back in the underworld, Ereshkigal awakens happy; she bathes and calls for hospitality to be readied for her lover. Namtar announces that Nergal has gone. She rages; she weeps; she wants him back. "Her tears ran down the sides of her nose ... 'my voluptuous lover'!" She falls from her chair; her eyes rain tears (ibid.: 519).

Namtar volunteers to go up again to find the scoundrel and bring him back. Ereshkigal tells him to say first to the heaven gods that she has never had a lover nor did she have any childhood pleasures as she was always queen of the dead. He is also to say that if Nergal is not returned to her, she will let the dead rise up to outnumber and devour all the living.

Namtar is received with all respect. He looks around but does not recognize the disguised Nergal. He returns empty-handed and mentions the deformed god to his queen. Ereshkigal understands the ruse. Namtar returns to the Great Above. Ea/Enki convinces Nergal he can be king of the netherworld if he goes below. He returns to the land of the dead. His clothing is surrendered at the seven gates. His nudity here is not the naked state of the dead, but sexual. He startles the queen of the dead. In some versions he roughly pulls her off her throne and makes passionate love with her for seven days and nights (sealing a marital pact?). In other texts, he is ready to cut off her head but when she proposes marriage he releases her and they share rulership. Anu sends a message: "That god whom I sent to you, let him dwell with you forever (ibid.: 523)." Patriarchy has usurped the underworld.

And what happened to death mother Ereshkigal, she, who was "given" the underworld in the deep dark earth womb? She became fearsome and demonized. She, once as beautiful as her "sister" Inanna, she who had rituals and temples in her name, she who is Inanna in her polar life-death opposites ever interchanging; she who is Queen of the realm of rest between returns, is imprisoned by human fear. Death is isolated from life. Death mother is given a dreadful role to play.

We remember Inanna, the story of life, goddess, and women. We forget Ereshkigal who is our own deep and dark story of losses. Maureen Murdock, in her *Heroine's Journey*, invites women to go deep into that darkness to meet our self who lives in the house of shadows. Our descent to the goddess of the/our underworld is an initiation point of our journey; we free both Ereshkigal and ourselves. We uncurse the dark. (Murdock 1990: 93:)

Nothing about her is menacing,
I feel her deep sense of sadness …
I am terrified by her power.
 "You can help me," she says.
 "No, I can't."
 "Of course you can," she booms.
 "By your presence they can no longer hold me. As each of my daughters comes to me of her own free will I am released."

CHAPTER 12

Warrior Goddess

War is bloody. Women's menstrual flow is both powerful and bloody. Lion, as carnivorous prey animal, is Inanna's emblem. Big cats accompany the mother goddess for countless millennia in the Ancient Near East, Old Europe, and Africa. Blood on prey animals' muzzles matches the blood show on vulvas; vulva is a "mouth." During menses women are powerful; they are taboo, sacred even, and no man can see them or touch them. Inanna/Ishtar is generally depicted nude as war goddess. She is accompanied, rides, or is drawn by lions. She bristles with weapons held and on her back — some of the "arrow" shafts in her two quivers end in snake heads and flower buds. She carries a lion-headed mace; she stares at the viewer with large all-seeing kohl-lined eyes.

Nudity in battle takes courage! Is the nudity left over from the early universal nude Great Mother? When mother goddess appears in her beautiful enticing young form, does her nudity imply sexuality? Is war sexy? The other possibility is that during menstrual seclusion both woman and goddess disrobe. Menstrual blood is taboo (sacred) and feared by men. The nude goddess indicates that she accompanies the king during her moon blood time. She is powerful, taboo, and scary.

SALTU (DISCORD)

Foster's anthology (2005: 97-106) includes a praise hymn for Ishtar from the time of Hammurabi. Ishtar is too noisy, too ready to fight; she is even aggressive against Ea (Enki) who has endowed her with her warrior spirit. Enki gathers the gods. Something must be done to calm her warring behavior! He takes dirt from his fingernails seven times and adds spittle. He creates a creature as big and feisty as Ishtar. Her name is Saltu ("discord"). She comes into being in an uproar; fierce and spoiling for a fight. Ea (Enki) shouts over her fearsome noise that she is to go rudely to her look-alike opponent and goad her to fight. He suggests that perhaps the goddess is too much for Saltu who then goes defiantly in search of Ishtar. The goddess has heard that another is approaching to fight her and sends her messenger, Ninshubur, to investigate. Here her messenger is male but in Sumerian texts the vizier is female. He goes and is surprised at what he finds. The opponent looks exactly like Ishtar! He reports back to the goddess and tells about Saltu's fierceness. The goddess flies into a rage.

Ishtar rightfully accuses Ea of this creation. Ea explains he did it to get her to alter her behavior; Saltu's purpose is to show Ishtar what she looks like as the "Mad Dancer in Battle." When she, Ishtar, agrees to calm down, her double will go away. Ishtar agrees. "The lioness Ishtar quieted, her heart was appeased." Ea keeps his word. Saltu disappears. He further requests that once a year people go to the streets and dance madly and wildly so Ishtar remembers how she once acted. "Let it be yearly, let a whirling dance be established among the feast days of the year. Look about at all the people! Let them dance in the street. Hear their clamor!"

INANNA AND EBIH

The goddess is "destroyer of *kur.*" *Kur* is "mountain." Inanna destroys a mountain. In the "Inanna and Ebih" text, she smashes it to the ground because it attacked her city; it was hostile and disobedient.

She roars like a lion. The poet describes her destructive storm power and noise as she destroys the enemy. Inanna is also called a "big wild-ox" ready to attack the *kur*, the hostile mountains. The wild "ox" here would have to mean an intact bull and not "ox" as is our term commonly used for castrated bulls that pull plows. Inanna is "an awesome lion" that kills the hostile and disobedient with "venom." Whether the "venom" is toxic anger or poison as from a serpent is unclear, however, lion demons with dragon and serpent aspects are depicted in seals.

Figure 47. Inanna and Her Lion-griffon

War deities grow out of political change and divine attributes. Men invent war. War is noisy and destructive. People know mothers defend their young. The goddess is imagined as a warrior — she is a Great Mother who defends her children greatly. Goddess is converted from a defender of her people into an instrument of war. Inanna uses her weather, storm, lightning and thunder, flood, blood (women's blood), lion, and fierceness in defense of her people. Ishtar, though equivalent as the maid form for fertility, is from a rougher more aggressive nomadic herding people. When the two goddesses merge, Inanna/Ishtar is a war goddess who leads the charge.

Excerpts from a Hammurabi inscription on a stele that accompanies the "laws of Hammurabi" (1792-1750 B.C.E.) are informative. The king's cosmic commissions, his deeds of conquest are listed. Ishtar is no longer the source of kingship, as Inanna/Ishtar has been for millennia. King Hammurabi claims his kingship is bestowed by three gods: Anu, Enlil, and Ea. Usurpation is nearly complete. Ishtar is only a war and sex goddess. The successful campaigns to conquer large land areas in all direction are described. "The epic spirit, the true lyricism displayed in these lines was in the service of propaganda, masking, though not completely, the dreary procession of plunder, destruction, and deportation that went along with these conquests (Foster, 2005: 126 citing A. Finet, *Le Code de Hammurapi*, 1998: 10:)." He says he rules all the four world regions and is Ishtar's favorite. (ibid.: 131, 134:)

> I am Hammurabi the perfect king, ... I found the way
> out of numerous pressing crises, I made light come out upon
> them. With the mighty weaponry that Zababa[79] and Ishtar
> bestowed upon me, with the superior insight that Ea ordained
> to be mine, with the capability that Marduk gave over to me,
> I expelled enemies north and south, I extinguished warfare,
> I brought happiness to the people, I made all the people of
> the realm to lie down in green pastures, I allowed no one
> to alarm them.
>
> ...
>
> May Ishtar, mistress of battle and combat, who bares
> my weapon, my protective spirit who loves my reign, curse
> his kingship in her angry heart and furious rage. May she
> turn his good fortunes to bad, may she break his weaponry
> on the field of battle and strife. May she stir up against him
> mutiny and insubordination. May she fell his warriors, may
> she let the earth gorge their blood, may she cast them down,
> one after another, into a heap in the open country, may his
> soldiers receive not quarter! May she deliver that man into

---

[79] first born of Enlil who is a war god; Zababa is also Inanna/Ishtar as a war goddess

his enemies' power and lead him off in fetters to the land
that was at war with him!

Hammurabi intended perpetuity for his laws. His stele includes an invocation to the major deities to inflict punishment on any king who ever interferes with them.

In a 13th century B.C.E. text, an Assyrian victory over Babylon is described, a king is praised, and the part played by each of the major gods is included (ibid.: 313). Ishtar receives only one mention as a warrior goddess. Her lead-line, usually carried coiled in a circle, is seen in imagery to denote rulership. Text and seals have Inanna/Ishtar leading captives with her line as one would lead oxen. Inanna also uses the line to lead her bull of heaven. Geshtinanna, the Lady Grapevine of heaven, has a vine line connecting heaven and earth. Inanna/Ishtar is equated with Geshtinanna as they are both queen of heaven and earth. They move freely between the two regions. Line and vine connect earth and heaven; line also measures and in peacetime is used to build and rebuild. In this text, the goddess's line is a "jump rope" game — war is her game (ibid.: 313). Ishtar flails her jump rope and drives her warriors berserk!

Ishtar is mentioned last in the Assyrian text of the divine warriors participating in war. Her attributes of sexual arousal have extended to arousal for fighting. Life is turbulent. She is established as goddess of love and war — both are unsettling; both are unpredictable. She is called "fickle," changeable, and contrary. She is blamed for losing battles by just walking away from her beloved king. "God(dess) is on our side" is a common presumption. In the Ancient Near East, the terrible consequences of war are the doings of the gods and Ishtar. Kings and men are blameless.

Weather deities are the logical war deities. Inanna is Queen of Heaven, equal, at least, to An(u), "heaven." Spring storms come from wide low black clouds rising above the horizon. Storms thunder and flash. Heavy rainfall, floods and winds destroy. Storm is zoomorphic thunderbirds, the Summerian Imdugud bird, and one of Inanna's emblems. The storm cloud rising on the distant horizon resembles the wide wingspan of a black eagle. Thunder sounds like roaring lions. The symbol of storms becomes Imdugud/Anzu bird imagined as a black eagle with a roaring lion head. When eagles are shown with knees spread wide, this is the attack position of the actual bird. Imdugud appears frequently as an emblem of her in cylinder seals, with or without Inanna. This is her storm power, her raging, her noise; the sound and destruction of war.

When patriarchal desire for conflict and conquest took over, defense became offense. Besides mother protection, other attributes that "logically" connected Inanna/Ishtar with warfare are menstrual and birth blood power, the noise of her spring thunderstorms (Imdugud bird), and the death aspect of Great Mother receiving the dead for renewal into her womb tomb. "Ishtar, mistress of turmoil, aroused him (the king) to strife (ibid.: 325)." Poor innocent king, bad Ishtar made him do it! Men go to war and temples are built or rebuilt when a deity tells a king to act. The king is also a priest and the one most worthy of divine whispers. The following is a dedication of a Kassite king's temple building at Uruk for Anu and Ishtar. It pledges the king's support. The inscription reads (ibid.: 365-6:)

... To Ishtar, the most great lady, who goes at my side, who maintains my army, shepherds my people, subdues those disobedient to me.

... The king gives land to Ishtar's temple [equivalent to a square of about 20 kilometers to a side measured by the amount of barley needed to seed the land] an area of 216,000 kor using a ratio per surface unit of 30 quarts of seed barley, measured by the large cubit, to Ishtar I granted.

3 kor of bread, 3 kor of fine wine, 2 (large measures) of date cakes,[80] 30 quarts of imported dates, 30 quarts of fine(?) oil, 3 sheep per day did I establish as the regular offering for all time.

---

[80] known also as Ishtar or Lady cakes; kor/kur is a measurement of 300 liters

> I set up boundary stones in all directions and guaranteed the borders. The towns, fields, watercourses, and unirrigated land and their rural settlements did I grant to Ishtar, my lady. Whosoever shall arise afterward and shall alter my deeds and change the command that I spoke, shall take out my boundary stones, shift my boundary lines, take away the towns, fields, watercourses, and non-irrigated lands, or the rural settlements in the neighborhood of Uruk, or cause (another) to take (them)away, or who shall attempt to convert them to state lands, may Ishtar, the most great lady, not go at his side in battle and combat, but inflict defeat and heavy losses upon his army and scatter his forces!

I resisted Inanna as war goddess in the evolution of the peaceable farming goddess. I even considered downplaying her warrior activities, but this is a biography. Her big story requires full disclosure. There was a need for a warrior goddess then and there is need for a warrior goddess now.

Patriarchy declared war on women millennia ago. Our earth home needs defending. I now easily imagine Inanna as a warrior. She sees all. She sees the abusers, the incesters, the rapists, the pedophiles, the domestic violence in our homes and communities. She sees the conscienceless deaths of non-combatants and combatants alike. She stands beside women. She reminds us to say NO! She watches as we too tie up our sandals and run out together saying NO! We say NO! in our families, communities, workplaces and in the world. We fight to recover from patriarchal domination. Inanna encourages us to lead and press for change. She, even she, was forced by king-pleasing priests' stylus to do a king's bidding in offensive acquisition-wars. But remember, she often quit the king and left him mid-battle without explanation. When that happened, he lost the battle.

Inanna loves her people and her land. Her women warriors, the sturdy and brave among us, are rising to be noisy and strong against the lopsided rule of unwisdom and uncaring; against the ruin being visited on our planet and atmosphere. Consider: Inanna, Life, is within every woman. The next chapter will give good reason to tie up those sandals, paint lightening bolts on your brows, practice your voice of thunder, hoist your quiver, grab your mace, and don't forget the lions!

CHAPTER 13

Patriarchy and the Sacred Woman

Fear is the basis of the whole — fear of the mysteries, fear of defeat, fear of death. Fear is the parent of cruelty, and therefore it is no wonder if cruelty and religion have gone hand-in-hand.

Bertrand Russell

The best that can be said of patriarchy is that it has already happened and now we begin recovery. We know that male-only rule is destructive; its missteps and blatant abuse of life, power, religion, women, the planet, minorities and those colonized are experienced and recorded globally. Male supremacy's stewardship is a dangerous and dismal failure. We read the evidence. We observe the actions of politics, corruption and abuse of power.

Reactionary male-based religions pressure our legal system; women's reproductive rights are again threatened; two millennia of religious dogma is pushing education towards a new dark age; we know countless people die for too many avoidable reasons; we witness tyrants, wars, conflicts and political threats. We hear lies everywhere.

There is hope. We are shaking out of the cog and safety of directed group work and mentality. Cog work is based on obedience. Obedience replaces creativity. Technologies developed during recent decades are used to expose truths previously suppressed; we network with like-minded concerned people around the world. Suppression of information is dropping; exposure of menace, illegal behavior, cover-ups, and formerly closeted dirty secrets is imminent.

Religious male-only ideology suppresses nature, humane-ity, and good sense. To accomplish the suppression requires muscle, force, intimidation, threat, punishment, and infliction of a great deal of guilt and fear. Men spent the last five millennia perfecting their position.

As patriarchy replaces partnership in the Ancient Near East, whose voice is left to oppose? Goddess is diminished and demonized. Women are silenced and "given" into marriage as business deals by their fathers or brothers. They are sold into marriage for a bride price and taken from their families as chattel to the husband's family. Women are displaced and isolated in strange male-controlled households and made to serve the entitled men, who in turn serve "superior" men. The big "superior" men are served by everyone. Sumerian for "big man" is *lu-gal.*

The early cities and settlements of Sumer are guided by the women and men elders. A second collective governing body is added — men who carry weapons. During times of threat, the elders select a man to lead the defense. For the duration of conflict, that man holds absolute rule. When war becomes pandemic, part-time leaders with temporary absolute rule became full-time absolute rulers. Kramer suggests that men experiencing absolute power would find relinquishing that role difficult and most likely would keep conflict or threat of danger on-going to make their part-time rulership permanent. Y-ness being Y-ness usurps peace, cooperation, inclusion, and participation and replaces them with constant conflict and absolute rule.

Y-ness also systematically takes over the long-established sensible, reasonable, and inclusive divine feminine by imitation, gender-flipping, demotion, minimization, and marginalization of the sacred feminine, one aspect, one goddess at a time. Y-ness wants freedom from the female voice and power that modifies Y-behavior and is spoken by both human and divine woman. Excepting where she-ness could not be pared away:

423

pregnancy, birth, lactation, childcare, food preparation, and vulvas; men and their gods take over.

Absolute secular rule is not enough for patriarchy. The alpha ruler is first bound to the religious center as a ruler-priest, a priestly king. He presides over the temple, assisting and serving the divine presence who owns the settlement or urban center. Religion and politics are interwoven. Absolute rulers move into their own palaces that rival and surpass temple grandeur; they also proclaim their own divinity. The divine status begins through association with the most powerful deities. Inanna reigns long and ranks high. Having sex with Inanna as her statue, proxy priestess, or queen representing the goddess is for fertility of the land and the way to sit the throne. The throne belongs to the goddess. A ruler is chosen by the goddess. He is her Dumuzi-beloved.

The renewal of fertility in the land is an annual event. The king has to please her once a year. He does not rule if he does not please her. Men, being men, enlarge sex, a natural expression, into a big event. The sexual prowess of the king brings fertility to the land. Under the old traditions, city elders grant temporary emergency rulership. Permanent rulership is ordained only by the goddess and only for a year. Rulership through the sacred feminine is one of goddess's ME. That too is revised and taken from her during the progression of patriarchy.

OVERVIEW OF THE TAKE OVER

Men take over when women's powerful solidarity is broken. We can no longer say NO! and say it together. Taking away our NO! means open season on sexual opportunism for men.

The subliminal message for my generation coming into biological ripeness in the late 1950's and early 60's was: when married we couldn't/ shouldn't say NO! as husbands have rights to sex on demand. The Christian wedding vows of the day included the woman agreeing to "love, honor and *obey*" the husband and were called "holy matrimony."

Patrimony is what is inherited from the father or male lineage, so why does matrimony mean marriage and becoming a husband's property? Matrimony should mean the wealth, wisdom, honor and voice inherited from our mother's lineage. When men own woman's body, and this is a the crucial thrust of patriarchal domination, then woman is without power or voice. The result of denying and dishonoring that deeply archaic women's rightful status is that men remain unwise and even dangerous without women's wisdom, voices, guidance, stories, and NO!

Patriarchy derailed humane creative potential. Two millennia of church fathers stunted humane evolution. The emphasis on technology is playing out in front of us. The good, the bad, and the ugly aspects of technology. It webs us together and reveals vast stores of knowledge. It kills people efficiently with guns, weapons, vehicles, and poisons. It also saves tiny babies. We can do our shopping and banking in our bathrobe and slippers. That same technology can steal our identity. The humanities are losing funding in colleges and universities in favor of technology and science, schools are failing their students, workers are laboring harder for less dollar value, the wealthiest get more and minimum wage is unlivable. Humane-ity is *not* on the table.

Men set a dangerous time in motion for us and our planetary home. Y-ness tyrannically dominates and avoids the modifying X-ness within themselves and women. Aggression, deadly competition, destruction, murder, rape, and domination grew and spread like plague. What happens when Y is crowned king of people, lands, and celestial realms is that old stories are edited. Wise women's influence, alive into historical times of Sumer, is overrun and forgotten. The Great Creatress is 'heroically' murdered.

Women of the Ancient Near East became sequestered. They were imprisoned in their women's quarters that were once their sacrosanct place of solidarity during their menses, their moon blood, blood so creatively powerful that women used the ritual around it to create culture. When women are removed politically, culturally, socially, economically and from sacred story, humankind suffers. X-ness is replaced by misogynous Y-patriarchy.

Male-only rule left written records of Y-ness in its extreme behaviors. Re-read what Y-ness has wrought from the records. There is record of constant warring, inquisition, witch trials, greedy colonization, muscular religious fanaticism, eighteenth, nineteenth, twentieth, and twenty-first century holocausts of ethnic groups in the Americas, Europe, Asia, Africa, Australia, and Indonesia. Within recent generational memory, we have the twentieth century's holocaust of Jews and others deemed unworthy to exist, culminating centuries of pogroms and intentional removal of inconvenient people. We have this century's Twin Towers 9-11 attack by religious fanatics of a heavy-handed manipulated version of religious ideology. Through five millennia we have record of religious believers and tyrannical rulers bringing mayhem, death, and murder into everyday life. Dominator world cultures touch and affect everyone, not only the obvious victims.

An Ancient Near Eastern wisdom proverb on gain and loss reads: "You find something, it gets lost. You discard something, it is preserved forever (Foster, 2005: 431)." Women found the goddess. We lost her model of humaneness when dominator maleness discarded her but she is preserved forever in our DNA, in our dreams, art, and memory. Our shared universal unconsciousness knows that domination by maleness and its Y-behaviors is wrong.

BIOLOGY OF DOMINATION

Dominator cultures (also called patriarchy and androcracy) of the Ancient Near East began as an unchecked misstep over 5,000 years ago. Conflict and wars result from a fear-filled response to climate changes, population increase, and decrease of available water. The Tigris and Euphrates riverbeds shift unreliably and inundate or move away from the large settled centers. The rivers flow shallowly over the flat southern Mesopotamian plains. Major fears arise over requirements of growing urban centers for food and water and the appeal and envy of cities and their concentrated wealth inviting conflict and raids. Raiding 'barbarians' of less urbanized and more nomadic cultures swept from desert, sea, mountains, and arid plains to take rather than merge.

Desperate times inspire fear. For men, fear results in desperate aggressive measures. Difficult terrains and extreme climates produce cultures with male domination and fierceness (Inuit, Australia Aborigines, mountain and desert dwellers). Harsh conditions bring out fear in men; fear teamed with the Y chromosome fuels aggression, violence, and destruction. Dr. Brizendino, in her book *The Female Brain*, states that male brains dedicate two and one half times more space to sex drive and aggression then does the female brain.

Intrinsic X-ness has the potential of cooperation, inclusion, and creative problem solving. The more difficult the situation, the more women's wisdom and voices are needed. Unfortunately, the more frightened men are, the less they can respond to non-violent biophilic solutions.

Water availability and rights cause tension. Unmet survival needs produce fear and desperation. Fear, in Y chromosomal response, moves quickly to anger; anger becomes aggression, destruction, violence, murder, and organized murder — war. The X chromosome is imbedded with nurturing, caring, inclusiveness, and has evolved over millions of years of our species' successful survival. Men have one X and women have two. Which gender is the obvious choice for deciding, guiding, participating, and cooperating with inclusivity, caring, and life affirming problem solving?

Harsh conditions, overpopulation, and resource depletion require action and decisions. When women are no longer included and heard; when sex is no longer sacred; when men wrest reproductive rights, both body and offspring, from the women, a serious misstep is taken. If women have voice and societal power, missteps can be redirected, corrected, or resolved in a biophilic manner. When men act alone, unmodified, unsupervised, and unwilling to take advisement, life on earth is usurped by male leadership. Ability to creatively react to climate changes and conflict; willingness to seek peace, reconciliation, cooperation, and inclusion; honoring woman's body; culture and gender partnership; and viewing life as sacred — all of these are lost.

People know they must tend the land around them; they know that most mothers are amazing, necessary, and wise. "Women have a special intelligence."[81] "Men must be very afraid of us or they would not try so hard to keep us down."[82]

The full and inclusive wisdom woven into women-based goddess myth is erased during the last centuries of the last millennium B.C.E.. An obscure god is elevated; over time all other gods are eliminated. Yahweh/Jehovah is a jealous and wrathful god. His priests and scribes write that he said so himself. Divine power is concentrated into a single off-planet god, who is invisible, who rules above earth, who deems earth and women to be inferior to heaven and men. Men's god gave earth to his sons to dominate. He spoke to and through his special sons.

The new god is fabricated from the attributes previously assigned to the big gods of earlier pantheons. He is incomplete. He lacks reproductive functions. His fixed "word" replaces the natural creativity of human experience. In the early centuries of the Common Era, natural sex is made unnatural, unholy. Male sexual desire is blamed on woman the temptress, the daughter of Eve. Sex and hunger drives all animals — we are a little twig on the primate branch of the animal kingdom part of the tree of life. Denial and repression of natural sexuality replaces the modification and self-discipline known by women to be a human responsibility. The evolving god does not like women. Eve and her Eve-lets are to blame because of the apple and snake business. Priestly editors and religious philosophers write misogyny into their texts through the words they create for their god named God. If the same effort used to manipulate and institutionalize male domination by Y-males had been applied to partnership and conflict resolution, our world would be far different today. Domination begets domination. Domination is a fatal disease.

Denial and repression ignore the basic problem facts. The Y chromosome is for fertilizing woman's eggs. The Y chromosome is the reason male bodies look as they do with generally stronger muscles, coarser body hair, larger frames and jaws, and a greater tendency for

---

[81] Orvilla Palmer Rogers in conversation 2014

[82] Margaret Palmer Seibel in conversation c.1950. My mother's family is matristic. The women are wise.

aggression and fighting. A fertilizer for eggs is required to continue a species. That is the good part. The bad part is that Y-ness is limited by its purpose. Human Y-ness retains the vestiges of chimp and ape male behavior but with a big brain — the combination can be lethal. Human females, the double X ones, learned millions of years ago to work together and share food-gathering, care and protection of young. This is also a vestige from our primate cousins. The second good part is that luckily, men also have a single X with the potential to act humanely and modify Y-behavior. The bad news is that many men do not give their X a chance to flourish.

Male fear turns into anger, anger becomes aggression, aggression causes destruction and violence; life is destroyed. All manner of strange excuses, fabricated reasons and blame emerge to support Y-behavior. Women use female solidarity to create culture and modify male Y-behavior. Men in power use male solidarity to rid themselves of women's influence, wisdom, and expectation that men can modify their domineering Y-ness.

I have no doubt that in all eras, some humans fell in love and kind men abounded. Alpha Y-only-based behavior of a few determined dominating men undermines the cooperative and peaceful directions of the many. In the Ancient Near East, Y-ness took over the biophilic direction of women who guide our species toward cooperative partnership with both genders. Fear of death and fascination with causing death in quantity to serve a few alpha males changes egalitarian partnership to a culture of domination and death. Necrophilia took over biophilia.

Human brains have the potential to create. That creative potential can express positively, biophilicly and creatively — or veer off in a destructive, selfish, death-dealing direction. It is up to the wise ones of both genders to guide us, just as Sumer had their elders for deciding what action to take. Wise women and men once combined their wisdom and guided Sumer for who knows how many millennia. The X chromosome is the guidance system. Xness is humane. Humane is the feminine of human. Women have two Xs; men have one X. The X chromosome, unlike the Y, evolved as maternal responsibilities increased. Millions of years ago, maternal care emerged out of necessity for our species' continuation. Biological pressure led to genetic change for a species' survival. The successful mutations survived and became part of our species' evolution.

Biological evolution is not learned, it is inherited, passed along as a given to enhance survival. Maternity lives in the X chromosome. It is the X in men that guides their own Y chromosome behavior *if* it is invoked.

Primates developed on their own branch of the mammal limb of the tree-like appearance of charted biological evolution. The chimp branch forked several times; one grew larger-brained upright-walking bipeds. We are the most recent twig of the primate branch. Homo sapiens sapiens. The name of our species, given by men of course, is Homo — "man," not both genders but maleness defining what is human, and sapiens — "wise." Double "sapiens" does not mean really wise men. It indicates our subspecies, the modern humans.

Our experimental species survived because of successful long-involved and responsible tending by mothers, the same women who also created culture. Women globally explained life as a Great Mother who is like themselves but never dying and very big. I suggest we rename our species: *Homa* sapiens sapiens for the very wise women.

WOMEN INCLUDE WHILE PATRIARCHY EXCLUDES

Women added male figures to the first big story. Men were neither banished nor excluded from women-created culture nor from sacred woman's story. They were included; that was the point! A sacred partnership between women and men, goddess and her beloved consort, was established. The survival of our species was nearly parthenogenetic — compare the male's few minutes of participation to a decade and half of woman's responsibility. When male as catalyst was understood, maleness was included.

In time, partnership was not enough for a few men who wanted absolute rule and control of everything and everyone and not for altruistic reasons. The tippy-top of patriarchal hierarchy is for the tyrant;

for him and only him. Everyone else in this unnatural arrangement is controlled by fear, threat, aggression, violence, and pain. Atrocities and destruction are committed so a few men can sit at the top of an unstable structure for a short time until they in turn fall to more aggressive men. A tyrant in charge will dominate, squandering life and resources, just to be on top a bit longer.

If a behavior is beneficial for a species, it continues. If a survival danger looms, the species adapts, mutates. Men are the unnatural current "owners" of human culture. X-ness is both beneficial behavior and our viable potential. Y-men went to war against women, nature, and of course each other. Dominators dominate woman and nature; the Christian Bible texts assure men that they have dominion over nature and women. This is an unnatural assumption. Men write and believe what they will but species biology is another matter. Jenny Graves, Australian geneticist, examined the demise of the human Y chromosome. At present, it is smaller than the X; it contains only the secondary sex characteristics and unassigned "junk" DNA. The old Y is in demise. New possible Ys are occurring. Infertility is on the rise as the constant XX is selecting viable new Ys. Y, and not X, is undergoing demise and mutation. Is that a natural species renewal event or did the pressure of life under threat developed by male rule cause the biological pressure and mutation; the ongoing demise of the Ys as we know it?

Caring for life is natural, making death is unnatural. Late in the last millennium B.C.E., dominators promoted the idea that women were not men, therefore women were not human; only man was human, only man had a soul. Once those ideas were muscularly institutionalized, "man" stood for the noun that meant *all* humans — all who *were* human, meaning the men. "Mankind" further implied "all" humans; "all" who are fully human; that narrowed the field to white men. Women, indigenes, people of colors, and selective ethnic others were considered not mankind; those who qualified were men but not necessarily kind. Those who were not fully human had few or no rights. There was doubt that women and both genders of other than Caucasian-believers in (misguided) Christianity have souls. Y-ness arrogantly believed that woman is the root of all men's problems; every misogynist knew he was victimized by women.

Aristotle taught that mothers were not the *real* parents of babies. In the face of the natural and obvious facts, he nevertheless said that men were the only parents and women merely the incubators of mighty man-seed. Men owned the offspring. Women were animals and had to be controlled, punished, and severely dealt with "for their own good." Women were said to be evil and lustful because they were natural and close to earth; they connected with earth-based deities, aka Life. All chthonic deities were made into demons by men. Women's wisdom, intuition, and herbal knowledge are long-held womanly practices. Those qualities and abilities were made *unnatural*, works of the devil, and were to be punished. (See punishment methods below.) Abuse begot abuse and it was administered guilt-free. It was necessary since women and others who are not white males, have no souls and are animals to be dominated and used. Only four centuries ago in our country, Protestant elders (male) met in the New England colonies to vote whether or not women had souls.

Modern humans have the same brainpan size we had when we emerged only seventy to one hundred millennia ago. The larger brainpan size accommodates the large brain size. If brains were any larger, the infant could not be successfully birthed and mother and baby would both die. Because our infants are delivered at an early stage of development, they require a long long time of dependency. We are here thanks to an unbroken chain of caring mothers.

Women's blood show caused both fear and envy in men which was perhaps encouraged by the women to influence the men into cooperation and participation. Over time, rising male alphaism retold the first mythic story, reducing sacrosanct blood to pollution and impurity, and turning women's seclusion in the women's taboo quarters into full-time imprisonment under male domination. Harem means "forbidden," as in: "no men." Devolved male fantasy converted it to a place of women in a man's private haven available for sex on demand. Men's excuse for owning the harem/women's quarters and the institutionalized everyday separation of women away from the world was that women needed protection because women were imagined to have uncontrolled lust. Women also needed protection from other men. Why is it that men, knowing the possible bad behavior of men, do not do something to change male behaviors instead of preventing women free access to opportunity, expression, and movement?

In 2014 an international attempt was made to name rampant rape during war a war crime. African boys and men in some war zones are promised rape as the privilege of conquest. The rape of women and children, the depravity of unmodified out-of-control males acting with impunity, is generally unchanged and unchallenged since humane-ity, Xness, was pushed aside during at least the last 5,000 years. Contemporary women have recently attempted to internationally do something about the the wartime rapists. They asked international cooperation and support that wartime rape be treated as a war crime and not a benefit enacted with impunity. Many countries already have that law but neither investigate nor exact punishment.

Perversion occurs when natural behavior is thwarted. When maleness is unmodified, when it acts with impunity and supports its own terrible inclinations of Y-behavior crowned king, we get what we have: constant conflict, global alphaism, and rule by the tippy-top of hierarchal political, social, religious, and education institutions. Women everywhere are suppressed by Y-domination. Fundamentalist religious beliefs are used to shore up support for control of women and our bodies in every area of the globe. Equality in opportunity is not yet a reality in this country even with women's hard won gains. Women's conditions in third world countries are bleak and horrifying. Women suffer the effects of unmodified maleness acting with impunity. Men, even wise ones, cannot subdue the Y-domination alone. It is up to women to steadily assert the pressure for partnership cultures. Partnership is the way of the distant past and possible future.

Y-alpha men act with impunity. They dominate men as well as women. Change is slow and will come through pressure from women and men in partnership, in solidarity ... again. Y-men will not change voluntarily; the dominator role suits them. Those on top will not change social order.

My mother was born only months after women got the right to vote with the 19th amendment to the constitution in 1920. The rights of all male citizens born here to vote, regardless of race, has been the law since 1869. Many states managed to intimidate, threaten, make rules of land ownership, literacy, and poll tax charges to keep African American men from voting. The white male establishment did nothing to prevent the illegal acts. In 1965, the Voting Rights Act was passed, yet there are still "shame states" who actively make voting difficult for black and Latino voters.

In 1923, Alice Paul proposed the Equal Rights Amendment for equality of rights regardless of gender or race. She led the fight up to 1972 when the senate and house of representatives passed the amendment. Three-fourths of the states, thirty-eight, are required to sign it for ratification. In 1977 the last state to sign, Indiana, brought the count up to thirty-five. In 1972 a guideline of seven years for ratification was imposed. That timeline has been extended. Since it is not part of the amendment it leaves confusion about the validity of those states that had already signed and the five who have rescinded. In 1980 the Republican party removed the ERA from its platform. Anti-feminist and other political groups held sway over the remaining states refusing to ratify the amendment for varied reasons including that it would allow for gay and lesbian rights, same sex marriage, and equal rights for transgendered people in: Alabama, Arkansas, Arizona, Florida, Georgia, Illinois, Louisiana, Mississippi, Missouri, Nevada, North Carolina, Oklahoma, South Carolina, Utah and Virginia. The most important reason for ratification is that if the amendment is in place, tight scrutiny is applied in the legal system protecting rights of everyone regardless of gender identification and race. Without it, protection is sketchy and depends on the whims of each state.

Y-men neither listen to the women nor imagine a need to change. The good thing about men not taking women seriously is that we can get a good deal of work accomplished before they pay attention to our intentions. My generation witnessed racial inequality addressed and brought forth the second wave of feminists.[83] My ex-husband got two thing out of the 70's wave of feminism: women burned their bras (they didn't) and a divorce. Women can bring about change. We just need to get men's boots off our necks — we can do the rest. Imagine Inanna, glaring and standing naked atop her lion-dragon, leading the way!

A crime procedural audiobook (Patricia Cornwell, *Dust*) had a profiler say that horrific murderers are men playing God. Because they can not "create" they do the other act that God does — "destroy". This strikes a chord. Over time, city-kings of the Ancient Near East declared themselves divine. The goddess is Life. She represents the creation of life and cannot be erased. When gods take over creation, it is only through the assistance of birth goddesses. By the last millennium B.C.E., Marduk creates everything but uses the slain body and blood of Tiamat that he, the hairy hero-god, flayed apart (but did not kill). Men/ gods have no wombs so they cannot create life without the feminine. What men and their gods mirroring Y-men's behavior can do alone is destroy.

Patriarchy's version of divine power, their Y-ness, is destruction. The story of Erra, an Akkadian god of parched lands, floods, weather, and war, demonstrates this. Marduk reigns as chief god and is tricked by Erra into leaving his dais to get his statue refurbished. (The deities are present in their statues.) Erra promises to run things properly in Marduk's absence. Left alone, Erra causes wars, devastation, and plagues; cities go to ruin and fields grow nothing. When he is finally convinced that he has done enough rabble-rousing, inciting, violence, and "filling the river with corpses," he simply says that's how he is: "When I am enraged, I devastate people." Erra is not punished. A praise for Erra is sung at the end of the composition (Leick 1991: 57-59). Similarly, Enlil orders the great flood since previous suffering ordered up by Enlil as punishment for the noise of the too-numerous humans is not effective — the people must die. The people petition their goddess to relieve

---

[83] The first wave of feminism in the USA occurred in the mid-nineteenth century and is remembered especially by the Women's Rights convention in 1848 at Seneca Falls, New York. One third of the signers of the document were men. The women's rights movement grew out of women promoting abolition of slavery.

their suffering. The people also petition the goddess to intercede with the punishing gods who tell divine kings to go to war and destroy cities and all who live there. Later alpha-male hegemony in the pantheons became monotheistic Yahweh, self-proclaimed jealous and wrathful god, who orders smiting and destruction as well as punishment for human misbehavior no matter how slight.

Rhythmic rise and fall is natural. A rise and fall vegetation god is lamented by woman and goddess alike; together they share grief over lost children; they weep together, the demigod is restored, and fertility manifests. Gaining rulership and eventual divinity by consorting with the goddess is part of the annual ceremony— until both goddess and woman are deleted from a partnership role. Partnership culture, both personal and social, was authored by women long ago. It is natural, practical, and functional. Y-ness requires modification by X-ness so that life is honored and our earth is tended with good stewardship. Everyone benefits. Domination culture benefits only the few. Male domination is unnatural. It is rule by the Y chromosome, which is only designed for fertilization. It is self-serving and death-making. Thankfully the Y is in demise. But the question is: can our beautiful planet survive until the new versions of Y, biologically modified by nature to keep our species alive, sorts itself? Jenny Graves, in her lecture — "The Demise of the Ys from a Feminist Perspective" — says it's up to women to select from the new versions nature is trying out and we must select wisely.

Under male domination, people suffer, Earth is devastated, water is polluted, and species die-off occurs in overwhelming numbers. Even when evidence is in-the-face apparent, it is ignored. Plunder of resources continues. President Obama's State of the Union address, January 2015, was dissected on NPR by a republican senator who not only didn't want federal guidelines for minimum wage, "as the states know what their people need," but added that the only way people can be better employed is to reduce the protection of land, nature, and worker guidelines regulating business because it costs too much money to come into federal compliance and that is bad for business! That shortsightedness is rampant. Here there is no big-picture viewing,

436

just the narrow laser glance to make certain the *lu-gals,* big-men, have a full wallet.

We have the creative potential of our large brains and X's intuitive genius to solve problems without war, killing, and taking. Ask the women! Men hiding behind religion force women to bear countless children. Women are *not allowed* to own their bodies, their reproductive rights. Women are *not allowed* to say NO! to unwanted sex and pregnancies. Women are forced into unending, unwanted, unplanned, unwise, unsafe pregnancies. Why, when overpopulation is so obvious a problem, are the male-based religions insisting on more babies popping out at an alarming rate by closing off access to birth control or termination? Here is a novel idea — what about self-control of men's own sexual urges, demands, and expectation of fulfillment of those impulses? Y is responsive to its own desires and does not take responsibility for our species and our world.

A PARTIAL LIST OF INDICTMENTS
AGAINST PATRIARCHY

Under Y-male rule's horrific domination behavior, their dogma and actions are easily found in records, texts, laws and sacred literature. Evidence for indictment of patriarchy for actions against humanity is well recorded. Because the culture of my experience is nominally "Christian," and this chapter is meant to be brief, I will list a few indictments against the fathers of Christian churches in Western culture.

I believe that the early beginning of what came to be called Christianity was humane and egalitarian. The philosophy of the prophet Jesus touched hearts and gave hope. Women were included as equals (See chapter 14). Christianity was usurped by maleness within 200 years of its beginning. The new religion was embraced by Y-men who interpreted and wrote religious tracts far from the original philosophy and teachings. Some men hid behind the religion to commit atrocities. Forced conversions grew into the Inquisition, witch hunts, trials, and burnings for financial gain and satisfaction of sadism. Women were most frequently the victims. Holocausts, colonization, and misused political power were supported by male-based religions. The Christian religion, under male control, reverted to reducing the female half of the species to near-animal status who lacked souls and needed domination by men. Fathers owned the family. Women were erased, silenced, controlled, and blamed. Suppression, repression, oppression of women, minorities and colonized people were a given. Y-male control of everything and hiding behind the major male-based religions, has set the potential evolution of our species back 2,000 years.

Remember, during Inanna's reign, religions did not compete. Throughout the Ancient Near East and its rising patriarchy, the conflict issues were not liturgical. Religious intolerance was not the reason to have a war. People freely worshipped their pantheons of choice. With the rise of the Hebrew single-god, religious rightness and wrongness was born. Once Yahweh was declared supreme, the one and only from a widening epicenter, religious competition was declared. Sacred groves and wooden pillars, representing the goddess for millennia, were burned. Guilt was instilled in the people — if one person did a wrong thing against Yahweh the community could expect a smiting. Jesus, a Jewish prophet (not a dynastic priest), taught his message of love, kindness, simplicity, and inclusion — all humane qualities. His following was hungry for all he taught after centuries of monotheism of a wrathful god and dynastic priests. Women supported the prophet Jesus financially, listened to his words and became teachers. Mary Magdalen was both partner and teacher. She was the bride to his bridegroom of the Song of Songs; like Inanna and Dumuzi. (More on Mary Magdalen in chapter 14.) After seven decades, the orally transmitted new philosophy was written down from memories several times removed. Some of the writing put the teachings off track. The revisions concretized into institutions. Within two hundred years, Y-men following the new religion had removed women from the ranks of teachers and high position. Church fathers picked through available religious tracts, edited or deleted some, and authored all manner of male-slanted texts. Forced conversions gave worshippers of competing ideas and divinities a choice to convert or die. Some chose to die.

Religion became useful for controlling the masses. Religion in the hands of only men was ripe for manipulation, propaganda, power and wealth accumulation. Within a few centuries, the stage was set and readied for horrific sadism. What was done in the name of faith made the male-owned Church one of the greatest mass murderers in history. Gone was the easy access between worshipper and that one's divine metaphor of choice. Gone was the feminine influence both sacred and human. Gone was humane-ity. Yes, beautiful passages of the beginning teachings were remembered and recorded, but too much was interpreted to keep men on top. Woman was diminished and sacred woman abolished.

People turn toward wisdom and comforting. Long ago, when stars were many and people few, women everywhere settled on a metaphor for the life force they experienced. They named life "mother." She mirrored women. Women created first culture and first awareness of a big story, a myth that expressed life. Great Mother was humane, cyclic, and explained life, death, and return. She did not tell her worshippers to go and smite and murder and burn people at the stake. She did not hate men as churchmen hate women.

Part one, Life, of this biography portrays the slow demise of goddess and erasure of women's voice. This chapter of part two, Death, has death no longer cyclic, but literally the death of people burned as holocaust (holocaust is burned offering to a deity). The European Inquisitions lasted six centuries. Cruel and sadistic men used religious dogma to gain power and wealth. Their concocted dogma was merely another tool for inflicting pain and control over the many by the few top alpha Y-men. Y-men abused religion and people. With no wisdom, guidance, and voice of women, men devolved religion into a weapon of mass destruction and self-aggrandizement as the following informational details exemplify.

SELECTIVE INDICTMENTS

In 298 C.E., Roman emperor, Diocletian, in a time of many faiths tolerably practiced, requested that Christians present at a sacrifice add a pinch of incense as was required by all in attendance to receive good omens. Their refusal resulted in an increase of "pagan" priest and Christian conflicts. Five years later, the "pagan" priests called for the closing of Christian churches. Three Christian eunuchs in the palace set several fires and were executed. Martyrs came into fashion. Gnostics criticized the martyrdom. Christians came to oppress other Christians. The church fathers even made children suffer to save their souls. They sacrificed the children to their version of a deity. Centuries later the same accusation was used by Christians against Jews as an excuse to persecute them. "In the matter of intolerance Christianity differed from all pagan religions, and surpassed Judaism; in that it stood in direct opposition to the spirit of the age (diverse faith tolerance) (Walker 1983: 600 citing S. Angus, *The Mystery-Religions.* 1975: 277)."

Would-be martyrs counted on emperor Julian to give them persecution and martyrdom. Though he disliked the fanatic Christians, Julian did not persecute. Gregory of Nazianzus, unable to get the emperor to attack Christians, complained: "He begrudged to our soldiers the honor of martyrdom." The tolerant Julian was mysteriously killed; a Christian was suspected. The report of Marcus Aurelius killing forty-eight Christians in 177 C.E. is unverified; it is reported by one Eusebius who used "holy lying" — lying was permissible if it "glorifies the Christian faith (Walker ibid.: 601)." Martyrdom faded for several centuries and when it was revived, fellow Christians did the deed. Christians warred against Christians and "infidels" alike. Zealotry massacred thousands of "heretics" in Asia Minor. Children and women were tortured until they "accepted the Host of the true faith." Christians were also tortured for being tolerant of "pagans" in their communities.

After the Church gained enough power it became a "reign of terror" against "pagans" and other Christians contrary to the Church's orthodoxy. Christian zealots tortured women to make them leave their goddess. A description of persecution in Asia Minor written in 386 C.E. reads (ibid.: 602 citing J.H. Smith, *The Death of Classical Paganism*.166:)

> The monks say they are making war on the temples but their warfare is a way of pillaging what little poor unfortunates do have, the produce of the fields and the cattle they feed ... They grab people's land, claiming the place is sacred ... They who (as they say) give honor to their god by fasting are getting fat on the wretchedness of others.
>
> And as for those others, the victims of such a sack, if they go to town, to a 'shepherd' — he will be called that, though he may not be a good shepherd precisely — and tell him, weeping, of their injustices suffered the shepherd will approve of the pillagers, and chase their victims away, saying that they should count it a gain that they have not suffered worse.
>
> If they hear of a place with something worth raping away, they immediately claim that someone is making sacrifices and committing abominations, and pay the place a visit.

Innocent I, fifth century, said "God gave the church the right to kill." The use of the sword was sanctified against those who would not "bow the neck" to "God's bishops, priests, and deacons (as that person) is guilty of insubordination against God and must suffer the death penalty (ibid.: 601 citing Pagels 1979: 34)."

Pope Innocent III wrote: "Anyone who attempts to construe a personal view of God which conflicts with Church dogma must be burned without pity." He established the Medieval Inquisition 1198-1216.

In 1229, the Church institutionalized the Inquisition. Canons were written that anyone harboring a heretic could lose all property and work for even slight suspicion. The Inquisition filled the coffers of the Church and the purses of the inquisitors.

Pope Innocent IV in 1252 sanctioned sadistically-inspired torture chambers. The devices were inscribed with: "Glory be only to God."

The priests were considered near god-like and curses from priests were feared. Every faith not Christian was demonic. The Reformation protestants were also victims. Children as young as two were made to confess. They could also be tortured and prosecuted. The black-robed and cowled inquisitors were adept at making innocent people confess. The torture was so painful, gruesome, and humiliating that victims confessed to anything to stop the pain, naming anyone, including family and friends, as heretics. Children of murdered victims were set loose in the streets to beg. No one dared help them as they might come under the notice of the inquisitors.

Pope Gregory IX told German Conrad Marburg to "not to punish the wicked but as to hurt the innocents with fear." Marburg said: "I would gladly burn a hundred innocents if there was one guilty among them."

Spain was the only western European country with a multi-religious and racial make up — Jews and Moors lived alongside Christians as an educated elite. The Jewish financiers and intellectuals were protected by the crown. By the late 1300s, restrictions rose against Jews. The black plague came and Jews were blamed for bringing the sickness to kill off Christians. Pogroms began. Large numbers of Jews and Moors converted out of fear, though many continued to practice their religions secretly.

The Spanish crown appealed to Pope Sixtus IV for Inquisition rights to go after the suspicious converts, the *conversos*. Two papal bulls[84] granted the request though the pope later regretted the decision that gave up his control in the Tribunal of the Holy Office of the Inquisition in Spain. Once the crown took charge, the red-robed priest/father inquisitors received compensation from the confiscated goods; the lion's share went to the crown and a small portion to the accuser. Those with wealth were targeted. One head inquisitor specialized in accusing wealthy women. Over time, he had placed fifty women in solitary confinement so he could rape them and of course confiscate their

---

[84] 'Papal bull' comes from Latin *bulla*, a round seal. A document with a papal seal is a papal bull.

wealth. The Spanish inquisition prosecuted converted Jews and Moors (Islam) with the excuse of unifying Spain and ridding it of insincere converts. The Catholic Spanish government got wealthy. Queen Isabella was convinced to expel 160,000 Jews; many were Spain's financiers and so her country's finances were hurt. The accused and banished educated elite left Spain with a deficit of intellectuals. Jews, Moors, protestants, homosexuals, criminals, and inconvenient others were victims. Fear was rampant. The crown got wealthy.

The Spanish victims were paraded to the stake for burning; this was called *autos-da-fe*, an act of faith. The events were as well attended as a bull fight. One *autos-da-fe* marched fourteen protestants to their stakes and publicly burned them alive. Many more were accused than were burned. While some records are available, as with all inquisition and witch hunt times, a great number of records have been destroyed by the tides of time and wars washing over the continent. Estimates range between 3-5,000 executed by the Spanish Inquisition between 1540-1700 C.E.. Those who were accused number 13,100 on surviving records but countless more were never recorded or named in lost documents. The Spanish Inquisition was officially closed in 1834.

The Roman Inquisition of 1542 was established as a Holy Office. Its intention was to go after protestants. Its name was changed in 1903 to Supreme Sacred Congregation of the Holy Office, and in 1965 to Congregation for the Doctrine of the Faith. Overseeing the behavior of priests is one of its official duties. It seems to have lost effectiveness. It was responsible for protecting pedophile priests by moving them from parish to parish to cover up their molestations. The priestly crimes were not reported to the police.

The Inquisitions spanned six centuries. Estimates of deaths from execution vary widely from a few thousand (claims of Catholic Church) to numbers in the millions. Victor Hugo estimated the number to be five million. The truth is somewhere between. The tally for people executed does not count deaths during terrible tortures, filthy imprisonments, suicides, and the dependents who died of neglect and hunger with no means of support after the property and wealth of their parents were confiscated and people were afraid to intervene. The tools used by the inquisitors of the Catholic Church[85] to get "confessions" are disgusting, sadistic, and demonic. Burning, torture, beating, suffocation, sexual perversions, and inflicting prolonged intense pain by the fathers of the Church and select others portray the devolution into sadistic perversion.

The following list of Inquisition torture tools is included as evidence of what Y-men are capable of when left to their own counsel and not held responsible for stewardship as shepherds of the people. This version of sadistic religion is the extreme opposite of sacred feminine religion. It is a disturbing array of horrors. Drawings and etchings of the time leave no details to the imagination. The victim is almost always shown naked.

The rack is best known but other diverse perverse instruments were also in use. A victim was tied to the rack and stretched until all major joints were dislocated or else the accused was tied to a table so a pendulum with a sharp edge on its underbelly swung while slowly lowering to cut the abdomen deeper and deeper. The stocks that held a prisoner at the shoulders and ankles were also favored; the victim's feet were covered with lard and a brazier was placed near the feet to blister and burn the the skin. This was used especially for women and children.

Another practice was water torture. A funnel was placed in the mouth and throat and water was poured in until the stomach burst. A special torture for women resembles the speculum used for gynecological examination gone mad. It has sharp points on rounded ends. Its shape gave it its name: the pear. It separated wider and wider apart until the woman's mouth or vagina was torn apart.

Two wheel tortures were also popular. The first was spiked and rotated with the victim tied to it so the victim was pierced by the spikes. The second version rolled over the victim. Blocks of wood were placed under the joints of the tied-down accused and a wheel with a steel rim rolled over the body crushing the joints. A German chronicler witnessed the second wheel torture: "the victim was transformed into a huge screaming puppet writhing in their own blood. It (the person) looked like a sea monster with four tentacles and raw slimy shapeless

---

[85] Franciscan and Dominical priests dominated the field of inquisition specialists.

flesh, mixed with splinters of bone (bibliocapleysdes.net/vatican/'esp-vatican29.htm#the%20church).”

The breast ripper was a clawed tong to rip off breasts for heresy, blasphemy, adultery, and witchcraft. It was also used when the torturing inquisitors experienced arousal while plying their horrors. Their arousal was blamed on the woman victim and proved that she was evil so a breast might be ripped off for punishment.

Hanging cages were suspended outside town halls, aristocrat's palaces, halls of justice, and cathedrals. Nude victims were put into the cages, hoisted above street level, and left to die exposed to the elements with neither food nor drink. Slow death by strangulation, garroting, was improved by adding a spike that separated cervical vertebrae as it tightened. The head crusher did just that. The accused's chin was placed on the lower shelf of the torture device; a metal cap sat on the head. The two sections were ratcheted together like a book press. The victim's teeth were crushed into the jaw bone, eye sockets broken, and brain crushed within the fractured skull. The iron maiden was a two-sided hinged device with spikes placed on both sides of the interior. The standing victim was penetrated as it closed. Death in the embrace of the iron maiden was slow.

The Judas cradle was a hoist holding the nude victim over a pointed pyramid. The legs were either weighted to the side or the ankles tied and suspended forward by ropes. The accused was then lowered over the point that entered the anus of men or the vaginas of women. The source article comments: “with their muscles contracted, they were usually unable to relax and fall asleep (ibid.).” Imagine that!

“The tortures took high advantage of positions of authority to indulge in the most pornographic sessions of sexual control over heretics (ibid. citing Anne Barstowe).” Wealth gained through confiscation of the accused's property was perhaps the greatest impetus for the Inquisition. Greed was followed by mislead religious zealotry and satisfaction of warped sex and pornographic sadism. The earlier heretics were wealthy. Inquisitor Eymeric bemoaned: “In our day there are no more rich heretics … it is a pity that so salutary an institution as ours should be so uncertain of its future (ibid.).”

And then religious misogyny invented witch hunts. From the 15th through the 18th centuries, for 300 years, Christian zealots hunted primarily women. The witch hunts began first in Europe and spread around the globe everywhere Christians converted and colonized. The Catholic Church first invented the concept of devil worship and then used it as an excuse to rid itself of more victims. R.H Robbins describes the witch hunts as: "the shocking nightmare, the foulest crime and deepest shame of western civilization (ibid.)."

A physician who attended women in "witch prison" described the accused and persecuted women as "driven half mad" in the dark squalor of the dungeons. The women were taken for tortures until most agreed to anything to make the torture and horrific conditions stop (ibid.). Please know that if a woman survived the tortures she lived only long enough to be brought to the stake and publicly burned alive. In case the carted victim screamed out her innocence and what was done to her to the waiting crowds, her tongue might be cut out or a wooden gag placed in her mouth. In Toulouse, the inquisitor Foulques de Saint-George made a 'visit' to women held in solitary-confinement so often — rape of the accused victims with impunity was a privilege of officials — that suspicion arose that he trumped-up charges for his sexual gratification. The citizens took the dangerous step to collect evidence against him.

Sexual abuse by the Catholic Inquisition was accepted practice. The physical world was dominated by men and what happened in the physical world stayed in the physical world. Women were Eves — all of them. When the torturers were sexually aroused, the victims were blamed. When the torturers' penises hardened during their sadistic work, it could not be their own sadistic excitement. No. The women did it to them and so punishment, sexual perversion, and torture ramped up. Pinchers, pliers, breast rippers, and heated iron prods were used to attack the women's offending breasts and genitals. All the above tortures are found in drawings and etchings of the time and illustrate the victims, generally nude, in all manner of torture machines and procedures. Drawings and etchings of the time showed hooded and robed creatures doing the deed while other men, not in robes, watched.

Old women, wise women, healer and plant medicine women were suspect and accused. Reginald Scott penned in 1584: "It is indifferent to say in the English tongue: 'She is a witch' or 'She is a wise woman.'" Prior to the reformation, ordinary people used the village healer women and men and not the priests or Church licensed "physicians." The "physicians" put the healing into God's hands. One of the Church "physicians'" treatment was to pack an infected wound with manure. If God deemed one worthy of saving, that one would get better. One accused woman was seen bathing children during a plague in London and was killed as a witch since no one bathed; bathing was considered unnatural. Every village had their healers and herbalists with effective remedies. Some may have chanted healing words while working. Wise women and healers were targeted by the Church because they were effective, respected and gave women too much power. When males took over healing, the west lost its valuable plant medicine traditions and countless people died of the Church-endorsed physicians' ineptitudes.

Misogynistic male-based religion has no end of rationale for bad behavior toward woman. Every misogynist believes he is a victim of women. In the second century C.E., Clement of Alexandria wrote: "Every woman should be filled with shame that she is a woman." Boethius, a sixth-century Christian philosopher, wrote: "Woman is a temple built on a sewer." In the sixth century, bishops voted at the Council of Macon to decide if woman have souls. Tenth century Odo of Cluny stated: "To embrace a woman is to embrace a sack of manure." Thomas Aquinas (thirteenth century) decided that God made a mistake when he created women. "Nothing (deficient) or defective should have been produced in the first establishment of things; so woman ought not to have been produced then." (He does not consider how he might then have ever existed.) Lutherans at Wittenberg had a debate on whether or not women were actually human at all (ibid.)!

Orthodox Christians hold all women since Eve responsible for sin. The biblical apocrypha states: "of woman came the beginning of sin and thanks to her, we all must die." Two pope-pleasing monks authored the *Malleus Maleficarum*, a handbook for identifying witches, which includes deeply misogynistic excuses for the torture and burning of mostly women. Church fathers reasoned with that old ruse of Adam birthing Eve via God from first-man's rib, and concluded that women are therefore "imperfect animals" and "crooked," "while men belong to a privileged sex from whose midst Christ emerged." (If Adam lost a rib in the deal, wouldn't he be the imperfect one?) The two woman-hating monks also claimed that women are more concerned with sex than are men. King James I claimed a woman is twenty times more likely to be a witch than a man. Eighty to ninety per cent of those prosecuted were women. The king wrote in his *Daemonologie*: "Loathe they are to confess without torture." Imagine that!

The following details are included to bring the witch hunt craze into focus. Those who write and re-write history add heroic sheen to their interest group and remove what is unfavorable to their religion, gender, or politics. The recorded facts must be kept and remembered. Men invented war, the Inquisition, elaborate sadistic tortures, and burning people alive in the name of their religion's version of a single male deity. They first created the idea of "devil worship" so to use it as excuse to eliminate witches (women), they created and perfected witch hunts, they protected their sadism and woman-hating by writing church cannons for legal misogyny, murder, and confiscation of property. Priests, bishops, and inquisitors acted with impunity. By 1520, France had witch burnings in nearly every community. At Leith, Scotland, nine women were burned together (1664). Bishops lead the hunts. In Neisse in Silesia an executioner invented an oven for roasting people. In nine years he roasted 1000 victims including children between the ages of two to four.

In England, 70,000 were killed as witches after 1573 and 40,000 between 1600-1680. 3000-4000 died during Cromwell's tenure. In Scotland, over 17,000 died between 1563 and 1603. Scotland's final witch execution was in 1727.

France saw 900 executed by Nicholas Remy in fifteen years. 80 were burned alive in one fire in 1574 at Valery-en-Savoie. Over 200 were executed in Labourt, 1619. In Lorraine, 900 were killed. The last witch execution in France was in1745.

Germany recorded 133 burned in one day at Quedlinburg in 1589. Between 1626-1629, 168 burned in Miltenberg. 274 died at Bamberg between 1627-1631, while another source recorded approximately 22,000 in the same locale between 1610 and 1680. The last German witch execution was in 1775.

Witch hunts and executions are recorded in Europe, North America, Australia, South America, Iceland, and anywhere the Church reached. In our New England, protestant sects actively persecuted victims with 29 of the accused hung. The last witch execution in this country was in 1692.

In addition to Inquisition and witch hunts, religious wars broke out. The thirty-year war of 1618-1648 began when Holy Roman Emperor, Ferdinand II, king of Bohemia, set out to establish his lands as fully Catholic. Protestant nobles of Bohemia and Austria fought back but lost after five years of war. For the next twenty-five years, political opportunists used religion as the basis for territorial expansions. Three religious sects vied for dominance: Roman Catholicism, Lutheranism, and Calvinism. The armies were considered mercenaries and the crowns did not pay the soldiers so they plundered and ravaged the countryside and towns they passed through. Europe's population was decimated to half.

Another indictment exposes a recently revealed but hardly new problem — enough victims have come forward to confirm allegations of thousands of pedophile priests. UK's Daily Mirror writes: "Damning reports by the UN this year have accused the Vatican of 'systematically' adopting policies that allowed priests to rape and molest thousands of children over decades and failing to report allegations to the authorities they transferred offenders to new dioceses where they could abuse again." The article quotes Pope Francis: "One in fifty priests is a paedophile. 2% carried out child abuse ... many more in the Church are guilty of covering it up." Since the 1980s, abuse by priests in the US and Canada surfaced. Ireland and twelve other countries in the 1990s reported priest-abuse. Ireland has revealed thousands of victims. The

Catholic hierarchy is charged with long-term abuse, cover-up and not reporting sex abuse to authorities.[86]

Religion as an excuse for violence continues. NPR reported that 5000 deaths occurred in jehad attacks in the month of November, 2014. Religion is used as the reason behind hatred and killing. Islam is the excuse to kidnap hundreds of African schoolgirls, murder health workers, kill school children, deny rights to women, enslave, and kill innocent people. Male-based religions allow horrific acts against humanity with righteous impunity. Lord John Acton wrote to a bishop in 1887: "Power tends to corrupt, and absolute power corrupts absolutely." English prime minister, William Pitt the Elder, wrote in 1770: "Unlimited power is apt to corrupt the minds of those who possess it." Abigail Adams wrote: "all men would be tyrants if they could."

This book's story is focused on what happened to the sacred feminine, Inanna, Queen of Heaven, Queen of Earth, and to women. When the sacredness of life, anthropomorphized as goddess, is lost, Xness is defeated and Y-males demonstrate they are not fit to decide the world view. I did not include secular political war's enormous death counts, maimed lives, deaths of non-combatants, destruction of land, cities, art, and waste of resources. Further dominator abuse of power is in the last chapter with women's efforts to right the wrongs.

Imagine: if men had not forced the sacred feminine into near extinction; if men continued to listen to women's wisdom and guidance in creative problem-solving instead of solving every perceived threat with intimidation and war; if teachings of love and cooperation had not been abused and twisted into trumped-up reasons to kill, torture, and dominate in the name of a re-made male-only-based deity; if intellectuals and healers had not been singled out for extermination; if women's reproductive rights had not been stolen; if women had not been diminished into chattel at best and burned alive or hung as witches at worst; if children who were persecuted and tortured or left alone to

---

[86] December 12, 2014 www.dailymail.co.uk/news/article-2690575/Pope-Francis-admits-two-cent-Roman-Catholic-priests-paedophiled-interview-Italian-newspaper.html

beg in unsympathetic cities had lived; if all the hate, murder, torture, and abuse in the name of men's God had not occurred, what might our world be like now?

When men invented war, gained absolute rule, and ownership of women, they did so by eradicating the sacred feminine. Without divine protection, women have no voice and no higher authority to confer their wisdom and warnings. Men began to kill, rape, and destroy the cultures of others. Overwhelming male domination causes die-off of creativity, safety, well being, and life. As one dominator culture declines and tumbles, new dominators replace the old order. Joseph Campbell writes the hero's journey as circular tale. After facing adversity and receiving help and enlightenment, the actualized hero returns home, gets rid of the old king and the old way, and reigns long enough to become the mirror image of the old king. The hero is then confronted and loses his kingdom to a new returning hero. What will it take for the next new order to be birthed with woman's voice, wisdom, and self-ownership? What will culture with woman's inclusiveness and biophilic devotion to life look like? It can happen. An awareness of woman, both human and divine, is rising. I imagine a bit of Inanna in every woman.

There *is* change afoot! Women and sacredness of life are rising; dreams, symbols, and expressions of the first principle, the feminine, are stirring. Awake women, balanced men, and divine feminine consciousness are returning. We are remembering. We are voicing our wisdom and taking action. We are saying NO! We are practicing creative problem-solving, conflict resolution, and peace and reconciliation. We remember — we are all connected. It is up to a partnership culture to find a new direction for living on earth.

The master's tools will never dismantle the master's house.
Audre Lorde

Part III

RETURN

Return to the roots of culture, of story, of religion, and there you will find the women. As strong and obvious facts return, so too do women. When awareness of a sacred woman, Life, and the ever present goddess, is "allowed," women's worth and history return. When a woman sees her image and wisdom mirrored onto life so big, she is the Great Mother, she returns to her self who would have been before patriarchy. Remember the cycle: Life-Death-Return.

CHAPTER 14

Woman Sacred and Human(E) in Ascendancy ... Again

Loved by kings and heroes, glorified by poets and bards, adored by man and beast, Inanna is the very epitome of the liberated woman, the ideal divine patroness for the current "women's lib(eration)" movement. Bright, brave, ambitious, aggressive, vindictive, but lovable and desirable nonetheless, she allowed no one, neither man nor god, to stand in her way, say her nay.

Samuel Noah Kramer, *From the Poetry of Sumer*

INANNA RETURNS

Storyteller and folklorist Diane Wolkstein read professor Samuel Noah Kramer's Sumerian translations and loved Inanna as did he. She asked that he do a book on Inanna. He agreed a book was a good idea and that they do it together. The collaboration of storyteller and Sumerologist resulted in *Inanna; Queen of Heaven Queen of Earth* and Inanna's story returned to popular culture.

Over time Inanna/Ishtar was demoted to love and war goddess; she no longer bestowed kingship. She was declawed and defanged; she is remembered in recent times, if at all, as Ishtar or as her exported Mediterranean goddess of sentimental love, Aphrodite. Mother Goddess made a strong return by popular demand during the European Dark Ages in the guise of Virgin Mary, mother of Jesus. She represents motherly love for everyone. Virgin originally meant "not owned by a man" — not "married." Originally, virgin has nothing to do with sex, only non-ownership. Mary was not married to Joseph prior to Jesus' birth.

Inanna's name ascended back above the horizon only one hundred years ago with the decoding of the Sumerian cuneiform script. Her equivalent, Ishtar, had continued with some name recognition but as a faded, defunct goddess of questionable qualities. Aphrodite is a polite love goddess and Venus lingers vaguely as love, the planet, and a pretty sculpture without arms. Inanna is said to be a prototype for Aphrodite, Venus, and even Isis. She is present as life, she is life as metaphor, she is life anthropomorphized. We moderns did not know her early Sumerian name, we heard only whispers of her as Ishtar, Aphrodite, and Venus. I knew her as Starlight Starbright. My mother pointed out evening star and taught me to wish on her. Since early childhood, I search the twilight sky and send her wish-prayers. In times of despair, she is my default for petitioning help. I knew her before I knew her name and story.

Two thousand years ago an influential Roman jurist, Ulpian, a human rights pioneer, said that justice is female and depends on "the feminine nature principle, which has a profounder kinship with the *natura iustum* (that which is just by nature) than does the male sex, with its greater susceptibility to the principle of domination." Pythagoreans taught that *iusticia* and *aequitas* (justice and equity) are "innate attributes of the feminine nature principle (Walker: 1983. 485-6. citing Bachofen, *Myth, Religion and Mother Right*. 1967: 189)." The Roman jurist recognized the positive feminine principle and difficulty with the male principle of domination, yet domination grew and grew.

Patriarchy was strong two millennia ago; the acknowledgement above of Ulpian and the Pythagoreans was encouraging, but conditions worsened. In the first four centuries of the Common Era, patriarchal opportunism unified behind a religious idea that was soon forced on the many. Male solidarity was engineered to keep the elite on top, women out, and power concentrated in a carefully selected canon. This was not at all the intention of the prophet who spoke of kindness and compassion, who spoke with men and women equally, who taught about human potential and forgiveness. Who spoke of his divine father as a loving god who was not the threatening, wrathful, follow-me-or-else god of other itinerant lay prophets of his time.

LOST OPPORTUNITY

A teacher appeared whose religious philosophy would later be called Christianity. His was a small voice among the many. He said he spoke the words of his god. The prophet Jesus was only one of the itinerant teachers wondering about the Near East, Persia, and the Roman Empire who also spoke words given them by one of the pantheonic gods. Ordinary men claimed intimate communication with one god or another. The idea of a "'true religion' was unknown to the ancients. The newly acclaimed 'true religion' began to be called Christian after 'Christ came in the flesh' (Walker 1983: 467).[87]"

I am including here a brief overview of highlights (or lowlights) of the continued usurpation of the sacred and human woman to lay a foundation for a model of return and to encourage ascendancy of that ideation in our present time.

Bourgeault describes the teachings in the Nag Hammadi gospels of Thomas and Philip, found in 1945 in an Egyptian desert, and the Mary

---

[87] Walker cites Doane, T. W.. *Bible Myths and their Parallels in Other Religions.* pp.409-11

Magdalene gospel found in a Cairo market in 1896[88] and sold as a text from an Eastern mystic tradition. The word "gnostic" is associated with the three gospels but was never a religion — Gnosticism. The East's cosmovision, *gnosis* — knowing, is defined by Rami Spairo as: "not only an altered state of mind (moving from narrow to spacious), but an altered trait of behavior, moving from selfishness, fear, and narcissism to justice, compassion, and humility." [89] That definition is far different from the Greek and Western version of *gnosis* via Plato that had to do with the freeing of the immortal soul from matter. Obviously the early church fathers went with Plato. Matter is bad, spirit is good. The three gospels that were outlawed and hidden away "belong to the wider tradition of universal wisdom, or *sophia perennes*, with its notion of conscious integral transformation where 'right practice' is wisdom while Christian-Greek-West promotes 'the right belief' needed for 'salvation' (Bourgeault 2010: 40)." The "right practice" does not mean deny the body, nor is it gained through initiation. The three lost gospels in their few pages hold the early story and not the master story contrived by sons of patriarchy.

I believe the beginning teachings were beautiful. The teacher was accessible, women and men came to learn, to be disciples together. A new version of the old story of partnership, that woman had began long ago, humane-ity was brought forth. The story revealed a big picture of human potential. The disciples, according to the newly found gospels, were men and women as equals. This was the old and long forgotten idea and must have surprised the well engrained attitudes of the patriarchal Near East and Roman Empire of the day. In less than two centuries after Jesus's immediate inner circle were gone, discord and revision were rampant. The first teachers had gone off in all directions with their sister-wives with varying degrees of understanding of the teachings. Many forms of Christian sects abounded.

---

[88] The Mary Magdalene Gospel was found in 1896, unpublished until 1955, translated from German two decades later and did not reach general readership for an additional two decades.

[89] Bourgeault 2010: 39 citing Rami Sapiro. *The Divine Feminine in Biblical Wisdom Literature.* 2005: xvii

I write this book as a woman from a western culture. This chapter will weave the lost, maligned, and suppressed story of the familiar Western religion with Inanna's story and the return of women, human and divine. It is the book's intention to re-story Inanna from her dusty burial. Cynthia Bourgeault, Episcopalian priest, states that her goal in writing her book, *The Meaning of Mary Magdalene; Discovering the Woman at the Heart of Christianity*, is "to repair the damage caused by a heavy handedly patriarchal (and at times flat-out misogynist) ecclesiastical tradition and reclaim Mary Magdalene's legitimate role as a teacher and apostle (ibid.: x)." Virgin Mother Mary fared far better than did Mary Magdalene.

GODDESS RETURNS AS VIRGIN MARY

Try as the men did who took over original Christianity, the idea of a mother goddess who heard, loved, and cared for her people remained in people's hearts. Following the fall of Rome, literacy was no longer taught in the former Roman Empire. The priests who were literate did not teach the populous reading and writing. They controlled the interpretation of written doctrine and kept the lucrative service of letter and contract writing in their hands. The aristocracy was also generally illiterate.

During the Dark Ages (no writing), Europe's people returned to a mother goddess. The available safe equivalent to a mother goddess is the mother of Jesus, Mary or Mariam, of Ephesus. We learn very little of her in the Christian biblical texts. We are told she was not married to Joseph so the church fathers could avoid questions of fatherhood. However, inadvertently, this detail also equates Mary with the young goddess of the east who also has a consort and not a "husband." The deified son story, Jesus, is based on the Ancient Near East's vegetation demigod Dumuzid or Tammuz. He dies and is resurrected on the spring equinox. Easter, from Ester, from Ishtar, is a moon-based celebration. *Christos* means "healing-moon-man," son of the *alma* ("moon-maiden") (Walker 1983: 464). Inanna is moon-based as is mother goddess. Virgin

Mary is often painted with a new crescent moon. Easter is not fixed annually as is Christmas fixed on the 25th day of December, replacing the winter solstice as Jesus' birth date.

Virgin originally meant a woman not married, i.e., not *owned* by a man. "Virgin" did not mean "chaste." Strong goddesses were not married. Inanna was bride but never made into an obedient wife by power-pirating patriarchy. Ishtar, Aphrodite, Venus, and Artemis were not captured by men's gods. Hera was "married" off to Zeus but theirs was an uncomfortable union.

Great cathedrals and little churches are named for the Virgin: "Our Lady of" many holy glories and places, extol her attributes — the same compassionate and intercessional qualities of Sumerian Inanna but without her naked sexy feistiness. People remember in their core that mother, Goddess Mother, is with them in times of trouble. Maid Mary, Virgin Mary is sanitized Inanna/Ishtar/Great Mother. Virgin Mary represents maternal compassion, suffers as her people do, and loves every one of them regardless of gender or circumstance — just as Inanna loves her people and they love her. Virgin Mary is tame and called pure, meek, and mild. Inanna is purely Inanna and is neither meek nor mild. Mother Mary gave birth to a vegetation god, who was born, died and resurrected as all vegetation gods die and are born again at the winter solstice. Madonna (beautiful mother) paintings of later Christianity often include Inanna's emblems of crescent moon, evening star, rosettes, and sea.

Strange male-born twisted tales were added to accommodate theologians' unnatural rationale. Their God's divine baby is accomplished through divine intervention; there is no sex involved because, within two centuries of the Jesus teachings, sex is deemed sinful while celibacy is holy. Sex as sin is a major contribution of the Christian patriarchs. Mary had to be immaculate and born also of an immaculate birth (no penis involvement) before bringing forth her own child's immaculate birth. Ascetics in Christianity are creative in their avoidance of admitting to a penis on their God. Bizarre images emerged including: semen leaving God's mouth through a tube that ducked under Mary's skirt, a dove carrying God's semen to her in its beak, and Gabriel holding God's semen in his mouth "to be filtered through the sacred lily (vaginal symbol) before entering Mary's body through her ear (Walker 1983: 605)!"

Women have gained pulpits in protestant sects but are no where close to ordination in the Catholic Church. The reason given is that men resemble Jesus and can speak as/for him but women are not men and do not resemble Jesus. Ah, but what of the Marys? The early church had strong opposition to Mother Mary's popularity since she was reminiscent of the long-lived triple mother goddess. Inanna's epithets are also Mother Mary's when Mary is called: Queen of Heaven, Empress of Hell, and Lady of All the World. In time, to make certain that Mary was absolutely immaculate, she was assigned a mother, Anne, who is directly borrowed from the Ancient Near East. Sumerian for "heaven/sky dome" is "an". When deified, "an" is found in Antu (feminine of An), Anath, Anat and (N)in-anna that became Inanna. They are all Queens of Heaven. They are all Mother or Mistress of all the Gods. Inanna is the distant mother of Virgin Mary. Joseph Campbell writes (1959: 139-40:)

> A number of the typical and apparently perennial roles of this mother-goddess can be learned, furthermore, by simply perusing the Roman Catholic "Litany of Loreto," which is addressed to the Virgin Mother Mary. She is there called the Holy Mother of God, the Mother of Divine Grace and the Mother of Good Counsel; the Virgin Most Renowned, Virgin Most Powerful, Virgin Most Merciful, Virgin Most Faithful; and she is praised as the Mirror of Justice, Seat of Wisdom, Cause of Our Joy, Gate of Heaven, Morning Star, Health of the Sick, Refuge of Sinners, Comforter of the Afflicted, and Queen of Peace; Tower of David, Tower of Ivory, and House of Gold.

Early woman and goddess alike are connected to water, rain, and the sea. Mary, Mari, Marian, Miriam, Maria are names of the sea. Her robe is blue; she wears a pearl necklace and sea foam. Mary/Mari is

Mother of the Seas; she keeps similarities and fragments of the universal goddess trinity. She is part Mari, Inanna, Aphrodite-Mari, Ishtar, Juno the Blessed Virgin, Isis as Stella Maris, Maya the Oriental Mother of the Redeemer; Moerae (triune of Fates) and the Great Goddess in general as Queen of Heaven, Queen of Earth, and Queen of the Underworld. She is easily recognized from Part I of this book. Mary is described as being the Juno-Artemis-Hecate triad in the *Speculum Beatae Mariae.* (Walker 1983: 603 citing Emile Male. *The Gothic Image. 1958:* 235, 238:)

> (She is) Queen of heaven where she is enthroned in the midst of the angels, queen of earth where she constantly manifests her power, and queen of hell where she has authority over the demons ... (she is a primordial being) created from the beginning and before the centuries.

The patriarch of Constantinople, in 717 C.E., called her Lady All-Holy and Lady Most Venerable. He reasoned that since she is God's mother, he must obey her, that redemption came through her. An Archdeacon of Evreux said his people considered her equal to or more than God. People of the Middle Ages perceived God as the punisher and Mary as the protector-defender. A sixteenth century woodcut shows God firing arrows of war and pestilence into the world with a message inscribed on the woodcut — a plea for Mary to stop him (Walker 1983: 604). "Mary stands for Mercy, and it is only because of her influence at court, not because of love or goodwill on God's part, that heaven is within reach (Ashe 1976: 203)."

Remember the god Enlil in Sumer? He was credited for causing droughts, pestilence, and floods. Pleas went out to Inanna to calm the wrath of the gods and "to say them nay!" Other Christian patriarchs set out to make Mary only human and therefore not to be worshipped. Epiphanius demanded: "Let the Father, the son and the Holy Spirit be worshipped but let no one worship Mary" (Walker 1983: 603). Anastasius stated: "Let no one call Mary the Mother of God, for Mary was but a woman, and it is impossible that God should be born of a woman (ibid.)." A sect, the Marianites, was persecuted into the fifth century. They believed Mary was the truly divine one. "Mariolatry has plagued Christian Patriarchy throughout its history, as the popular need to worship the Mother-figure always arose unbidden (ibid.: 603)." Christian doctrine does not allow Mary to be placed above Christ, "yet the vitality of Christ's own church has often seemed to depend on her rather than him ... without her he would probably have lost his kingdom (Ashe 1976: 236)." Mary Daly writes a similar statement (Daly 1973: 92:)

> The church seemed doomed to failure, destined to go down to bloody death amidst the bleeding corpses of its victims, when the people discovered Mary. And only when Mary, against the stern decrees of the church, was dug out of oblivion to which Constantine had assigned her and became identified with the Great Goddess was Christianity finally tolerated by the people ... The only reality in Christianity is Mary, the Female Principle, the ancient goddess reborn.

WOMEN NEED A QUEEN OF HEAVEN

Mary is a construct of all the goddess mothers who birthed sons/gods in religious stories of the ancient world. The Church's dichotomy of saying "yes" to Mary and "no" to Mary, all the mountains of text for and against her, the grand intricate astounding stories to justify the arguments of both sides, and the speculations of the rise of Mary and the sects nominally Christian who worshipped primarily her — all of this rationalizing in texts is aptly summed up as "only a bad reason for things believed from a deeper motive: the ineradicable presence of female divinity (Ashe 1976: 213)." Her people wanted Mary deified. The church fathers outline three requirements for deification: immortality (requires a declared assumption and this was made official in 1950), sinlessness (granted her by declaring her own immaculate conception), and omniscience which is denied by the church but granted by the people.

463

Theologians of the thirteenth century reasoned: "Mary's mortality should bring more women to obey the church, because the king of heaven is no mere man but a mere woman is its queen. It is not a mere man who is set above the angels and all the rest of the heavenly court, but a mere woman is; nor is anyone who is merely man as powerful there as a mere woman (Walker 1983: 606)."[90] The important part of the quote to note is: "should bring more women to obey the church." Pope John XXIII, apparently received a direct message from Mary about that and claimed: "The Madonna is not pleased when she is put above her son."

Madonna had ways of going over the heads of the church fathers. Guerber, in his *Legends of the Rhine*, 1895, writes of a penniless beggar who prayed to the Virgin Mary for aid and then played his fiddle for her. She was so pleased that she gave the beggar one of the golden shoes from her statue. He was caught with the priceless shoe and sentenced to death. He prayed to her again as he was taken to the scaffold. Mary publicly gave him her second golden shoe. The beggar was released but the shoes were locked up in the priests' treasury in case she should be tempted to give her golden shoes to some other beggar seeking her help.

Mary and Inanna love everyone, as do countless other mother goddesses. It is the way of the mother. Mary was portrayed leaning on a balance scale determining a final reckoning — the weight of good compared to bad life-time deeds. The scale shows a few things on the good side and much more on the bad side. She leans on the good side and tips the scales; the sinner's few good acts outweigh the bad and that one escapes damnation! Some priests said even terrible sins could be neutralized by doing service or making something for the Virgin. Mary once did battle with forces of evil but this was conveniently not remembered (ibid.: 608). "The people needed a queen of heaven (ibid.: 608)." [91]

Cathedrals were built for Mary over earlier goddess sites and collectively called "Our Ladies" and "Palaces of the Queen of Heaven." In Rome the Santa Maria Maggiore covers the cavern of Magna Mater

---

[90] Walker cites Vern Bullogh. *The Subordinate Sex*. pp. 169-70
[91] Walker citing Rudolf Augstein. *Jesus Son of Man*. p. 302

(Great Mother). Santa Maria in Aracoeli was built over the temple for Tanit; other Italian Mary churches were placed over Juno, Isis, Minerva, Diana, and Hecate sanctuaries. One church name even tells us she is Holy Mary over Minerva (Santa Maria Sopra Minerva) (ibid.).[92] Chartres has a black Mary statue in the grotto under the cathedral. Isis and Aphrodite sites were rededicated to Mary and Cypriots interchanged the names of Mary and Aphrodite. Aphrodite is the Greek version of Inanna.

Inanna and Mary both evoke devotion and inspiration. They are the muses of creativity. Goethe writes of Mother Mary: "Supreme and sovereign Mistress of the World! … Oh Virgin, in the highest sense most pure, oh Mother, worthy of all our worship, our chosen Queen, equal with the gods." Inanna's scribal poets could not have said it better! An eighteenth century theologian writes: "at the command of Mary all obey, even God." Five millennia earlier Inanna's theologians said: "No god could say her nay!"

Historian Henry Adams believed that regardless of how diminished Christianity's divine mother is, she "offered the only hope of spiritual comfort in an alienated technological age." He further recognized that men have given their work, and life involvement over to machines "but did not have the life-sense to save the race. In their blind pride over their scientific facilities, they would cling to the insensate mechanisms they had created, making them go faster and faster, though incapable of applying the brakes." Adams recognized further that a counterbalance to chaos was another sort of energy — life energy, erotic love energy, reproduction and creation energy. He invoked "woman's faith in her own creativity, in all the ramifying, formative processes of life, above all, those of sex, love, and motherhood." He addressed the Virgin Mary: "I feel the energy of faith, not in the further science but in you (ibid.: 612)."[93]

Mary is called Ecclesia — "the Church" — which includes buildings and church organization, yet the church is absolutely male-run. The recently restored frescos in the Catacombs of Priscilla from the first several centuries of our Common Era, are recently unveiled by

---

[92] Walker citing E. Wilkens. *The Rose-Garden Game.* p.69
[93] Walker citing Lewis Mumford. *Interpretations and Forecasts.* p. 363

the Vatican. Photographs of the paintings from the catacombs under Rome are revealing. A painting in the "Queen of the catacombs" shows Mary nursing her babe as all Madonna goddesses do. Most amazing are paintings showing women teaching and giving blessings with the hand mudras now used only by ordained priests. The conclusion any viewer would reach is that women were active as teachers, as priests (priestesses) in the early Christian religion. Women in religious roles of the Catholic Church, nuns and lay, now advocate for ordination rights. Since the church continues to hold "women in low regard", women are not granted the ordination rite to become priest(ess). When asked about the obvious role of women in beginning Christianity, as verified by the frescos, a Vatican source denied that women ever had teaching or priestly roles and said that this speculation is "sensationalist fairy tales".[94] The frescos were restored; they were known to exist. Given the secretive nature of the Vatican to control information that does not support official dogma, it is surprising that they were revealed to the public. Perhaps the patriarchs do not have eyes to see.

"Sensationalist fairy tales" indeed! Evidence is recently available that another Mary, Mary Magdalene, was a teacher, a disciple, a financial supporter, a favorite, and wisest of Jesus' community. She was also his wife, bride, and companion. She is called the apostle of the apostles because Jesus first appeared to her and she, above the rest, understood the teachings. An opera was commissioned by the San Francisco Opera company based on the Gospel of Mary Magdalene. When Mary meets the resurrected Christ; he sings of his love for her, and asks that she teach what she learned from him *and* what he learned from her.

SEX AND THE CHURCH — MARY MAGDALENE

Theologians and worshippers of old were at ease with the goddess as maid-mother-crone, life-death-return, all in one. Western minds have difficulty grasping that all goddesses are one goddess, all her

---

[94] http://politicalblindspot.com/vatican-catacombs-paintings-discovered-shoe-female-priests/ pp. 2-5

names and epithets are aspects of the one. Goddess flows through cycles and mirrors women in all phases of her life. Because people wanted Mary or else they would revert back to their "pagan"[95] mother goddess, the Christian patriarchs settled on a pure adolescent virgin for Mary's image. She is meek and mild and will do the bidding of God. She is impossible for women to model since we can never be so pure, and that is the point. For some reason, the beautiful, lusty, ripe, nude goddess of the Ancient Near East with abundant luxurious head and pubic hair, singing a song to her vulva, facing her viewer frontally while holding a perky breast in one hand, leading a lion and/or holding unwomanly weapons in the other, was frightening to church fathers. They demonized the goddess original and sanitized her Mary stand-in when they had no choice. The church fathers do not like women. They wrote passages that say women are triply cursed: when barren, when they conceive, and, when they give birth, the third curse is labor pain. There is no comparable curse for men.

The effort to vilify sex by church fathers, is unending. Men, especially priestly men, seek to control the lives, thoughts, bodies and freedoms of women when their own lack of self control is legion. One such maligned and important woman is Mary Magdalene. Christian women theologians agree that to stay within a male-based religion, women theologians have three choices. The first is to make-do, just accept, or look for the pockets of pro-woman passages and reinterpret texts where possible. The second is to dig and research and find new aspects of what exists, new information, return what was deleted, and find and reveal facts that ease the male bias to lead the faith toward partnership based on the earliest beginning of the Christian story. The third choice is to give up on Christianity and create a new system based on reflections of the sacred feminine. The research for this last chapter, the ascendency of goddess and women … again, gave me pause. I was fully in favor of the third way, but theologians and interested others, researching into Mary Magdalene, her times, her teaching, and her place in the early days of the new religion gave hope to the second choice for

---

[95] Pagan is used as any religion other than Christian.

those wishing to restore the lost story and remain within Christianity. The evidence is compelling. It is being advanced and read; I have not heard that Inquisitors and witch hunters are re-employed … yet.

Margaret Starbird has done remarkable work with her delving into Mary Magdalene using only biblical and historical resources. She presents compelling arguments to redefine Mary Magdalene and to see her as a human woman enacting the ancient partnership of the sacred marriage, the *hieros gamos*, as a living symbol. Mary Magdalene is a necessary consciousness to change the outdated dysfunctional masculinized church. There is reason to hope. Pope Francis is appointing one lay woman to an important committee and is listening to lay and religious woman leaders. However, fundamentalist protestant sects are likely a mission impossible for change. Catholicism at least has Mary as a beginning reference. Protestants deleted her as a sacred influence centuries ago. Mary Magdalene, the priests assure us, is a reformed prostitute. Everyone has heard that, but it is not true.

Misogyny, in a few early centuries of the common era, removed sacred and human woman from men's "master story." The ancients knew that without a catalyst, the earth and woman's procreative powers lay fallow, barren. Without the feminine, nothing will grow, the land and people die. Long ago women crafted partnership, the *hieros gamos.* It is the acknowledged partnership that assigns to the man protection of the woman, the earth (always feminine), and creative life energy. The story Starbird weaves has veracity. She not only reassembles Mary Magdalene's existence and importance but sees her as the piece missing in the Christian religion, the healing that is needed.

I would expand that importance to global significance. Every early belief system developed a *hieros gamos*, a divine couple of creative energy; every creation myth begins with a Great Mother Creatress who brings forth the earth and heaven and the gods. In every language "earth" is feminine. We, again, are in desperate need of the feminine brain, wisdom, and voice.

Male-run religion becomes the fist of politics, the excuse for war and killing, the aggression of colonization, the behind-story of political decisions. Male-based religion invents the reasons to hate other people;

the reasons to diminish women, sacred and human. The way out of global insanity is up to aware women and balanced men. Resurrecting Mary Magdalene from lies and denials is a basic and large piece of her restoration. Bourgeault notes the "undercutting" of Mary Magdalene's authority and her role as the "apostle of the apostles" that resulted from "a deepening sickness of the soul already visible in the Western church by the end of the patristic era (Bourgeault 2010: 23)." Is the patristic era ended?

Mary Magdalene is the beloved of the teacher, Jesus. Her name, Mary, derived from the name of the queen Mariamne, incarnate of Goddess Mari. Mari was widely worshiped in the Ancient Near East as the sea chambers of birth, Mother Sea, and a great fish who gave birth to the gods. Her second name, Magdalene, does not come from her assumed town of birth, Magdela, as is the popular belief. Magdalene means "she of the temple-tower." The temple in Jerusalem had three towers; one had the name of the queen who represents the goddess, the tower of the feminine. Enough is found to assure us that Mary Magdalene was a real woman, educated, and likely a priestess of the tower. She knew the anointing ritual — anointing has several connotations: anointing initiates during the sacred marriage ritual and oils anoint the dead for easy passage into the afterlife. Messiah means "the anointed one." A messiah requires anointing to be the "anointed one." Mary Magdalene anoints Jesus in the books of Matthew, Mark, Luke, and John.

The biblical cannons contain four gospels written forty and more years after the death of Jesus. The story of him and his teachings vary but there are four events that each of the four gospels contain; one of those describes a woman who anoints Jesus from her alabaster jar of oil/ perfume. She is sister of Lazarus and Martha; she is Mary Magdalene. She is said to be a redeemed prostitute but that is misogynistic fantasy. Nowhere, biblically, is that description mentioned. Mary Magdalene listens and talks with Jesus, she is his bride, they are the same participants in the ancient *hieros gamos* partnership of Inanna and her shepherd king Dumuzi. Together, spiritually and sexually partnered, their joy of being each other's beloved fills the land with love, growth and creative fertility.

Mary Magdalene and the sister-wives of the disciples walked with the men, learned with the men and taught with the men. The story told was a return to the sanity, compassion, wisdom, egalitarian partnership — women as equals. Everyone was welcome. There were no threats or forced conversions. There was no dismissal of women. Jesus brought forth the feminine. Mary Magdalene was his wife and more. Bourgeault calls the quality of their shared love as the "unitive power of redemptive love" and "beatific communion" with the sacred beloved (ibid.: 28). It is "beatific communion" that allows Mary Magdalene to hear Jesus after his resurrection and before his ascension. The most profound teaching came through her to the disciples from the spirit of Jesus. Leloup writes, citing the Gospel of Philip (Leloup 2002: 10:)

> The Lord loved Mary more than all the disciples and often used to kiss her on the mouth. When the others saw how he loved Mary, they said "Why do you love her more than you love us?" The Savior answered them in this way: "How can it be that I do not love you as much as I love her?"

So were they married? Did they have sex? Starbird, Bourgeault, and Leloup, refer to the societal fact that Jewish men of the day were not complete, not fully a man, unless they were married. Sumerians had the same idea. To teach in the temple, a man had to be fully a man. Jesus taught in the temple. He was fully human. Furthermore, the sacred marriage was deeply instilled in the Near East Semitic tradition. The temple in Jerusalem had three chambers for offerings: the Holy Place, the Holy of Holies, and the Holiest, the Bridal Chamber, the heart of the temple. The Holiest part of the temple in Jerusalem has to do with the *hieros gamos,* the bridal chamber. Inanna's temples too had her bridal chamber. Leloup explains the chambers: at the Holy place, one is first purified (water), renewed, cleansed by anointing (sacred fire), and accepts the Eucharist to better focus and take on a new perspective. A door then opens to the second chamber where all is clear and exposed; here bias and what limits growth is burned away in order "to bring the dark, hidden secrets of the soul to light, so that they can be immobilized (Analogue 68 of the gospel of Philip). Here the veil that keeps an individual from knowing his or her true Self is lifted. Stripped of the egoic self and exposed to the light, one is restored to 'fullness of being,' that is, to one's True Self, which makes the initiate ready to enter the Bridal Chamber." The readied individual, still separate from the divine, enters the chamber to experience a transformation that erases the duality into a unified consciousness. The transformation is only for those who already understand un-duality. That one then enters into a sacred embrace (Bourgeault 2010: 133).[96]

What does this mean? Leloup writes: "The mystery which unites two beings is great; without it the world would not exist (Leloup 2002: 23)." The gospel of Philip states that the "pure embrace" (limited to the heart) is infinitely the more powerful, "its image, however, is found in physical sexual union (Bourgeault 2010: 135)."

The Church fathers were wrong. The early teaching was not celibacy good, sex bad. If one has done the work to become fully human, to know one's true Self and become aligned to that clarity, then holiness can move through physical union. The problem lies in sex without the hard work of becoming aligned. Did Jesus and Mary Magdalene, or did they not, share bodies as well as hearts? Jesus is declared "at once perfect in his divinity and perfect in his humanity" by the Council of Chalcedon (451 C.E.) (ibid.: 142). I imagine them in their Bridal Chamber, in a divine embrace, of body, mind, and spirit. I imagine the Church fathers of the future rescinding the unhealthy emphasis on celibacy great! sex terrible! The Church has already rescinded the part about Mary Magdalene being a reformed prostitute but that memo was not spread vigorously.

Sacred beings are entirely holy, including their bodies.
Gospel of Philip, Analogue 60

"Not only was Miriam (Mary) of Magdala a woman, she was a woman who had access to sacred knowledge (Leloup 2002:13)." In her time, men studied the mystical Torah and women did not. Mary Magdalene broke societal traditions. She had great strength and inspiration to be as she was. The reluctance of the male disciples to accept her as an equal is easy to imagine. What is worse for the other disciples is that after the

---

[96] Bourgeault citing Ward Bauman. *Luminous Gospels*. p. 79

resurrection and before the ascension, Mary was in communication with Jesus and they were not. She used the *nous*. "In the ancient world, the *nous* was seen as 'the finest point of the soul' … (that) gives us access to that intermediate realm between the purely sensory and the purely spiritual … the imaginal (or the mundus imaginalis) (ibid.:13-14)."[97] Mary asked questions and the resurrected Jesus answered.

Once upon a time, that imaginal communication between deity and mortal was how sacred scripts came into being and divine messages were delivered. The *mundus imaginalis* bridged the invisible and visible, the spirit world and the corporal world. Mary continued teaching the disciples through the forty days before the ascension. The other disciples did not understand all the teachings at a deep level. They were jealous of her connection with the master and her understanding of what he had not taught them. In the end, Peter and Simon Peter deny her. She weeps, not because they hurt her feelings and reject her, but because they do not understand all of the teaching. She weeps for them. The disciples and their sister-wives went forth in every direction to teach. Each one taught what that one understood. Many sects arose around the region.

What was lost through time and determined deletion has partially returned. The recovered Mary Magdalene story is pieced together from scattered biblical mentions and deduced from social and historical texts of the time. She also returns in the three hidden-away gospels of Thomas, Philip, and Mary Magdalene. These gospels were rejected and destroyed when official canon selection choices were made. For nearly two thousand years, Mary Magdalene's presence was lightly scattered through the New Testament gospels and prophesied in the Old Testament in the book of Micah, though priestly editors diligently rid their texts of her importance.

Mary the Virgin survived and was elevated by popular demand. Since sex was deemed unredeemable and evil, it needed to be removed from the vicinity of Jesus. If he were sexual, that meant sex was redeemable. By declaring Jesus celibate, they had credence to demand celibacy of the prelates and condemn both sex and women. They could

---

[97] Leloup citing Henry Corbin, *The Voyage and the Messenger.* pp.117-134

not allow a bride for Jesus. They could not allow a woman to be the apostle of the apostles. They could not allow a woman to be a teacher. They could not allow a mortal bloodline to flourish. They could not allow the old *hieros gamos* to survive. As a result, denied sexuality has sickened the West's primary religion. Women are despised and reduced to silenced brood mares. Priestesses are a joke and goddess is demonized. Only men's great fear of women and the sacred feminine could fuel the fiery hate and denial of Eve, goddess in general, Mary Magdalene and by extension — and all women. All the brides are in exile. There is no partnership of creating. Without the sacred partnership, the land and people will die. The role of the bridegroom is protector of the land, the bride and the bride's people. The role of the bride is to initiate, with sacred oil and with her body, the bridegroom into his potential creative power. What was a once a yearly cycle for return and reunion of the beloveds has been delayed two thousand years.

Figure 48. Inanna and Dumuzi, the *Hieros Gamos*

Mary Magdalene has both a sacred and human role as did priestesses of Sumer when they, as Inanna, sprinkled the cedar oil and made joyful love with the consort-proxy of the demigod-beloved of their goddess. The goddess, through her priestess, selected a man to protect her and her land — she *is* the land. He praises her and gives her gifts. They retire to her bed, her garden, her holy chamber. She anoints him with special perfumed oil and her body. The love, pleasure, and joy of their copulation and their resulting energy of procreation spreads through the land. The chosen consort rules for another vegetation cycle as the shepherd of her flock. The king *is* the vegetation god Dumuzi and the priestess *is* Inanna. They are each other's beloved. They bring about fertility and new cycles through sex, through partnership. This is the old story of partnership. *Hieros gamos.* Sacred marriage. Sacred pleasure. Sacred Bride and Groom. Woman and man. Together again. The visible and invisible, the spiritual and physical, the cosmos and humanity is bridged.

Jesus appears first to Mary Magdalene after his resurrection. The vegetation god traditionally reappears to the mother-beloved after a time of being "dead". The very same story of a demigod's death and resurrection is in the Inanna and Dumuzi liturgies and the Eleusinian, Orphic, and Osirian mysteries. Early Christian "Gnostic" writing includes the idea that a great goddess of silence, Sige, is the origin of the Creative Word. She births Sophia, who is Wisdom and Knowledge. Sophia is both mother and spouse of God. "Gnostic" women were ecclesiastically equal with men in status, teaching, praying and baptizing.

The "Gnostics" believed that a world soul inhabited and embraced everything. Some "Gnostic" sects believed "the true revelation of esoteric Christianity came through a woman, the 'apostle to the apostles', Mary Magdalene, Jesus's beloved (Walker: 1983, p. 344)." The Roman (orthodox) Christian Fathers hated the presence of female divinity, female authority and the non-separation of "sinners" from the world soul. Instead, the church fathers said sinners had to be punished in "hell" and they would not go to heaven. Goddess, woman's participation in teaching, and alchemical research into natural science (because it required the participation of woman and her menstrual blood) were all heretical and had to be stamped out (Walker 1983: 345,346).

WOMAN IN ASCENDANCY ... AGAIN

In the concluding pages, we will move forward in time and consider some of the progress women have made on our return and ascendancy. Abigail Adams, well educated and capable, ran the family's farm estate and administrated the family's financial matters while her husband, John, worked to get our fledgling country up and running. She wrote to him while he attended the First Continental Congress:

> Remember the ladies, and be more generous and favorable to them than your ancestors. Do not put such unlimited power into the hands of the husbands. Remember, all men would be tyrants if they could ... If particular care and attention is not paid to the ladies, we are determined to foment a rebellion, and will not hold ourselves bound by any laws in which we have no voice or representation.

John did not listen to her. Women did not get the vote for another century and a half. The first wave of feminism "fomented" into a women's bill of rights in 1848, at Seneca Falls, New York; a third of the signers were men. The 19th amendment, giving women the vote, was finally passed and ratified in 1920. Only one of the women who began the fight for woman's vote was still alive when the amendment was added to the Constitution. Alice Paul proposed the Equal Rights Amendment in 1927. It finally passed both the house and senate in 1972. Three fourths of the states, thirty-eight, are required to ratify it into an amendment. The reason for the ratification is to give serious scrutiny to equal rights protection of everyone regardless of gender or race. Without the amendment, states conduct gender and race business as usual. In 1972, twenty-seven states ratified; the thirty-fifth ratified in 1977. The ERA is still not an amendment. Anti-feminists and other political groups fight it. The republican party has removed the ERA issue from its election platform. We must continue to foment!

Women are raising their voices again. Early partnership forged by our foremothers is moving again into consciousness. Male-only dominator culture is a death sentence. It always was. Men without women's awareness and natural relational interest, revert to aggression and domination. Women did not exclude men. The point of creating culture was securing male participation and cooperation. It still is. Male dominator culture works diligently to destroy women's long-ago established relational partnership culture. The dominator goal is *the polar opposite* of women's culture, with Y-male emphasis on selfishness, elitism, and death; not life and inclusion. The patriarchal goal is dismissal of the female gender from any influence or position of importance, the silencing and exclusion of women and the demonization and eradication of sacred woman. Y-ness perfected supreme rulership of domination over the last 5,000 years — but a conquerer is on top only until he is not.

The animal nature of the Y chromosome combined with a creature with a big brain is dangerous. In the world of non-human primates, females can refuse sex even with the alpha male. Rape is observed only very rarely. In the animal world, males do not attack females even if provoked. Lucky female animals. A U.N. survey (see Eve Ensler's site on One Billion Rising) reported that one of every three women will experience rape, incest, and/or physical abuse in her lifetime. Eve Ensler inspired the first worldwide "One Billion Rising" event on Valentines Day, 2013. She invited women to dance in the streets to acknowledge the criminality, rapes and silenced dirty secrets of their perpetrators. They danced to acknowledge and support the one billion harmed. (If the world population is rounded off to six billion, then women number about three billion, and one of every three is one billion.) There is no need to stage a one billion rising event in the animal world as animal males do not behave like human Y-men.

Our only hope is to change back to a partnership culture through the awake women and balanced men. Balanced men are the portion of the population the Y-men consider meek and mild, feminine and womanly — *as if these qualities were terrible weaknesses.* They are not weak! They are the real and certain strengths of our species. The hairy heroes destroy us and our planet. If "the meek shall inherit the earth," will it be the return of X's influence present in both genders and in double portion in women? (Read "meek" as: caring, compassionate, wise, biophilic, protective, inclusive, cooperative, and sustaining life-affirming values — just as early women designed culture.) Or might the Biblical prophesy mean the "meek" will be moths, morning glories, and pond scum?

Inanna gives the ME, the civilizing powers, to her people; her protagonist god Enki wants them for himself (see chapter 2). Woman-based culture shares knowledge; male based religion keeps it for itself as did the "Christian" Church keep literacy for itself after Rome fell in 476 C.E.. The church fathers methodically removed traces of the feminine from its selected and edited male-orientated texts and put priests between their singular god and the often forcibly converted followers. The purpose of force, coercion, and threat is control. If a belief feels true, it requires no force or threat to exist. Earliest Christianity, in its beginning, was direct, kind, humane, inclusive, and held that woman followers were important. Mary Magdalene is not a reformed whore. She is beloved of the man Jesus, the wandering Jewish prophet. Within a few centuries, maleness revamped the unwritten story, arranged second and third-hand memories to male advantage, edited and selected texts for the official canon, destroyed the gospels of other Christian sects, rid the new religion of ordained woman teachers and erased the egalitarian status of women followers. Goddess and women share everything with their children; gods and men do not.

A new cycle of necessary awareness of women's influence is returning. Women's sacred understanding never died. Goddess symbols linger just out of focus, just off-stage. Great Mother's story is whispered at the well and wafts in wisps of dream and intuition. Listen to the women as their wisdom is unsilenced; there is hope. Humane-ity is rising again. The rising is no less than a revolution; a revolution without murder. It is a revolving, turning, cycling movement. Revolutions use expressive symbols and slogans. Humane-ity, X-ness, symbolizes a sacred theme of

"Life." Life is a sacred Great Mother. The goddess is stirring and women are stepping from the margins, from seclusion; separateness is forgotten. We meet at the well. Our voices are heard, again.

Women are researching, creating, and authoring change. That change takes back our bodies, minds, expression, and long-denied spirituality. We are human, not because we use tools, but because we tell stories. People tell stories that mirror human behavior. We recognize others and ourselves in a story's characters and their actions. We resonate with the familiar. We pass wisdom along with image and story. We desire to live life to its fullest and wisest potential.

Religion means "bound to". We are bound to this beautiful planet by life and by living. It is up to us to choose how we live and what we are "bound to." The dominator male-directed major religions fail to honor life and planet. Their godhead is off-planet, unseen, unprovable and favors "his" sons; he is unknowable excepting for a few of the "sons" who assure us the soul's big job is to discard the physical world. Consider: being human is a hard job but the physical world is where we learn, create, evolve. We do not need to apologize for being in the human condition. We cannot consider it unholy. We cannot just mark time suffering until we are freed to move to out of the physical world! Life is sacred.

Feminine influence rises again, Phoenix from her ashes. Repressed memory is surfacing; oppressed women of the West are finding their voice in relative safety. That relative safety is not global. The collective strength of women and caring men ripples out. With that combined strength, there is hope for all life. That hope is the return of woman's innate concern for life, wisdom, and the honored archaic voice of sacred and human women. She-ness returns in dreams and creative expression; awake women and balanced men again bring forth their wisdom and voice. Worldwide, people are dreaming the sacred feminine. Jungian analyst, Marian Woodman, writes in her foreword for *The Black Madonna Within,* by Tataya Mato (1994: xiii:)

> Why is she a Madonna? As an image of femininity ... she
> is more than a beautiful mother. She embodies a divine calm,

a concentrated awareness of herself. She is an incarnation of divine energy ... she is a bridge to the creative source.

Why is she dark? Individuals blessed with her presence in their dreams love her at a personal, heart level. The radiance that shines through her darkness is magnetic. Through her austere and loving discipline, she can teach us how to transform dark, opaque, inert matter into the flowing energy of the sacred temple in which we dwell ... at the same time (we) learn to honor the sacred temple called Earth. Psychologically, darkness suggests that which is still unknown to the consciousness ... Our survival, both as individuals and as a planet, depends on recognizing the light that shines in her darkness.

Why is she appearing in contemporary dreams? In past centuries, she was known to many saints and artists ... now she demands, often through illness, that we recognize her. Dreamers who are being instructed ... are being told ... there is no time to waste. She ... opens a vision of planetary harmony. Loving her is experiencing the light that shines in her darkness.

Women and men are dreaming in goddess. Over the last four decades I dream-experienced her three times as Black Madonna, three times as Kwan Yin, three times as a huge orange python, once each as Crone, Great Sow, Ouroboros, dancing white bear, and white snow owl. I dreamed Inanna and women dancing in bright colored flounced goddess dresses; each dress was a solid red, yellow, green or blue. She and they danced in a walled garden swirling, hands raised high. I saw Inanna's true dance — not the imposed dance of war.

In a rather spectacular dream, I was in a large restaurant (representing the storehouse) and Inanna/prime creatress came through the ceiling-high doors as a huge dragon. There was a little box strapped on her back full of portly men. They held onto ropes tied to her neck. They thought they had control of her. She scraped the men off her back as she dove out through a wide window and into the ocean. In the next dream scene, she was a giant sea serpent in my actual seaside cove. Her head rested on shore. The tide was low. Neighborhood men came with their rifles. I said NO! don't shoot. I sent one of the men to my kitchen for a sharp knife. They thought I was going to kill her myself. I took the knife and sawed through the many old ropes tied tight around her neck, strangling and silencing her. The ropes piled up at my feet. I freed her from the many attempts of men to capture her. The tide was rising. She lifted her head, held my eye gaze for a moment and turned her great long body back to sea. The ropes at my feet had little bags caught amid the strands of clinging seaweed. I opened one and found several smooth deep red stones. They resembled blood clots. They were the treasure she protected. Blood, birth, creation, life-power — she was Nammu, Sumerian creatress mother of whom Inanna is the maid aspect. She is first snake. She is the energy behind this book.

I remember each goddess dream in exquisite detail. At first, when she came I did not know who she was. She revealed her identity in time. She came and assisted the healing of my burdened life. She came and my paintings began to tell stories of divine woman and sacred earth. She came and I committed daily to immerse in the study and research of her story. She came and inspired, perhaps insisted, that I discover and write the story of a Great Mother Goddess who grew out of the deep earth, dark sky, women's bodies and blood, and our humane-ity. She came and I already knew her as Starlight, Starbright. She came and I learned her name. Inanna.

We heal by remembering and dreaming and creating. We create our myths. "To create a myth, that is to say, to catch a glimpse of a higher truth behind a palpable reality, is the most manifest sign of the greatness of the human soul, and the proof of its faculty of infinite growth and development (Goblet d'Alviella, *The Migration of Symbols*. 1894: 3)." The template of biophilic possibilities is here, within us. Memory of goddess's myths is in our X chromosome, the "realm of silence (Depak Chopra)," "the archetypal realm (Jung)."

Women tend, mend, befriend, and defend their young and dependent others; we once held high position and status. After millennia (generally rounded off to five) of a gender-specific dark age, women return through their efforts and struggles to own their bodies, have a voice, research, make legislative change, promote inclusivity, embrace diversity, awaken cultural awareness, replace domination with partnership, steward ecology and activate support for healthy human and planetary life. Woman's return is not yet global but it is rising. That hopeful manifestation is important for human-time but perhaps not for earth-time. If wise women (and men) are not able to influence the sorry state of global domination, our future is finite. Without humans exploiting and overcrowding her, earth will go on; bruised and scarred to be sure. Earth will re-group and support her new creations. If we fail and biology marks us for extinction, will other primates step forward to do a better job than our last millennial efforts? Will whales practice pod partnership in the quiet recovering seas, singing their songs of new safety and remembering the old destructive horrors of mankind? Will clever carrion crows continue cawing their observations of humans long after the last of us has turned to dust? Will humans have so poisoned the earth and her air that all life dies but for sturdy pond scum, that is, if it can find water?

The feminine voice of wisdom is alive; it *is* life, women are life-orientated and goddess *is* Life. Goddess has many epithets describing her as Life. Eve's name shares Arabic word roots with "teaching", "snake", and "life". Goddess is All life, All Mother Life, All Maternal Being, Creatress, Goddess Mother of the Universe, Great Womb, Lady Birthgiver, Life, Mamma, Matrix, Mistress of Life, Mother Belly, Mother Earth, Moon Mother, Mother of Life, Mother of the Land, Mother Undefiled, Original Mother Without a Spouse, Queen of Heavenly Midwives, Queen of Life and Death, She Who Creates the Seed, Strength of Life, Thought of Life, Universal Mother, White goddess of Life-in-Death and Death-in-Life, Woman with Four Hundred Breasts, Womb of Creation, Womb of Matter and World Shaper. Wise woman knowing is expressed as life, love of life, compassion, nurturing, protection, and support of life. Life is a sacred woman; love of life is biophilia.

RENEWAL OF THE *HIEROS GAMOS* —
RETURN OF PARTNERSHIP

Imagine a revolution of returning partnership. It will take decades and generations to re-root, but not millennia. We have the template encoded in our ancient memory, our cell memory, our collective unconscious. This new partnership revolution has record of what went wrong and where we must be especially vigilant. Dominators fear change in their status. They fight, threaten, hurt, isolate, and kill challengers. They make laws and religious interpretations to support their illogical and unfounded belief in male superiority and the right to rule and own any and every thing. When the oppressed stir, the dominators backlash. The up-close experience of dominator behavior, spousal abuse, is readily recognized; it is no longer the husband's and father's right to beat and abuse with impunity, protected by male-run cultures. Rape, incest, child molestation, and spousal abuse are no longer our society's dirty secrets. The rule of thumb, an English ruling that said a man could legally beat his wife and children with a stick no thicker than his thumb, in its time was upheld as remarkable leniency. Look at men's thumbs and imagine the damage a stick that size inflicted! Dominator abuse is evident in physical, mental and emotional guises in families, institutions, corporate work places, and in fundamental religious beliefs that control women and women's bodies while extolling male rights of superiority.

First writing recorded the organized diminishment of women, both sacred and human in the texts and art of the Ancient Near East. From then onward we have patriarchy's own record of people enslaved, starved, tortured, and murdered; people targeted for genocide, deported for slave labor, and selected for containment and extermination. Those practices continue in many dominator cultures. Male infants are preferred because men want sons. The preference for sons is promoted as sons are valuable for rulers to use for war and labor. Daughters are property to sell into marriage. China's recent one-child policy resulted in gynocide by aborting or abandoning girl babies and children by the millions so the fathers could try again for a son. There is now a gender imbalance in

China with an increase in male crime rate and suicides among women. The result of decrease in available females is that the crime rate rises. The only-child sons are pampered and spoiled. A term was coined in China for their resulting behavior: "the little emperor syndrome." The entitled, spoiled, and unwilling-to-work sons are of no help in a society top-heavy with an aging population and reduced workforce of young people.

However, there is hope. Women continue to survive, think and express. In the last two centuries enough women came together with their wisdom and raised voices to awaken others into consciousness. The first wave of feminism in the mid-nineteenth century grew out of the abolishment of slavery movement. Like early women, the feminists gathered in solidarity. Women are again speaking out. They feel and think deeply — they are "flinking."[98] They are challenging male-favored laws, male impunity, Catholic priest pederasts, rape and abuse. They continue working toward pay and opportunity equality. Domination culture is exposed. The alternative — partnership — is promoted.

Come. Women are meeting again at the well. Women are protesting as informed activists. Women continue to do what they are doubly evolved to do. They care deeply for life. Women have been without a sacred symbol of evolved humane X-ness for over two millennia, but the sacred feminine is too sensible and too deeply enmeshed within human development and subconscious memory to die. The sacredness of life is X-ness. Great Goddess is the image and symbol for life. Women are rising. Women and Divine Woman are in ascendancy ... again.

I have told you an old story about a goddess, holy Inanna. Her story is also your story. We are finding our way out of domination. We are finding our story through the efforts of mostly woman researchers. Science is giving us evidence to overcome male-made myths and perceptions. The lost story of woman, sacred and human, is returning. We reach and teach each other as we did in our sacrosanct women's quarters in the Ancient Near East. We have our counsel of wise women. Our daughters are cherished. They learn the sacredness of body and spirit; they sing their

---

[98] a term coined by professor Phyllis Brazee, University of Maine, Orono

bridal songs of partnership. We have strong brave women as inspired models; we have the renewal of woman's spirituality. Women, life, divine feminine, and feminine principles are in ascendancy ... again.

I wanted to know Inanna and found woman's brave history. We share one story; it is both sacred and human. Our instinctual XX-ness, teamed with our big brain, steps into a new expressive feminine consciousness. Long ago we did not just live out our days. We considered what we observed about being alive. Life stirred within us and was born. We nurtured and cared for new life for years. We gathered with other women. We bled with other women and moon. We recognized a life force energy. We revered life. Life was all around us: earth and mountains and rivers and seas and sky and moon and stars. We named the bigness Mother, Great Mother. For most of the time of modern humans, women's every age and function was mirror-projected to cosmic proportions as the universal Mother goddess. We imagined her. We said NO! together. We and she, with her many thousands of names and epithets,[99] guided both halves of humanity into partnership.

When stars were many and people few, women guided our experimental new species away from extinction. Now, when people are many and and stars are few —as most are unseen through polluted air — we need remember that we have the template within us of guiding leadership. I give you Inanna's story and invite you to remember her and yourself. Imagine her, strapping on her sandals and stepping onto her starlight path to stand beside you. She comes with her lions purring and growling. She leads the bull of heaven by its nose lead-line, tamed. She laughs; her joy is of our return. We gather again at the well; we dance, sing, express. She brings us her MEs. She always brings her MEs to the people, but first she brings them to those who are remembering. We try on her MEs: rulership, high priestess, crown, truth, loosening of the hair, the art of lovemaking, forthright speech, adoring speech, songs, the art of the elder, the art of power, the arts and crafts, healing,

---

[99] The author found 9,000 goddess names.

procreation, counseling, heart-soothing, giving judgements, making decisions, the art of kindness, the art of assembling a family, a secure dwelling place, and sitting on a throne. Do you remember what Inanna said to the thieving god Enki who took her ME? She got him roaring drunk, he "gave" them (back) to her and she said: "I take them!" Women must now accept our worth, intelligence, bodies, and powers and say: "I take them!"

In the early days of research, I wanted Inanna to be only loving, compassionate, beautiful, and kind; outspoken and sexy were fine but I resisted her warrior title. I reconsider. We are defensive warriors, defending our children fiercely — now we extend our defensiveness, as does Inanna, from the personal child to the plight of humankind, to all life. It is the same protective tend, mend, befriend, defend we already own in our XX-ness. We defend life. Inanna reminds us we too are warriors, but bloodletting is not our weapon, nor are lies, intimidation, enslavement, torture, or terror. Our greatest weapons are solidarity and speech. Y-men fear our potential to tame them into humane beings; they want to silence our NO! We say NO! again in solidarity in enough numbers for safety. Men envied our creativity. They stole our time, energy, and story; our love, bodies, and voices, but we are rising again like evening star.

Goddess Inanna is Queen of Heaven, Queen of Earth, evening star, morning star, fertility, love, allure, sex, storehouse, herds, and agriculture; protector of widows, orphans, prostitutes, captives, and anyone who needs her; defender, decree-maker, and holder of all the civilizing powers. Our beautiful goddess fastens her sandals to smite a dishonoring mountain, sings a song to her vulva, and steps out of the crumbled ruins of millennial dust and back into our hearts. She brushes away several thousand years of diminishment, slander, and banishment. She bathes in pure water. She fixes gold vulva ornaments into her luxurious shining hair. She decides whether to wear nothing at all or the flounced gown and robes of queenship. Her attendants place beads on her neck and jewels of allure on her breast. Her robe is either of the old days, sheepskin, or woven of brightly dyed red or blue wool and adorned with gold rosettes and stars. She applies kohl to her all-seeing eyes, she turns and stares out; she sees and hears us.

Inanna never backs away from challenge. She lets out her lioness roar. She challenges malignant change. We hear her speak through ancient cuneiform texts. Inanna is love, and creativity. She is leader, judge, and decision-maker. She is elderly people giving counsel. She is the art of culture and civilization. She is sorrowful laments and joyful hearts. She is fire and safety, she is lion and consternation. Inanna is both sides of an issue. She is complete. She is reality. She is nature. She is human nature. She is renewal. Life is birth, death, and return. Cycles incorporate both sides of nature's seasons, of life and death, and of human behavior. Patriarchal domination of the last five thousand years is the dark side of human behavior. The great wheel turns. Awareness of a sacred feminine is emerging again. Inanna is returning to us.

Out of the translations, an amazing sacred woman appears. She is far older than first writing. She is supreme for thousands of years. She is involved in everything important. While she reigns, women are represented. When her story is stolen and her roar silenced, women become the property of men. Inanna, Queen of Heaven, Queen of Earth and almost everything, is reduced to goddess of sentimental love; her fertility and sexual power is only associated with sex as prostitution; she is demoted to goddess of the desperate women selling themselves at taverns and the city walls. She is blamed for causing war. She is systematically sanitized; defanged and declawed. Her faded ghostly shade appears as the lovely Aphrodite and Venus; as Virgin Mary meek and mild, and wish-receiving evening star. Her burial dust falls away; what was forgotten is remembered. Her past and our past are present. Come, we gather again in private seclusion and at the public well. We parade before her at new moon; we appeal to her evening star; we walk away free from the strongholds of domination, we are un-silenced; we roar!

Look again at Inanna's images and emblems. Find the ones that resonate with you. Embrace them. Reread Inanna's titles and epithets. Sacred woman mirrors human woman. She and we are of the same star stuff. I invite you to find Starlight, Starbright in the purpling of night and allow her to inspire and guide you. Let your heart speak to her, recognize her in yourself, and if you have forgot her prayers, her hymns, her exaltations, just say: "Starlight, Starbright, first star I see tonight, wish I may, wish I might, have the wish I wish tonight." She will call you home to rest and dream; she will whisper guidance for the coming day.

In the tradition of ancient scribes of Sumer who dedicated their completed tablets to their goddess, I will end:

THIS IS A PRAISE SONG TO HOLY MAID INANNA

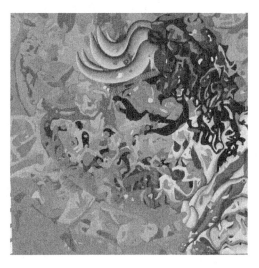

Figure 49. Inanna Evening Star

EPILOGUE

Today ends a full year of writing; composing and composting nine years of research. The book is completed December 22, 2014; a new crescent moon sliver and evening star appear together near the horizon. Inanna calls me home to rest and dream and imagine a new world. Crescent new moon is her festival day — I will meet you there!

Years ago, at a holistic nursing seminar, we viewed a Canadian documentary about witch hunts: "The Burning Times." We wept. As healers, as caregivers, as women with specific views of spirituality, we acknowledged that we likely experienced burning first-hand in earlier life times. I had dreamed glimpses of those events; the phantom smell of smoke haunted my childhood.

When this book was nearing completion and committed to publication, I developed sleep disturbing anxiety. Researching, writing, painting, and counseling from my seaside acre are safe, but I was about to go brazenly public with criticism of Y-maleness in general and theologians in particular. I had researched and written to retrieve, express, and promote the return of women both sacred and human. I assured myself that none of those responsible for domination and oppression would ever read these pages. The book would be as invisible to them as I am, gray-haired, 72, living with a cat, considering ideas, writing in the predawn and welcoming the sunrise. I also talk to evening and morning star, write poetry to the moon, and dream occasionally in goddess, but never a god. I write for women, so we remember to work for change both above and below the radar. The burning times are past and documented, but … do you smell smoke?

NOTES AND ADDITIONAL MATERIAL

RECIPE FOR INANNA/ISHTAR DATE CAKES

Ancient Sumerian recipe for date cakes/lady cakes/Ishtar cakes served in temples and palaces (Nemet-Nejat 1998: 158:)

1 sila butter
1/3 sila white cheese (soft farmer cheese, not aged)
3 sila dates
1/3 sila raisins

add "excellent" finely ground wheat or barley flour (The flour measurement is left up to the cook.)

(A sila is a measurement equalling 0.850 liters or one-fifth of a gallon.)

Shape mounds like a flat bread. Bake in clay bread-oven until set (any oven at 350 degrees should work). The batch size for this moist sweet chewy dense cake should serve a fair-sized new moon festival day.

GLOSSARY

(Inanna's numerous names and epithets are
found at the end of chapter 12)

Abzu/Absu: primeval sea and subterranean "sweet water" sea, home
of Nammu who created heaven and earth from the abzu/abyss.
Humans were also created from the rich fertile marsh clay of the
Abzu. It is home to Enki, son of Nammu.

Akkad: variant of **Agade**, the city founded by Sargon the Great; after
Sargon unified north and south Sumer, the land was called Sumer
(south) and Akkad (north).

ala-**drum**: *ala* is a tambourine attached to a drum head.

Amaushumgalanna: another name for Dumuzi, also written as
Ushumgalanna; literally "Mother-Dragon of Heaven" (Kramer
1956, 1981: 358). I found this curious but considered that Inanna is
of the primal great mother, Sumerian Nammu, who is imagined as
a great serpent prime creatress and serpent became dragon. Inanna
is called the dragon of the gods in her warrior aspect; the gods are
born of the mother goddess. Universally, the son born of the great
mother becomes consort of her maiden self for fertility in the land.

An: (also **Anu**), from '*an*' meaning heaven. He is the earliest sky-god
and first consort for Inanna. He fades in time to be a benevolent
king of the gods who makes decrees. An ancient proverb says he
makes the decrees but Inanna tells him what to decree.

Antu: female sky, epithet of Inanna.

Anunna-gods: (also **Anunnaki**), name of sky-gods, some of whom in time populated the Nether World; they are seven "greater gods" compared to the Igigi-gods, the "lesser gods" who worked for the Anunna-gods before humans were created to do all the labor. Inanna leads the seven Anunna-gods in decree making; they are honored by the seven fires lit on the walls of her temple and indicate the seven stars of the Pleiades.

Anunnaki: (see Anunna-gods).

Anzu: a later name for the Sumerian thunderbird, Imdugud. (See Imdugud.)

Apsu: (see Abzu)

Asushunamir: "impersonator", a transgendered or transvestite male, considered sacred in Inanna's temple because this one bridges two worlds: male and female. Bridging two worlds gave special status that allowed safe entry and return from the underworld — a feat no ordinary living human could accomplish. He is sent by Enki to Ereshkigal to secure Inanna's release. Ereshkigal lets Inanna go but curses the "impersonator" to a hard life of prostitution at the city wall and abuse from the public.

Atrahasis: ("exceedingly wise") is the Sumerian Noah prototype. Originally, the story goes, people are created to work for the gods without limits to their life span; they are also created noisy. They are so noisy and numerous that Enlil ordered various attempts to kill them off because they disturbed his rest. Enki is fond of one man and connives to give him a message to build a boat and load it with the man's family and animals of the steppe before a great flood came. Atrahasis follows Enki's instructions and his boat and life sealed within survive. Thereafter life limits are decreed by the birth goddesses. Some women would go to the temple and practice celibacy to keep the population under control. Death, stillbirths, aborted pregnancies, and disease are introduced to keep the human population down.

Baba: (see also Bau), Baba is an early goddess, a fertility manifestation of great mother and frequently used in personal names. She is goddess of fertility and abundance; she participates in the "sacred marriage". She is associated with the evening star and called consort

493

of An. Baba has her own temple in the Uruk temple precinct and is one of Inanna's names in poems (Leick 1991: 23).

bala-priest: by the time of Enheduanna, temple liturgy was copied and shared in temples. This indicates a uniformity of religious practice. The bala-priests spent time in the temples of the cult-center city, Nippur.

Bau: a goddess from Lagash, generally a healing goddess (see also Gula) and an equivalent of Inanna.

Belili: old woman who hides Dumuzi in one of the Inanna descent poems.

Belet-ili: sister of Tammuz; equivalent of Inanna/Ishtar and Gestinanna.

Bull of Heaven: curved horns and white animals were first associated with the moon goddess. The wild bulls of the Ancient Near East were formidable and an obvious metaphor for raw power. The bull belonged to the moon and to the constellation, our Taurus, that rose when plowing and planting time began. The chief god of the Sumerian pantheon, An, claims the Bull of Heaven is named for him. Dumuzi is called Inanna's wild bull, and Inanna herself is compared to a wild bull when she is a warrior. The Bull of Heaven is mentioned as Ereshkigal's consort. Gilgamesh kills the Bull of Heaven in a late text.

Damu, Danu: early date palm god who did not die and resurrect as did Dumuzi because dates are available year long.

Dumuzi: an early shepherd-king of Uruk (Erech), whose myth possibly evolved from Damu. He is likely the first king consort of Inanna; he became a demigod, i.e., he dies at the end of the harvest and reappears in the spring, resurrected.

Ea: (see Enki)

Eanna: "House of Heaven", Inanna's temple in Uruk. She is the tutelary owner of the city. The Eanna precinct grew to encompass 25% of her city. An is her consort in Uruk (the city is also called Unug or Erech).

Ebih: mountains northeast of Sumer that Inanna flattens because they (the mountain people) are disobedient and did not bow down to her.

Ekur: "Mountain House", built up on rubble of previous temples; it rises high. It is Enlil's temple in Nippur but it was not always his.

In one story Enki invents aborted pregnancies so Ninhursaga's city would depopulate, fall, and Enlil could take over her temple.

Enheduanna: *en*-priestess (highest ranking) of Nanna, moon god, in Ur — his celibate symbolic human consort. She is the earliest acknowledged poet/writer whose known surviving compositions number around forty. Her writing style was imitated and her tablets were copied for over a millennium in scribal schools; she was well educated and the daughter of king Sargon the great. Her fluency in both Akkadian (a Semitic language) and Sumerian and her ability to weave the old Sumerian myths within the work she created for numerous temples and deities has led to speculation that her mother was Sumerian. Her father the king claimed Ishtar as his personal goddess and merged her officially with Inanna. Enheduanna wrote three important poems for Inanna. Sargon unified the north and south; he sent his only daughter south to Ur and Uruk to oversee the temples there. For 500 years, women of the ruling families held the position of *en*-priestess to the moon god.

Enki: (*en*, chief and *ki*, earth) tutelary deity of Eridu, a southern city in the marshland. The first tutelary divine of Eridu was likely Nammu who created everything from the Abzu, the sweet ground water, the sea primeval. Enki is called the son of Nammu which is a way for gods to usurp goddess territory. He is often imaged inside a square "fish house", but he always has two streams of water with fish issuing from his shoulders as the Tigris and Euphrates rivers. He is called the god of wisdom, cleverness, trickiness, and magic.

Enkidu: is created to equal Gilgamesh in size and strength to be a companion to the ill-behaved king of Uruk. He is born in the wild, ran and plays with the animals of the steppe; he helps animals escape from hunters' traps. One of Ishtar's sacred temple harlots is sent to seduce Enkidu, tame him, and initiate him into civilization. Mission accomplished, she brings him back to Uruk where his first act is to stop Gilgamesh from raping brides. Following that, they wrestled to a draw and became fast friends. He is wiser than the king who does not listen to Enkidu's good advice.

Enlil: (*en*, chief and *lil*, air) first son of earth (Ki) and heaven (An) and was generally in charge of the Sumerian Pantheon. He carries out orders for his distant father, An. He authors the punishing destructions against humans, including the deluge.

Enmerkar: a pre-flood king of Uruk and one of the contesting kings in the story of "Enmerkar and the Lord of Aratta".

Ereshkigal: death mother and one of the oldest goddesses. She is "sister" of Inanna and the third aspect the great mother creatress, Nammu. Ereshkigal is beautiful, weeps for her dead children, has rebirth symbols (cowrie shells), and, in the old days, tends our dead until they renew, return. Patriarchy changed the netherworld to a doomed place of no return and replaced her with gods.

Eridu: (Eridug) Southern city bordering the marshland, home of Enki. It is considered the oldest of the Sumerian cities.

Etana: appointed first king of the first city by Inanna. He takes part in the story of Imdugud (eagle) and snake where, after swearing a pact of friendship and hunting together to feed their young, eagle eats snake's children. A punishment is enacted where eagle is captured, put in a pit and his pinion feathers cut. Etana is without heirs and dynastic kingship requires a son. If he rescues eagle, the bird will take him to get the plant of fertility. After several high flying acrobatic attempts to get Etana to heaven and Inanna, they succeed. Etana peeks into the window of her heavenly home, sees her sitting on a cushion with a lion at her side, and makes the request. The tablet fragments end here but the plant must have been successful as other tablets refer to a son of Etana.

Gatumdug: a mother goddess equivalent to Inanna

Gestinanna: "Lady Grapevine", sister to Dumuzi, offers herself to replace Dumuzi when he is condemned to the underworld; a compromise is reached by Inanna where Dumuzi will be in the underworld half a year and Gestinanna will be there the other half year. She is sometimes the equivalent to Inanna.

giparu: area of the temple where the *en*-priestess resides in the women's quarters. Inanna also make judgments from the giparu and, in a late addition to the Gilgamesh Epic, king Gilgamesh wants entry to take over her giparu. The giparu/women's quarters is sacrosanct/taboo for men to enter.

Gilgamesh: (Bilgames in some Sumerian texts) was an Early Dynastic king of Uruk. His hero status is told in five different stories now known as the Epic of Gilgamesh. He is worshipped like a god at several cities including Uruk and Nippur.

Gudea: an *ensi* (a ruler, governor, but not a king) of Lagash and known as a temple builder.

Gugalanna: Great Bull of Heaven, is the constellation Taurus rising at the time of plowing, sometimes consort to Ereshkigal, and associated with An. A god-consort can be called "wild bull of heaven" and Inanna is like a wild bull in her war goddess role.

Gula: a healing goddess, associated with dogs. Dogs are carrion eaters and bring the spirits of the dead to the death goddess or guard the spirit making its way to her. She is imagined with a dog head in some images but is more often accompanied by them.

hierodule: is a sacred consort, who brings fertility and grants rulership through an annual sexual union.

huluppu tree: is a wetlands tree, possibly willow or popular.

Humbaba (Huwawa): guardian of the cedar forests in Lebanon where the goddess has her throne. Gilgamesh and Enkidu attack and kill the guardian, cut down the forest, and sing heroic Gilgamesh songs about the conquest. Humbaba does not attack them; though terrible in appearance, he is not aggressive.

Igigi-gods: a class of Sumerian gods, sometimes called the "lesser gods"; in the creation-of-man epic they do the labor on earth for the big gods before humans are invented.

Imdugud: Sumerian thunderbird. Black storm clouds rising over the horizon, stretched low and wide, resemble the black eagle with wings spread. Thunder is indicated by using a lion's head for growling thunder. The bird is synonymous with Inanna's storm power and eventually with her war persona. Storms are noisy and destructive as are wars. Many stories have Imdugud playing a variety of roles: stealing the tablet of destinies, taking Etana to heaven, and accompanying warrior deities.

Inanna: read the book!

Irinni, Irnina: names for Inanna used by early translators. (See Inanna's numerous names, titles, and epithets at the end of chapter 10)

Ishara: Akkadian and Syrian "Lady of love"; goddess of fertility and the marital bed.

Ishtar: Semitic equivalent of Inanna, varying only in her more aggressive and waring personality.

Ki: means earth; she is the chthonic mother goddess.

Kul(l)ab(a): the area of Uruk where the cultic sanctuaries are located.

Kur: mountain.

Lilith: (*lil* is Sumerian for air, wind), she a wilderness version of early Inanna, a hybrid bird-goddess with wings and owl talons for feet. Her wings give her access to heaven and earth. Lilith has her own cult centers. Over time, Lilith is demonized and goes from wind maiden to evil wind that brings diseases into the city; she is then said to steal babies. She played a walk-on roll in the Biblical version of Adam and she walked off because he wanted to be on top, sexually dominating her. In the Semitic story, she is then sexually frustrated and would steal men away in their dreams, i.e., she is blamed for their nocturnal emissions.

Lord of Aratta: the ruler of a mountain city, Aratta (not yet found), who needs grains from Uruk and contests with king Enmerkar of Uruk who wants timber and silver from the mountains. A wise woman sage of Uruk explains to the two kings that trade will solve the problem and war is averted.

lu-gal: big or great man

Lulal: Inanna's warrior son, worshipped in Bad-tibira.

Mammu: (see Nammu)

Marduk: elevated to chief god of the Babylonian pantheon.

ME: (pronounced 'may') the powers, rules, and contradictory aspect of human life. The concept of ME is so vast that the Sumerian word is used rather than a less encompassing word in translation. (*ME* is also written *me* or *Me* in translations.)

mundus imaginalis: communication that bridges the seen and the unseen, see also *nous*.

Nammu: Sumerian prime singular creatress who alone creates heaven and earth from the abyss, the primeval sea. Nammu is referred to as a serpent and serpent is the metaphor for the umbilical cord, the vaginal snake of life. She is mother of the gods. The serpent metaphor became a dragon. This author feels strongly that Inanna is the maid, potential fertility aspect of Nammu; Ereshkigal is the death mother of the global great mother creatress triad. Nammu represents: life, death, and return. Early Ubaidian snake goddesses are found in graves in Sumer and Enheduanna refers to Inanna as "first snake" and one who "wears the robes of the old, old gods". Inanna is also called "dragon of the gods". Tiamat is the Akkadian equivalent of Nammu.

Namtar: Ereshkigal's vizier, administrative assistant.

Nanse, Nanshe: a marsh goddess having to do with fish, birds, and moral conduct; she is described with the same powers as Inanna.

Nanay: is described like Inanna with great attractiveness and allure. She represents the evening star, and in Babylonia, she wears a beard as does Ishtar as masculine morning star. She is listed beside Inanna in the offering tablets of Uruk; she is an equivalent of Inanna and possibly a goddess of people emigrating to Uruk.

Nanna: moon god who took precedence over the moon goddess as patriarchy took over; also known as Akkadian Suen/Sin.

Neolithic: "New Stone Age" began c. 9000 B.C.E. in the ancient Near East with farming, animal husbandry, trading and permanent settlements.

Nergal: a chthonic god of the earth and underworld, who has his own cult centers. He is variously a god of war, disease, and pestilence as well as fertility, vegetation and light.

Nibru: (also known as Nippur) is a city in northern Sumer where a large number of tablets are found. It is a large cult and intellectual center. Enlil is the tutelary owner.

nin: originally only meant lady or queen (Kramer and Jacobsen); over time the word expanded to also mean lord; many god names begin with Nin-. The author asks: did these gods arise after the masculine gender inclusion or are these names the result of gender-flipping a goddess and keeping her "queen" name?

Ninazu: underworld god.

Ninegala: (Lady of the Palace, the big house) used for both Inanna and the palace queen during the sacred marriage rite. This could mean that the queen herself was Inanna's proxy for the *hieros gamos*.

Ningal: (great queen or lady) moon goddess, and interpreter of dreams; usually said to be the mother of Inanna and Utu, the sun god. She was worshipped at Ur.

Ningirsu: a warrior god of Lagash.

Ninhursag(a): a birth goddess, equated with Ninmah and Aruru. She is humiliated at her own party celebrating the birth of humans when Enki unfairly wins a drunken contest with her. Either accidentally caused by drunkenness, or on purpose to explain imperfect humans, Ninhursag's handicapped people she creates are found suitable occupations by Enki. When it is Enki's turn, because he can't carry a pregnancy, he invents the aborted fetus. The back story is that he wants to get the goddess out of her temple, Ekur, in Nippur, so Enlil can take it. The aborted fetuses cause depopulation and her own city dies. Enlil takes over her temple. She runs away to the foothills where she will not see Enki ever again. Her name became Ninhursaga, Queen of the Stoney Ground.

Ninlil: (Lady Air) also known as Sud; is a grain and birth goddess, consort with Enlil, and mother of Nanna the moon god.

Ninmah: (exalted lady), a birth goddess.

Ninshubur: sukkal/vizier of Inanna, Queen of the East, Lady Dawn; she slashes at the monsters that Enki sent when the two goddesses left in the boat of heaven after Inanna got her MEs (back).

Ninsianna: Inanna's name as the planetary star, our Venus.

Ninsun: Lady Wild Cow, dream interpreter and goddess mother of Gilgamesh.

Nintu: Lady who gives birth.

nu-gig: sacred or taboo, class of temple women who wear an ornamental yoke with *shuba* gemstones draped around their necks. Inanna also wore one.

Ninurta: (Lord Earth) storm, war, and farm god; the "farmer of Enlil". He was responsible for the "life-giving semen". He brought irrigation to the land, put game in the forests and plants in the steppes. He is son of Ninlil. When his mother comes to congratulate him on his splendid accomplishments, he gives her the stoney ground with growing plants (spring) and changes her name to Ninhursag. She is the second goddess to be renamed Ninhursag.

Nippur: Enlil's city; the cult and intellectual center where a large collection of preserved tablets were found on shelves like a library.

nous: is access to the immediate realm between the physical and spiritual worlds, see also *mundus imaginalis*.

Paleolithic: Old Stone Age, gatherer-hunter groups followed animal and plant cycles using mostly stone tools, from c. 700,000 to 9000 B.C.E. in the ancient Near East, when early permanent settlement began with plant cultivation, animal domestication, and trade.

Saltu: the exact double of Ishtar created to match the goddess's noise and warring and make her cease her bad behavior.

Sargon the Great: a Semitic king who goes from being cupbearer for his predecessor to the first king to unify Northern and Southern Sumer. He establishes his own city Akkad/Agade and is the father of Enheduanna, *en*-priestess, devotee of Inanna and the first acknowledged poet/writer.

Shamhat: temple harlot of Inanna's temple who initiates Enkidu from his innocence in nature into human culture by way of sex, food, and communication. Enkidu and Shamhat then go to Uruk where he has a somewhat taming influence on Gilgamesh.

Shara: tutelary deity of Umma, said to be Inanna's son.

Shukaletuda: "spotty", the gardener's inept son who rapes Inanna while she sleeps in the shade of his father's trees. He was hidden by his father and Inanna caused all sorts of disasters until he was delivered up to her. He does die (as humans will do) but strangely, we hear Inanna say his name will be remembered in song.

Sin: moon god, a variant of Suen. See Nanna.

Suen: moon god, see Nanna.

Tammuz: beloved consort of Ishtar for the agricultural year; equivalent to Sumerian Dumuzi.

Tiamat: Semitic equivalent to Nammu. (See Nammu.)

tigi-**harps**: instruments for laments.

Ubaidians: a place name used for the non-Semitic people preceding the Sumerians from the first discovery site. Traces of their culture are found along the coast of the Arabian peninsula extending north along the Euphrates and Tigris rivers. Ubaidian pottery was found below the earliest Sumerian level at Ur, under eight feet of silt that indicates a deluge. The Ubaidians had a developed culture when the Sumerians arrive. Their small temples are found below the earliest Sumerian sites. The merging of the two non-Semitic agricultural groups creates the beginning of the most brilliant civilization of Mesopotamia. Tigris and Euphrates are Ubaidian names for the rivers.

Ur: important Sumerian city of the south, and location of the Nanna (moon god) temple complex where Enheduanna is *en*-priestess.

Uruk: (Erech), southern Sumerian city where Inanna is tutelary goddess along with her consort An. It is the location of the large temple precinct area of Inanna/Ishtar, the Eanna, House of Heaven.

Utu: sun god, said to be brother of Inanna.

vizier: administrative assistant for a deity, also *sukkal*.

SUGGESTIONS FOR FURTHER READING

Inanna:
 Meador: *Inanna, Lady of Largest Heart*
 Wolkstein and Kramer: *Inanna Queen of Heaven and Earth*

Sumerian Poetry and Literature:
 Black, Cunningham, Robson and Zalyme: *The Literature of Ancient Sumer*
 Foster: *Before the Muses*
 Jacobsen: *The Harps that Once …*
 Kramer: *From the Poetry of Sumer*

Sumerian Life:
 Bottero: *Everyday Life in Ancient Mesopotamia*
 Kramer: *History Begins at Sumer; The Sumerians; Their History, Culture, and Character*
 Van de Mieroop: *A History of the Ancient Near East*

Sacred Feminine (General):
 Baring and Cashford: *The Myth of the Goddess*
 Frymer-Kensky: *In the Wake of the Goddess*
 Gimbutas: *The Language of the Goddess; Civilization of the Goddess*
 Meador: *Uncursing the Dark*, and *Princess, Priestess, Poet*
 Perera: *Descent to the Goddess*

Women's Studies and Spirituality:

Brizendino: *The Female Brain*

Daly: *Gyn/Ecology; Beyond God the Father*

French: *A History of Women in the World* (4 volumes, very comprehensive)

Miles: *Who Cooked the Last Supper?*

Reed: *Woman's Evolution*

Stone: *When God Was a Woman; Ancient Mirrors of Womanhood*

Walker: *The Woman's Encyclopedia of Myths and Secrets* (Loaded with interesting facts!)

Sexuality and Menstruation:

Buckley and Gottlieb: *Blood Magic; the Anthropology of Menstruation*

Eisler: *Sacred Pleasure; Sex, Myth, and the Politics of the Body*

Fisher: *Woman's Creation; Sexual Evolution and the Shaping of Society*

Grahn: *Blood, Bread, and Roses* (how women created culture)

Knight: *Blood Relations* (how women created culture, comprehensive)

Leick: *Sex and Eroticism in Mesopotamian Literature*

Mary Magdalene:

Bourgeault: *The Meaning of Mary Magdalene*

Starbird: *The Woman with the Alabaster Jar; Mary Magdalene, Bride in Exile*

Mythology (General):

Frazer: *The New Golden Bough*

Graves: *The White Goddess*

Harrison: *Prolegomena* (brings in the feminine back story of mythology)

Kramer: *Mythologies of the Ancient World*

ANNOTATIONS FOR DRAWINGS AND PAINTINGS

(All drawings and paintings are by the author.
To view the paintings in color, visit sandrabartheimann.com)

Cover Art: Painting by Author, *Inanna*, acrylic on panel, 30"x30".

Title Page: Drawing from a photograph of a stele of Gudea fragment, 22nd century B.C.E., the Louvre; figure 288, page 234, in Parrot: *Sumer the Dawn of Art.* The goddess is identified as Bau, an Inanna equivalent.

Drawings from photographs; the left and center figures are identified as snake goddesses from the Baghdad Museum; figure on right is from a photograph of an early Ishtar, terra-cotta, Sumerian, in Louvre collection; page 57 in the *New Larousse Encyclopedia of Mythology.*

Drawing from a photograph of a terra-cotta figure from Ur, Old Babylonian Period, in collection of the British Museum, London.

Drawing from a photograph of a baked clay snake goddess, from a Ubaidian grave; figure 15, page 47, in Lloyd: *The Archaeology of Mesopotamia.*

debated calling all of the area outside the sphere the abzu/apsu since some poems said rain was the outer water leaking from the outer primordial sea through the cloud breasts of a heavenly goddess; it was from the *abzu* that Nammu created heaven and earth. Did she use all of it or is it like our vast deep space surrounding our earth today?

Drawing From a photograph of a cylinder seal impression, Mesopotamian, Akkadian, c. 2200-2159 B.C.E., British Museum, London BM 89115; figure 139, page 213, found in Aruz: *Art of the First Cities*. From left to right: Nintur, weather god, with arrows (lightning) and lion (thunder), Inanna, Utu, sun god, with his saw to open the mountains to enter the underworld at night from the west and open his way up in the east at dawn, and Enki, god of sweet water, with two flowing streams for the Tigris and Euphrates rivers.

Drawing composite is from photographs: woman in foreground from first half of the third millennium, marble votive statue, Iraq Museum, Baghdad; figure 140, page 111 of Parrot: *Sumer Dawn of Art*. Male figure drawn to her left from a photograph of a gypsum votive, Mesopotamia, Nintu temple, Early Dynastic II, c. 2650-2550 B.C.E., Worcester Art Museum, Massachusetts; figure 24b, page 60, from Aruz: *Art of the First Cities*. Figures in the background drawn from a photograph of assorted figurines from the Abu temple, Tell Asmar, Early Dynastic I-II, c. 2900-2550 B.C.E.; figure 25, page 60 of Aruz: *Art of the First Cities*.

Painting by author, oil on canvas, 48"x48".

Painting by author, acrylic on canvas, 24"x 24".

512

BIBLIOGRAPHY

Aldington, Richard and Delano Ames, Translators. 1959, 1986. *New Larousse Encyclopedia of Mythology*. NY: Crown Publishers

Aruz, Joan, ed.. 2003. *Art of the First Cities*. New Haven and London: Yale University Press

Ashe, Geoffrey. 1976. *The Virgin*. NY: ARKANA Routledge & Kegan Paul Inc.

Atkinson, Clarissa W., Constance H. Buchanan and Margaret R. Miles. 1985. *Immaculate and Powerful*. Boston: Beacon Press

Bahrani, Zainab. 2001. *Women of Babylon; Gender and Representation in Mesopotamia*. London and NY: Routledge

Baring, Anne and Jules Cashford. 1993. *The Myth of the Goddess; Evolution of an Image*. London, New York: Penguin Group

Bendt, Alster. 2005. *Wisdom of Ancient Sumer*. Bethesda, Maryland: C. D. L. Press

Berger, Pamela. 1985. *The Goddess Obscured*. Boston, MA: Beacon Press

Bernal, Martin. 1991. *Black Athena; the Afroasiatic Roots of Classical Civilization*. London: Random House

Bertman, Stephen. 2003. *Handbook to Life in Ancient Mesopotamia*. Oxford: Oxford: Oxford University Press

Biaggi, Christina. 1994. *Habitations of the Great Goddess*. Manchester, Connecticut: Knowledge, Ideas and Trends

Black, Jeremy. 1998. *Reading Sumerian Poetry*. Ithaca, NY: Cornell University Press

Black, Jeremy and Anthony Green. 1992. *Gods, Demons and Symbols of Ancient Mesopotamia*. Austin, Texas: University of Texas Press

Black, Jeremy; Graham Cunningham, Eleanor Robson, and Gabor Zalyome. 2006. *The Literature of Ancient Sumer*. Oxford and NY: Oxford University Press

Bottero, Jean. 1987. *Mesopotamia: Writing, Reasoning, and the Gods*. Chicago, London: The University of Chicago Press

Bottero, Jean. 1992. *Everyday Life in Ancient Mesopotamia*. Baltimore, Maryland: the Johns Hopkins University Press

Bottero, Jean. 2001. *Religion in Ancient Mesopotamia*. Chicago: University of Chicago Press

Bourgeault, Cynthia. 2010. *The Meaning of Mary Magdalene*. Boston and London: Shambhala Publications, Inc.

Bowen, Catherine Drinker. 1968. *Biography: the Craft and the Calling*. Boston and Toronto: Little, Brown and Co.

Briffault, Robert. 1927. *The Mothers; a Study of the Origins of Sentiments and Institutions. Volumes I, II, III*. NY: J.J. Little and Ives Company

Brizendino, Louann. 2006. *The Female Brain*. NY: Broadway Books

Buchanan, Briggs. 1981. *Early Near Eastern Seals in the Yale Babylonian Collection*. New Haven and London: Yale University Press

Buckley, Tomas and Alma Gottlieb. 1988. *Blood Magic; the Anthropology of Menstruation*. Berkeley and Los Angeles: University of California Press

Cameron, Averil and Amelie Kuhrt, eds.. 1983. *Images of Women in Antiquity*. Detroit, Michigan: Wayne State University Press

Campbell, Joseph. 1959. *Primitive Mythology; the Masks of God*. Harmondsworth, UK: Penguin Books

Campbell, Joseph. 1949, 1968. *The Hero With a Thousand Faces*. Princeton, NJ: Princeton University Press

Campbell, Joseph. 1964. *Occidental Mythology*. NY: Penguin

Campbell, Joseph. 1968. *Creative Mythology; the Masks of God*. Harmondsworth, UK: Penguin Books Ltd.

Campbell, Joseph. 1974. *The Mythic Image*. Princeton, NJ: Princeton University Press

Campbell, Joseph. 1986. *The Inner Reaches of Outer Space*. NY: Harper & Row, Publishers

Campbell, Joseph. 1988. *The Way of the Animal Powers, Part I and II*. NY: Harper & Row publishers

Campbell, Joseph. 1990. *Transformations of Myth Through Time*. NY: Harper & Row, Publishers

Campbell, Joseph. 2013. *Goddesses; Mysteries of the Feminine Divine*. Novato, California: New World Library

Christ, Carol P.. 1987. *Laughter of Aphrodite*. San Francisco: Harper & Row, Publishers

Collon, Dominique. 1987. *First Impressions; Cylinder Seals in the Ancient Near East*. Chicago: University of Chicago Press

Dalley, Stephanie translator. 1989. *Myths from Mesopotamia*. Oxford: Oxford University Press

d'Alviella, Count Goblet. 1956. *The Migration of Symbols*. NY: University Books

Daly, Mary. 1993. *Beyond God the Father*. Boston: Beacon Press

Daly, Mary. 1990. *Gyn/Ecology*. Boston: Beacon Press

Daly, Mary. 1992. Outercourse: *The Bedazzling Voyage*. NY: Harper Collins

De Riencourt, Amoury. 1983. *Woman and Power in History*. Bath, UK: Pitman Press

Eisler, Riane and David Loye. 1990. *The Partnership Way*. NY: Harper Collins Publishers

Eisler, Riane. 1996. *Sacred Pleasure; Sex, Myth, and the Politics of the Body*. (no city given): Harper One

Electronic text Sumerian Dictionary http://psd.museum.upenn.edu/epsd/nepsd-frame-html.

Eliade, Mircea. 1959. *The Sacred and the Profane; the Nature of Religion*. San Diego, NY, London: A Harvest/ H.B.J. Book, Harcourt Brace Jovanovich, Publishers

Eliade, Mircea. 1978. *A History of Religious Ideas*. Chicago: the University of Chicago Press

Fisher, Elizabeth, 1979. *Woman's Creation: Sexual Evolution and the Shaping of Society*. NY: McGraw-Hill Book Company

Foster, Benjamin R.. 2005. *Before the Muses*. Bethesda, Maryland: CDL Press

Fox, Milton, Patricia Egan, and Alice Roberts, eds.. (No date given) *Treasures of Prehistoric Art*. NY: Harry N. Abrams, Inc.

Frankfort, Henri. 1954. *The Art and Architecture of the Ancient Orient*. London: Penguin Books, Ltd

Frankfort, Henry, H. A. Frankfort et al. 1977. *The Intellectual Adventure of Ancient Man*. Chicago and London: the University of Chicago Press.

Frazer, Sir James George. 1958. *The Golden Bough*. NY: The MacMillan Co.

Frazer, Sir James George. 1959. *The New Golden Bough*. NY: Griterion Books, Inc.

Frazer, Sir James George. 1996. *The Illustrated Golden Bough*. UK: Soft back Preview

French, Marilynn. 2002. *A History of Women in the World*. NY: The Feminist Press

Friedrich, Paul. 1982. *The Meaning of Aphrodite*. Chicago: University of Chicago Press

Frymer-Kensky, Tikva. 1992. *In the Wake of the Goddesses*. NY: Fawcett Columbine

Gelb, I.J.. 1970. *Texts Sargonic in the Louvre Museum: Material for the Assyrian Dictionary, No. 3*. Chicago: University of Chicago Press

George, Andrew, translator. 1999. *The Epic of Gilgamesh*. London: Penguin Books Ltd.

George, A.R.. 1993. *House Most High; the Temples of Mesopotamia*. Winona Lake, Indiana: Eisenbrouns

Giedion, D.. 1962. *The Beginnings of Art, Part I*. NY: Bollingen Foundation, Distributed by Random House

Gimbutas, Marija. 1974, 1982. *The Goddess and Gods of Old Europe: Myths and Cultic Images*. Los Angeles: University of California Press

Gimbutas, Marija. 1989. *The Language of the Goddess*. NY: Harper & Row Publishers

Gimbutas, Marija. 1991. *Civilization of the Goddess*. NY: Harper Collins

Gimbutas, Marija. 1999. *The Living Goddess*. Berkeley: University of California Press

Godon, Elinor. 1989. *The Once and Future Goddess*. San Francisco: Harper San Francisco

Goldenberg, Naomi R.. 1979. *Changing of the Gods; Feminism and the end of Traditional Religions.* Boston: Beacon Press

Gottschall, Jonathan. 2012. *The Storytelling Animal.* NY: Houghton Mifflin Harcourt Publishing Co.

Grahn, Judy. 1993. *Blood, Bread, and Roses; How Menstruation Created the World.* Boston: Beacon Press

Graves, Robert. 1948. *The White Goddess.* NY: Farrar, Strauss & Giroux

Griffin, Susan. 1978. *Woman and Nature.* NY: Harper & Row, Publishers

Groenwgegen-Frankfort, H.A.. 1951. *Arrest and Movement.* London: Farber & Farber

Gunter, C.Ann ed.. *Investigating Artistic Environments in the Ancient Near East.* Washington, D.C.: Smithsonian Institution

Hallo, William W. and J.J.A. Van Dijk. 1968. *The Exaltation of Inanna.* New Haven &London: Yale University Press

Harding, Esther M.. 1990. *Woman's Mysteries ancient and Modern.* Boston: Shambhala

Harrison, Jane Ellen. 1903, 1991. *Prolegomena.* Princeton, NJ: Princeton University Press

Harrison, Jane Ellen. 1905. *The Religion of Ancient Greece.* Elibron & Elibron Classics

Harrison, Jane Ellen. 1913, 1918. *Ancient Art and Ritual.* London, NY, Toronto: Oxford University Press

Harrison, Jane Ellen. 1928. *Myths of Greece and Rome*. London: Ernest Benn. Ltd

Hawkes, Jacquetta. 1968. *Dawn of the Gods*. NY: Random House

Hrdy, Sarah Blaffer. 1999. Mother Nature; *Maternal Instincts and How They Shape the Human Species*. NY: Ballantine Books

Hrdy, Sarah Blaffer. 2009. *Mothers and Others*. Cambridge, Massachusetts, London: Belknap Press of Harvard University Press

Husain, Shahruku. 1997. *The Goddess*. Boston, NY, Toronto, London: Little, Brown and Company

Jacobsen, Thorkild. 1970. *Toward the Image of Tammuz and Other Essays on Mesopotamian History and Culture*. Cambridge, Massachusetts: Howard University Press

Jacobsen, Thorkild. 1976. *The Treasures of Darkness, a History of Mesopotamian Religion*. New Haven and London: Yale University Press

Jacobsen, Thorkild. 1987. *The Harps that Once. . . ; Sumerian Poetry in Translation*. New Haven: Yale University Press

James, E.O.. 1994. *The Cult of the Mother-Goddess*. NY: Barnes and Nobles

Jung, Carl G.. 1964. *Man and His Symbols*. NY: Dell Publishing Co. Inc.

Kampman, Marcella. 2008. *Inanna, Goddess of Love*. Calgary, Canada: Bayeux Arts, Inc.

Knight, Chris. 1991. *Blood Relations*. New Haven and London: Yale University Press

Koltuv, Barbara Black. 1986. *The Book of Lilith*. Berwick, Maine: Nicolas-Hays, Inc

Kondoleon, Christine ed. *Aphrodite and the Gods of Love*. Boston: MFA Publications

Kramer, Samuel Noah. 1945. *Enki and Ninhursag; a Sumerian 'Paradise' Myth*. New Haven, Connecticut: American Schools of Oriental Research

Kramer, Samuel Noah. 1956. *History Begins at Sumer*. Philadelphia, Pennsylvania: University of Pennsylvania Press

Kramer, Samuel Noah. 1963. *The Sumerians; Their History, Culture, and Character*. Chicago: the University of Chicago Press

Kramer, Samuel Noah, ed.. 1961. *Mythologies of the Ancient World*. Garden City, NY: Anchor Books

Kramer, Samuel Noah. 1961. *Sumerian Mythology*. NY: Harper & Brothers

Kramer, Samuel Noah. 1969. *The Sacred Marriage Rites: Aspects of Faith, Myth, and Ritual in Ancient Sumer*. Bloomington, Indiana and London: Indiana University Press

Kramer, Samuel Noah. 1979. *From the Poetry of Sumer; Creation, Glorification, Adoration*. Los Angeles and London: University of California Press

Kramer, Samuel Noah and editors of TIME-LIFE-BOOKS. *Cradle of civilization*. NY: Time Incorporated

Langdon, Stephen, 1909. *Babylonian Liturgies; Sumerian Texts from the Early Period*. Paris: Libriarie Paul Gethner

Langdon, Stephen. 1909. *Sumerian and Babylonian Psalms*. Paris: Libriarie Paul Gethner

Langdon, Stephen. 1914. *Tammuz and Ishtar*. Oxford: Clarendon Press

Langdon, Stephen. 1919, reprinted 2010. *Sumerian Liturgies and Psalms*. Memphis, Tennessee: General Books LLC

Langer, Susanne K.. 1943,1947. *Philosophy in a New Key*. London: Harvard University Press

Leick, Gwendolyn. 1991. *A Dictionary of Ancient Near Eastern Mythology*. London and NY: Routledge

Leick, Gwendolyn. 1994. *Sex and Eroticism in Mesopotamian Literature*. London and NY: Routledge

Leick, Gwendolyn. 2001. *Mesopotamia; the Invention of the City*. London and NY: Penguin Books

Leloup, Jean-Yves. 1997,2002. *The Gospel of Mary Magdalene*. Rochester, Vermont: Inner Traditions.

Leon, Vicki. 1997. *Uppity Women of Medieval Times*. Berkeley, CA: Conari Press

Lerner, Gerda. 1986. *The Creation of Patriarchy*. NY, Oxford: Oxford University Press

Levi- Stauss, Claude. 1978. *Myth and Meaning*. NY: Schocken Books

Liverani, Mario. 2006. *Uruk, the First City.* (Translated by Zainab Bahrani and Marc Van de Mieroop) Sheffield, UK and Bristol, Connecticut: Equinox

Lloyd, Seton. 1978. *The Archaeology of Mesopotamia.* London: Thames and Hudson

Markale, Jean. 1997. *The Great Goddess.* Rochester, Vermont: Inner Traditions

Marks, John. 1987. *Love and Death in the Ancient Near East.* Guilford, Connecticut: Four Quarters Publishing Co.

Marshack, Alexander. 1972. *The Roots of Civilization.* NY: McGraw-Hill Book Company

Mato, Tataya. 1967. *The Black Madonna Within.* Chicago and LaSalle, Illinois: Open Court

May, Rollo. 1991. *The Cry for the Myth.* NY, London: W. W. Norton and Company

Meador, Betty De Shong. 1992. *Uncursing the Dark.* Wilmette, Illinois: Chiron Publications

Meador, Betty De Shong. 2000. *Inanna, Lady of Largest Heart.* Austin, Texas: University of Texas Press

Meador, Betty De Shong. 2009. *Princess, Priestess, Poet.* Austin, Texas: University of Texas Press

Mellaart, James. 1967. *Catal Huyuk.* NY: McGraw-Hill Book Company

Metzner, Ralph. 1994. *The Well of Remembrance.* Boston & London: Shambala

Meyers, Carol. 1988. *Discovering Eve; Ancient Israelite Women in Context*. Oxford and NY: Oxford University Press

Miles, Rosalind. 1988, 2001. *Who Cooked the Last Supper? The Women's History of the World*. NY: Three Rivers Press

Minden, M., J. Geller, J. E. Wansbrough. 1987. *Figurative Language in the Ancient Near East. Guildford, UK: School of Oriental and African Studies*, University of London; Biddles Ltd.

Mitchell, Stephen. 2004. *Gilgamesh*. NY, London, Toronto, Sydney: Free Press

Monaghan, Patricia. 2000. *The New Book of Goddesses and Heroines*. St Paul, Minnesota: Llewellyn Publications

Moortgat, Anton. 1967. *The Art of Ancient Mesopotamia*. London and NY: Phaidon

Murdock, Maureen. 1990. *The Heroine's Journey*. Boston: Shambhala Publications

Nemet-Nejat, Karen. 1998. *Daily Life in Ancient Mesopotamia*. Westport, Connecticut, London: Green-Wood Press

Oppenheim, A. Leo. 1967. *Letters from Mesopotamia*. Toronto and Chicago: University of Chicago Press.

Oxford Electronic Text Corpus of Sumerian Literature: http://www-etcsl.orient.ox.ac.uk/catalogue/

Pagels, Elaine. 1988. *Adam, Eve, and the Serpent*. NY: Vintage Books

Pagels, Elaine. 1995. *The Origin of Satan*. NY: Random House

Parrot, Andre and George Salles eds.. 1961. *Sumer, the Dawn of Art*, NY: Golden Press

Patai, Raphael. 1967, 1990. *The Hebrew Goddess*. Detroit: Wayne State University Press

Perera, Sylvia Brinton. 1981. *Descent to the Goddess*. Toronto: Inner City Books

Pfeiffer, John. 1982. *The Creative Explosion*. NY: Harper & Row, Publishers. Inc.

Plaskow, Judith and Carol P. Christ. 1989. *Weaving the Visions*. NY: Harper & Row, Publishers Inc.

Pollack, Rachel. 1997. *The Body of the Goddess*. Shaftesbury, Dorset: Element

Pollock, Susan. 1991. "Women in a Men's World. Images of Sumerian Women". in: Curo, Joan M. and Margaret W. Denkey, eds.. 1991. *Engendering Archaeology; Woman and Prehistory*. Oxford and Cambridge: Blackwell Publishers

Pomeroy, Sarah B.. 1975. *Goddesses, Whores, Wives, and Slaves: Women in Classical Antiquity*. NY: Schocken Books

Pritchard, James, ed.. 1975, 1992. *The Ancient Near East Volumes I and II*. Princeton, N.J.: Princeton University Press

Qualls-Corbett, Nancy. 1988. *The Sacred Prostitute Eternal Aspect of the Feminine*. Toronto: Inner City Books

Reed, Evelyn. 1974. *Woman's Evolution*. NY, London, Montreal, Sydney: Pathfinder

Reiter, Raina R. ed.. 1975. *Toward an Anthropology of Women*. NY: Monthly Review Press

Rosaldo, Michelle Zimbolist and Louise Lamphere, eds.. 1974. *Woman, Culture and Society*. Stanford, California: Standard University Press.

Schmandt-Besserat and S.M. Alexander. 1974. *The First Civilization; The Legacy of Sumer*. Published by The University Art Museum and the University of Maryland, exhibition catalog.

Sefati, Yitzhak. 1998. *Love Songs in Sumerian Literature*. Bar- Ilan University Press, Jerusalem: Graphit Press Ltd.

Seton, Lloyd. 1978. *The Archaeology of Mesopotamia*. London: Thomas and Hudson Ltd.

Sjoberg, Ake W. and E. Bergmann. 1969. *The Collection of the Sumerian Temple Hymns*. Locust Valley, NY: J.J. Augustin Publisher

Sjoo, Monica and Barbara Mor. 1987. *The Great Cosmic Mothers*. NY: Harper SanFrancisco

Starbird, Margaret. 1993. *The Woman with the Alabaster Jar; Mary Magdalene and the Holy Grail*. Rochester, Vermont: Bear & Co.

Starbird, Margaret. 2005. *Mary Magdalene, Bride in Exile*. Rochester, Vermont: Bear & Company

Stone, Merlin. 1976. *When God was a Woman*. Orlando, NY, London: A Harvest Book Harcourt, Inc

Stone, Merlin. 1979. *Ancient Mirrors of Womanhood. Vols. I and II*. NY: New Sibyline Books

Sanday, Peggy Reeves. 1981. *Female Power and Male Dominance; on the Origins of Sexual Inequality.* Cambridge: Cambridge University Press.

Taylor, Shelley E.. 2002. *The Tending Instinct; Women, Men, and the Biology of our Relationships.* NY: Time Books, Henry Holt and Company, LLC

Thompson, William Irwin. 1981. *The Time Falling Bodies Take to Light.* NY: St. Martin's Press

Tigay, Jeffrey H.. 1982. *The Evolution of the Gilgamesh Epic.* Philadelphia: University of Pennsylvania Press

Van de Mieroop, Marc. 2011. *A History of the Ancient Near East.* Oxford: Blackwell Publishing

Van de Mieroop, Marc. 1999. *The Ancient Mesopotamian City.* Oxford, UK: Oxford University Press

Visicato, Giuseppe. 2000. *The Power and the Writing: the Early Scribes of Mesopotamia.* Bethesda, Maryland: C.D.L. Press

Walker, Barbara G.. 1983. *The Woman's Encyclopedia of Myths and Secrets.* NY: Harper & Row

Walker, Barbara G..1987. *The Skeptical Feminist.* NY: Harper & Row, Publishers San Francisco

Walker, Barbara G.. 1988. *The Woman's Dictionary of Symbols and Sacred Objects.* NY: Harper One

Walker, C.B.F.. 1987. *Reading the Past Cuneiform.* Berkeley and Los Angeles: University of California press/ British Museum

Ward, William Hayes. 1910. *The Seal Cylinders of Western Asia.* Washington, D.C.: Carnagie

Watanabe, Chikako E.. 2002. *Animal Symbolism in Mesopotamia.* Wien: Institut fur Orientalistik der Universitat Wien

Weigle, Marta. 1982. *Spiders and Spinsters.* Albuquerque: University of New Mexico Press

Wolkstein, Diane and Samuel Noah Kramer. 1983. *Inanna Queen of Heaven and Earth.* Cambridge, San Francisco, London: Harper & Row Publishers

Woodman, Marion. 1990. *The Ravaged Bridegroom; Masculinity in Women.* Toronto: Inner City Books

Woodman, Marion. 1993. *Conscious Femininity.* Toronto: Inner City Books

Woolley, Sir Leonard, 1929, 1950. *Ur of the Chaldes.* Harmonsworth, Middlesex: Penguin

Woolley, Sir Leonard. 1961. *Mesopotamia and the Middle East.* Baden-Baden, Germany: Holle Verlag G.M.B.H.

Woolley, Sir Leonard. 1965. *The Sumerians.* New York and London:W. W. Norton & Company

Wunderlich, H.G.. 1975. *The Secret of Crete.* London: Souvenir Press Ltd.

Zettler, Richard L.. 1992. *The Ur III Temple of Inanna at Nippur.* Berlin: Altorientalieches Seminar und Seminar, fur Nordirasialische der Freien Universitat

CPSIA information can be obtained at www.ICGtesting.com
Printed in the USA
BVOW04*1955061016

464370BV00005B/143/P